ACCOUNTING
for the
HOSPITALITY
INDUSTRY

ACCOUNTING for the HOSPITALITY INDUSTRY

Elisa S. Moncarz
Nestor de J. Portocarrero

School of Hospitality Management
Florida International University

Prentice Hall

Upper Saddle River, New Jersey 07458

Library of Congress Cataloging-in-Publication Data

Moncarz, Elisa S.
    Accounting for the hospitality industry / Elisa S. Moncarz, Nestor de J. Portocarrero.—
3rd ed.
        p. cm.
    Rev. ed. of: Financial accounting for hospitality management. ©1986.
    Includes index.
    ISBN 0-13-973884-3
    1. Hospitality industry—Accounting.   2. Hotels—Accounting.   3.
Restaurants—Accounting.   I. Portocarrero, Nestor de J.   II. Moncarz, Elisa S. Financial
accounting for hospitality management.   III. Title.

HF5686.H75 M66 2002
657'.837—dc21

                                                                            2002019848

Editor-in-Chief: Stephen Helba
Executive Assistant: Nancy Kesterson
Executive Acquisitions Editor: Vernon R. Anthony
Director of Manufacturing and Production: Bruce Johnson
Associate Editor: Marion Gottlieb
Editorial Assistant: Ann Brunner
Managing Editor: Mary Carnis
Production Liaison: Adele M. Kupchik
Marketing Manager: Ryan DeGrote
Production Management: Karen Berry
Manufacturing Manager: Ilene Sanford
Manufacturing Buyer: Cathleen Petersen
Creative Director: Cheryl Asherman
Senior Design Coordinator: Miguel Ortiz
Cover Design Coordinator: Christopher Weigand
Formatting: Pine Tree Composition, Inc.
Copyeditor: Erica Orloff
Printer/Binder: Courier Westford
Cover Designer: Amy Rosen
Cover Image Credits: Calculator close-up: SuperStock; service desk bell: Francisco Cruz, SuperStock
Cover Printer: Coral Graphics

Pearson Education LTD.
Pearson Education Australia PTY, Limited
Pearson Education Singapore, Pte. Ltd
Pearson Education North Asia Ltd
Pearson Education Canada, Ltd.
Pearson Educación de Mexico, S.A. de C.V.
Pearson Education—Japan
Pearson Education Malaysia, Pte. Ltd

10 9 8 7 6 5 4 3 2
ISBN 0-13-973884-3

Contents

Preface

Accounting for the Hospitality Industry is designed to provide students with an advantageous mix of accounting theory and practice and is tailored to the special needs of the hospitality service industries. Much of the content of this book is the result of the authors' extensive experience as professional accountants, as professors in the accounting and finance program of the School of Hospitality Management at Florida International University, as authors of other hospitality-related textbooks, and as developers of WebCT-based courses that are taught over the Internet. Collectively, the authors have been teaching accounting and finance at Florida International University's School of Hospitality Management for almost fifty years. This book represents a melding of their opinions and expertise.

Most of the existing books dealing with introductory accounting are not suitable for students of hospitality management because they focus on techniques, tools, and procedures that are mostly applicable to manufacturing firms, retail firms, or other non-hospitality industries. This book gives attention to the unique accounting and operating characteristics that are of major concern to managers in the hospitality industry in the new millennium, and in so doing it fills a great need in the industry.

Ever since the authors published their earliest book, *Financial Accounting for Hospitality Management* in 1986 (published by AVI Publishing Company, which was later acquired by Van Nostrand Publishing Company), the book has consistently maintained a unique appeal to students because of its clarity and depth. Students found the book helpful in their studies and as an ongoing supportive resource in their successful careers. While some of this information is included in this text, the data has been further clarified, restructured, or updated as a result of new thinking and developments affecting the hospitality and financial environment.

As a result of globalization, hospitality managers can no longer count on working primarily in the mostly stable North American environment. They must operate in countries with different laws, economic systems, and accounting systems. Furthermore, the North American business climate is itself impacted by the rest of the world in an unprecedented manner. Hyperinflation and overbuilding in the 1980s and the lack of financing and industry slowdown in the early 1990s led hotel firms with large amounts of property, purchased many years ago, to sell these properties and place more emphasis on management rather than ownership. E-commerce places new accounting demands on hospitality businesses as it introduces new ways of generating sales, as well as more scientific ways of handling accounts receivable and inventories. Outsourcing their support services, especially involving e-commerce, is now an option that hospitality firms must consider if they are to remain competitive, for which it is essential to know the true cost of in-house services. Greater per-worker productivity and trends in demand, largely the result of the Internet's impact on the hospitality industry, force companies to restructure—requiring, also, a restructuring of their accounting systems and procedures.

Recent statistics and forecasts indicate that the hospitality industry will face an ever more fluid and changing environment in the future. Exchange rate risks will be a growing concern, and, most recently, if the risk of energy deprivation grows, it will force hospitality firms to consider internal sources of power. Future industry focus on maximizing the firm's value requires the manager to understand operations, the business environment and how to make risk management decisions. This understanding comes only from a thorough knowledge of accounting terminology, accounting systems, and accounting controls. Indeed, the manner in which management is capable of dealing with such future uncertainties, including changes in economic growth and increased government regulations, will make the difference between business success and failure.

In addition to the aforementioned challenges stemming from its operating venue, the hospitality industry also faces unique challenges posed by the following internal, distinctive characteristics:

1. It is labor intensive.
2. It is capital intensive.
3. It is highly leveraged.
4. It has its own Uniform Systems of Accounts.

Because labor costs consume approximately one third of every revenue dollar, managers must be able to understand the accounting controls essential to avoid the disproportionate growth of such a large expense category. Furthermore, low-cost competition from countries with lower labor costs reduces profit margins. Managers must also be able to understand the accounting calculations and the accounting terminology that accompany the financial negotiations necessary to obtain the large amounts of capital needed by firms in this industry. Finally, the use of high leverage adds considerable risk to hospitality firms, which requires them to walk a financial tightrope between maximizing growth without exceeding their ability to meet their debt obligations. Frequent interest rate changes make this even more difficult. They require that managers be aware of the accounting impact of these changes on their business and on how interest rates affect their company's leverage. As stated above, knowledge of accounting terminology, accounting systems and accounting controls is essential under such circumstances in order to minimize the risks posed by the increasingly fluid economic and business environment as well as the shrinking margins introduced by global competition. This book is designed to make the first step towards acquiring this knowledge and expertise easily understandable, and it is designed, as well, to give recognition to the hospitality industry paradigm, its unique needs, and its unique system of accounts.

WHO CAN BENEFIT FROM THIS BOOK?

This book is primarily designed to meet the needs of future hospitality managers, as well as those who are currently in the industry and did not have the opportunity to become familiar with accounting prior to becoming managers of hospitality firms.

It will help those already in management to develop a better understanding of the origin of accounting information and its uses, which are essential for managers, or future managers, to be able to:

1. Better evaluate their own performance,
2. Evaluate the performance of managers whom they supervise,
3. Know what information an accounting system is capable of providing to improve decision-making, and manage a firm more efficiently,
4. Acquire a basic understanding of how financial statements are used to make decisions about the future of the organization,
5. Discuss his, or her, firm's accounting system knowledgeably with the firm's stakeholders.

Thus, it is uniquely suited for management development programs.

It is also designed to enable students with no accounting background to become acquainted with the accounting process and the information an accounting system is capable of providing. The text can be used by:

1. Students in first-semester accounting courses offered by four-year hospitality management education programs, or by
2. Junior colleges offering hospitality-related programs leading to an associate degree, or by
3. Graduate students of hospitality management who have had limited exposure to business and accounting.

Since the sections of this book are, for the most part, independent of each other, the book can be easily adapted to the requirement of any appropriate accounting course in a hospitality management program by omitting or extending one or more chapters.

No previous exposure to accounting or business is required prior to using this text.

FEATURES OF THIS BOOK

One of the major advantages of this book is that it is organized into three sections, each of which may be taught independently of the others. Section I provides the required background for understanding accounting. This includes introducing the student to accounting terminology, the basic accounting concepts, various forms of business entity that are used in the hospitality industry, and the accounting cycle. Section II deals with a more elaborate discussion of the major financial statements. Section III explains some selected, commonly-used accounting processes in greater detail than they are presented in Section I.

Section	Title	Chapters
I	The Accounting Framework and Procedures	1–8
II	Financial Statements	9–10
III	Selected Topics	11–13

In addition to presenting a clear and comprehensive discussion of financial and managerial topics geared to the hospitality industry, this textbook includes other important features, such as:

1. A step-by-step explanation of the accounting cycle of a hospitality service-type business in Section I.

2. A very innovative way of emphasizing the importance of matching expenses against revenues to help students understand the process of adjusting the trial balance.

3. An in-depth examination of the statement of income based on the Uniform System for the Lodging Industry (ninth revised edition), presented in Section II.

4. A more detailed treatment of special topics (presented in Section III). These topics include payroll accounting, receivables, inventory, payables, property and equipment, corporation accounting and financial analysis.

5. Develops student expertise in several areas and provides limited practice in using accounting information for managerial purposes.

6. An extensive glossary of new items, presented at the end of each chapter, and an index that appears at the end of the book, serve as useful reference tools by enabling readers to locate key accounting and business terms easily.

7. Use of simple, straightforward language throughout the book.

8. A discussion of appropriate provisions of the wage-hour law and payroll tax laws affecting the hospitality industry.

9. Inclusion of a brief explanation of Canadian payroll taxes in response to the request of Canadian adopters of our earlier book.

10. A chart of accounts based on a slight simplification of the Uniform System of Accounts for the Lodging Industry (see Appendix A).

11. The "why" and "how" of accounting concepts and procedures is emphasized throughout the text.

12. A review of major disclosures found in financial statements of hospitality firms.

13. Full recognition, where appropriate, of current pronouncements of the Financial Accounting Standards Board and other authoritative bodies.

14. A complete set of financial statements of the hospitality firm Outback Steakhouse is included in Appendix B.

Assignment material may be selected from questions, exercises, and problems at the end of most chapters to accommodate a wide variety of student comprehension and interest. Questions provide a review of the key ideas and major points covered in the text, whereas exercises and problems are more comprehensive in scope and are arranged in order of increasing difficulty. Problems are grouped under separate headings for shorter problems and for longer problems. The framework for solving these exercises and problems in Excel spreadsheet format is provided online for student use.

SUPPLEMENTARY MATERIALS

An Instructor's Solution Manual containing responses to all questions, and solutions to all exercises and problems, is available to adopters. PowerPoint slides are also available for instructors' use. These PowerPoint slides will include chapter material using innovative ways to present concepts from the text.

A Student Exercise Workbook, presented in Excel format, is designed to facilitate the students' learning process. All three supplements can be accessed and downloaded from the book's website, *www.prenhall.com/moncarz.*

In conclusion, this book is designed not only to teach accounting and accounting procedures, but more importantly, a major objective of this text is to make students aware of the importance and usefulness of accounting to hospitality industry managers. It is designed to defeat the natural objections that non-accounting students have to learning a subject as unconventional as accounting.

ACKNOWLEDGMENTS

We wish to acknowledge the role played by the thousands of former students in our Accounting for Hospitality Industry classes at Florida International University's School of Hospitality Management, many of them currently holding key positions in the hospitality industry worldwide. We want to express our sincere thanks to each of them. We are confident that this book will continue to provide our future students a solid accounting foundation that should help them to achieve their goals and become leaders in the hospitality industry of the twenty-first century.

SPECIAL THANKS

We wish to express our sincere appreciation to our spouses, Dr. Raul Moncarz and Maria Esperanza Portocarrero, and to our children for their patience and understanding. They always support us with encouragement and motivation to complete a long and arduous task. This book is dedicated to them.

THE ACCOUNTING FRAMEWORK

Accounting as the Basis for Management Decisions | 1

The learning objectives of this chapter are:

- To introduce accounting as a system used by decision-makers.
- To focus on accounting as "the language of business."
- To contrast financial accounting and management accounting.
- To understand the role of organizations in the management information system.
- To provide an overview of the management information system.
- To introduce the three basic financial statements.
- To understand the major forms of business organizations.

Accounting is a system for collecting, summarizing, analyzing, and reporting, in monetary terms, information concerning an organization, and supplying that information to decision makers. The information provided by the accounting system must be useful and relevant to the users of the accounting data. These users are generally classified into two categories: (1) the organization's management, that is, those individuals charged with the responsibility for directing the operations of the business enterprise, and (2) outsiders, that is, investors, creditors, government, employees, credit unions, and others interested in certain financial aspects of the business.

This book will focus on the accounting system from the point of view of the hospitality manager as the user of accounting information. We shall not, however, discuss the managerial uses of accounting information in the hospitality field until the student has a good understanding of what accounting information is and why it is essential for the successful operation of lodging, foodservice, and travel organizations.

As a starting point, this chapter examines the major features and the basic objectives of both the accounting system and hospitality organizations. We proceed by identifying and analyzing the main characteristics of the three basic forms of legal organizations: sole proprietorships, partnerships, and corporations. To that end, we examine the main advantages and disadvantages of each and the main differences between them. Finally, we discuss the hospitality manager's need for accounting information. Key accounting terms and basic financial statements are also introduced in this chapter.

ACCOUNTING: THE LANGUAGE OF BUSINESS

The main purpose of accounting is to provide the information necessary to the organization's management to enable it to plan and control its business activities. Implicit in this objective is the idea that accounting is a very important management tool. Accordingly, accounting has been referred to as "the language of business" because it is the primary means of communicating business information.

Learning accounting is like learning a new language. If hospitality managers are to effectively use accounting information, they must acquire an adequate understanding of the accounting system, including its nature and limitations. Because good decisions require proper analysis of accounting data, the hospitality manager who lacks training in accounting is unable to identify all the pertinent elements of the decision-making process, and thus it is highly doubtful that he or she can function as an effective manager.

USERS OF ACCOUNTING INFORMATION

As stated earlier, the principal user of accounting information is the organization's management. The type of accounting data needed by hospitality managers depends on a number of factors, such as the location and class of the operation. For instance, the manager of a small hotel operation requires less accounting information than the manager of a large hotel chain, which is far removed from direct contact with day-to-day operations. However, regardless of the type of accounting data needed, every hospitality firm uses accounting information to measure business success and to select the best possible alternative in attaining company objectives. Present and prospective hospitality investors need information on how well a firm is doing before they decide whether or not to sell or buy company stock. At the same time, bankers and other hospitality lenders are concerned with granting and renewing credit to hospitality organizations, and they depend largely on accounting data to evaluate of the risks involved in making loans and extending credit. Because of the capital-intensive nature of the hospitality industry, it becomes extremely important for hospitality organizations to maintain themselves in good financial condition in view of the aforementioned evaluations conducted by both investors and creditors—the main suppliers of funds. It is interesting to note that external users of accounting information view the organization's management as information providers. Investors, creditors, and other users of accounting information have certain expectations about how the management of the hospitality firm should perform. When they receive accounting data describing how management has actually performed, they use these data as the basis for making economic decisions. Consequently, hospitality managers are held responsible for the accounting data used by outside parties.

THE DISTINCTION BETWEEN MANAGEMENT ACCOUNTING AND FINANCIAL ACCOUNTING

Management accounting is concerned with the internal uses of accounting information by the manager. Financial accounting, on the other hand, provides information for both internal and external uses and is based on a set of principles and a number of ground rules designed to enhance and clarify communication between the business and parties external to the business.

The two kinds of accounting are obviously related, in three basic ways:

1. All accounting is essentially financial in nature, in that it is stated in terms of money.
2. Management is responsible for the content of both management and financial accounting reports.
3. Both management and financial accounting rely upon the accounting information system.

Based on the foregoing, obviously the use of managerial data must be preceded by an adequate understanding of financial accounting.

ORGANIZATIONS AND THEIR STRUCTURE

Before studying how accounting is used in business, we must first discuss the nature of business. Organizations can be defined as distinct entities—a person or persons with stated purposes, operating in some definable environment. A university providing educational services is an organization, as are an attorney offering legal services and a hotel operation providing lodging and food services.

All of the different types of organizations operate in an environment by interacting with each other in various kinds of quid pro quos (something for something). These quid pro quos, or equal exchanges of values between organizations, are known in accounting as business transactions. For example, a hotel maid, as an employee, provides cleaning services in return for a paycheck from the hotel organization (employer).

Accounting deals with the essence of business activity: economic exchange interaction between organizations. In accounting, we have to decide for which organization we are accounting. It is desirable at this point to discuss the basic structure and objectives of the hospitality organization.

The primary purpose toward which the hospitality organization works is to provide services to the general public. A hotel operation offers lodging and food-services for a fee. Similarly, a travel agency provides travel services and receives a commission fee in return. Hence, the common objective of all hospitality firms is to provide services with a mind to earning a profit. The management of the firm is charged with the responsibility of conducting the day-to-day activities according to established goals that the organization desires to achieve, such as a good reputation and dependability and, more recently, social responsibility; but the primary objective is to achieve an adequate return on the investment made by the owners of the company.

In planning, controlling, and carrying out specific functions within the organization, three different levels of management exist: top management, middle management, and lower management. The president and vice president(s) of the company, as members of top management, guide the overall direction of the hospitality firm while relying on middle and lower management to plan, coordinate, and control at their management levels, in keeping with the established policies of the organization. In this connection, line and staff unit relationships govern the basic structure of the organization. Line authority is directly related to the specific goals and objectives of the organization. The staff units, on the other hand, exist to provide services to other units and to top management.

Consider the organization chart of Apache Hotel, a medium-sized hotel operation, shown in Exhibit 1–1. This chart tells us, for example, that the general manager has line authority over all departments of the operation. He or she has the overall responsibility for seeing that services are offered timely and properly. The manager of each unit has line authority over the staff. For example, in this chart we see that the chef has line authority over cooks, baker, and pastry chef,

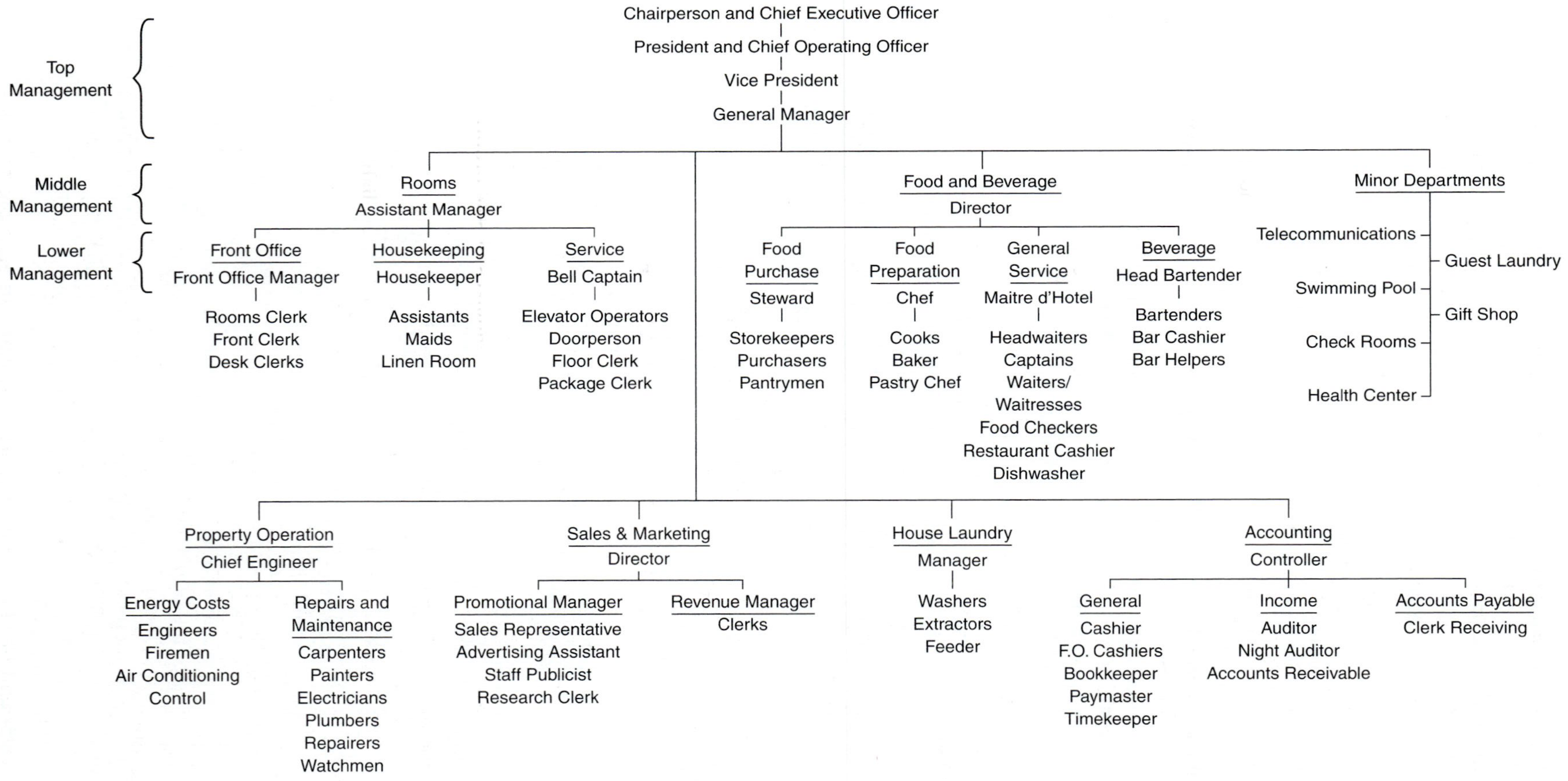

Apache Hotel Organizational Chart

Top Management
- Chairperson and Chief Executive Officer
- President and Chief Operating Officer

Middle Management
- Vice President
- General Manager

Lower Management

Rooms — Assistant Manager
- **Front Office** — Front Office Manager
  - Rooms Clerk
  - Front Clerk
  - Desk Clerks
- **Housekeeping** — Housekeeper
  - Assistants
  - Maids
  - Linen Room
- **Service** — Bell Captain
  - Elevator Operators
  - Doorperson
  - Floor Clerk
  - Package Clerk

Food and Beverage — Director
- **Food Purchase** — Steward
  - Storekeepers
  - Purchasers
  - Pantrymen
- **Food Preparation** — Chef
  - Cooks
  - Baker
  - Pastry Chef
- **General Service** — Maitre d'Hotel
  - Headwaiters
  - Captains
  - Waiters/Waitresses
  - Food Checkers
  - Restaurant Cashier
  - Dishwasher
- **Beverage** — Head Bartender
  - Bartenders
  - Bar Cashier
  - Bar Helpers

Minor Departments
- Telecommunications
- Swimming Pool
- Check Rooms
- Health Center
- Guest Laundry
- Gift Shop

Property Operation — Chief Engineer
- **Energy Costs**
  - Engineers
  - Firemen
  - Air Conditioning Control
- **Repairs and Maintenance**
  - Carpenters
  - Painters
  - Electricians
  - Plumbers
  - Repairers
  - Watchmen

Sales & Marketing — Director
- **Promotional Manager**
  - Sales Representative
  - Advertising Assistant
  - Staff Publicist
  - Research Clerk
- **Revenue Manager**
  - Clerks

House Laundry — Manager
- Washers
- Extractors
- Feeder

Accounting — Controller
- **General** — Cashier
  - F.O. Cashiers
  - Bookkeeper
  - Paymaster
  - Timekeeper
- **Income** — Auditor
  - Night Auditor
  - Accounts Receivable
- **Accounts Payable** — Clerk Receiving

Exhibit 1–1 Apache Hotel organizational chart.

and has the final responsibility for food preparation. If any problems in the area of food preparation arise, the chef is expected to be aware of them and take appropriate corrective action. In turn, the chef is responsible to the food and beverage director, who, in turn, is responsible to the general manager for the overall performance of the food and beverage departments.

TYPES OF BUSINESS ORGANIZATIONS

The three major forms of business organizations are the sole proprietorship, the partnership, and the corporation. Many small hotels, restaurants, and travel agencies are first organized as sole proprietorships or partnerships. Although there might be fewer hospitality corporations, they transact more business than all the partnerships and proprietorships combined.

The Sole Proprietorship

A sole proprietorship is a business owned by a single person. Typically, the individual proprietor originally finances the hotel or restaurant by using his or her personal savings, supplemented by bank or government loans.

The proprietorship form of legal organization is the simplest form of organization for a hospitality firm, since no formal procedures are needed to establish the business. The owner/operator is only required to comply with specific state and/or local licensing laws in order to start selling goods and services to the public. The business entity itself generally has no reporting requirements separate and distinct from those incumbent upon the owner, nor does it have any limitations that the owner would not have. In view of the fact that there is but one owner, the sole proprietorship provides total control over resources and operations. All profits belong to the owner/proprietor, with no need to share them. Moreover, the total control held by the proprietor facilitates the decision-making process, since there is no need to deal with differences of opinion in day-to-day operations, and there are no co-owners to consult in establishing policies or making other business decisions.

The proprietorship is not in and of itself subject to taxation. However, the annual federal and state tax returns filed by the owner must include the income or loss from the business. Thus, the income tax rate applicable to the sole proprietorship is determined on the basis of the owner's total income from all sources and his or her total deductions. The two principle disadvantages of sole proprietorships are limited life and the unlimited liability of the owner. Upon the death or retirement of the owner, the current business must be dissolved inasmuch as there are normally no provisions for the continuity of the business. Furthermore, unlimited liability makes the owner of a sole proprietorship personally liable for the firm's actions and debts. This means that the owner's personal assets are legally available to satisfy business debts.

Another disadvantage of a sole proprietorship is that it depends solely on its own operations and the financial capabilities of its owner. Since the sole proprietorship is an unincorporated business owned by one individual, it becomes very hard to raise large amounts of capital. Because of these drawbacks, it is almost impossible for a sole proprietorship to expand rapidly. It simply cannot obtain the large amounts of funds necessary for the rapid construction of new hotels, restaurants, and travel agencies or for the renovation of existing ones. It is very difficult for an organization with a limited life, whose assets may serve as collateral for the owner's other businesses, to borrow large sums of money.

Advantages and Disadvantages of Sole Proprietorships. To summarize, the principal advantages of the sole proprietorship form of legal organization are:

1. Ease of formation. Proprietorships are simple to establish since there is no need to comply with the federal and state laws applicable to partnerships and corporations.
2. Control over operations. Because there are no co-owners, the owner/operator has complete control over daily operations, thereby speeding up the decision-making process.
3. No sharing of profits. All the profits of the business belong only to the owner.
4. Simplicity. Proprietorships are subject to less government regulations than partnerships and corporations.
5. Taxation. A proprietorship's income is not subject to separate taxation. However, owners must include the applicable business income or losses in their personal tax returns. Since a corporation's income is taxed twice, once at the corporate level and again when dividends are paid, a sole proprietorship is usually more economical tax wise, if the owner does not wish to leave profits in the business.

The main disadvantages of the sole proprietorship are:

1. Limited life. Death or bankruptcy of the owner results in the dissolution of the business.
2. Unlimited liability. The owner is personally liable for the firm's debts and actions.
3. Difficulty in raising capital. Rapid expansion of proprietorship operations is very difficult to achieve because a sole proprietorship does not have access to large amounts of borrowed money or investment by other owners.

The Partnership

A partnership is an association of two or more persons to carry on as co-owners of a business for profit. Two or more persons called the partners therefore own the partnership. It is a somewhat more formal type of legal organization than the sole proprietorship but much less formal than a corporation is. Currently, small hotels, restaurants, travel agencies, and other hospitality service companies that want to combine the managerial ability, hospitality industry experience, and capital of two or more persons extensively use it.

While the partnership can be based on an oral understanding between partners, written agreements are highly recommended. The partnership agreement should include, as a minimum, the following:

- Name of partnership and business location
- Name of each partner
- Amount contributed by each partner
- Each partner's salary
- Procedures for dissolution of partnership
- Partnership duration, if applicable
- Procedure for division of profits and losses between partners

Like a proprietorship, a partnership is simple to organize and is subject to few government regulations. It also has limited life. Death, bankruptcy, or withdrawal of a partner results in the dissolution of the business. Similarly, admission of a new partner to an existing partnership either by contribution of capital or by acquisition of an interest from an old partner requires the formation of a new partnership. The law regards the partnership as a proprietorship with more than one owner. A partnership cannot sue or be sued. In addition, it cannot enter into contracts and is not subject to taxation. The law views all business transactions as acts of the partners as individuals.

The individual partners' actions thus can actually obligate the business if they are performed within the scope of the partnership. Additionally, each partner becomes personally liable for the business. Like proprietorships, the partnership form of legal organization has unlimited liability. The partnership is jointly and individually liable for the debts of the partnership; in other words, in the event that the partnership is unable to pay its debts, the partners' personal assets will be available to satisfy creditors' claims.

Partners can distribute profits or losses from the business in many different ways. If no prior agreement exists, the profits are divided equally among the partners taking into consideration some pertinent factors:

- Each partner's capital contribution
- The time spent by each partner in the business
- Goodwill contribution by each partner
- Each partner's special ability and experience in the field.

As indicated before, partnership income is not subject to taxation, but all partners must include their share of profits or losses in their individual tax returns and pay income taxes using the applicable personal income tax rate. (Of course, partners can use partnership losses to offset other income on their personal tax returns.)

Advantages and Disadvantages of Partnerships. The main advantages of the partnership form of business organization are:

1. Ease of formation. Partnerships are relatively easy to organize, being subject to few government regulations.
2. Opportunity to combine capital, hospitality industry experience, and managerial ability of two or more persons. For this reason, it is a very common form of organization used by small restaurants and hotels.
3. Partnership income is not subject to taxation. Even though individual partners must include their individual share of profits or losses from the partnership in their personal tax return, the individual income tax is generally lower than the corporate tax rate.

The major disadvantages of the partnership form of legal organization are:

1. Limited life. Withdrawal, death, or bankruptcy of a partner will result in the dissolution of a partnership. Likewise, admission of a new partner ends the old partnership relationship.
2. Unlimited liability. Each partner is personally liable to creditors for debts incurred by other partners acting for the partnership.
3. Mutual agency. Each partner is an agent of the company and can obligate the partnership for his or her acts within the scope of the partnership business.
4. Difficulty in raising capital. Although it is somewhat easier for partnerships to obtain the capital required for expanding operations than it is for proprietorships, it is still difficult to raise huge amounts of partnership capital since the ability to do so is limited by the partners' personal wealth and borrowing power.

The Corporation

A corporation is considered a legal person, separate and distinct from its owner. The most famous definition of a corporation was included in the Dartmouth College Case Decision by Chief Justice John Marshall in 1819: A corporation is "an artificial being, invisible, intangible, and existing only in contemplation of law." Thus, a corporation is a multiple-owner organization that is recognized as a separate legal entity by law. Accordingly, it can enter into contracts and can sue or be sued. Since the corporation is a legal person, a corporate officer signing a loan as agent for a corporation is not putting personal assets at risk. The corporation is responsible for its own acts to the extent of its own assets only, not those of the individual stockholders. Thus, one of the main reasons for incorporating a partnership or proprietorship is to protect the owners' personal assets from losses beyond the amount invested in the business.

The owners of a corporation are called shareholders or stockholders, inasmuch as the ownership interest in the company is evidenced by readily transferable shares of stock issued (sold) by the corporation. The shareholders of a corporation control the regular operations of the business only indirectly by electing a board of directors, who actually manage the corporation. In this management capacity, the board of directors selects the corporation's officers, who run day-to-day operations as well as establish general corporate policies. This circuitous route notwithstanding, ultimate control of a corporation rests with the shareholders.

Corporations are incorporated under the laws of one of the fifty states or the federal government. Generally, hospitality industry corporations are chartered by the states. They are limited in their activities to those stipulated in the charter. The process of incorporating a hospitality business involves paying legal fees, as well as incorporation fees to the state, in order to secure the charter. All these payments are referred to as organization costs and are initially recorded as assets since they have a future value to the business.

Unlike the partnership and proprietorship forms of business organization, the corporate form facilitates acquisition of the large amounts of capital needed for expansion. This can be accomplished through the sale of additional shares of stock to new owners by issuing stock certificates representing their interest in the enterprise and the means by which ownership can be easily transferred in the future. Since the borrowing capacity of a profitable corporation is far greater than that of a proprietorship or a partnership because of its limited liability, building new hotels or restaurants, renovating old ones, and purchasing new equipment as means of expanding existing operations are greatly facilitated by using the corporate form of legal organization.

Since corporations have several owners, it is usually necessary to establish a management team, which may or may not include one or more owners, to carry on the operations of the business. The members of this management team composed of corporation officers and employees, act as agents for the corporation and conduct its business as a separate legal person with the same rights, duties, and responsibilities of a natural person. A shareholder (not an officer of the corporation) has no power to bind the corporation to contracts, unlike a partner or a proprietor. In addition, shareholders enjoy limited liability, which means that they are protected from personal losses beyond the amount of their investment. In contrast with partnerships and proprietorships, corporate income is subject to taxation, that is, corporations are required to pay income taxes and file separate tax returns. Shareholders do not have to include their corporation's net income in their personal tax returns except for those earnings actually paid out to them in the form of dividends. Accordingly, corporate income may be taxed twice: First the corporation's income is taxed, and then, if dividends are declared, these are taxed again, this time to the shareholders.

Advantages and Disadvantages of Corporations. The advantages of the corporate form of legal organization are:

1. Limited liability. The special legal status enjoyed by corporations acts as a barrier to protect the owners/shareholders from losses beyond the amount of their investment.
2. Indefinite life. Unlike proprietorships and partnerships, the life of the corporate form of business organization is not affected by the withdrawal of a shareholder in any way since the corporation is treated legally as if it were a person separate from its owners.
3. No mutual agency. Shareholders who are not legal agents or officers are unable to bind a corporation by their actions. If they own many shares, they may bear a strong influence on its management team but cannot unilaterally bind the corporation legally without the specific authorization of the corporation itself.
4. Ease of obtaining additional capital. Corporations are aptly structured for borrowing large sums of money. They also have a legal structure that enables them to sell small ownership interests (shares) to the general public.
5. Ease of transfer of ownership interest. Since ownership of the corporation is via shares of stock, it is simple to transfer ownership interest. Shareholders can ordinarily sell their shares to others without obtaining the company's approval, whereas a sole proprietor cannot sell partial interests in a business, nor can a partner sell a partnership interest without dissolving the partnership.
6. Separate legal entity. By virtue of its special legal status, a corporation has the power to buy, own, or sell property. Furthermore, it can enter into contracts, and can sue or be sued.

The principal disadvantages of the corporate form of legal organization are:

1. Double taxation. Corporate income is initially subject to the payment of income taxes by the corporate entity itself, and then shareholders are required to pay income taxes on the portion of corporate earnings distributed to them in the form of dividends.
2. More government control. Corporations are governed and influenced largely by federal government regulations.
3. More costly to organize. The establishment of a corporation entails the payment of legal fees and state charter fees.
4. More involved decision-making process. In corporations, important business decisions may be quite time consuming. They usually must be referred up the chain of command, often necessitating the agreement and final approval of the board of directors of the corporation.
5. Dilution of earnings and control. A typical corporation has a large number of owners/shareholders, who must share the earnings and control of the corporation with many other owners.

ACCOUNTING AS AN INFORMATION SYSTEM

Information is one basic resource that hospitality organizations use in managing their affairs. In addition to accounting, which is a very significant part of the management information system, hospitality managers also rely on data from related fields in their decision-making process, including economics, marketing,

Input - - - - - - - - - - - - ▸ Process - - - - - - - - - - - - - ▸ Output
Source Documents   Reduction of Data   Information to
                    (Accounting Cycle)   Management

Exhibit 1–2   The accounting system.

and personnel information. Just as management can be viewed as a system, accounting can also be seen from a systems viewpoint.

As Exhibit 1–2 shows, the inputs to the accounting system are source documents (checks, sales, purchase invoices, and the like) that serve as evidence that a business transaction took place. For that reason, business transactions have been regarded as the raw material of the accounting system. It is self-evident that understanding business transactions is essential in learning accounting, that is, knowing what happened with reference to a specific event, all of which requires the clear identification of the values of what is given and received as a result of the business transaction. For instance, if a restaurant borrows $20,000 from a bank for thirty days, the restaurant has received cash with a value of $20,000. On the other hand, the restaurant has given written promise to repay the $20,000 in thirty days, the value of which must aggregate the same dollar amount.

Once business transactions are identified, they are recorded and summarized to show the progress and position of the firm. This is accomplished by completing the sequence of steps known as the accounting cycle. In effect, the accounting cycle involves processing the raw material of the accounting system (business transactions) in order to get the output or end product, which is information to management in the form of financial statements and other accounting reports.

The basic steps of the accounting cycle include the recording phase, commonly referred to as bookkeeping, which is often confused with the overall accounting function. Accounting, however, goes beyond the bookkeeping function, which is mechanical in nature. Accounting's analytical function is primarily the design of specific accounting systems and the preparation, analysis, and interpretation of accounting data as presented in the financial statement produced by the accounting system.

FINANCIAL STATEMENTS

Financial statements (the output or end product of the accounting system) represent means of transmitting to management and other interested parties a concise picture of the profitability and financial condition of a business entity. The three major financial statements are the balance sheet, the statement of income, and the statement of cash flow. Together these financial statements summarize all the business transactions included in the detailed accounting records of the company.

The balance sheet shows the financial position of a company at a particular point in time. It will answer questions such as what resources are owned by the company, which are called assets, or what amounts are owed by the company, which are called liabilities. It is also referred to as a position statement or statement of condition. Furthermore, it is of great interest to management and outsiders as an indicator of the financial strength of the firm.

The statement of income reflects the results of the operations of a company during a specific period of time, better known as the accounting period—a month, a quarter, and a year. It will indicate whether management has achieved its primary objective—earning an adequate profit for the owners of the company during the accounting period. A profit is earned when revenues, the inflow of assets received in exchange for services rendered, is greater than the items consumed (expenses) in the process of rendering these services. These concepts are expanded upon in later chapters.

In addition to the balance sheet and the income statement, a third basic financial statement is the statement of cash flow. The latter summarizes the operating, financing, and investing activities of management during the accounting period. Also, it is used by hospitality managers in the planning of future investment projects, as well as in making major financing decisions, which are of utmost importance to the hospitality industry as a result of its large capital requirements.

The three aforementioned financial statements are prepared in accordance with a set of conventions called generally accepted accounting principles (GAAP). These principles, and the related concepts to which they are directed, represent the foundation of accounting. They will be discussed in more detail in Chapter 2. Because of the unique features of the hospitality industry, and particularly departmentalized operations for some segments of the industry, some industry associations have developed uniform systems of accounts to be used in the preparation of financial statements. In Section 2, we shall discuss in some detail the basic guidelines underlying the preparation of the statement of income according to the Uniform System of Accounts for the Lodging Industry, which underwent a major revision in 1997 and was approved by the American Hotel and Motel Association.

THE HOSPITALITY MANAGER'S NEED FOR ACCOUNTING INFORMATION

As we have already noted, it would be impossible for a hospitality industry organization to carry out and fulfill its basic goals without good accounting information. To give a specific example of how accounting information aids hospitality management, consider the following situation:

Madison Inn is a medium-sized hotel operation, headed by Ms. Rose, its general manager. The company employs sixty-five people, who are working toward the principal objective of the organization—earning an adequate profit by providing lodging and food services. Madison Inn owns land and a building in which the hotel operates, and the furniture and fixtures used in its operations. Additionally, it has cash in a bank account, office and housekeeping supplies, and food that is offered for sale. All of these items represent the resources that Madison Inn needs to conduct its business.

What accounting information does Ms. Rose need in order to conduct business activities and make the necessary economic decisions of the Madison Inn organization? In essence, she needs accounting information to direct daily operations, to plan future operations, and to select the best alternative in the solution of operational problems. Specifically, she will need to know the contribution of each department of the hotel to total earnings, the amounts owed by customers, the amounts owed to each purveyor and the date payment is due, the amount of cash in the bank at any particular time, and the future cash requirements. These are just some examples of the types of accounting information required by Ms. Rose for directing a smooth operation. Without receiving adequate accounting information, on a timely basis, Ms. Rose's decisions may fail to achieve the basic objective of maximizing the owner's return on investment.

The higher the level of authority and responsibility, the greater the need for accounting information. Nevertheless, middle and lower management also depend upon accounting records in decision making. For instance, the house-keeper of Madison Inn needs to know what supplies are on hand and what items are needed so that additional quantities can be ordered. Sometimes, hospitality management relies upon the expertise of professional accountants to meet its need for accounting information. The Certified Public Accountant (CPA) is the recognized professional accountant. Required to hold a CPA certificate indicating the attainment of specific educational and professional criteria, the passing of the CPA examination, and complying with ethical and technical standards enforced by this profession, the CPA furnishes auditing, tax, and other accounting services. While CPAs are also engaged to provide advice and consultation on various management problems, they do not make management decisions. Therefore, responsibility for the contents and integrity of the financial statements ultimately lies with management.

In summary, the primary aim of accounting is to provide useful and relevant information to management as an aid to decision-making. On this basis, hospitality managers are not interested in accounting as an end in itself but as a necessary step toward using financial statements and other accounting information for decision-making purposes. Regardless of the degree of assistance provided by professional accountants, obtaining the knowledge that is so indispensable to successfully operating the hospitality firm requires that each manager possess an adequate accounting background.

SOME KEY TERMS INTRODUCED IN THIS CHAPTER

1. **Accounting.** A system for collecting, summarizing, analyzing, and reporting, in monetary terms, information concerning an organization.
2. **Accounting cycle.** The processing of the raw material of the accounting system in order to obtain the output of the system, which is information to management and others in the form of financial statements and other reports.
3. **Accounting period.** The segment of time selected to measure the results of operations. This is usually one year, although it may be a month, a quarter, or a semi-annual period.
4. **Assets.** Future values or resources owned by the business.
5. **Balance Sheet.** A financial statement that reflects the position of a business at a point in time.
6. **Board of Directors.** The governing board of a corporation elected by the voting stockholders.
7. **Bookkeeping.** The record-keeping, or initial, phase of accounting.
8. **Business transactions.** The raw material of the accounting system involving an equal exchange of value between organizations.
9. **Cash Flow Statement.** A financial statement that summarizes the operating, investing and financing activities of management by showing sources and uses of cash.
10. **Certified Public Accountant (CPA).** The recognized professional accountant who provides auditing, tax, consultation and advisory services.
11. **Corporation.** A multiple-owner organization that is recognized as a separate legal entity.
12. **Creditor.** A person or company to whom a debt is owed.
13. **Earnings.** The excess of revenues over expenses.
14. **Expenses.** Goods or services consumed in operating a business.
15. **Financial accounting.** Accounting information for both internal and external users.

16. **Financial statements.** The output or end product of the accounting system, representing means of transmitting to management and other interested parties a concise picture of the profitability and financial condition of a business entity.
17. **Generally Accepted Accounting Principles (GAAP).** Set of ground rules or conventions that have received substantial support from an authoritative source.
18. **Income.** *See* earnings.
19. **Income Statement.** A financial statement that reflects the results of operations of a company for a certain period of time.
20. **Liabilities.** Claims of creditors against assets, representing amounts owed by the business.
21. **Limited liability.** Owners are not personally liable for the debts of the organization.
22. **Management.** Group of people in a firm who are responsible for planning, controlling, and directing business activities.
23. **Management accounting.** The accounting procedures primarily concerned with the internal uses of accounting information by management.
24. **Mutual agency.** All partners' responsibility for an individual partner's business actions in a partnership.
25. **Organization.** Distinct entity with stated purposes operating in a clearly definable environment.
26. **Partnership.** An association of two or more persons to carry on as co-owners of a business that is not organized as a corporation.
27. **Profitability.** Measure of a company's ability to generate earnings from its available resources.
28. **Proprietorship.** *See* sole proprietorships.
29. **Quid pro quo.** Something for something; equal exchange of values inherent to business transactions.
30. **Revenue.** An inflow of assets in exchange for goods and services.
31. **Sales.** *See* revenue.
32. **Shareholders.** *See* stockholders.
33. **Sole proprietorship.** An unincorporated business owned by one individual.
34. **Source documents.** Written documents that serve as evidence that a business transaction took place, such as bank checks, purchase invoices or cash register tapes.
35. **Statement of Cash Flow.** *See* Cash Flow Statement.
36. **Stockholders.** Owners of a corporation.
37. **Transactions.** *See* business transactions.
38. **Unlimited liability.** Owners are personally liable for the debts of the business.

QUESTIONS

1. What is accounting?
2. What is the main purpose of accounting?
3. Name and describe which groups are the primary users of accounting information.
4. What is the main difference between management accounting and financial accounting?
5. What are the similarities between financial accounting and management accounting?
6. Describe how a hospitality firm can use accounting information as a basis for making business decisions.
7. What is an organization?

8. What is the main objective of a hospitality organization?
9. What is a business transaction?
10. What is the input of the accounting system?
11. What is the output, or end product, of the accounting system?
12. Name and describe the three basic financial statements.
13. Why must a hospitality manager have a basic understanding of the accounting system?
14. Who is responsible for the information contained in the financial statements?
15. Contrast bookkeeping and accounting.
16. What are the major advantages and disadvantages of the sole proprietorship form of business organization?
17. What are the major advantages and disadvantages of the partnership form of business organization?
18. What are the major advantages and disadvantages of the corporate form of business organization?
19. What are three unique characteristics of each of the three forms of business organization?
20. Which is the most important form of business organization in the United States in terms of economic power?

EXERCISES

1. The Lafitof Amusement Park is organized as a corporation. Indicate whether the following statements are true or false.
   (a) There is no need to have a board of directors since one of the characteristics of a corporation is that it has a management team separate and distinct from the owners.
   (b) The owners are personally liable for the corporation's debts.
   (c) The owners must include their portion of the corporation's income on their personal tax return.
   (d) It will be relatively easy to expand because of access to capital.
2. What financial statement(s) would you use to verify each of the following:
   (a) The earnings of Apache Hotel decreased 50 percent during the year.
   (b) Apache Hotel invested $100,000 in a new convention hall during the current accounting period.
   (c) Apache Hotel borrowed $80,000 to make the above investment.
   (d) Apache Hotel sold an old freezer during the current accounting period.
   (e) Apache Hotel repaid $10,000 during the current accounting period.
3. Name five potential users of financial statements and indicate why they may be interested in them.
4. Name five source documents and explain their function.

SHORT PROBLEMS

1. Identify three business transactions for the Madison Inn. Explain why these transactions might affect the balance sheet and/or the income statement of Madison Inn and state the value(s) received and given for each transaction.
2. Visit a fast-food restaurant. List all the sources of revenue you think it has. Now list all of the products and services that you think are consumed by the business (expenses) in the process of generating the above revenue. What is the name of the financial statement that includes the two lists?
3. Visit another fast-food restaurant. List as many resources (assets) as you think the restaurant owns. Then list all the things they may have purchased

on account (credit). These are the restaurant's liabilities. What is the accounting name for the financial statement that includes these two lists?

LONG PROBLEMS

1. The Apache Hotel operates a parking lot on some adjacent land, which it rents from its owner under a five-year lease agreement dated January 1, 2009. Consider the following information:

   1. Apache Hotel installed a lighting system on the parking lot at a cost of $10,000, on January 5, 2009.
   2. Rent payments on the lease are $12,000 per year.
   3. Apache Hotel paid an attendant on an hourly basis according to the number of hours punched on his time card. During 2010, this payment amounted to $12,000.
   4. The electricity paid for lighting the parking lot amounts to $11,000 per year.
   5. The hotel spent $2,000 during 2009 to repair the parking lot. It borrowed the money from Second National Bank and paid $200 interest on the loan in 2010.
   6. During 2010, 36,500 cars used the parking lot, paying an average of $1.00 per car. The parking attendant gave each customer a receipt.
   7. The Apache Hotel sold a fixed number of parking spaces to another hotel on the other side of the lot for a $9,600 yearly fee. During 2010, monthly invoices of $800 were sent to the hotel.

   Required:
   a) Describe all of the transactions you can identify for the year ending December 31, 2010, that are strictly related to the operations of the parking lot.
   b) Name the source documents that are likely to be involved in each transaction.
   c) Determine the parking lot's results of operations for the year ending December 31, 2010 (i.e., did it generate a profit? If so, how much?).
   d) Were there any transactions that took place in 2009 but were not repeated in 2010? Do these transactions benefit the parking lot during 2010? What would you call the items owned by the parking lot as a result of these transactions?

2. (a) List the assets or resources of a hypothetical person (possibly a friend of yours). Then list all the person's debts (the amounts you think they owe).
   (b) Calculate the difference between what they own and what they owe. Decide on a name to be used for this difference.
   (c) What is the accounting name for the two lists you made in (a).

3. (a) List as many sources of imaginary revenue as you can think of for a hypothetical person during a month (possibly a friend).
   (b) List as many items consumed (expenses) as you can think of for this same person during this same period.
   (c) Calculate the difference between the person's revenue and expenses. What is this difference called in accounting terminology?
   (d) What are (a), (b), and (c) above called in accounting terminology when you put them together?

4. Madison Rose is thinking about developing a new restaurant concept: Madsy's Restaurants. She is not sure whether to have the restaurant company set up as a proprietorship, a partnership, or a corporation.

   Required:
   Identify the advantages and disadvantages of the different forms of business organizations and make a recommendation to Ms. Rose.

Basic Accounting Concepts 2

The learning objectives of this chapter are:

- To describe the major reference sources of GAAP.
- To explain the basic accounting concepts that relate to the balance sheet.
- To explain the basic accounting concepts that relate to the income statement.
- To introduce the fundamental accounting equation.
- To understand how transactions affect the fundamental equation and the balance sheet.
- To understand the presentation of the owners' equity section of a balance sheet for all three types of business organizations discussed in Chapter 1.

Simultaneously with the recognition of accounting as a system that provides the financial information necessary for making certain business decisions, the need arises for guidelines to ensure the usefulness and reliability of this accounting information.

In Chapter 1, we saw that the main purpose of accounting is to accumulate information concerning the financial activities of a business organization in a manner that will permit its meaningful summarization in the form of financial statements. Obviously, there cannot be widespread understanding of financial statements unless they are prepared in conformity with a body of generally accepted rules or conventions.

These rules or conventions are called Generally Accepted Accounting Principles, better known by their initials GAAP. All GAAP are oriented toward several basic concepts. GAAP interpret the manner of applying these concepts in specific accounting situations, thereby providing the basis for accounting practice.

In this chapter, we first describe the major reference sources used to decide whether or not a particular accounting treatment has substantial authoritative support and thus merits application as a GAAP. In so doing, we review the main organizations authorized to formulate GAAP. We then explain seven of the basic accounting concepts on which GAAP are based, and which relate principally to the preparation of the balance sheet. The dual-aspect concept of accounting, in particular, is the subject of extensive review, which results from the fact that all business transactions have a dual aspect. We demonstrate that the balance sheet is also based on the dual-aspect concept.

The remaining basic accounting concepts, those more directly applicable to the measurement of business income are then discussed. They serve as guidelines for the proper recognition of revenues and expenses and thus are emphasized in the preparation of an income statement.

We conclude this chapter with the illustration of the owners' equity section of a balance sheet for all three types of business organizations: sole proprietorships, partnerships, and corporations.

GENERALLY ACCEPTED ACCOUNTING PRINCIPLES

In essence, GAAP are those principles that have received substantial support from an authoritative source. The primary organization responsible for developing GAAP in the United States in the past has been the American Institute of Certified Public Accountants (AICPA). Although the 1933 and 1934 securities laws gave the U.S. Securities and Exchange Commission (SEC) the authority and responsibility for the development of GAAP, the SEC informally delegated most of this responsibility to the AICPA. Nevertheless, the SEC has been exerting an ever-increasing influence upon the development of accounting principles, especially in the recent past, because of a growing feeling that the accounting profession has not acted at all times in the best interests of improved financial disclosure. As a result, the SEC has become more involved in the development of its own acceptable accounting principles as formulated in Regulation S-X and in the SEC Accounting Releases.

Up to 1973, GAAP were most heavily influenced by the Accounting Principles Board (APB) of the AICPA. From 1973 to the present, the Financial Accounting Standards Board (FASB) has been primarily responsible for developing GAAP. The FASB, which is part of the Financial Accounting Foundation, an institution that is independent of all professional accounting groups, was created by the AICPA as successor to the APB, which was disbanded in 1973, in order to improve the confidence of investors and other users of financial statements. Since the APB was composed of accounting professionals who donated their efforts on a part-time basis, the output of the APB was in many instances insufficient to satisfy the members of the business and investment communities.

The APB issued 31 opinions and 15 accounting research studies prior to its dissolution. At this writing, the FASB has issued over 130 statements. All opinions, research studies, and statements issued by the APB and the FASB are currently part of GAAP and therefore are considered to have authoritative support unless they have been superseded by a subsequent FASB pronouncement. The FASB is constantly responding to new accounting problems as they arise by amending and enlarging the body of GAAP.

Although entities in the hospitality industry are not legally required to conform to GAAP, there is a strong presumption of misrepresentation in the financial statements if an entity does not. In fact, the financial statements of most hospitality industry firms of any substantial size are examined by independent certified public accountants (CPAs), who are required to issue an opinion regarding the fairness of presentation in these statements. If the CPA's opinion is to be unqualified, it must include a clear affirmation of the financial statements' conformity with GAAP. Material departures from GAAP must be spelled out in the CPA's opinion letter accompanying the financial statements. Thus, they become a matter of public knowledge, affecting how investors, creditors, and other interested parties view the company.

It is important to note that although the external auditor, who must be a CPA, is responsible for conducting an independent examination of the financial statements in order to express an opinion, the responsibility for the preparation and integrity of those financial statements rests with management.

BASIC ACCOUNTING CONCEPTS

As already mentioned, all GAAP are derived from an underlying structure of concepts. They provide the basis for accounting practice and consequently referred to as basic features, principles, postulates, fundamentals, or conventions. The seven basic accounting concepts underlying the preparation of the balance sheet are:

1. Business entity concept
2. Money measurement concept
3. Objectivity concept
4. Going-concern concept
5. Cost concept
6. Conservatism concept
7. Dual-aspect concept

Business Entity Concept

The business entity concept indicates that a hospitality organization will be viewed, for accounting purposes, as a unit independent from its owners. In other words, the firm is considered an economic unit that stands on its own, and therefore, when recording financial information, the activities of the hospitality firm must be kept separate and distinct from personal finances of its owners. For example, the personal automobile of a hotel owner (Mr. X) should not be included among the resources owned by the hotel organization. X Hotel should be recognized as a separate entity on its own right, separate and distinct from Mr. X, its owner. Although Hotel X and Mr. X may not be separate entities from the legal standpoint, the resources assigned to Hotel X for its exclusive use must be accounted for as if they belong to Hotel X separately from Mr. X's other personal resources.

The debts of a business must also be reported separately from the debts of the owner. This means that even if there is no legal distinction between Hotel X and Mr. X, only those debts of Mr. X that are directly related to the hotel business may be included in the hotel's financial statements.

Money Measurement Concept

Accounting is concerned with the recording of facts that can be expressed in monetary terms. Without such a standard of measure, accounting reports would not be very meaningful, for they would include such diverse items as 8 trucks, 18,000 square feet of building space, and 100 acres of land, with no statement of their value in terms of a common monetary unit.

In the United States, financial statements are expressed in terms of U.S. dollars. This common denominator enables the quantification of the effects of a wide variety of financial transactions. Use of the dollar as a measuring unit assumes that it is an unchanging yardstick, a stable-measuring unit. Unfortunately, we all know that a dollar in the year 2000 does not have the same purchasing power as a 1970 or 1980 dollar. The rather significant inflation (increase in prices resulting in decreased purchasing power of the dollar) of the late 1970s and early 1980s created concern over the validity of considering the dollar a stable measuring unit.

Several techniques have been devised to adjust financial statements in order to compensate for the changing value of the dollar. However, GAAP still requires the use of the money measurement concept, which assumes a stable monetary unit.

Objectivity Concept

In order to ensure the necessary reliability of the information disclosed in financial statements, the accounting measurements must be objective and verifiable; that is, free from bias and subject to verification by an independent third party, usually an auditor. Some accounting measurements are very easily verified, but many measurements on financial statements contain elements of judgment and thus need to be systematized so that others repeating the same rational process will obtain the same measurement results. In any event, the amounts reported should not be biased by the subjective judgments of management. For instance, objective verifiable evidence in processing the purchase of inventory will include a vendor's invoice showing that the purchase was actually made.

Going-Concern Concept

In the absence of evidence to the contrary, the assumption we make in the accounting process is that the hospitality entity will continue in operation indefinitely. It follows, therefore, since the business is not to be sold or liquidated, that there is no need to record current replacement values (market values) or liquidating values.

The going-concern concept, also known as the continuity concept, influences the measurement process. Under this assumption, we show the resources owned by the business (land, buildings) at their original cost, inasmuch as they are not going to be sold. Instead, we assume that these resources are used in the regular operations of the business. Hence, the current resale value of these resources is irrelevant in the measurement process.

When there is good reason to believe that the going-concern concept is no longer applicable to a particular firm, then management is required to measure the resources owned by the business at their liquidating value. Using liquidation values is seldom justified—a firm must be in partial or total liquidation before a firm's resources may be so valued.

Cost Concept

The cost concept is very closely related to the going-concern concept. It states that cost is the proper basis for accounting for the resources owned by the hospitality organization. As we learned in Chapter 1, these resources are called assets.

Assets represent future values (resources) owned by the business. Cost is defined as the price paid to acquire an asset. The acquisition cost of an asset will remain in the accounting records until the asset is sold, expires, or is consumed by the business.

For example, a piece of land acquired by a hotel in 1990 for $100,000 would appear on the balance sheet at its acquisition cost until sold by the hotel. If in 2003 the land could be sold for $200,000, no change would be made in the accounting records to reflect this fact. The land would still appear on the balance sheet at its acquisition cost of $100,000.

It follows from the cost concept that the amounts at which assets are listed in the accounting records do not indicate what these assets are worth except at the time they were acquired. In fact, at the initial recording of a transaction historical cost usually is the same as the fair market value. However, as time passes, the cost and fair market value will more than likely differ because of changes in a particular market or to inflationary and recessionary trends in the economy as a whole.

Conservatism Concept

Conservatism represents a departure from the cost principle when convincing evidence exists that cost cannot be recovered. It is a judgment exercised in evaluating uncertainties, in order to avoid self-serving exaggeration. In a technical sense, conservatism means selecting the method of measurement that yields the least favorable immediate results. Traditionally, this attitude has been reflected in the working rule, "Anticipate no gains, but provide for all possible losses."

In applying the conservatism concept, assets are to be written up (recorded at a higher value) only upon an exchange, but they might be written down (recorded at a lower value) without an exchange. For instance, consider lower-of-cost-or-market rules in recording food or beverage inventories. Inventories are written down when replacement costs decline, but they are not written up when replacement costs increase. For additional discussion of inventories, see Chapter 11.

The conservatism concept, however, should not be used to justify an unwarranted reduction in the asset costs and earnings of an entity. An example of this is provided by the FASB in its Statement of Accounting Concept No. 2. This statement interprets the conservatism concept in the specific area of estimates of future events. If two estimates of future payment, one greater than the other, are equally likely to occur, conservatism requires the use of the lesser estimate. If, however, the greater future payment estimate is more likely to happen, it will be more objective to use the greater estimate rather than the lesser. Consequently, the application of the conservatism concept does require the use of prudent judgment in evaluating the uncertainties and risks inherent in business situations. A deliberate understatement of the assets and earnings of the firm, which goes contrary to the facts, as they are likely to evolve, should be avoided.

DUAL-ASPECT CONCEPT: THE FUNDAMENTAL ACCOUNTING EQUATION

The dual-aspect concept is based on the fact that there are ownership claims to all things of value. This can be expressed in the form of the fundamental accounting equation:

$$ASSETS = EQUITIES$$

If a hospitality entity buys a car for $5,000 cash, the asset's value is recorded as $5,000. The entity has the right of ownership over the car for an equal amount of $5,000. This ownership right is called the owner's equity in the car. If, however, the entity borrows $3,000 to buy the car, then the lender of this money has a claim against the car in the amount of $3,000. At the same time, the owner's claim is reduced to $2,000 ($5,000 − $3,000). The claims of lenders against the assets of a firm are called liabilities. After taking into account the claims of lenders, the fundamental accounting equation becomes:

$$ASSETS = LIABILITIES + OWNERS' EQUITY$$

If we substitute the amounts from our hypothetical car purchase, the equation will be expressed as:

$$ASSETS = LIABILITIES + OWNERS' EQUITY$$
$$\$5,000 \text{ (Car)} = \$3,000 \text{ (Amount borrowed)} + \$2,000$$

As we can see, all assets of the business are claimed by someone—either by the owners or by outside parties, known as creditors. Assets are all the resources owned by the hospitality entity. These may consist of money (cash), land, buildings, equipment, and other property or property rights. Liabilities are the claims of creditors (lenders) against the assets of the hospitality firm. Creditors have a claim against these assets until amounts they loan to the entity have been repaid.

Examples of liabilities include accounts payable (amounts owed to suppliers) and notes payable (amounts owed to the bank).

Owners' equity represents the claims of the owners of the hospitality organization. It is also referred to as capital or stockholders' equity, depending on the type of legal organization used by the entity. The owners' equity can be determined at any time by subtracting the liabilities from the assets. The fundamental accounting equation can be rearranged in the following manner:

$$OWNERS'\ EQUITY = ASSETS - LIABILITIES$$

This illustrates the residual owners' equity. That is, owners have claims on the assets of the hospitality business only after the creditors' claims have been fully satisfied.

At the inception of a hospitality firm's life, the owners' equity is represented by the original investment made by the owners in the business. Subsequently, owners' equity may increase with additional owners' investments. Further, an entity generates a profit when it earns more assets than it consumes.

This net increase in assets belongs to the owners of the entity, so that earning a profit also increases the owners' equity of an entity. On the other hand, since losses produce a net decrease in the assets of an entity, they diminish owners' equity. We can say that business profits belong to the owners just as owners are negatively affected by losses. In other words, owners reap the fruits of profits earned by the entity but must also bear the brunt of losses.

Accordingly, when a firm earns assets, we say that it is receiving revenue, whereas when a firm consumes assets we say that it is incurring expenses. Usually, a hospitality firm earns assets by selling food and beverages or by selling a service, such as temporary lodging. Revenues and expenses can be said to be logical extensions of owners' equity. Revenues represent an increase in the entity assets resulting from the sale of goods or services and, consequently, they will increase owners' equity. In the process of earning these revenues, assets are consumed, resulting in a corresponding decrease in owners' equity. Thus, expenses represent the costs incurred by the hospitality entity in earning revenues and tend to decrease owners' equity. Similarly, when assets earned are distributed to the owners of the firm in some form (usually money), this also logically produces a decrease in owners' equity.

The fundamental accounting equation forms the basis of the double-entry accounting system. All transactions will have a dual effect on the equation, maintaining its equality at all times. The sum of the claims of creditors and owners must always equal the total assets of a hospitality industry entity. Therefore, a transaction that increases an asset must, in turn, increase a liability or owners' equity and/or decrease another asset. For example, if Aric's Hotel borrowed $2,000 from a bank, the assets (cash) of the business would increase $2,000, while the liabilities (notes payable) would also increase by $2,000. If Aric's Hotel buys a refrigerator for cash, one asset (cash) decreases while another asset (equipment) increases. In both instances, the fundamental accounting equation remains in balance.

Effect of Transactions on the Fundamental Accounting Equation

As noted before, business transactions affect elements on both sides of the fundamental accounting equation equally. Thus, while the total assets of a business may increase or decrease the change will always be accompanied by a corresponding change in liabilities and/or owners' equity. In accounting, this condition of equality must always exist. To illustrate the fundamental accounting equation further, we analyze the following three transactions for BB Hotel, which is a sole proprietorship:

June 1: (a) Mr. Bryan Bober invested $100,000 cash in the business.
2: (b) BB Hotel paid $1,000 cash for housekeeping supplies.
3: (c) BB Hotel purchased $30,000 worth of furniture and equipment on account.

Transaction (a)—Invested cash. Mr. Bryan Bober made a contribution or investment of cash to start his BB Hotel business. The dual-aspect of this event is that BB Hotel now has an asset, cash, of $100,000, and Mr. Bober, the owner, has a claim against this asset, also of $100,000. This transaction would be shown as follows:

$$\frac{\text{Assets} \quad = \text{Liabilities} + \text{Owner's equity}}{100,000 \text{ (cash)} = \quad 0 \quad + \quad 100,000}$$

Transaction (b)—Paid cash for housekeeping supplies. BB Hotel purchased housekeeping supplies for cash, exchanging one asset for another. The total amount of assets did not change, but now there are two assets, cash and housekeeping supplies inventory. Owner's equity was not affected by this transaction. The effects of transaction (a) and (b) on the fundamental accounting equation are shown below:

	Assets	= Liabilities +	Owner's equity
	Cash + Housekeeping = supplies	0 +	100,000
(a)	+100,000 + 0		
(b)	−1,000 + 1,000	= 0 +	0
	+99,000 + 1 000	= 0 +	100,000

100,000 Assets = 100,000 Equities

Transaction (c)—Purchase of furniture and equipment on account. BB Hotel purchased furniture and equipment on credit. An asset (furniture and equipment) is increased and a liability (accounts payable) also increases. The owner's equity is not affected. The overall effect on the fundamental accounting equation of the BB Hotel produced by the transactions is shown below:

	Assets			= Liabilities +	Owner's equity
	Cash	Housekeeping supplies	Furniture & equipment	Accounts payable	
(a)	+100,000			= 0 +	100,000
(b)		−1,000 + 1,000		= 0 +	0
(c)			+30,000	= +30,000 +	0
	99,000 +	1,000	+30,000	= 30,000 +	100,000

130,000 Assets = 130,000 Equities

We can now see how the property values (assets) of a hospitality firm can be determined at any point in time by adding the claims of creditors (liabilities) and the claims of owners (owners' equity) against these assets. It is also evident that at every step of the accounting process, the equality of the fundamental accounting equation is maintained.

We can now begin to understand why the fundamental accounting equation is the basis for the preparation of one of the basic financial statements—the balance sheet. The balance sheet is often referred to as the position statement because it reflects the financial position of a company at a single point in time. This statement includes the assets of the firm and the claims against those assets (liabilities and owners' equity) on a specific date. In the above illustration, the balance sheet of BB Hotel as of June 3, 2010 would show the following information summarized according to the fundamental accounting equation:

BB HOTEL
Balance Sheet
June 3, 2010

Assets		Liabilities & Owner's Equity	
Cash	$ 99,000	Liabilities	
Housekeeping supplies		Accounts payable	$30,000
inventory	1,000	Owner's equity	
Furniture and equipment	30,000	Bryan Bober, capital	100,000
Total assets	$130,000	Total liabilities & owner's equity	$130,000

Illustrative Problem

We continue analyzing the effect of typical transactions on the fundamental accounting equation by reviewing several transactions for a newly formed restaurant. These business transactions are events that affect the financial condition of the business. They are explained below and analyzed in Table 2–1. Mr. David Ricardo and Ms. Lisa Montcalm formed a partnership, David and Lisa's Restaurant, which was engaged in several transactions during the first two weeks of operations. These transactions are presented on the following pages. (Refer to Table 2–1 for the analysis of the effect of each of these transactions on the fundamental accounting equation.)

1. Mr. Ricardo and Ms. Montcalm invested $5,000 each to start David and Lisa's Restaurant. The total investment of $10,000 is deposited in a bank account opened in the name of the restaurant. The asset (cash) and the owners' equity are increased.

2. A bank loan of $30,000 is negotiated, and the proceeds of the loan are deposited in the organization's bank account. The bank, calling for annual interest of 12 percent, issues a note. An asset (cash) increases and a liability (notes payable) also increases.

3. A lease is signed, for a fully equipped building for two years, with the right to renew for two additional years. The annual cost is $24,000, payable monthly in advance. The first month's rent ($2,000) is paid. An asset (cash) decreases and an expense (rent expense) increases, causing a corresponding indirect decrease in owners' equity.

4. Food inventory is purchased for $2,000. Supplies require cash payment by new accounts, and so payment is collect on delivery (COD). An asset (food inventory) is received in exchange for another asset (cash).

5. Sales for the first week were $1,000: $500 in cash, $300 paid by credit cards, and $200 on open account. Assets (cash and accounts receivable) increased and revenues (food sales) increased, resulting in an indirect increase in owners' equity. Accounts receivable reflects the future value received by the restaurant in the form of the customer's understanding to pay for the food and services received when due, according to the applicable credit terms.

6. A beverage license application is filed. The year's fee is $1,200 payable with the application. Since David and Lisa's Restaurant is making an advance

Table 2–1. Transaction analysis for David and Lisa's Restaurant (dates as indicated)

Date, Feb., 2007	Transaction	Assets Cash	Accounts receivable	Food inventory	Prepaid expenses	Land	Equipment	Liabilities Accounts payable	Notes payable	Mortgages payable	Owners' Equity Ricardo capital	Montcalm capital	Revenue/(expense)
1.	Owners' invested cash	10,000									5,000	5,000	
2.	Borrowed $30,000 from bank	+30,000 40,000							+30,000 30,000		5,000	5,000	
3.	Paid one month's rent	−2,000 38,000							30,000		5,000	5,000	−2,000 Rent expense (2,000)
4.	Purchased food inventory on a COD basis	−2,000 36,000		+2,000 2,000					30,000		5,000	5,000	(2,000)
5.	Sales for first week	+500 36,500	+500 500	2,000					30,000		5,000	5,000	+1,000 Food sales (1,000)
6.	Prepaid beverage license fee	−1,200 35,300	500	2,000	+1,200 1,200				30,000		5,000	5,000	(1,000)
7.	Cost of food sold	35,300	500	−400 1,600	1,200				30,000		5,000	5,000	−400 Cost of food sold (1,400)
8.	Prepaid insurance premium	−2,400 32,900	500	1,600	+2,400 3,600				30,000		5,000	5,000	(1,400)
9.	Purchased land	−2,000 30,900	500	1,600	3,600	+20,000 20,000			30,000	+18,000 18,000	5,000	5,000	(1,400)
10.	Cash received for first week's credit card sales	+285 31,185	−300 200	1,600	3,600	20,000			30,000	18,000	5,000	5,000	−15 Credit card fees (1,415)
11.	Purchased kitchen equipment on account	31,185	200	1,600	3,600	20,000	+2,000 2,000	+2,000 2,000	30,000	18,000	5,000	5,000	(1,415)
12.	Sales for second week	+1,200 32,385	+1,300 1,500	1,600	3,600	20,000	2,000	2,000	30,000	18,000	5,000	5,000	+2,500 Food sales 1,085
13.	Cost of food sold	32,385	1,500	−1,000 600	3,600	20,000	2,000	2,000	30,000	18,000	5,000	5,000	−1,000 Cost of food sold 85
	Closing balance	32,385	1,500	600	3,600	20,000	2,000	2,000	30,000	18,000	5,000	5,000	85

Total assets: 60,085

Total liabilities and owners' equity: 60,085

payment for an item having a future value to the business (the right to sell alcoholic beverages for the specified time period), they are acquiring an asset. This type of asset is commonly referred to as a prepaid expense because payment is made before the expense is incurred. It will become an ordinary expense gradually as its benefits are consumed by the restaurant in the generation of revenues, which will occur as the license expires during the course of the year. Consequently, this transaction results in one asset (prepaid expenses) being exchanged for another asset (cash).

7. Food costing $400 was consumed in making the sales for the first week. An asset (food inventory) is decreased and expenses (cost of food sold) increased because of the consumption of the food in producing the aforementioned sales. The increase in expenses will cause an indirect decrease in owners' equity inasmuch as expenses decrease owners' equity.

8. David and Lisa's Restaurant purchased a two-year fire insurance and liability policy for $2,400, paying cash. Again, the business has acquired a future value—two-years' insurance protection—by making an advance payment. Thus, the insurance protection bought with the $2,400 premium is an asset that falls within the previously described asset category of prepaid expenses. Consequently, one asset (prepaid expenses) is exchanged for another asset (cash).

9. The partners agree to purchase a future building site. The cost is $20,000. They pay $2,000 down and give a 10-year, 15 percent mortgage for the balance. One asset (land) increases, another asset (cash) decreases for the cash paid out, and a liability (mortgages payable) increases as a result of the written promise to repay the mortgage loan in 10 years.

10. The credit card company sends a $285 check in payment for credit card sales during the first week ($300). The remaining $15 is the 5 percent fee the credit card company charges for collection. One asset (accounts receivable) is decreased, another asset (cash) is increased, and there is an increase in an expense (credit card fees) resulting in a decrease in owners' equity.

11. Kitchen equipment is purchased on account for $2,000. An asset (equipment) increases and a liability (accounts payable) also increases.

12. David and Lisa's Restaurant is doing splendidly. The second week's sales are $2,500: $1,200 in cash, $500 on open account, and $800 in credit card sales. Two assets (cash and accounts receivable) increase in the presence of revenues (food sales). As previously explained, revenues are earned assets and therefore also increase owners' equity.

13. Food costing $1,000 was consumed in making the second week's sales. Assets (food inventory) decreased and expenses (cost of food sold) increased. This increase in cost of food sold expense results in a decrease in owners' equity.

From the foregoing illustrative problem, it is evident that every recorded event affects at least two items, in essence, changing both assets and equities (liabilities and owners' equity). Therefore, every accounting transaction can be analyzed in terms of its effect on the balance sheet.

We now carry out the illustrative problem one step further by demonstrating how a balance sheet can be prepared from the transaction analysis shown in Table 2–1, since it is an expanded version of the fundamental accounting equation.

Now that all the transactions have been analyzed and recorded in terms of their effect on the fundamental accounting equation, as well as their balance sheet

DAVID AND LISA'S RESTAURANT
Balance Sheet
February 13, 2007

Assets		
Cash		$32,385
Accounts receivable		1,500
Food inventory		600
Prepaid expenses		3,600
Land		20,000
Equipment		2,000
Total assets		$60,085
Liabilities & Owner's Equity		
Liabilities		
Accounts payable		$ 2,000
Notes payable		30,000
Mortgages payable		18,000
Total liabilities		50,000
Owner's equity		
David Ricardo, capital	$ 5,000	
Lisa Montcalm, captial	5,000	
	10,000	
Net income for the period ended		
February 13, 2007	85	
Total owner's equity		10,085
Total liabilities & owner's equity		$60,085

Exhibit 2–1   Balance sheet for David and Lisa's Restaurant as of February 13, 2007.

effect, all the necessary information is available for the preparation of the balance sheet.

We utilize the information from the column headings of assets, liabilities, and owners' equity. In the case of the owners' equity section of the balance sheet, it is necessary to show the owners' investments separate from the earnings of the period (excess of revenue over expenses), commonly called net income. This detailed owners' equity information is usually shown as a separate supporting statement known as "the statement of owners' equity."

The balance sheet for David and Lisa's Restaurant is presented in Exhibit 2–1. It reflects the financial position of the restaurant as of February 13, 2007 (the balance sheet date) by listing individually all resources owned by the organization (assets) and the claims of creditors and owners against those resources (liabilities and owners' equity).

THE MEASUREMENT OF BUSINESS INCOME

The measurement of business income is the main focus of the income statement, which summarizes revenues and expenses over a stated period of time. Hence, the determination of the point in time when each revenue and expense should be recognized and the allowable amount of revenue and expense are of crucial importance in determining the net income or net loss for the period.

The prime objective of a hospitality firm is to earn a profit (net income) for its owners, thereby providing an adequate return on the owners' investment in the business (return on investment, ROI). This objective is achieved primarily by providing services to its customers. A hotel firm offers lodging, food, and telephone services, among others; a restaurant provides a dining experience to its patrons; a tourism organization offers travel services, and so on. All these examples illustrate the revenues earned by hospitality-oriented organizations by providing services to customers. Consequently, when a company sells its services (or goods), assets (mainly cash or accounts receivable) are received by the company in exchange. As we already know, assets received in exchange for goods and services sold are called revenues. Revenues will result in a corresponding increase in net income and ultimately in owners' equity.

The hospitality firm has to use certain items in operating the business and providing the aforementioned services to its customers. These items represent the costs of doing business, or expenses, and include the cost of goods and services consumed (incurred) in generating revenues. For instance, a travel agency consumes the services of its employees (salary and wage expenses), the service of a utility company (electricity expense), and so on.

An income statement is prepared by listing the revenues earned during the period and the expenses incurred in earning those revenues during the same period. The basic accounting concepts relating to the measurement of income must serve as guidelines for the proper recognition of revenues and expenses, thereby ensuring accuracy and uniformity of income measurement. They are 1) time period, 2) realization, 3) matching, 4) consistency, and 5) materiality.

Time Period Concept

Even though business activities are considered to continue forever (in accordance with the going-concern concept discussed earlier, the income statement reports revenues, expenses, and resulting net income only for a convenient segment of time. The main reason for subdividing the life of an enterprise this way is to provide management and other users of accounting information with periodic reports that will serve as a basis on which to evaluate the firm's progress.

The segment of time selected to measure the results of operations of a hospitality organization is called the accounting period. It may cover one month, three months (a quarter), or one year, and represents the interval of time over which the transactions are recorded and summarized in order to prepare the basic financial statements, which is done at the end of the period. Whereas the balance sheet, as we saw, is prepared as of the last date of the accounting period, the income statement includes the business activity over the entire accounting period being reported on. Because of this, the income statement is considered a flow statement. For external reporting purposes, the accounting period is usually one year, which may or may not coincide with the calendar year. When a twelve-month period other than a calendar year is used, it is called a fiscal year. Usually when fiscal year accounting period is selected, it is based on an entity's natural business year. A natural business year ends when business activity is at its lowest point, thereby facilitating the measurement of business income.

Accounting statements for periods shorter than one year are called interim statements and are used primarily for internal management information purposes. Many hotels and restaurants prepare monthly and/or quarterly interim statements. Also, publicly held companies (those owned by the general public) are required to submit quarterly statements to the SEC in addition to their annual reports.

In sum, the time period concept states that the results of operations will be measured over specific intervals of time.

The Realization Concept

The realization concept dictates the recognition of revenue. It requires that revenue be recognized at the time it is earned, which generally occurs when a sale of a product is made (formally, when title to goods is transferred) or services are rendered: Recognition is the process of formally recording or incorporating an item in the financial statements of an entity.

Based on the realization concept, the receipt of cash is not a determining factor in the recognition of revenues. Revenues are to be assigned to the accounting period in which they are earned, regardless of when cash is actually collected. For instance, the sale of a hotel room on credit terms (on account) will be recognized as revenue by the hotel in the period when the customer receives the services, as opposed to the period when cash is actually collected. When the hotel customer pays the amount due (at some future date), the amount collected is not considered revenue but is treated instead as an exchange of two assets (a decrease in accounts receivable and an increase in cash).

In practice, the moment when revenue must be recognized is often called the point of sale and is subject to the following conditions:

- The earning process is essentially complete.
- Its exchange value can be objectively determined.

Based on the realization principle, revenues received in advance may not be recognized in the current period. Customers' deposits, for example, do not fulfill the requirements for revenue recognition since the earnings process is not essentially complete. Thus, when a hotel receives a deposit to be applied against a future reservation, the deposit does not represent revenue but is considered unearned income (deferred income) since services have not yet been rendered. It represents an increase in assets (cash) and liabilities (unearned income). When the customer applies a deposit to an actual room rental, then and only then will the hotel recognize the revenue.

Occasionally, problems arise in applying the realization concept to practical situations. One typical example of a difficult revenue recognition situation in the hospitality industry is accounting for franchise fee revenue. Generally, the sale of a franchise results in the hotel or restaurant chain receiving an initial fee plus a percentage of annual gross revenue over the life of the franchise in exchange for granting certain rights and performing specified services, such as assistance in site selection or supervision of construction activity. The initial fee may call for a down payment at the time of signing the franchise agreement and the balance in equal installments over a specified future period. In deciding when the initial fee revenue should be recognized, several alternatives are available:

1. When the cash is received (cash basis)
2. At the inception of the franchise (when the agreement is signed)
3. Spread over the life of the franchise agreement
4. When substantial performance has occurred

Current accounting authorities require alternative (4), which normally has taken place when the franchise begins operation. This alternative seems to fulfill the revenue recognition criteria better than do the others, that are based on the assumption that the earnings process is virtually complete when a franchisee opens for business.

Matching Concept: The Accrual Basis of Accounting

The matching concept deals with the recognition of expenses. Just as revenues are to be recognized when earned (the realization concept), the matching concept calls for expenses to be recognized when consumed (incurred) in the process of generating revenues. Furthermore, expenses are to be matched (offset) against the revenues they helped produce during each accounting period. As with revenues, expenses are recognized when incurred, regardless of whether or not cash is paid out. Salaries and wages, for example, are recognized as expenses in the period the employee services are received, even though this might not be the same period in which payment for those services is made.

Although expense recognition will normally follow revenue recognition, as noted earlier, some problems do occur in determining when certain revenues are to be recognized. Furthermore, it may also be difficult to determine exactly which expenses have been incurred in producing revenues in a given accounting period. This means that perfect matching is quite difficult to achieve. Nonetheless, it is essential to match revenues and expenses over time in order to ensure the proper measurement of periodic business income.

In the process of recognizing expenses, one of the problems encountered is that not all costs can be directly assigned to specific revenues. Some expenses may only have an indirect relationship with revenues. Three different standards can be applied to determine whether an expense should be recognized in the current period, as follows:

1. The expense is directly associated with revenues of the period.
2. The expense is directly associated with the accounting period itself.
3. The expense cannot be associated with the revenues of future periods.

Use of the first standard for recognizing expenses implies a direct relationship between expenses and revenues. This direct relationship may also be considered causal in nature. For instance, a commission paid by a hotel for a particular booking should be reported as an expense in the same period that the revenue from the room sale is reported.

Use of the second standard relates to the recognition of expenses that are not directly associated with specific revenue transactions but have contributed to the earning of revenues in general. Thus, they are said to be costs of doing business. General and administrative costs such as professional fees may not be directly associated with any one sale during the period. Nevertheless, these expenses are essential to the operation of the hospitality service firm. Some of these expenses may benefit several accounting periods and may therefore require allocation to the periods that they benefit. For example, an annual insurance premium paid in advance (prepaid insurance) must be allocated as an expense to the monthly periods that it benefits. We cover the systematic allocation of these costs in later chapters.

Use of the third standard for recognizing expenses implies that even though an expense does not produce a benefit in the current accounting period, it is reported as an expense simply because it cannot be associated with the revenue of future periods. In other words, there is an immediate recognition of a de facto consumption of an item that does not benefit the current or future periods. The expensing of spoiled food held in inventory is an example of the immediate recognition of an expense that cannot be associated with revenues of the current or future periods. Assets (food inventory) have been consumed (spoiled) without producing revenues since the food cannot be sold in the current or future periods.

Application of the matching concept in the measurement of income is at the heart of the accrual basis of accounting. The determination of periodic business income is based upon the proper matching of expenses incurred during the period against the revenues they help earn. The process of expense recognition can also be visualized in terms of offsetting efforts (expenses) against the rewards (revenues) of the period. This results in the determination of business success (net income) or failure (net loss) for the specified period of time.

Consistency Concept

The consistency concept requires an entity to give the same accounting treatment to similar events in successive accounting periods. Only when this concept is applied can meaningful comparison be made between accounting periods. Consistent application of accounting methods and procedures increases the usefulness of financial statements to a firm by facilitating the identification of trends within the firm. It should be noted that consistently applying accounting methods and procedures does not, in and of itself, allow comparisons among different firms. Diversity in utilizing accounting methods and procedures is acceptable among different firms, as long as the methods and procedures used are compatible with GAAP. Within each individual firm, however, consistency in their application is imperative.

The concept of consistency does not, however, preclude all changes in accounting methods and procedures. If there is good reason for changing procedures, it should be done. Such changes may be needed to adapt to a changing environment or to conform to new pronouncements of the FASB or the SEC. If a change is deemed necessary, however, the responsibility for justifying it lies with management. The nature of and justification for a change in accounting principle and its effect on net income should be disclosed in the financial statements of the period in which the change is made. The justification for the change should explain clearly why the newly adopted accounting principle is preferable. Changes in accounting methods and procedures should therefore not be taken lightly.

Materiality Concept

Accounting only deals with significant information—there is no reason to be concerned with what is not important. Therefore, insignificant items are not considered in applying the basic accounting concepts. To determine materiality, the size of an item must be considered in relation to the size of the business (i.e., within the economic environment of the firm). An item that is material to one firm may not be material to another.

Consider the following example: A travel agency acquires twenty pencils at a cost of $3 for use in its office. In theory, the acquisition of these items represents an acquired future value (an asset). However, since the amount is considered insignificant, the $3 would be charged to current operations (expensed) and would be included on the income statement of the period as part of miscellaneous expenses. This concept permits a firm to account for amounts that it considers immaterial, in the most efficient and economic manner, rather than the one that is most theoretically correct.

Management is responsible for determining materiality. The decision of what is and what is a not material calls for the exercise of judgment and common sense, within the context of a particular firm. Therefore, the relative importance of any event must be evaluated in relation to the firm where it occurs, and this requires prudent judgment. Expensing $2,000 worth of miscellaneous equipment may be considered immaterial for a very large publicly held company such as McDonald's Corporation. The same amount, however, would be considered material for a small restaurant or hotel and should be recorded as an asset.

OTHER CONCEPTS OF INCOME MEASUREMENT

The accrual basis is considered the most accurate basis of income determination since it provides for the matching of expenses against revenues during each accounting period. This accounting method conforms to GAAP, but other bases of income determination are also used under special circumstances.

Under the cash basis of accounting, revenues are recorded only when cash is received while expenses are recognized only when payment is made. Nonetheless, the cash basis of accounting is only permitted by GAAP when revenues and expenses materially coincide with cash receipts and payments only permit it. For example, a small restaurant selling for cash only and paying wages and supplies with cash may use the cash basis rather than the accrual basis of accounting.

Income measured for tax purposes is governed by regulations established principally by U.S. Congress, the tax courts and the Internal Revenue Service. Tax basis for income measurement may not agree with earnings before taxes as reported on a hospitality firm's income statement. As we learned earlier, net income is determined by the proper application of GAAP. Conversely, taxable income is based on the tax code and reported to the government on a form called a tax return.

ILLUSTRATIVE INCOME STATEMENT

The information used in the transactional analysis for David and Lisa's hypothetical restaurant (Table 2–1) will be used again here to demonstrate how an income statement can be prepared. In the process of doing so, the effect of revenue and expenses on owners' equity will be considered in order to understand why these income statement elements are subdivisions of owners' equity.

Although we illustrated the preparation of the balance sheet by directly referring to the transactional analysis worksheet, in practice the income statement is normally prepared first. It is necessary first to calculate the amount of net income (revenues less expenses), which is then added to the beginning owners' equity. By adding net income to beginning owners' equity, we calculate the amount of owners' equity at the end of the accounting period covered by the income statement. In Table 2–1, revenues are indicated by a plus (+) sign and expenses are indicated by a minus (−) sign based on the fact that revenues increase owners' equity, whereas expenses decrease it. Accordingly, net income will increase owners' equity; on the other hand, net loss will decrease owners' equity. The income statement for David and Lisa's Restaurant is shown below:

DAVID AND LISA'S RESTAURANT
Income Statement
for the Period Ended February 13, 2007

Revenues		
Food sales		$3,500
Total revenues		3,500
Expenses		
Cost of food sold	$1,400	
Rent	2,000	
Credit card fees	15	
Total expenses		3,415
Net income		$ 85

BB HOSPITALITY COMPANY
Statement of Income
for the Years Ended December 31, 2005 and 2004

	2005	2004
Revenues		
Net Sales	$84,600	$75,600
Other income	80	100
Total Revenues	84,680	75,700
Costs and Expenses		
Cost of food sold	20,000	16,000
General and		
Administrative	45,000	42,000
Interest expense	1,000	800
Other expenses	100	70
Total	66,100	58,870
Income before income taxes	18,580	16,830
Income taxes	5,400	4,130
Net Income	$13,180	$12,700

Exhibit 2–2 Example of a comprehensive Income Statement.

Comprehensive Income Statement Illustration

The income statement for David and Lisa's Restaurant is an oversimplified version of an actual income statement. A more comprehensive income statement is presented in Exhibit 2–2. (The income statement will be covered in greater depth in Chapter 10.)

In Exhibit 2–2, the presentation of two successive years (2005 and 2004) permits a comparison of the company's performance between years, and thus enhances the use of financial statements for decision-making purposes. Note that the income tax is considered an expense of doing business for the corporate form of legal organization.

OWNERS' EQUITY IN THE BALANCE SHEET

The form of legal organization determines the manner of reporting owners' equity on the balance sheet. In fact, the accounting and legal differences between the three main forms of business organization are reflected in the owners' equity section of the balance sheet. We shall therefore turn our attention to the balance sheet and discuss the manner of accounting for owners' equity under each form of business enterprise.

Owner's Equity for Proprietorships

Since there is only one owner, it is very simple to account for owner's equity and present it on the balance sheet of the sole proprietorship. Basically there is only a single account, the owner's capital account, to deal with. All entries affecting owner's equity are recorded in this account, which includes owner's investment(s) in the business, withdrawals, and business income or losses. A breakdown of the different sources of changes in the owner's capital account that have occurred from the date of the preceding balance sheet is often included in the company's balance sheet. Nonetheless, a separate statement of owner's capital (or owner's equity) is considered a better presentation. Such a statement might look as follows:

STATEMENT OF OWNER'S CAPITAL
for the Year Ended December 31, 2007

Beginning balance, December 31, 2006	$10,000
Add: Net income for the year 2007	3,000
Less: Withdrawals for the year 2007	1,000
Ending balance, December 31, 2007	$12,000

The balance sheet will only show the ending balance of $12,000. Withdrawals represent the amount of cash or other property taken by the owner from the business for personal use. They are treated as a reduction of the owner's equity in the business. Proprietors have the power to remove cash or other assets from the business for personal use at any time.

The owners' equity of a partnership is similar to that of a proprietorship except that each partner has a separate account, including the same details as the proprietor's capital account (net income, withdrawals, and investments).

Owners' Equity for Corporations

Since the owners of a corporation are the shareholders (or stockholders), the owners' equity section of a corporate balance sheet is commonly referred to as shareholders' equity (or stockholders' equity). It is divided into two major subdivisions in order to differentiate between the owners'/shareholders' investments in the business and the accumulated earnings retained in the firm since the company's formation. The paid-in capital represents the sources of invested capital, including common stock, preferred stock, and additional paid-in capital (see below). When a firm has issued only one class of stock it is referred to as common stock (or simply capital stock). Hence, the common shareholders are considered the true owners of the corporation. Some corporations issue another class of stock, preferred stock, as an additional source of capital. The preferred shareholders, as the name implies, have certain preferences on earnings distributions and upon liquidation of the firm.

Different types and classes of capital stock (in both common and preferred stock) can be issued, each having its own special features. For instance, there is par and no-par stock. Most stocks have a par value, which is an arbitrary value assigned to one share of stock either by the corporation or the board of directors. No-par stock has no specific value per share assigned to it. Additional paid-in capital reflects the portion of paid-in capital that exceeds the par value of the capital stock.

The second source of shareholders' equity is retained earnings. It represents the total of all previous years' net income that has not been distributed as dividends. By not distributing earnings to the shareholders as dividends, the enterprise is in a position to use this retained income as a source of capital for future growth.

A separate statement of retained earnings is prepared summarizing the changes that have taken place during the period. The main items included in the statement of retained earnings are:

- Beginning balance
- Net income or (net loss) for the period
- Dividends declared during the period
- Ending balance

Accordingly, the balance sheet will only include the ending balance of retained earnings. If there is a negative balance in retained earnings, we use the term deficit to refer to it. This will be the result of accumulated losses exceeding accumulated income, and it will be shown as a reduction of shareholders' equity on the corporate balance sheet. An illustration of a simple statement of retained earnings follows:

FRB RESTAURANTS, INC.
Statement of Retained Earnings
for the Year Ended December 31, 2007

Beginning balance, December 31, 2006	$65,000
Add: Net income for the year 2007	$28,000
	$93,000
Less: Dividends declared	$8,000
Ending balance, December 31, 2007	$85,000

As previously noted, the ending balance of retained earnings reflects the net amount of accumulated income, not paid out in the form of dividends since the company was first organized. The following is an illustration of the shareholders' equity section of the FRB Restaurants, Inc. balance sheet as of December 31, 2007:

FRB RESTAURANTS, INC
Shareholders' Equity
December 31, 2007

Common Stock, $1 par value; authorized	
issued and outstanding 50,000 shares	$50,000
Retained earnings	85,000
Total Shareholders' equity	$135,000

The above illustration is a simplified version of the shareholders' equity section of a corporate balance sheet. Many corporations include other equity accounts such as additional paid-in capital, preferred stock and treasury stock. In the above example, the shares of common stock were sold at par, and so there was no need to present additional paid-in capital. We shall cover other corporate accounts in future chapters.

Moreover in the remaining chapters, while we shall occasionally include illustrations and problems concerning sole proprietorships and partnerships, our emphasis will be on the corporate form of legal organization since the corporation is the major form of business enterprise in terms of economic power in the United States.

SOME KEY TERMS INTRODUCED IN THIS CHAPTER

1. **Accounting Principles Board (APB).** A committee of the American Institute of Certified Public Accountants (AICPA) that was responsible for the formulation of accounting principles before it was replaced by the Financial Accounting Standards Board (FASB).
2. **Accrual basis of accounting.** The recognition of revenues when earned and expenses when incurred regardless of when cash is received or paid.
3. **Accounts payable.** Amounts owed to suppliers for goods or services purchased on credit.
4. **Accounts receivable.** Amounts owed by customers for goods or services sold on credit.

5. **Additional paid-in capital.** The portion of paid-in capital that exceeds the par value (or stated value) of the issued shares of both common and preferred stock.

6. **American Institute of CPAs (AICPA).** The foremost national association of certified public accountants.

7. **Business entity concept.** An accounting premise that indicates that an organization is viewed as a unit independent from its owners.

8. **Cash basis of accounting.** A basis of accounting under which revenues and expenses are recognized when cash is received and paid.

9. **Conservatism concept.** When evaluating uncertainties, selecting the method of measurement that yields the least favorable immediate result in order to avoid self-serving exaggeration.

10. **Consistency.** An accounting concept that requires an entity to give the same accounting treatment to similar events in successive accounting periods.

11. **Cost.** Price paid to acquire resources owned by the organization (or assets), representing the proper basis to account for those resources.

12. **Debt.** An amount owed; an obligation.

13. **Dividend.** The distribution of corporate earnings to stockholders as a return on their investment in the company.

14. **Dual-aspect concept.** An accounting premise that is based on the fact that there are ownership claims to all things of value.

15. **Financial Accounting Standards Board (FASB).** An independent board responsible, since 1973, for establishing Generally Accepted Accounting Principles.

16. **Going-concern concept.** For accounting purposes, the assumption made is that the business will continue in operation indefinitely.

17. **Historical cost.** *See* original cost.

18. **Inventory (e.g., food, beverage).** Goods purchased but not yet used to generate revenues.

19. **Matching concept.** An accounting principle requiring that costs necessary for the generation of revenue be matched (offset) against the revenues they helped produced in the determination of periodic net income.

20. **Materiality concept.** An accounting concept that deals with significant information: accordingly, insignificant items might be ignored in applying the basic accounting concepts.

21. **Money measurement concept.** Accounting is only concerned with the recording of facts that can be expressed in monetary terms, as opposed to using physical or other units of measurement.

22. **Net income (or net earnings).** The excess of revenues over expenses.

23. **Net loss.** The excess of expenses over revenues.

24. **Notes payable.** Obligations evidenced by a promissory note.

25. **Objectivity concept.** An accounting concept requiring that accounting measurement is free from bias and subject to verification by an independent third party.

26. **Obligations.** Liabilities of the company.

27. **Owners' equity.** Owners claims on the assets of the business after the creditors' claims have been fully satisfied; residual equity. The owner's equity for a sole proprietorship is called owner's capital; the owner's equity for a partnership is called partners' capital and the owners' equity for a corporation is called shareholders' (or stockholders') equity.

28. **Partners' capital.** *See* owners' equity.

29. **Par value.** An arbitrary value placed on a share of stock at the time the corporation seeks authorization of the stock; usually determines the legal capital of the corporation.

30. **Preferred stock.** A class of capital stock that possesses certain preferences over common stock in earnings distributions and in the event of liquidation of a corporation.
31. **Prepaid expenses.** Items paid in advance that will benefit future accounting periods, for example, prepayments for insurance, rent and licenses.
32. **Profits.** *See* earnings.
33. **Promissory note.** A formal, or written, promise to pay a specific amount on a specific date, which may or may not include interest.
34. **Realization concept.** An accounting principle requiring revenues to be recognized at the time they are earned, rather than when payment is collected.
35. **Recognition.** The process of formally recording or incorporating an item in the financial statements of the company.
36. **Retained earnings.** The cumulative earnings of a firm since its formation, net of any amounts paid out to shareholders in the form of dividends.
37. **Securities and Exchange Commission (SEC).** A federal agency responsible for protecting the interests of investors in publicly held companies by regulating the sale and exchange of most securities.
38. **Shareholders' (or stockholders') equity.** The owners' equity section of a corporate balance sheet. *See also* owners' equity.
39. **Withdrawals.** Cash or property taken out by proprietors or partners for personal use.
40. **Time period concept.** An accounting concept stating that the results of operations of a company are to be measured over specific intervals of time (e.g., month, quarter, year).

QUESTIONS

1. What are basic accounting concepts, and why are they needed?
2. What organization is currently primarily responsible for developing GAAP?
3. What are the basic accounting concepts most applicable to the balance sheet?
4. What are the basic accounting concepts most applicable to the income statement?
5. What concept states that the resources assigned to a business for its exclusive use must be accounted for separately from the assets of the owner of a business? Would your answer change if you were told that legally those assets still belong to the owner of the business?
6. What concept assumes that a business organization will continue operations indefinitely?
7. What basic accounting concept(s) does (do) not permit showing assets at their current market value when a business is not in liquidation?
8. What basic accounting concept allows you to mark down assets under certain circumstances? Does it also allow you to mark up assets when their current value is greater than their cost?
9. Based on what concept would you require clear-cut evidence that a transaction had taken place in order to justify recording the transaction?
10. What is the fundamental accounting equation? How is it related to a balance sheet?
11. How many types of equities are there? Name and describe them. What effect do they have on the fundamental accounting equation? What is another name for assets minus liabilities?

12. What is the difference between an asset and an expense?
13. What is revenue? Name two sources of revenue for (a) a hotel and (b) a restaurant.
14. How does the matching concept relate to the realization concept?
15. How does net income affect owners' equity? How does a net loss affect owners' equity? Explain.
16. How do we calculate owners' equity at the end of the accounting period?
17. Is every cash receipt a revenue? Is every cash expenditure an expense? Explain.
18. What types of business organizations are likely to present a statement of owners' capital? a statement of retained earnings?
19. What is the main difference between the owners' equity section of a corporation's balance sheet and that of a partnership or sole proprietorship?

EXERCISES

1. Give an example of a transaction that might have the following effects:
   (a) Increase owners' equity and decrease a liability
   (b) Decrease an asset and decrease a liability
   (c) Decrease owners' equity and decrease an asset
   (d) Increase one asset and decrease another asset
   (e) Increase an asset and increase a liability
2. Match the appropriate letter(s) reference(s) to each of the following statements. A letter may be used more than once, or not used at all. Use the letter (h) for "none of the above."
   (a) Business Entity
   (b) Consistency
   (c) Going-Concern
   (d) Cost
   (e) Dual-Aspect
   (f) Realization
   (g) Conservatism
   (h) None of the above
   _____ Food Inventory is reported at the lower of cost or market at the end of the reporting period.
   _____ Land is reported on the balance sheet at its acquisition price even though its economic value has risen.
   _____ Assets = Liabilities + Owners' Equity
   _____ Sales of rooms on credit are reported on the income statement
   _____ Accounting is only concerned with significant information.
   _____ To facilitate comparability we give the same accounting treatment to similar events from one period to the next.
   _____ In the absence of evidence to the contrary, we record assets on the balance sheet at their historical cost.
3. State whether each of the following can be used as conclusive evidence that the company is earning a profit. Explain.
   (a) Increase in total assets
   (b) Increase in accounts receivable
   (c) Increase in owners' equity
   (d) Increase in net income
   (e) Increase in cash
4. The basic accounting equation can be expanded to include revenues and expenses. For the following transactions use this expanded accounting

equation to determine the missing amounts on each line of the table below.

	Assets	= Liabilities +		Owners' equity		
			Invested capital +	**Revenues** −	**Expenses**	
(a)	400,000	= 300,000	+ 80,000 +	30,000 −	?	
(b)	?	= 200,000	+ 300,000 +	50,000 −	100,000	
(c)	1,000,000	= ?	+ 600,000 +	0 −	0	
(d)	180,000	= 110,000	+ ? +	50,000 −	40,000	
(e)	100,000	= 60,000	+ 25,000 +	? −	30,000	

5. Prepare an income statement based on the following items:

Rent expense	$100	Supplies expense	$55
Insurance	50	Payroll expense	200
Utilities	90	Laundry expense	45
Sales	1,100	Cost of food sold	350
Interest expense	55	Interest income	90

6. (a) What basis of accounting is the statement below structured upon?
   (b) Could it be used as an income statement for the month of March? Explain.

SOLE BROTHERS FISH RESTAURANT
Statement of Cash Receipts and Expenditures
for the Month Ending March 27, 2000

Receipts	
Cash sales	$181,000
Collections on credit sales	17,500
Owners' investments	6,000
Total receipts	204,500
Expenditures	
Inventory purchases (cash)	180,000
Owners' withdrawals	3,000
Payments of accounts payable	15,000
Payroll expense	55,000
Utilities expense (including a $1,000 deposit)	2,500
Rent for March, April, May, current year	3,000
Total expenditures	258,500
Excess of expenditures over receipts	($ 54,000)

SHORT PROBLEMS

1. Prepare a balance sheet for Handy Andy's fast-food parlor at August 31, 2005 from the following accounts (Andrew Runn is the owner of the company):

Andrew Runn's capital (end of period)	$87,000
Land	$40,000
Taxes payable	$ 5,000
Prepaid expenses	$ 4,000
Accounts receivable	$15,000
Cash	$10,000
Notes payable	$25,000
Accounts payable	$22,000
Equipment	$10,000
Building	$98,000
Inventory	$12,000
Mortgage payable	$50,000

2. Below is given the amount of Ryan Smith's (the owner) capital at the beginning and end of an accounting period. Subsequently certain transactions are presented that occurred during the period. Explain the effect of these transactions on owner's equity.

Beginning owner's equity $1,235

Ending owner's equity $2,466

(a) The company purchased a refrigerator for $560 cash.
(b) Ryan Smith took home the old refrigerator, which was recorded on the books of the company at $300 but had a current resale value of $350.
(c) Ryan Smith deposited $1,000 in cash in the company's bank account. The company signed a note promising to pay it back in 6 months.
(d) Ryan Smith withdrew $250 from the company's bank account for his own personal use.
(e) Ryan Smith brought a new sign he had at home to the business for its exclusive use. The sign had a current market value of $1,400.
(f) Ryan Smith invested an additional $1,000 in the business.
(g) The company borrowed $10,000 to buy land.
(h) The company reported a $619 loss from operations during the period.

3. XYZ Hospitality Company has the following assets and liabilities at the beginning of the year:

Assets $430,000   Liabilities $280,000

Calculate assets, liabilities, and owners' equity after taking into account the following transactions:
(a) A liability of $10,000 was paid off.
(b) Kitchen equipment worth $25,000 was exchanged for vehicles worth $25,000.
(c) The owner deposited $30,000 in the company's bank account.
(d) The company earned $50,000.
(e) The company purchased equipment for $20,000 in cash plus a note payable of $23,000.

4. The following is an abbreviated balance sheet for the Cargill Restaurant, which is owned and operated by Fred Cargill:

Assets		**Liabilities & Owner's Equity**	
Inventories	$150,000	Liabilities	
		Notes payable	$100,000
		Owners' Equity	50,000
Assets	$150,000		$150,000

If the restaurant sold all of its food and beverage inventories for:
(a) $100,000;
(b) $150,000;
(c) $200,000,
what would its balance sheet and income statement look like, assuming there were no other transactions?

LONG PROBLEMS

1. Indicate the basic accounting concept(s) applicable in each of the following situations. Explain the reason why the transaction might not be properly recorded.
    (a) Land is recorded at $100,000, what it cost 10 years ago, even though its current market value is $300,000.
    (b) A motel owner gave her manager a $200 petty cash fund to cover cash expenditures but failed to determine how much of these funds had been spent when she prepared the financial statements.
    (c) A travel agency pays two months' rent in advance and records the entire payment as "rent expense."
    (d) A hotel owner has decided to liquidate his hotel and requests his accountant to record the hotel's assets on the balance sheet at their current market value.
    (e) Food and beverage inventory purchased for $7,000 last year is now worth only $5,000. The accountant tells the restaurant manager that she must mark it down by $2,000 on the company's accounting books.
    (f) Joe Mix has two cars that belong to him. He wants to include them in the balance sheet of his Mix'em-Up Restaurant Company so that it will appear the company has more assets.
    (g) A catering contract was signed by a restaurant with a local tour bus company. The owner of the restaurant requested his accountant to include some future sales from this catering contract in the restaurant's current income statement to improve current earnings.
    (h) A hotel has extended credit to several guests, and the invoices sent them are still unpaid. In the past, the manager has never included the invoices as part of the hotel's sales until payment was received.
    (i) The owner of a travel agency does not want to prepare formal financial statements even though it has been a year since the agency was created. The owner says she knows it is not doing well and so wants to postpone preparation of financial statements until results will be favorable.
    (j) A large airline with $200 million in sales has customarily recorded equipment purchases of $1,000 or less as an expense. In order to avoid having to report a loss in the current period, management is considering changing this policy so that all equipment purchases above $200 will be included in the equipment asset account, and then switching back next year to the previous $1,000 cut-off amount.
2. (a) Prepare a schedule similar to the one in Table 2–1. Use multicolumn accounting paper. Create accounts as needed, placing the name of each account at the head of a column. Then list the following transactions of the MRB Beach Amusement Park, owned by Ms. M.R. Bober, indicating the effect of each transaction in the appropriate columns. If a transaction has no effect on the account listed in a column, enter a zero in that column.
    1. Ms. Bober invests $50,000 in cash and $30,000 in equipment.
    2. The amusement park sells $15,000 worth of tickets for cash.
    3. Salaries of $3,000 are paid.
    4. Rent in the amount of $1,000 is paid.

5. A new ride is purchased for $25,000; of this amount, $15,000 is paid in cash and a note payable is signed for the balance.
6. A $6,000 electricity invoice was received. It will be paid next month.
7. A $500 invoice for water was received and paid.
8. Tour tickets worth $3,000 are sold on credit.
9. Two old cars worth a total of $6,000 are exchanged for an air conditioner for the Funny House.
10. Office supplies worth $500 are purchased for cash; half will be consumed this period.
11. Advertising worth $1,000 was purchased, half in cash and half on account.
12. Ms. Bober withdraws $2,500.
13. Invoices for $3,500 are paid by the amusement park.
14. A $3,600 invoice for a full year's insurance policy ($300 per month) was received and paid.
15. Accounts receivable worth $2,000 were collected.
16. The $10,000 note payable in (5) expired and was renewed.

(b) Prepare an income statement and a balance sheet for MRB Beach Amusement Park.

3. John Fisher graduated from Florida International University School of Hospitality Management. Upon graduation, John decided to start a take-out restaurant. In the process of doing this, he executed the transactions listed below.

(a) Prepare a schedule similar to the one in Table 2–1. Create accounts as needed on multicolumn accounting paper by placing the name of each account at the head of a column. List the following transactions on this schedule, indicating the effect of each transaction in the appropriate columns. If a transaction has no effect on the account listed in a column, enter a zero.

1. As the initial investment in the company John Fisher deposited $150,000 in the company's bank account.
2. The company purchased $5,000 worth of food and beverages for future consumption. The purchase was made with 20 percent cash and 80 percent credit.
3. The company purchased equipment for $2,000 cash.
4. The company purchased land for $40,000 and a building for $90,000, by making a $30,000 down payment and signing a mortgage note payable in the amount of $100,000 for the balance.
5. Sales during the first week were $5,000, all cash.
6. Food and beverages worth $1,500 were consumed in making these sales.
7. Office supplies worth $300 were purchased for cash.
8. The company paid salaries in the amount of $600.
9. The company received an invoice for water of $50 and paid on the same day.
10. The company received the electricity invoice for $200, but did not pay it immediately.
11. The company sold $1,500 worth of food and beverages to a local business on credit.
12. The company consumed $500 worth of food and beverages in making the above sale.
13. Invoices due were paid, totalling $20,000.
14. The company took advantage of a discount price and paid a trash collection fee of $1,200 for the entire year. At the time this amount was recorded, one month's service had already been received.

15. The company collected $750 on previous credit sales.

16. John Fisher withdrew $1,000 from the company's bank account for his personal use.

(b) Prepare a balance sheet and an income statement for the restaurant.

4. (a) Describe each of the transactions of the Ship's Hull Restaurant (owned by Mr. Hull) indicated in the table below and identified by number in the left-hand column.

(b) Prepare a balance sheet and income statement for the restaurant based on these transactions.

Note: Assume revenues are generated by food sales.

Assets		Liabilities		Capital	Revenue	Expenses	
Name	Amount	Name	Amount			Name	Amount
1. Cash	+20,000			+20,000			
2. Equipment	+30,000						
Cash	−10,000	Notes payable	+20,000				
3. Land & building	130,000	Mortgages payable	+100,000	+30,000			
4. Inventory	+20,000						
Cash	−10,000	Accounts payable	+10,000				
5. Cash	+15,000				+30,000		
Accounts receivable	+15,000						
6. Inventory	−9,000					Cost of sales	−9,000
7. Cash	−8,000					Payroll	−8,000
8.		Accounts payable	+1,000			Utilities	−1,000
9. Prepaid rent	+2,000						
Cash	−2,000						
10. Cash	+3,000	Unearned revenue	+3,000				
11. Cash	+4,000	Accounts payable	+4,000	*Borrowed Money*			
12. Cash	+7,000						
Accounts receivable	−7,000						
13.		Accounts payable	+500			Supplies	−500
14.		Accounts payable	+800			Laundry	−800
15. Equipment	−5,000						
Cash	+2,000	Notes payable	−3,000				
16. Cash	−2,500			−2,500	*Owner decided to pay themselves.*		
Totals	+186,500		+128,300	+47,500	+30,000		−19,300

ASSETS $186,500 = LIABILITIES Plus OWNERS' EQUITY $186,500

5. Head up a sheet of paper as indicated below and record the following trans-actions by adding or subtracting them in the appropriate columns. Place the name of the asset, liability, or owner's equity item for which you are making an entry in the column headed "name" and the letter representing the trans-action in the column marked "transaction." Then prepare a balance sheet and income statement reflecting the results of these transactions.

Transaction	Assets		Liabilities		Owner's equity	
	Name	Amount	Name	Amount	Name	Amount

(a) Jim Stiel, the owner, invests $20,000 in cash in his catering business, Jim Stiel's Catering. He also contributes a refrigerator, with a market value of $600, to the business.

(b) The business entity paid the rent for the building it occupies. It has a one-year lease. A payment of $500 for the current month and another payment of $500 for the twelfth month was made.

(c) The company purchased supplies for $200 on credit.

(d) The company borrowed $1,000 from the bank against a note payable.

(e) The company rendered catering services amounting to $7,000, of which 40% of the sales are credit sales, the remainder cash sales.

(f) The company purchased food and beverages worth $5,000 on account.

(g) The company consumed $3,000 from food and beverage inventory in making the sales specified in (e).

(h) The company consumed 50% of the supplies purchased in (c) in the cur-rent accounting period.

(i) The company paid payroll of $2,200.

(j) The company received invoice for water consumption during the pe-riod, $150.

(k) Jim Stiel withdraws $800 in cash for his personal use.

(l) The company received and paid electricity invoice for $280.

(m) The company collected $1,600 of the account receivable.

(n) The company paid $2,100 of the accounts payable.

(o) The company paid $200 of the notes payable.

(p) Jim Stiel withdraws $1,500 for his personal use.

Processing Business Transactions | 3

The learning objectives of this chapter are:

- To understand the nature of business transactions.
- To reinforce the understanding of the accounting equation in analyzing business transactions.
- To identify and examine the steps of the accounting cycle.
- To review the first step of the accounting cycle—analysis of business transactions.
- To identify the role of business transactions as the raw material of the accounting process.
- To understand the value(s) received and the value(s) given inherent to business transactions.
- To introduce the second step of the accounting cycle—journalizing.
- To apply the rules of debits and credits.

In order to make full use of accounting information in management decisions, we must know how to analyze the output of the accounting process in order to evaluate the performance and financial condition of the hospitality entity. Understanding accounting depends greatly on the ability to analyze business situations and recognize business transactions when they occur—to "know what happened."

Knowing what happened for accounting purposes requires: (1) Identifying the value(s) given and the value(s) received in each transaction, and (2) determining the dollar amounts to be entered in the accounting records in order to record these value exchanges. Once we have analyzed and recorded the business transactions, it is not difficult to summarize data into meaningful categories for management information purposes.

As mentioned in Chapter 1, the accounting system consists of input, processing, and output. The input of the accounting system consists of source documents such as checks, time cards, and purchase and sales invoices, which record the fact that a business transaction has taken place. In this chapter, we shall first explain the nature of these business transactions, and see how they are the raw material of the accounting process. Second, we shall begin to examine the accounting cycle with multistep actions. The first step of the cycle is identifying and understanding business transactions through a procedure known as transactional analysis. Finally, we shall introduce the second step of the accounting cycle—journalizing, which is covered in greater detail in Chapter 4.

BUSINESS TRANSACTIONS: THE RAW MATERIAL OF THE ACCOUNTING PROCESS

We learned in Chapter 1 that accounting is a system for collecting, summarizing, analyzing, and reporting (in monetary terms) information about an organization; that is, it is a system for keeping track of value exchanges between organizations. These value exchanges are known in accounting as business transactions. Business transactions are events that take place in the life of a business and that result in an equal exchange of values. They may involve investing in the business, selling goods (food and beverages, for example) or services, paying bills, purchasing needed items from vendors, or collecting receivables.

In order to record these transactions, a bookkeeper or accountant must be informed that they have taken place. Source documents will provide such information; that is, they constitute the evidence of completed transactions, which is the basis for processing them in the accounting system. For example, when an established restaurant purchases food or beverage for its inventory, it normally buys it on account and receives an invoice, which becomes the basis for processing the purchase transaction. When the invoice is paid, the check issued by the restaurant will serve as proof that a cash payment transaction has been completed. Likewise, employee time cards or time sheets are very important source documents in a hospitality firm because of the labor-intensive nature of the industry. They reflect the expenditure of time as a basis for the processing of payroll transactions.

For each business transaction that occurs, a source document is received and created. These documents not only serve as objective evidence that transactions have taken place, but they also indicate the amounts to be recorded, in keeping with the objectivity concept of accounting. They provide the opportunity to capture all of the information necessary for processing within the accounting system. We can see how understanding business transactions is basic to the acquisition of accounting knowledge—they are the raw material of the accounting process. For example, in a restaurant, a chef processes raw materials—food ingredients, such as vinegar, paprika, raw meat, cooking oil, pepper, and garlic—in order to deliver the final product to the restaurant's customers—a prepared meal. Similarly, the raw material of the accounting process, business transactions (cash receipts, sales, purchases, payments), must be processed by the bookkeeper or accountant through the accounting system in order to obtain its final product—financial statements and other periodic reports for the use of management and other decision makers.

THE ACCOUNTING CYCLE

The accounting cycle represents the processing stage of the accounting system. This is the stage where business transactions are summarized and analyzed in order to obtain the output of the system.

The accounting cycle consists of seven steps, as shown in Exhibit 3–1. Many hospitality firms operate with annual accounting periods, and thus apply the accounting cycle steps on an annual basis by closing the books once a year. However, most large hospitality firms, and some small ones, may also prepare interim reports (monthly, quarterly, etc.); thus, they will perform these steps for the interim period(s) in addition to the year-end.

As we saw in Chapter 2, if the annual accounting period ends on December 31 it is called a calendar year. However, some firms may follow a fiscal year coinciding with their natural business year, in which case the annual accounting

STEPS	COMMENTS
1. Identification and analysis of business transactions	Recognition of value(s) received and value(s) given.
2. Journalizing	Chronological recording of business transactions in a journal.
3. Posting	Transferring the information from the journal to the ledger.
4. Taking the trial balance of the general ledger	Ascertaining the equality of account balances in the ledger.
5. Adjusting the trial balance	Adjusting account balances at the end of the accounting period to reflect passage of time.
6. Preparation of financial statements	Using the financial statement worksheet to prepare the balance sheet and the income statement.
7. Closing the books	Preparing accounting records for the next accounting period.

Exhibit 3–1   The accounting cycle.

period will usually be selected to end when business activity is at its lowest point, thus facilitating the process of preparing financial statements.

IDENTIFYING BUSINESS TRANSACTIONS

All business transactions by definition involve a quid pro quo or equal exchange of values. That is, for every transaction there are one or more values received and one or more values given, and these values are equal. This can be represented by the value exchange equation:

$$values\ received\ (vr) = values\ given\ (vg)$$

To illustrate this concept, we refer again to the three transactions included in Chapter 2.

Transaction (a)—Invested Cash.   Mr. Bryan Bober invested $100,000 cash in his new BB hotel business. This transaction results in BB Hotel receiving a value, cash in the amount of $100,000, and giving in return an ownership share to the owner, Mr. Bober. Based on the equality of values exchanged, we conclude that assets increased $100,000, while owner's equity also increased in the same amount. In terms of the value exchange equation,

$$vr\ (cash) = vg\ (100\%\ ownership\ share)$$
$$\$100,000 = \$100,000$$

Based on the dual aspect of accounting, the effect of this transaction on the fundamental accounting equation was shown to be as follows:

$$A \qquad = L + \qquad OE$$
$$100,000\ (cash) = 0 + 100,000\ (capital)$$

where A is assets, L is liability, and OE is owner's equity.

Transaction (b)—Paid Cash for Housekeeping Supplies.   BB Hotel made a cash payment of $1,000 for the purchase of housekeeping supplies. The value received by the business consists of housekeeping supplies, an asset, with a value of $1,000. The value given in return would be cash, another asset, in the amount of $1,000. Again, in terms of the value exchange equation,

$$vr\ (housekeeping\ supplies\ inventory) = vg\ (cash)$$
$$\$1,000 = \$1,000$$

We had previously expressed this transaction in terms of the fundamental accounting equation as an exchange of the assets cash and housekeeping supplies inventory.

$$A \qquad\qquad = L + OE$$
$$0 \begin{cases} +1,000 \text{ housekeeping supplies inventory} \\ -1,000 \text{ cash} \end{cases} = 0 + 0$$

Transaction (c)—Purchase of Furniture and Equipment on Account. In this transaction, BB Hotel received furniture and equipment with a value of $30,000 (vr). In return for this vr, BB Hotel gave its promise to repay the $30,000 in the future, accounts payable (A/P). Note that this promise was given in the form of an understanding in the normal course of business by virtue of accepting X company's credit terms as a condition for the purchase of furniture and equipment. It is evident that the vr, furniture and equipment (an asset), is equal to the vg, accounts payable (a liability). This account payable reflects the fact that $30,000 is owed to X company, which now becomes a creditor of BB Hotel:

$$vr\ (furniture\ \&\ equipment) = vg\ (accounts\ payable)$$
$$\$30,000 = \$30,000$$

Furthermore, the effect of transaction (c) in terms of the fundamental accounting equation is:

$$A \qquad\qquad = \qquad L \qquad + OE$$
$$+30,000 \text{ furniture \& equipment} = +30,000 \text{ A/P} + \quad 0$$

In these three examples, we saw how every business transaction involved an equal exchange of values: The value received (vr) was always equal to the value given (vg). In each transaction, there was only one vr and one vg. However, many transactions involve two or more values received and/or two or more values given. In such cases, the equality of values exchanged will still prevail. Let us consider the following transaction:

Transaction (d)—Week's Sales. The sales of BB Hotel for the week consisted of $3,000 in cash sales and $5,000 in credit sales. In this case, there are two values received, cash and accounts receivable (A/R). An accounts receivable is the promise received from customers to pay a specific amount in the future, in this case $5,000, pursuant to BB Hotel's credit terms.

Consequently, transaction (d) involves the combination of two asset values received (cash $3,000 and accounts receivable $5,000) in the amount of $8,000. These values received will equal the value given by BB Hotel, services performed (room sales) in the amount of $8,000:

$$vr = vg$$
$$\$3,000 \text{ cash} + \$5,000 \text{ A/R} = \$8,000 \text{ room sales}$$
$$\$8,000 = \$8,000$$

The effect of the above transaction on the fundamental accounting equation is:

$$A \qquad\qquad = L + \qquad OE$$
$$3,000 \text{ cash} + 5,000 \text{ A/R} = 0 + 8,000 \text{ room sales}$$
$$+8,000 = 0 + 8,000$$

VALUES RECEIVED (DEBITS) AND VALUES GIVEN (CREDITS)

To summarize, step 1 of the accounting cycle entails recognizing that a business transaction affecting the financial condition of the hospitality firm took place. This identification process entails a two-stage analysis of each business transaction:

1. Determine the individual value(s) received (vr) and the individual value(s) given (vg) for each transaction. As we already know, all transactions involve an equal exchange of values based upon the quid pro quo (something for something) characteristic inherent in all business transactions. Thus, in every transaction vr = vg.
2. Analyze the effect of each transaction in terms of the fundamental accounting equation. That is, think through the effect of the transaction on assets, liabilities, and owners' equity, including the subdivisions of owners' equity: revenues and expenses.

After all the business transactions occurring in a particular accounting period have been recognized and analyzed, we are in a position to record, sort out, and summarize them. Before going on to these remaining steps of the accounting cycle, we shall enhance our understanding of step 1 by analyzing several business transactions.

Transactional Analysis

Hundreds, or even thousands, of business transactions may take place every day in an average hospitality firm, the volume depending on the size of the business. Some of the more typical of these transactions are identified and described in Exhibit 3–2, (1) in terms of their effect on the fundamental accounting equation and (2) in terms of their effect on the value exchange equation. The kind of analysis in Exhibit 3–2 is a specific example of transactional analysis in action.

AN INTRODUCTION TO JOURNALIZING

It is worth noting again that using transactional analysis to comprehend what happened with respect to one transaction or a group of related transactions is crucial and will considerably accelerate the overall learning process.

Having acquired a clear understanding of what happened in the business transactions of a particular period, we are ready to process these transactions through the accounting system. This takes us to step 2: journalizing. Journalizing is the chronological recording of business transactions in a journal, or keeping a business diary to record all values received (vr) and all values given (vg) for each transaction. The journal is often referred to as a "book of original entry" because it is the place where transactions are initially recorded.

We have learned that every transaction involves receiving one or more values and giving one or more values and that the total of values received must equal the total of values given. This is an appropriate point to become acquainted with accounting terminology: Values received are called debits, and values given are called credits, and so the value exchange equation can also be written:

$$debits = credits$$

By accounting convention, debit may be abbreviated to *Dr* and credit to *Cr*. In every transaction, therefore, $Dr = Cr$.

Typical business transactions | Effect on fundamental accounting equation | Values exchanged

Description	Type	A	=	L	+	OE*	VR	=	VG
1. Owners' investment in hospitality organization	Invested capital	+cash		0		+ owners' capital	Cash or other property		Ownership share
2. Borrowing money	Borrowed capital	+cash		+ notes payable		0	Cash		Promise to pay
3. Purchase inventory (supplies or inventory for sale) for cash	Purchase	+inventory −cash		0		0	Goods		Cash
4. Purchase inventory (supplies or inventory for sale) on account	Purchase	+inventory		+ A/P		0	Goods		Implied promise to pay
5. Cash sales	Sales	+cash		0		+ revenue	Cash		Goods (food sales, beverage sales) or services (room sales)
6. Sales on open account	Sales	+ A/R		0		+ revenue	Promise to pay (A/R)		Goods or services
7. Repay loan or pay for credit purchases	Cash disbursement	−cash		− A/P or notes payable		0	Note or promise to pay		Cash
8. Pay a cash expense	Cash disbursement	−cash		0		−expense	Use of goods or services		Cash
9. Renew bank note	Due date extension on borrowed capital	0		0		0	Continued use of money		Renewal of promise to pay
10. Withdrawal of money by owners	Cash disbursement	−cash		0		−withdrawal	Reduction of ownership share		Cash

*Remember that revenues increase OE and expenses decrease OE

Exhibit 3–2 Hospitality firm transactional analysis.

When journalizing business transactions, we record in the journal all values received by debiting the specific asset, liability, and owners' equity, revenue, or expense item(s). At the same time, we record all values given by crediting the appropriate asset, liability, owners' equity, revenue, or expense item(s). We shall now refer to these items as accounts. An account is a recording format for gathering and summarizing the effect of business transactions. There is a separate account for each type of asset, liability, owners' equity, revenue, and expense. We have already seen that for every transaction recorded in the journal, all debits must be equal to all credits. This is necessary to record the equal exchange of values in business transactions. This dual aspect of accounting, more importantly, is the basic premise supporting the double-entry accounting system.

The actual procedures to be followed in journalizing will be discussed in depth in Chapter 4. At this point, it is important only to recognize that if we learn how to determine what accounts are to be credited or debited, step 2 of the accounting cycle—journalizing—will become a fairly simple procedure.

Let us consider two examples of how we can determine what accounts need to be debited and what accounts need to be credited in recording business transactions in the journal.

Example 1. Borrowed $10,000 from the ABC Bank, signing a 90-day promissory note. A promissory note consists of a written promise to pay a certain sum of money on demand or at a specified future time. In this example, a written note promises to pay ABC bank $10,000 in 90 days from the date the money was borrowed.

The transaction involves a value received (the asset cash) in the amount of $10,000 and a value given (the promise to repay the note) in the same amount. Hence, the cash account is debited and the notes payable account (a liability account is credited since we debit value(s) received and credit value(s) given.

The journal entry will be shown as follows:

Dr	Cash	10,000	
Cr	Notes payable		10,000

Notice that the credit entry has been indented. This will be done at all times, as we shall see when we discuss journalizing procedures in Chapter 4.

Example 2. Paid Rent for the month, $1,000. The value received (rent expense) denotes that we have received the right to use the rented premises for a period of one month in exchange for the payment of $1,000. The cash asset reflects the value given in this transaction. Therefore, we must debit rent expense (vr) and credit cash (vg) or:

Dr	Rent expense	1,000	
Cr	Cash		1,000

Note that the effect of this transaction on the fundamental accounting equation is a decrease in cash (an asset) and a decrease in owners' equity. Nonetheless, we do not debit owners' equity. Instead, we debit rent expense since expenses produce decreases in owners' equity and we must have separate account(s) for expenses.

Traditionally, in order to learn how to record business transactions in a journal, students were asked to memorize certain rules (referred to as the rules of debit and credit) without any attempt to understand the logic involved in the development of these rules. It was simply stated that debits and credits had no meaning other than left and right since, as we shall see, debits are entered on the left side of an account and credits are entered on the right side of an account. However, we feel that to understand accounting it is not only necessary to understand the rules of debit and credit, but more importantly, to understand the logic behind these rules. That is why we used the "equal exchange of values" approach in our initial example of recording transactions in a journal. Understanding the inherent logic in the accounting system facilitates performing the accounting process and comprehending its output.

The general rules of debits and credits are shown in Exhibit 3–3. We can see that increases in asset accounts will be recorded by debiting the proper asset account, whereas decreases in assets will be credited to the proper asset account. This can be easily understood by recognizing that when an asset increases, the hospitality firm receives a value, a resource that will provide future economic benefit. For example, when food inventory is purchased for cash or on credit the firm receives a value, food inventory (an asset), which will have to be debited based on the rules in Exhibit 3–3.

The same rationale applies in the case of expenses. An increase in expenses signifies that a value has been received by the hospitality firm in the past and has been consumed in its operations. Therefore, the specific expense account representing the item consumed by the hospitality firm will be debited to reflect the value received by the business. For instance, when rent expense is incurred it means that the firm has received a value—the use of the rented premises for a particular period—and thus the rent expense account will have to be debited when recording the transaction in a journal.

Insofar as liability, owners' equity, and revenue accounts are concerned, increases will be recorded as credits to the respective accounts. This is based on the fact that the hospitality firm will give one or more values when there are increases in any of those accounts. When we make a purchase on credit, for example, the business will have to give a value, in the form of a promise to pay in the future, for the item purchased.

This results in an increase in the liability account, accounts payable.

The rules of debits and credits listed in Exhibit 3–3 can be easily remembered by referring to the fundamental accounting equation:

$$\text{Assets} = \text{Liabilities} + \text{Owners' equity}$$

Dr increases	Cr increases
Cr decreases	Dr decreases

In other words, asset increases are debited. Asset decreases, on the other hand, are credited, based on the fact that the business gives a value any time an asset decreases (in the form of a cash payment, land, furniture, or any other resource owned by the business).

At the same time, increases in liability and owners' equity accounts will be credited, recognizing that the entity has given a value in the form of a promise to pay (liability) or a share in ownership (owners' equity). Conversely, decreases in

Account	Debit	Credit
Asset	+	−
Liabilities	−	+
Owners' equity	−	+
Revenue	−	+
Expense	+	−

Exhibit 3–3 Rules of debit and credits.*

*A + indicates that the account has increased, and a − indicates that it has decreased.

these accounts will be debited, reflecting the value(s) received by the firm (a return to the firm of any previously given promise to pay, or a return of ownership share).

From the foregoing discussion we can conclude that there are two alternative approaches to journalizing, i.e., the process of identifying the particular accounts to which specific transaction amounts should be debited or credited.

The first approach is based on the logic of value exchanges (values received = values given). This approach is highly recommended because it touches the core of the accounting function: keeping track of value exchanges. The second alternative is based on the fundamental accounting equation. It involves memorizing the rules of debits and credits presented in Exhibit 3–3, and applying them in the process of journalizing. Relating these rules to the fundamental accounting equation should make them easier to remember.

If the student is able to analyze transactions effectively using the first approach, then the second approach is unnecessary. Because it provides a more fundamental understanding of the accounting function, the analysis of value exchanges is to be preferred. The rule of debits and credits method is presented, however, because many students find it easier to assimilate and it is still widely used in the study of introductory accounting.

Regardless of which approach is used, once students have learned to translate business transactions into specific accounts to be debited or credited with appropriate amounts, they will have mastered the journalizing process. This can only be accomplished by practicing the technique in the actual solution of problems.

Chapter 4 will provide the opportunity to put into practice the technique of journalizing. It will expand our coverage of journalizing procedures. A greater variety of transactions will be analyzed and illustrated in the process of explaining how they are to be recorded in the general journal, the simplest and most flexible type of journal.

SOME KEY TERMS INTRODUCED IN THIS CHAPTER

1. **Account.** An individual record of effects of transactions on each asset, liability, owners' equity, revenue, or expense item.
2. **Cr.** *See* credit.
3. **Credit.** Value(s) given in a business transaction: decreases in assets or expenses; increases in liabilities, owner's equity or revenues.
4. **Debit.** Value(s) received in a business transaction: increases in assets or expenses; decreases in liabilities, owner's equity or revenues.
5. **Dr.** *See* debit
6. **General journal.** A book of original entry used to record business transactions.
7. **General ledger.** A book of final entry, consisting of a group of accounts that constitute an organization's accounting system.
8. **Interim reports.** Financial reports that cover accounting periods of less than a year (i.e., a quarter).
9. **Journal.** A business diary used to record business transactions in chronological order.
10. **Ledger.** A book of accounts in which business transactions are posted after having been recorded in a journal.
11. **Posting.** The transfer of information recorded in a journal to a book of final entry known as the ledger.
12. **Trial balance.** A list of the debit and credit balances from the general ledger to ensure that total debits equal total credits.

QUESTIONS

1. What are the three stages of an accounting system? In which stage does the accounting cycle occur?
2. What are the various steps of the accounting cycle? List them in proper sequence.
3. What is transactional analysis? In what part of the accounting cycle does it occur, and why is it necessary?
4. What is the function of source documents? Name three source documents.
5. What is meant when it is said that a company operates on a calendar-year basis? On a fiscal-year basis? On a natural-year basis?
6. What is step 1 of the accounting cycle? On what basic accounting concept is it based? Under what circumstances are values received in a business transaction equal to values given?
7. What effect do values received have on each of the different elements of the fundamental accounting equation?
8. Why is it important to understand what happened in a business transaction?
9. How do revenues affect owners' equity? How do expenses affect owners' equity?
10. Define journalizing.
11. What are two different ways of understanding the process of journalizing?
12. State the rules of debits and credits.
13. What is the ultimate objective of the accounting system?

EXERCISES

1. Place the following steps of the accounting cycle in proper sequence and define them:
   (a) Adjusting the trial balance
   (b) Journalizing
   (c) Closing the books
   (d) Transactional analysis
   (e) Taking the trial balance of the general ledger
   (f) Preparing financial statements
   (g) Posting
2. For the following transactions state the values received and the values given:
   (a) Fifteen thousand dollars in cash is invested to start a company.
   (b) The company borrows $5,000.
   (c) Furniture is purchased in the amount of $2,000, paying $1,000 in cash and $1,000 on credit.
   (d) The company pays back $3,000 of the money it borrowed.
   (e) The owner transfers to this company $6,000 worth of equipment that was used by another organization owned by the owner.
   (f) Equipment is sold for $3,000, receiving $2,000 in cash and the balance on account.
   (g) The owner withdraws $1,500 in cash from the company for his personal use.
3. (a) Based on your answers to Exercise 2 indicate the effect of the given transactions on the accounting equation and express the values received and values given in terms of debits and credits. The first transaction is presented below as an example:

1. The $15,000 in cash received by the company represents an increase in assets. Increases in assets are recorded as debits. The $15,000 worth of ownership rights given represents an increase in owners' equity. Increases in owners' equity are recorded as credits.

(b) What general statement can you make concerning the procedure for recording values received and values given?

4. Suggest one transaction that may have caused the changes in the various elements of the accounting equation indicated in each case below:

	Assets	= Liabilities +	Owners' equity		
			Investment +	Revenues −	Expenses
(a)	+10,000	0	+10,000	0	0
(b)	+1,000	0	0	0	0
	−1,000				
(c)	+5,000	+5,000	0	0	0
(d)	+4,000	0	0	+4,000	0
(e)	−2,000	0	0	0	+2,000
(f)	−1,500	0	−1,500	0	0
(g)	0	+1,000	0	0	+1,000
(h)	0	−2,000	+2,000	0	0
(i)	−1,000	−1,000	0	0	0
(j)	+1,000	+2,000	−1,000	0	0
(k)	+4,000	+3,000	+1,000	0	0

SHORT PROBLEMS

1. Consider the following transactions of Delectable Restaurant. Determine the value(s) received and value(s) given for each transaction:
   1. Issued capital stock for cash, $100,000
   2. Borrowed money from Third National Bank, signing a note for $500,000
   3. Purchased land and building for $300,000, making a down payment of $50,000 and signing a mortgage note for the balance
   4. Purchased furnishings and equipment on account, $50,000
   5. Operating licenses are acquired; payment is included with the application, $300
   6. Purchased inventory in the amount of $3,000, as follows: $300 for cash and the $2,700 on account
   7. Recorded sales for cash, $1,000 and on account, $2,000

2. For each of the items presented below calculate the missing amount.
   1. Assets = $35,000, revenues = $15,000, invested capital = $16,000, liabilities = $19,000, expenses = ?
   2. Expenses = $8,000, invested capital = $4,000, liabilities = $16,000, revenues = $12,000, assets = ?
   3. Invested capital = $10,000, assets = $110,000, expenses = $35,000, revenues = $40,000, liabilities = ?
   4. Assets = $112,000, expenses = $560,000, liabilities = $73,000, revenues = $544,000, invested capital = ?
   5. Assets = $50,000, invested capital = $6,000, liabilities = $46,000, expenses = $10,000, revenues = ?

3. Consider the following transactions of the Short Stop Commuter Airline.
   (a) Determine the value(s) received and value(s) given for each transaction.
   (b) Determine the debits and credits needed to record each transaction.

1. The owner of the airline invested his light plane, worth $60,000, in exchange for 6,000 shares of $5 par common stock of the new company.
2. The owner loaned the company $10,000 in cash in exchange for a note payable.
3. The company purchased $4,000 worth of furniture for $3,000 cash, giving a note payable for the balance.
4. $2,000 worth of spare parts was purchased on open account with 30-day credit terms.
5. $3,000 worth of commuter services was sold on account to a corporation.
6. Salaries amounting to $1,500 were paid.
7. A six-month lease was signed for office space at $800 per month.
8. The current month's rent was paid and the sixth (last) month's rent was paid, both at the beginning of the month, making a total payment of $1,600.
9. An invoice for water amounting to $150 was received but not paid.
10. Cash sales amounted to $9,900.
11. $2,000 payment was received on the credit sales previously made.
12. Dividends of $3,000 were paid.
13. A $1,000 payment was made to creditors of the company.
14. An invoice for electricity amounting to $200 was received and paid.
15. An invoice for gasoline amounting to $1,200 was received and paid.

LONG PROBLEMS

1. The Restful Inn presents you with the following information:
   1. The hotel sold 5,000 shares of common stock at its par value of $1 a share.
   2. Land is purchased for $100,000 cash.
   3. A travel agency pays two months' rent in advance, $3,000.
   4. Credit sales for the week amounted to $40,000.
   5. The restaurant purchased $5,000 worth of food on credit.
   6. Cash sales for $10,000 were made.
   7. Furniture and equipment was purchased on credit, $20,000.
   8. The hotel receives a $10,000 payment against previous sales on account.
   9. Dividends in the amount of $1,000 were paid.
   10. A $1,000 payment was made on account.
   11. The hotel borrowed $30,000 from First National Bank, signing a note.
   12. An electricity invoice was received in the amount of $300. It will be paid next month.

   Required:
   (a) Determine the value(s) received and given for each transaction.
   (b) Determine the names of the account(s) to be debited and account(s) to be credited for each transaction.

2. For each of the following transactions, determine the following:
   (a) Type of business transaction
   (b) Effect on the fundamental accounting equation
   (c) Value(s) received and values(s) given
   (d) Account(s) to be debited and account(s) to be credited
      1. Mr. X invested $30,000 to start a new business, Hospitality Services, Inc.
      2. Ms. X withdraws money for personal use, $10,000.

3. Hospitality Services, Inc. sales for the day, $3, 000 in cash.
4. Purchase of inventory on account, $1,000.
5. Hospitality Services, Inc. borrowed $100,000 from a bank and signed a note.
6. Purchase of equipment on account, $30,000.
7. Sales on open account, $5,000.
8. Repay loan, $10,000.
9. Pay utility expense, $300.
10. Purchase supplies inventory for cash, $200.
11. Received water bill for $100. It will be paid next month.
12. Cost of inventory used in making food sales, $300.

3. Prepare a worksheet as shown below and enter the transactions of the Eversweet Coffee Shop listed subsequently. Write the name of the desired account in the appropriate account column and the amount in the corresponding amount column. Indicate increases in an account with a plus (+) and decreases with a minus (−) sign.

	Assets		Liabilities		Owner's equity	
Transaction	Account	Amount	Account	Amount	Account	Amount

(a) The coffee shop was established as a sole proprietorship with a deposit of $20,000 in its bank account made by the owner, Charles Greener.
(b) The coffee shop signed a 1-year lease for a location that had previously been used as a coffee shop and was almost fully furnished. The first and last month's rent was paid, a total of $2,000 for the 2 months.
(c) Some additional furniture and equipment was purchased for the coffee shop. The furniture cost $4,000 and the oven and refrigerator cost $6,000. Of the total $10,000 purchase, one half was paid cash and a note payable was signed for the balance.
(d) Food and beverages worth $4,000 were purchased on credit.
(e) Cash sales of $5,000 were made.
(f) Food and beverages worth $1,500 were consumed in making these sales.
(g) A local business opened an account and bought $500 on account. $150 worth of food and beverages were consumed in making these sales.
(h) $1,000 worth of supplies inventory was purchased on credit.
(i) A $1,300 payment was made on suppliers' accounts.
(j) An electricity invoice for $200 was received.
(k) Payroll of $280 was paid to the part-time help.
(l) A $400 payment was received as part payment on previous credit sales.
(m) An invoice for water amounting to $200 was received and paid.
(n) Charles Greener took home $500 worth of unprepared food and withdrew $500 in cash.
(o) The company paid $2,000 on the note payable it had previously signed.

4. (a) Prepare a worksheet as follows:

Transaction	Description	Assets			Liabilities			Owner's equity								
								Investment			Revenues			Expenses		
		Dr Cr	Acct	Amt	Dr Cr	Acct	Amt	Dr Cr	Acct	Amt	Dr Cr	Acct	Amt	Dr Cr	Acct	Amt

(b) Enter the following transactions of the Kirkshire Restaurant in the appropriate columns. First, describe each transaction in the description column, then enter a Dr or Cr in the Dr/Cr column, followed by the name and amount of the affected account in the next two columns.

1. Cash	+25,000	J. Kirkshire, capital	+20,000
		Notes payable	+5,000
2. Food inventory	+8,000	Accounts payable	+3,000
Cash	−5,000		
3. Furniture	+3,000	Notes payable	+7,000
Equipment	+4,000		
4. Cash	+2,500	Sales	+2,500
5. Cost of sales	+750	Food inventory	−750
6. Cash	−400	Payroll	+400
7. Accounts receivable	+1,000	Sales	+1,000
8. Cost of sales	+300	Food inventory	−300
9. Electricity expense	+200	Accounts payable	+200
10. Water expense	+100	Cash	−100
11. Cash	+400	Accounts receivable	−400
12. Food inventory	−150	Accounts payable	−150
13. Rent	+350	Cash	−700
Prepaid rent	+350		
14. Cash	+600	Customers' deposits	+600
15. Withdrawals	+1,000	Cash	−1,000

(c) After transcribing all transactions verify that the fundamental accounting equation applies to the column totals of your worksheet.

Journalizing, Posting, and Taking a Trial Balance | 4

The learning objectives of this chapter are:

- To expand our understanding of the second step in the accounting cycle—journalizing—by learning how to record transactions in the general journal.
- To learn the third step in the accounting cycle—posting from the general journal to the general ledger.
- To become familiar with the structure and format of the "T" account as a substitute general ledger account, and to learn how to calculate its balance.
- To learn to take a trial balance.
- To present some methods that will assist in discovering some of the errors that can occur in the accounting process.
- To briefly familiarize the reader with the general ledger format in a computerized accounting system in contrast to that in a manual system.

In the previous chapter, we analyzed transactions by learning that each transaction involves an equal exchange of values and that it is the dual-aspect concept of accounting that reflects this duality inherent in every transaction. It is the concept upon which the accounting rules of debit and credit are based. This approach enables us to understand that values received and values given ultimately underlie the rules of debits and credits and facilitate the understanding of how to record transactions much better than merely memorizing the rules of debits and credits.

Based on this concept, we learned that journalizing (step 2 of the accounting cycle) entails the chronological recording of business transactions in a journal by recording the value(s) received and the value(s) given for each transaction. As also noted, the values received are debited, whereas the values given are credited, and they must be equal in value,

$$Dr = Cr$$

Therefore, the journal is a business diary that records in chronological order all values received (*Dr*) and all values given (*Cr*) while maintaining the basic equality of value exchanges, and it must be designed to accommodate this dual aspect of every transaction. In fact, the word "journal" is derived from the Latin word for day and implies a daily recording of business transactions. In this chapter, we describe and illustrate the use of the general journal to record business transactions because it is the most flexible journal that can be used to record any type of transaction. However, there are other journals, with different formats,

(1)	(2)	(3)	(4)	
Date	Description	Ref.	Dr	Cr

Exhibit 4–1 General journal—sample page setup.

designed to record specific types of transactions more efficiently. These are known as special purpose journals and are described in Chapter 7.

THE GENERAL JOURNAL

Journals are described as books of original entry because they are the first place where transactions are recorded in an accounting system. The general journal is used to gather and record in an orderly fashion all hospitality entity transactions. A sample page of the general journal is shown in Exhibit 4–1. The general journal (GJ) consists of the following items:

1. The date column—used to show in chronological order when each business transaction took place.
2. The description column—used to indicate the names of the specific accounts being debited and credited as well as an explanation of the transaction.
3. The reference column (Ref)—to be used when transferring information from the journal to the book of final entry (the general ledger) by a procedure, to be explained later, called posting.
4. Debit (Dr) and credit (Cr) columns—used to enter the actual amounts being debited and credited.

RECORDING TRANSACTIONS IN THE GENERAL JOURNAL

Now that you are familiar with the format of the general journal we will proceed to learn the actual process of journalizing. As explained in Chapter 3, step 1 of the accounting cycle involves the analysis of each transaction in order to discern what values are received (Dr) and what values are given (Cr). We explained then that values received are recorded as debits and values given are recorded as credits.

Journalizing consists of entering these debit and credit amounts in the debit and credit columns of the general journal, along with the date of the transaction, the name of each account to be debited or credited, and below this a brief description of the transaction being recorded. This information for each transaction, when completely entered in the general journal, is known as a journal entry. No entry is made in the Ref. (reference) column during the journalizing step. But later, when these amounts are posted, during the third step in the accounting cycle, the number of the account to which each amount is posted is entered here.

These steps are summarized below (refer to Exhibit 4–1):

1. Enter the transaction date by writing the year in small numerals at the top of the date column (1) and the month and day on the first line of the date column. Normally, the year and month are not repeated for subsequent entries made on the same journal page.

2. Record the name(s) and amount(s) of the account(s) debited by entering the account name(s) in the description column (2) and the amount(s) debited in the Dr column (4). The dollar sign is omitted since it is understood that all amounts are in dollars.

3. Record the name(s) and amount(s) of the account(s) credited by *indenting* the account name(s) in the description column (2) and entering the amount(s) credited in the Cr column (4). As in step 2, the dollar sign is omitted.

4. Write an explanation of the entire transaction on the next line below the credit entry in the description column (2).

5. After all transactions are recorded we transfer the information from the journal to a book of final entry (the general ledger). This step is called "posting"—step 3 of the accounting cycle—and is explained later. During this third step, we indicate in the Ref. column (3) of the general journal the account number(s) being posted as evidence that the posting was actually made, and to serve as a reference indicating where the posting was made.

6. Verify that the total of the debits equals the total of the credits, i.e., that the journal entry balances. If it does not balance, a review of the original transaction analysis should be made. When only one debit and one credit entry exists, this step is not required. However, in the case of complex journal entries, where more than one debit or credit is included in a single journal entry, this precaution helps avoid wasting time later searching for errors caused by posting unbalanced journal entries.

Sample Journal Entry

To illustrate these steps we journalize the following transaction below.

April 5, 2005   Mr. Carlton invests $30,000 in his new travel agency, a sole proprietorship, by transferring this amount from his personal bank account to the travel agency's bank account.

The travel agency, an accounting entity separate and distinct from Mr. Carlton himself, receives $30,000 in cash. In exchange, it gives to Mr. Carlton ownership rights in the amount of $30,000. The value received, cash, must be debited to the cash account and the value given, ownership rights, is credited to Mr. Carlton's capital account. Exhibit 4–2 shows how this transaction would be recorded in a general journal. The procedure for preparing the journal entry is as follows:

1. The transaction date, April 5, 2005, is entered in the date column. Since this is the initial journal entry for the year, the year 2005 was written in small numerals above the first line of the date column. Since this is also the first journal entry for the month, April was written on the first line of the date column along with the date. For other entries on this same page the year and month are not repeated.

Date 2005	Description	Ref.	Dr	Cr
April 5	Cash		30,000	
	Mr. Carlton's Capital			30,000
	Initial Capital Investment			

Exhibit 4–2   Initial travel agency journal entry.

2. The cash account was debited $30,000. Thus, the name of this account was entered in the description column and the amount of the debit $30,000, in the Dr column. The dollar sign is omitted since it is understood that all amounts are in dollars.

3. Mr. Carlton's capital account was credited $30,000. Thus, the name of the account credited, Mr. Carlton's capital, was entered in the description column. *Remember, the names of the accounts being credited are indented to help distinguish them from accounts being debited.* The amount of the credit, $30,000, is entered in the Cr column. As in step 2, the dollar sign is also omitted.

4. An explanation of the transaction was written on the next line following the credit entry. Explanations of transactions should always be brief and to the point. In this case, three words suffice to describe the entire nature of the transaction: initial capital investment.

5. When these amounts are later transferred (posted) to the general ledger, the number of the account(s) to which they are posted will be entered in the Ref. column.

6. Since this journal entry has only one credit and one debit, it was not necessary to total the debits or the credits in order to verify that they are equal.

Illustrative General Journal

Now that we understand how to make a journal entry we shall reinforce our newly learned ability by analyzing the process of recording the following 16 varied events in the general journal of the Montric Restaurant. The Montric Restaurant is a partnership owned equally by Ms. Montcalm and Mr. Ricardo.

Events Affecting the Montric Restaurant—June 2005

1. June 1   Ms. Montcalm and Mr. Ricardo make the initial investment in their restaurant by depositing $2,500 each to open a separate bank account for the new accounting entity, the Montric Restaurant.

2. June 1   A bank loan of $10,000 is granted. The proceeds are deposited in the new entity's bank account. The note payable calls for simple interest at 12 percent per year (12 percent APR).

3. June 2   A lease is signed to rent a fully equipped building for use as a restaurant, during one year, with the right to renew for two additional years. The annual rental is $12,000.

4. June 3   The first month's rent, amounting to $1,000, is paid.

5. June 4   Food inventory is purchased for $1,800. Since suppliers insist on cash payment from new accounts, the purchase terms are collect on delivery (COD).

6. June 11   Sales for the first week of operations are $4,900. Of these sales $4,500 are in cash, $150 paid through credit cards, and $250 on open account to a local business.

7. June 11   Food costing $400 was consumed in making the above sales.

8. June 12   A two-year fire insurance policy is purchased by the restaurant for $960 and is paid in cash.

9. June 13   The restaurant purchases a plot of land on which to construct its own restaurant building. The total cost is $10,000. A down payment of $2,000 is made and a four-year, 10 percent mortgage note is given for the balance.

10. June 16   The partners each withdraw $1,000 for their personal use.

11. June 18   Ms. Montcalm takes food costing $50 home for his personal use. The retail price of this food is $140.

12. June 21   Eighty dollars is received in partial payment of sales on open account.

13. June 22   The electricity invoice arrives in the amount of $164. The partners decide to pay it later.

14. June 24   The cook is paid $4 per hour for the 120 hours he has worked.

15. June 28   The $164 electricity invoice is paid.

16. June 30   The water invoice for $40 is received and paid the same day.

The Montric Restaurant: Recording 16 Sample Events in the General Journal

As previously stated, these transactions are to be recorded in chronological order according to the date on which the transaction took place. The month will appear only on the first line of the general journal. Thereafter, all entries on the same page will include the day's date only. The year and the month will be repeated in transaction 9 because this will be the first transaction on the second page of the general journal. As always, values received are debited, values given are credited, and *values given* are *indented* when recorded in the general journal.

Event No. 1

June 1, 2005   Ms. Montcalm and Mr. Ricardo make the initial capital investment in their restaurant by depositing $2,500 each to open a separate bank account for the new accounting entity, The Montric Restaurant.

Values Exchanged.   An asset, cash in the amount of $5,000, is received by the restaurant in exchange for ownership rights (owners' equity accounts) of $2,500 each given to Ms. Montcalm and Mr. Ricardo. Values received are recorded as debits; values given are recorded as credits.

Rules of Dr and Cr.   Asset increases are debited and increases in owners' equity accounts are credited.

Journal Entry #1

Date 2005	Description	Ref.	Dr	Cr
June 1	Cash		5,000	
	Ms. Montcalm's Capital			2,500
	Mr. Ricardo's Capital			2,500
	Initial Capital Investment			

Event No. 2

June 1, 2005 $10,000 cash is borrowed and a note is signed.

Values Exchanged.   An asset, cash, in the amount of $10,000, is received by the restaurant in exchange for a promise to pay it back, notes payable (a liability).

Rules of Dr and Cr.   Asset increases are debits and liability increases are credits.

Journal Entry #2

Date	Description	Ref.	Dr	Cr
1	Cash		10,000	
	Notes payable			10,000
	Borrowed $10,000 from bank			

Event No. 3

June 2, 2005   A lease on the building is signed.

Values Exchanged.   No values are exchanged. This is merely an agreement to exchange values in the future.

Rules of Dr and Cr.   Not applicable—no transaction.

Journal Entry
None—no transaction took place.

Event No. 4

June 3, 2005 $1,000 is paid for the first month's rent of the leased building.

Values Exchanged.   The restaurant is receiving a service, the use of the building for one month, and gives an asset, cash, in exchange.

Rules of Dr and Cr.   Using rented space represents the consumption of a service, an expense. Increases in expenses are debited since we receive and use the right to occupy the premises for a month. An asset, cash, decreases, which is recorded as a credit.

Journal Entry #3

Date	Description	Ref.	Dr	Cr
3	Rent expense		1,000	
	Cash			1,000
	Paid first month's rent			

Event No. 5

June 4, 2005 $1,800 worth of food is purchased.

Values Exchanged.   An asset, food, worth $1,800 is received. Another asset of equal value, $1,800 in cash, is given.

Rules of Dr and Cr.   The increase in the asset, food inventory, is recorded as a debit, whereas the decrease in the asset, cash, is recorded as a credit.

Journal Entry #4

Date	Description	Ref.	Dr	Cr
4	Inventory–food		1,800	
	Cash			1,800
	Purchased food inventory			

Event No. 6

June 11, 2005   First week's sales are $4,900. Cash sales are $4,500 and credit sales $400.

Values Exchanged.   Two assets, $4,500 in cash and $400 in agreements to future payments (accounts receivable), are received. Food and related dining services worth $4,900 are given.

Rules of Dr and Cr.   An increase in assets, cash and accounts receivable, is recorded with debits. Goods and services sold are revenues, and revenues are recorded with credits.

Journal Entry #5

Date	Description	Ref.	Dr	Cr
11	Cash		4,500	
	Accounts Receivable		400	
	Sales			4,900
	Week's sales			

Event No. 7

June 11, 2005   The restaurant consumes food in the amount of $400 in making the week's sales.

Values Exchanged.   The restaurant receives the use of $400 worth of food. It gives up an asset, food inventory, in exchange.

Rules of Dr and Cr.   Assets consumed are expenses. Increases in expenses are recorded with debits. Decreases in assets, food inventory in this case, are recorded with credits.

Journal Entry #6

Date	Description	Ref.	Dr	Cr
11	Cost of food sold		400	
	Inventory–food			400
	Cost of week's food sales			

Event No. 8

June 12, 2005   A two-year fire insurance policy is purchased for $960 in cash.

Values Exchanged.   The restaurant receives a future value, insurance coverage during the next two years. In exchange, an asset, $960 in cash, is given.

Rules of Dr and Cr.   The insurance company's commitment to provide insurance coverage during the next two years is an asset that will provide future benefit, a prepaid expense. To increase the asset, prepaid expenses, its account is debited. To decrease the asset, cash, its account is credited.

Journal Entry #7

Date	Description	Ref.	Dr	Cr
12	Prepaid expenses		960	
	Cash			960
	Purchased fire insurance			

Event No. 9

June 13, 2005   Land worth $10,000 is purchased with a $2,000 down payment and an $8,000 mortgage note.

Values Exchanged.   An asset, land, worth $10,000 is received. In exchange another asset, $2,000 in cash, plus a liability, the promise to pay $8,000 in the future, are given.

Rules of Dr and Cr.   One asset, in this case land, increases and should be debited. Another asset, cash, decreases and is credited. A liability, mortgage notes payable, increases and is credited because liabilities increase with credits.

Journal Entry #8

Date	Description	Ref.	Dr	Cr
13	Land		10,000	
	Cash			2,000
	Mortgages payable			8,000
	Purchased land			

Event No. 10

June 16, 2005   Each partner withdraws $1,000.

Values Exchanged.   The restaurant receives a return of ownership rights, recorded through an account called "withdrawals," which will be later netted out against, and will reduce, the partners' capital accounts. In exchange, it gives each partner an asset, $1,000 in cash.

Rules of Dr and Cr.   Withdrawals is a contra-equity account because it increases with debits. The partners' capital accounts increase with credits so the withdrawal account operates counter to or "contra" to the partners' capital. The withdrawals account is debited and, when netted against the partners capital accounts, will decrease these accounts. The decrease in the asset account, cash, is recorded with a credit.

Journal Entry #9

Date	Description	Ref.	Dr	Cr
16	Montcalm's withdrawals		1,000	
	Ricardo's withdrawals		1,000	
	Cash			2,000
	Partners' withdrawals			

Event No. 11

June 18, 2005   Ms. Montcalm withdraws $50 worth of food.

Values Exchanged.   Withdrawals do not have to be made in cash. The restaurant is receiving a $50 reduction in ownership rights and is giving food, with a cost of $50, in exchange. The retail value of the food is not relevant since no retail sale was made.

Rules of Dr and Cr.   Again, the contra-equity account "withdrawals" is increased by debiting it. An asset, inventory–food, is credited, reflecting the asset decrease.

Journal Entry #10

Date	Description	Ref.	Dr	Cr
18	Montcalm's withdrawals		50	
	Inventory–food			50
	Partners' withdrawal			

Event No. 12

June 21, 2005   A client made a partial payment of $80 on his open account.

Values Exchanged.   The restaurant receives an asset, $80 in cash, and gives a reduction of the amount owing to it (accounts receivable) in exchange. Accounts receivable are "informal promises to pay" to the restaurant, given by customers. When a customer pays what is owed his or her informal promise to pay is no longer valid—it is "returned" to the customer.

Rules of Dr and Cr.   An asset, cash in this case, is increased. Another asset, accounts receivable, is decreased. Therefore, we debit the asset, cash, to record its increase, and credit another asset, accounts receivable, to record its decrease.

Journal Entry #11

Date	Description	Ref.	Dr	Cr
21	Cash		80	
	Accounts receivable			80
	Received payment on open account			

Event No. 13

June 22, 2005   An electricity invoice for $164 is received and will be paid later.

Values Exchanged.   This is a completed transaction because (1) we have consumed a service (electricity) and (2) we know the value of that service. In return for the electricity received, the restaurant is giving an implied promise to pay in the future, an account payable.

Rules of Dr and Cr.   When a service is consumed, it is an expense, which is debited. An implied promise to pay is an account payable, a liability, which is recorded as a credit.

Journal Entry #12

Date	Description	Ref.	Dr	Cr
22	Utilities expense		164	
	Accounts payable			164
	Receipt of electricity invoice			

Event No. 14

June 24, 2005   The cook is paid wages of $480 ($4 × 120 hours).

Values Exchanged.   The cook's services are received and consumed. In exchange, $480 in cash is given to the cook.

Rules of Dr and Cr.   A service consumed is an expense, and increases in expenses are debited. Cash, an asset, is decreased and thus is credited.

Transaction	Assets	Liabilities	Owner's equity			Values exchanged		Accounting entry	
			Capital	Revenues	Expenses	Values received	Values given	Dr	Cr
1. Partners invest $2,500 each in the restaurant	+5,000 cash	0	+2,500 Montcalm's capital +2,500 Ricardo's capital	0	0	$5,000 in cash	Ownership rights $5,000	5,000 cash	2,500 Montcalm's capital 2,500 Ricardo's capital
2. Borrow $10,000 from a bank	+10,000 cash	+10,000 notes payable	0	0	0	$10,000 in cash	Promise to pay $10,000	10,000 cash	10,000 notes payable
3. Lease contract is signed (no transaction involved)	0	0	0	0	0	None	None	None	None
4. $1,000 rent is paid	−1,000 cash	0	0	0	−1,000 rent expense	Use of building for one month with value of $1,000	$1,000 in cash	1,000 rent expense	1,000 cash
5. $1,800 worth of food is purchased COD	−1,800 cash +1,800 food inventory	0	0	0	0	$1,800 worth of food	$1,800 in cash	1,800 food inventory	1,800 cash
6. Cash sales of $4,500, credit sales of $400 are made	+4,500 cash +400 accounts receivable	0	0	+4,900 sales	0	$4,500 received in cash, plus agreement to pay $400 in the future	Food & related services worth $4,900	4,500 cash 400 accounts receivable	4,900 sales
7. Food that cost $400 consumed in making above sales	−400 food inventory	0	0	0	−400 cost of sales	Use of $400 worth of food	$400 reduction in food inventory	400 cost of sales	400 food inventory
8. A two-year fire insurance policy is purchased for $960	−960 cash +960 prepaid expenses	0	0	0	0	Right to future insurance in the amount of $960	$960 in cash	960 prepaid expenses	960 cash

#	Transaction								
9.	Land is purchased for $2,000 cash & an $8,000 mortgage note	−2,000 cash +10,000 land	+8,000 mortgage payable	0	0	0	Land worth $10,000	$2,000 in cash, promise to pay $8,000	10,000 land / 2,000 cash 8,000 mortgage payable
10.	Each partner withdraws $1,000 for his personal use	−2,000 cash	0	−1,000 Montcalm's withdrawals −1,000 Ricardo's withdrawals	0	0	Return of ownership rights worth $2,000	$2,000 in cash	1,000 Montcalm's withdrawals 1,000 Ricardo's withdrawals / 2,000 cash
11.	Ms. Montcalm takes $50 worth of food home	−50 food inventory	0	−50 Montcalm' withdrawals	0	0	Return of ownership rights worth $50	$50 reduction in food inventory	50 Montcalm's withdrawals / 50 food inventory
12.	$80 is received in partial payment of open account	+80 cash −80 accounts receivable	0	0	0	0	$80 in cash	$80 in reduction of accounts receivable	80 cash / 80 accounts receivable
13.	Received electricity invoice for $164, to be paid later	0	+164 accounts payable	0	0	−164 utilities expense	Use of $184 worth of electricity	Agreement to pay $164 in the future	164 utilities expense / 164 accounts payable
14.	Cook is paid $480	−480 cash	0	0	0	−480 payroll expense	Services worth $480 rendered by cook	$480 in cash	480 payroll expense / 480 cash
15.	Electricity invoice is paid, $164	−164 cash	−164 accounts payable	0	0	0	Reduction of amount owed to electric company, $164	$164 in cash	164 accounts payable / 164 cash
16.	Water invoice for $40 is received and paid	−40 cash	0	0	0	−40 utilities expense	Use of $40 worth of water	$40 in cash	$40 utilities expense / 40 cash
	TOTALS	23,766	18,000	2,950	4,900	20,184	37,038	37,038	37,038

Exhibit 4–3 Analysis of The Montric Restaurant's transactions.

71

Journal Entry #13

Date	Description	Ref.	Dr	Cr
24	Payroll expense		480	
	Cash			480
	Paid cook's wages			

Event No. 15

June 28, 2005   The $164 electricity invoice is paid.

Values Exchanged.   A reduction of amounts owed by the restaurant (accounts payable) is received in exchange for an asset, cash.

Rules of Dr and Cr.   Amounts owed are accounts payable, which are liabilities. Decreases in liabilities are debits. Asset decreases are credits. In this case, there is a decrease in both an asset, cash, and a liability, accounts payable.

Journal Entry #14

Date	Description	Ref.	Dr	Cr
28	Accounts payable		164	
	Cash			164
	Paid electricity invoice			

Event No. 16

June 30, 2005   A $40 water invoice is received and paid the same day.

Values Exchanged.   The consumption of $40 worth of water is recorded in exchange for an asset, $40 in cash.

Rules of Dr and Cr.   Services or assets consumed are expenses. Increases in expenses are debits. Cash, an asset, decreases and thus is credited.

Journal Entry #15

Date	Description	Ref.	Dr	Cr
30	Utilities expense		40	
	Cash			40
	Received and paid water invoice			

For the reader's reference the analyses of the above transactions have been summarized in Exhibit 4–3, where the reader may also verify that:

1. Total values received = total values given.
2. Total debits = total credits.
3. The fundamental accounting equation (assets = liabilities + owners' equity) was preserved.

Pages 1 and 2 of the complete general journal of Montric Restaurant appear on the left side of Exhibit 4–8. Notice that since transaction No. 9 (June 13, 2005) is the first entry on the second page of the general journal, the year and month are repeated.

At this point we have learned (1) to analyze transactions and (2) to journalize them by entering them in a book of original entry called a general journal. Nonetheless, the information included in the journal is not very useful because of the way the information is organized (in chronological order). It is very difficult to determine the effect of all the transactions in each individual account because there might be several entries affecting each account, some of which may be debits and some credits. To determine the value of an account from looking at journals we would have to memorize each transaction affecting that account in the journals and then mentally combine debit and credit amounts appropriately. This, of course, is impossible to do. Fortunately, the next step in the accounting cycle—posting to the general ledger—enables us to overcome this problem.

POSTING TO THE GENERAL LEDGER

Posting to the general ledger—step 3 of the accounting cycle—involves transferring the information recorded in the journal, or journals, to a book of final entry known as the general ledger. This is done by copying the debits and credits recorded in the journal for each account to a single place in the general ledger so that we can view the transactions affecting each account all together. Thus we can easily combine debits and credits and arrive at a balance for each account.

In other words, posting enables us to organize and summarize the debits and credits, which are entered chronologically in the general journal, in order to provide meaningful and useful information concerning each account individually, and all the accounts collectively. After all entries have been posted, the ledger provides a listing of the balances in all accounts, based on a summary of the transactions affecting each account.

The General Ledger

Therefore, the general ledger (GL), the book of final entry, consists of a group of accounts that constitute a hospitality organization's accounting system, each account with its own balance. It may be a book, a loose-leaf binder, a tray of cards, or on a computer disk, or, for pedagogical purposes, it can be a sheet of paper with several "T" accounts on it (to be explained later). No matter what its form, the general ledger summarizes the effect of the transactions recorded for each account. An accounting system will have a separate account for each type of asset, liability, owners' equity, revenue, and expense account. Typically, the general ledger accounts will appear in financial statement order, that is, first all the asset accounts, then liability accounts, then owners' equity accounts, then revenue accounts, and, finally, expense accounts. The actual number of accounts will vary from operation to operation, depending on the nature of the business, management's need for information, and the amount of expense management is willing to incur to obtain accounting information.

CHART OF ACCOUNTS

In order to facilitate finding general ledger accounts during journalizing, posting, and preparing financial statements, the hospitality organization normally creates a chart of accounts. This consists of sequentially listing all the firm's account names and assigning them appropriate numbers based on each account's correct position in the financial statements.

The balance sheet asset accounts are listed first, from top to bottom. Then the liability and owners' equity accounts are listed, from top to bottom. In keeping with the fact that revenue and expenses are a subdivision of owners' equity, these income statement accounts are listed after the owners' equity accounts in the same order in which they normally would appear on the income statement.

As stated earlier, these account numbers are entered in the Ref. column of the general journal to indicate that the corresponding debit or credit amount has been posted to the appropriate general ledger account. This serves as a reference for the reader of the journal pointing to which account was debited or credited.

Below is presented a simple general ledger account classification system:

Type of account	Account numbers
Assets	100 to 199
Liabilities	200 to 299
Owners' equity	300 to 399
Revenues	400 to 499
Cost of sales	500 to 599
Other expenses	600 to 699

Exhibit 4–5 shows a chart of accounts for the Montric Restaurant based on this classification. The accounts are listed as they would appear on the balance sheet and income statement to assist the reader in visualizing the relationship between account location and account number. Normally, however, charts of accounts are listed in a single column in sequential numerical order.

When preparing a chart of accounts some numbers should remain unassigned in each account category (cash, accounts receivable, inventory, etc.) to be utilized later should it be necessary to add new accounts in a category. The chart of accounts in Exhibit 4–4, for example, is poorly designed because it would present a problem if a second bank account were later opened. No numbers would be available to place the second bank account next to the first bank account where it logically belongs.

The chart of accounts shown in Exhibit 4–5, on the other hand, does leave some numbers available to add future bank accounts, as well as to add second or third accounts of any other account category that the restaurant may need to open.

Asset	Account Numbers
Cash	101
1st National Bank	102
Accounts receivable	103
Inventory–food	104
Inventory–supplies	105
Prepaid expenses	106
Land	107
Buildings	108
Equipment	109
Furniture & fixtures	110

Note that there would be no number available after #102 to assign to a second bank account. The second bank account would have to be assigned the number 111, placing it out of sequence with the other cash accounts.

Exhibit 4–4   Sample of a poorly designed chart of accounts.

Account	Number	Account	Number
Assets		*Liabilities*	
Cash	101	Accounts payable	201
Accounts receivable	104	Notes payable	205
Notes receivable	108	Mortgages payable	209
Inventory—food	115	Payroll payable	215
Inventory—supplies	119	Taxes payable	230
Prepaid expenses	125	Unearned revenues	249
Land	150		
Buildings	155	*Owners' equity*	
Equipment	160	Montcalm's capital	301
Furniture and fixtures	170	Montcalm's withdrawals	302
		Ricardo's capital	306
		Ricardo's withdrawals	307
		Revenues	
		Sales	401
		Expenses	
		Cost of sales	501
		Payroll	601
		Utilities	611
		Rent	680
		Insurance	683

Exhibit 4–5 Sample of a well-designed chart of accounts.

THE "T" ACCOUNT

As indicated before, a general ledger account may take many different forms. Its simplest form, which we shall use for teaching purposes, is the "T" account format. Sometimes this account format is used when discussing business over lunch and a napkin becomes a basic general ledger. It is, indeed, a very simple method of gathering and summarizing debits and credits in the general ledger accounts. The "T" account derives its name from its shape, resembling, as it does, the capital letter "T":

```
        (1)              (2)
       Cash            No. 101
      ──────────────┬──────────
        Dr          │    Cr
        (3)         │    (4)
```

The "T" account consists of four major parts. These four parts are described below and are identified numerically in the "T" account above:

1. The name of the account
2. The account number
3. The left side, known as the debit side (Dr)
4. The right side, known as the credit side (Cr)

Posting Procedures

The "T" account format will be utilized to explain the process of posting since this format will be used for learning purposes and in problem solving throughout the text.

The steps used in posting to the general ledger using the "T" account format, starting with the debit postings first, are:

1. Enter the source from which the transaction is being posted. So far, in this text, we have only identified one source, which is the general journal. Later, when we study special-purpose journals, you will learn that other sources can be referred to here. You should also mention the page of the source from which the transaction is being posted.

2. To the left of the Dr column of the "T" account to be debited, enter the date of the transaction as shown in the journal from which it is being posted.

3. Enter in the debit column of the "T" account the amount of the debit entry as shown in the journal.

4. Enter in the general journal Ref. column the number of the general ledger account to which the debit entry was posted. This step will serve as evidence that the journal entry was posted from the journal to the ledger, and will point the reader of the general journal to the corresponding account in the general ledger.

5. The preceding steps are repeated for the credit side of the journal entry, with the exception that we enter the date and amount in the credit column of the general ledger "T" account.

Once all journal entries have been posted from the general journal to the general ledger for a week, month, or any other period of time selected by the hospitality company, we must determine the balance of each account in the general ledger. We shall be guided by the basic rules of debit and credit in determining a general ledger account balance. That is, assets and expenses will have a normal debit balance since increases in these accounts are debited. Likewise, liability, owners' equity, and revenue accounts will normally have a credit balance because increases in these accounts are credited.

Accordingly, the balance of each account is found by adding the debits, adding the credits, and subtracting the smaller sum from the larger sum. For asset and expense accounts the larger total will normally be in the debit column, resulting in a debit balance. Similarly, for liability, owners' equity, and revenue accounts, the larger total will normally be in the credit column, resulting in a credit balance.

Exhibit 4–6 presents an example of a general ledger cash account in "T" account format with hypothetical amounts.

The main elements of a filled-in "T" account, such as the cash account above, are:

1. The name of the account (cash)
2. The account number (101)
3. The beginning balance (Bal. 6/1/07)

		(1) Cash			(2) No. 101
(3) Bal.	6/1/07		1,468		
(4)	6/2/07 GJ34		500	172	GJ35 (4) 6/3/07
(5) Totals			1,968	172	
(6) Bal.	6/3/07		1,796		

Exhibit 4–6 Sample general ledger cash account—"T" format.

4. The transaction dates and amounts debited and credited during the period and the source from which the transaction was posted. In this example, the source is the general journal (GJ). One posting comes from page 34 of the general journal and the other comes from page 35.

5. When there is more than one debit or more than one credit on one side of the "T" account and there is at least one offsetting debit or credit on the other side of the account, the totals of both debits and credits must be calculated and shown. If there is only one entry on each side, or there are several entries on only one side of the "T" account, simply calculate and show the balance on the appropriate side of the "T" account without including a separate line for totals. In these instances, a separate line for totals would be redundant.

6. The ending balance (Bal. 6/3/07)

In reviewing Exhibit 4–6 you should refer to the posting procedures and the procedure for determining an account balance enumerated earlier. Since the total debits (including the beginning debit balance) were larger than the total credits, we have an ending debit balance of $1,796 (total debits of $1,968 less total credits of $172).

Remember that if a "T" account only has one debit and one credit, or it only has entries on one side of the account, then a total line is not required. Only a balance is calculated and shown, as illustrated below:

	Prepaid Insurance		No. 126	
	6/1/07	600	50	6/30/07
Bal.	6/3/07	550		

Note: Once you have calculated a balance for an account you must not underline the balance. *Open balances should* never *have lines underneath them.* Lines are entered underneath a balance only after it is closed. Closing an account is a topic that will be explained later in the text. Until you learn how to prepare closing entries you should leave all balances without any underlines.

Posting Illustrated

The initial transaction of The Montric Restaurant will be posted here to the corresponding general ledger accounts in "T" account format to illustrate the posting process. The complete general journal entry is repeated here for reference:

A description of the posting process follows:

1. The source and the date of the debit transaction, GJ1 and 6/1/05, are entered on the left-hand side of the general ledger cash "T" account. GJ1 means that the information for this posting came from page 1 of the general journal. Later you will learn to use other abbreviations for postings from special-purpose journals.

2. The $5,000 debit to cash is entered on the left-hand side of the general ledger cash "T" account.

3. The number of the cash account, 101, is entered in the general journal Ref. column to indicate that the debit has been posted.

4. The balance is calculated for the cash account as of June 1, 2005. An increase in cash is debited, so the $5,000 transaction amount is added to the beginning zero balance, resulting in a debit balance of $5,000 as of June 1, 2005.

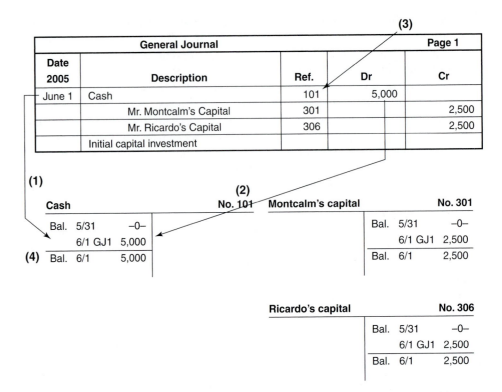

Exhibit 4–7 The Montric Restaurant—initial transaction posted to the general ledger in "T" account format.

The credit side of the entry is posted following this same procedure. All the subsequent entries would be posted in the same manner. The posting of all of The Montric Restaurant's transactions using the "T" account format is shown in Exhibit 4–8. In order to reinforce the understanding of the posting process, the reader should trace the remaining entries of The Montric Restaurant from the general journal to the appropriate general ledger accounts in Exhibit 4–8. When all the transactions for the period have been posted to the appropriate general ledger accounts, these accounts contain a summary of the impact on a business of all its financial activity during the period. Before they can serve as the basis for the preparation of financial statements, however, two more steps in the accounting cycle are required: step 4 of the accounting cycle—taking a trial balance of the general ledger; and step 5—adjusting the trial balance. The former step—the process of taking a trial balance—will be discussed next.

When Does Posting Take Place?

In manual systems, accounts were posted on a daily, weekly, monthly, or quarterly basis, or any time that the business selected. Usually, posting occurred at the end of each accounting period. Some computerized accounting systems update, or post to, the general ledger every time an entry is made in a journal. These systems are called "online" systems because they are continually posting and updating balances. Point-of-sales systems record sales as they occur at various sites throughout a hotel or restaurant. No documents need to be sent to the accounting department to be recorded there. Other computerized accounting systems are fed data in batches and must be instructed to post. Because it is not always up to date, this type of system is being discontinued in favor of online systems. At a minimum, a business must post all transactions every time financial statements are prepared, or its financial statements will be outdated.

TAKING A TRIAL BALANCE OF THE GENERAL LEDGER

In order to test the accuracy of debit and credit balances in the general ledger at the end of an accounting period, a trial balance is prepared. This consists of a list of all the general ledger accounts with their current balances as of the last day of the period. The balances of accounts with debit balances are added in a left-hand column, and the balances of accounts with credit columns are added in a right-hand column. Since debits must equal credits, the totals of the two columns will equal each other if the debits and credits of all journal entries are equal and if no single line of a journal entry has been left unposted.

Taking a trial balance does not detect postings to the wrong general ledger accounts, nor does it detect the omission of an entire balanced journal entry, or its double posting, nor does it detect equal errors in opposite directions. In any of the above cases, the trial balance will still balance. The trial balance will serve only as a partial proof of the arithmetic accuracy of the recording and posting process. Even though taking a trial balance does not eliminate the possibility of all posting errors, it does reduce this possibility considerably. It will detect debits that were posted as credits, or credits that were posted as debits. It will detect unbalanced journal entries, or incomplete posting of a balanced journal entry.

The trial balance is taken after the balance in each individual ledger account has been calculated. At this point the individual account names and numbers and their respective debit or credit balances are listed in separate columns. The debit and credit columns are totaled and should equal each other. If they do equal each other, the trial balance is said to be in balance. But, remember, for the reasons stated above, a balanced trial balance does not mean that no errors were made in the completion of the first four steps of the accounting cycle. It just means that if any errors were made, they were not the type of error that taking a trial balance will detect.

The procedure for taking a trial balance of the general ledger is as follows:

1. Set up a list with all of the general ledger account numbers on the left and names on the right in chart of account order.
2. Set up two columns to the right of this list. The left column should be headed Dr and the right column should be headed Cr.
3. Enter debit balances in the Dr column and credit balances in the Cr column.
4. Total the Dr column and the Cr column. The two totals should be equal, indicating that the trial balance balances.

The trial balance for The Montric Restaurant is shown in Exhibit 4–9. The accounts payable account does not appear on the trial balance since it has a zero balance. The electricity invoice that was originally entered in the accounts payable account was paid on June 28, 2005—prior to the end of the accounting period on the balance sheet date of June 30, 2005.

DISCOVERING ERROR SOURCES

As explained earlier, despite the fact that a trial balance balances, the existence of undetected errors and/or omissions is not precluded. As a method of discovering accounting errors the trial balance has three shortcomings:

1. Equal errors in opposite directions will compensate for each other without unbalancing the trial balance.

THE MONTRIC RESTAURANT
General Journal

Date 2005	Description	Ref.	Dr	Cr
June 1	Cash	101	5,000	
	Mr. Montcalm's capital	301		2,500
	Mr. Ricardo's capital	306		2,500
	Initial capital investment			
1	Cash	101	10,000	
	Notes payable	205		10,000
	Borrowed $10,000 from bank			
3	Rent expenses	680	1,000	
	Cash	101		1,000
	Paid first month's rent			
4	Inventory—food	115	1,800	
	Cash	101		1,800
	Purchased food inventory			
11	Cash	101	4,500	
	Accounts receivable	104	400	
	Sales	401		4,900
	Week's sales			
11	Cost of food sold	501	400	
	Inventory—food	115		400
	Cost of week's sales			
12	Prepaid expenses	125	960	
	Cash	101		960
	Purchased fire insurance			

Cash — No. 101

	Dr		Cr
6/1/05	5,000	6/3/05	1,000
6/1/05	10,000	6/4/05	1,800
6/11/05	4,500	6/12/05	960
6/21/05	80	6/13/05	2,000
		6/16/05	2,000
		6/24/05	480
		6/28/05	164
		6/30/05	40
Totals	19,580	Totals	8,444
Bal.	11,136		

Accounts Receivable — No. 104

	Dr		Cr
6/11/05	400	6/21/05	80
Totals	400		
Bal.	320		

Prepaid Expenses — No. 125

	Dr
6/12/05	960
Totals	960
Bal.	960

Accounts Payable — No. 201

	Dr		Cr
6/28/05	164	6/22/05	164
Totals	164		
		Bal.	0

Notes Payable — No. 205

	Cr
6/1/05	10,000
Totals	10,000
Bal.	10,000

Mortgages Payable — No. 209

	Cr
6/13/05	8,000
Totals	8,000
Bal.	8,000

Inventory—Food — No. 115

	Dr		Cr
6/4/05	1,800	6/11/05	400
		6/18/05	50
Totals	1,800	Totals	450
Bal.	1,350		

Land — No. 135

	Dr
6/13/05	10,000
Total	10,000
Bal.	10,000

General Journal

2005			Debit	Credit
June 13	Land	135	10,000	
	Cash	101		2,000
	Mortgage payable	209		8,000
	Purchased land				
16	Montcalm's withdrawals	302	1,000	
	Ricardo's withdrawals	307	1,000	
	Cash	101		2,000
	Partner's withdrawals				
18	Montcalm's withdrawals	302	50	
	Inventory—food	115		50
	Partner's withdrawal				
21	Cash	101	80	
	Accounts receivable	104		80
	Received payment on open account				
22	Utilities expense	611	164	
	Accounts payable	201		164
	Receipt of electricity invoice				
24	Payroll expense	601	480	
	Cash	101		480
	Paid cook's wages				
28	Accounts payable	201	164	
	Cash	101		164
	Paid electricity invoice				
30	Utilities expense	611	40	
	Cash	101		40
	Received and paid water invoice				

General Ledger

Montcalm's Capital — No. 301

		6/1/05	2,500
		Totals	2,500
		Bal.	2,500

Montcalm's Withdrawals — No. 302

6/16/05	1,000		
6/18/05	50		
Totals	1,050		
Bal.	1,050		

Ricardo's Capital — No. 306

		6/1/05	2,500
		Totals	2,500
		Bal.	2,500

Ricardo's Withdrawals — No. 307

6/16/05	1,000		
Totals	1,000		
Bal.	1,000		

Sales — No. 401

		6/11/05	4,900
		Totals	4,900
		Bal.	4,900

Cost of Food Sold — No. 501

6/11/05	400		
Totals	400		
Bal.	400		

Payroll Expense — No. 601

6/24/05	480		
Totals	480		
Bal.	480		

Utilities Expense — No. 611

6/22/05	164		
6/30/05	40		
Totals	204		
Bal.	204		

Rent Expense — No. 680

6/3/05	1,000		
Totals	1,000		
Bal.	1,000		

Exhibit 4–8 The Montric Restaurant—general journal and general ledger in "T" account format. The reader should verify that all postings not indicated by arrows have been made correctly from the general journal to the general ledger.

THE MONTRIC RESTAURANT
Trial Balance
June 30, 2005

No.	Account Name	Dr	Cr
101	Cash	$11,136	
104	Accounts receivable	320	
115	Inventory–food	1,350	
125	Prepaid expenses	960	
135	Land	10,000	
205	Notes payable		$10,000
209	Mortgages payable		8,000
301	Montcalm's capital		2,500
302	Montcalm's withdrawals	1,050	
306	Ricardo's capital		2,500
307	Ricardo's withdrawals	1,000	
401	Sales		4,900
501	Cost of food sold	400	
601	Payroll expense	480	
611	Utilities expense	204	
680	Rent expense	1,000	
	Totals	$27,900	$27,900

Exhibit 4–9 The Montric Restaurant—trial balance.

2. If a complete journal entry has been omitted entirely or posted twice, the trial balance will still balance because the debits and credits omitted or posted twice are of equal values. That is why it is important not to fill in the Ref. column of the general journal until after the debit or credit has actually been posted to the general ledger.

3. Finally, if a debit or a credit is posted to the wrong account, the trial balance will still balance. This is a very difficult type of error to detect, and there is no way to avoid it except by being careful.

If the trial balance does not balance, that is, the total of the debit general ledger account balances does not equal the total of the credit balances, this indicates one or more of eight types of errors or omissions:

1. The journalizing of one or more debits or credits has been omitted (unbalanced journal entry has been created).

2. The posting of one or more debits or credits has been omitted.

3. One or more debit or credit amounts have been journalized twice (unbalanced journal entry has been created).

4. One or more debit or credit amounts have been posted twice.

5. A debit entry has been journalized as a credit, or credit as a debit (unbalanced journal entry has been created).
6. A debit has been posted as a credit, or a credit posted as a debit.
7. An error in addition or subtraction has been made when calculating the balance of a general ledger account.
8. When you checked a journal entry to determine whether or not it was in balance, you totaled one side of the journal entry incorrectly.

In this case, you should follow the steps listed below to determine the source of the error or omission you have detected:

1. Repeat the addition of the trial balance columns.
2. If your additions are correct, recalculate the balances in the individual general ledger accounts.
3. If there is a difference, determine the amount. If the difference can be evenly divided by 9 then there is a high probability that either:
   (a) You moved a decimal point to the left, i.e., $10,000 was written as $1,000 or $100;

   or

   (b) You transposed two numbers by reversing their order, i.e., $480 was written as $840, $7,136 was written as $7,316, etc.

   When these two mistakes occur, the difference between the totals of the Dr and Cr columns of the trial balance is divisible by 9 without any remainder. Go back and verify that you transferred the appropriate general ledger account balances to your trial balance.
4. Divide the difference between the total of the Dr column and the total of the Cr column in half and look for the amount in the trial balance, or in one of the journal entries. If it appears, then most likely you have entered a debit amount as a credit amount or vice versa.
5. Retrace your postings from the general journal to the general ledger accounts.
6. Verify that your initial journal entries, as entered in the general journal, are in balance.

This process may appear simple when dealing with elementary textbook problems. In a real business situation, there may be several errors to find and many more transactions than those in our examples. Finding an error can become a very lengthy and time-consuming process. The best and most economical procedure is, therefore, to avoid errors by exercising care when performing accounting functions.

Two ways of reducing the probability of committing an error are:

1. Do not enter zeros in the cents columns of the general journal or general ledger—use a dash instead. This helps to minimize clutter in these columns and helps avoid confusing a zero with a six.
2. Do not use dollar signs in journals or ledgers. They add clutter and may be confused with numerals.

COMPUTERS IN ACCOUNTING

We have been studying the accounting cycle as it is performed in a manual accounting system. Today, because of the low cost of computers and computer accounting programs, almost every business, even the smallest businesses, use computers and have automated their accounting process to a greater or lesser extent.

Advantages of Using Computerized Accounting Systems

There are certain advantages to using computerized accounting systems. Some of these are enumerated below:

1. Computers facilitate the entry of data. It is faster to enter a journal entry through a computer than to write it by hand.
2. Computers warn you if you are about to enter an unbalanced journal entry.
3. If they are programmed properly, computers can eliminate posting errors.
4. Computers eliminate errors in the calculation of account balances.
5. Computers execute the entire accounting cycle much faster than if it were done by hand.
6. Computers print the financial statements much faster and more easily than if they are typed by hand.
7. Errors can be corrected much more easily when the information is stored in a computer because it makes corrections throughout the entire accounting cycle and prepares new financial statements for printing in a matter of seconds, or at most, minutes.

Computers Are Still Subject to the Accounting Process

Nevertheless, as managers you must understand the accounting process in detail for the following reasons:

1. A computer will only process what is input into it. If you or your employees enter improperly analyzed transactions, then you will obtain erroneous information from the computer. When entering transactions a computer does not tell you what account should be posted, for instance. Nor does it tell you how much should be posted to each account, nor when it should be posted.
2. We have not discussed adjusting entries yet—this is the next step in the accounting cycle. But when you learn to make adjusting entries, you will find that they are mostly based on a manager's accounting judgment rather than neatly determinable numerical facts. Computers cannot make judgment decisions because they do not understand opinions, nor can they weigh the intangible benefits or drawbacks inherent in different accounting decisions. Computers only process numbers. No doubt you are familiar with the term: GIGO—Garbage in, garbage out. If you don't enter correct information into your computer program you will obtain useless, or worse, misleading information from your computer.
3. Most computer programs today warn you if you are entering an unbalanced journal entry, but they do not prevent you from doing so. If you do not understand the consequences of entering an unbalanced journal entry, then you will obtain erroneous output from the computer.
4. Most importantly, computers do not change the rules of accounting. They just perform all the steps in the accounting cycle more quickly. Therefore, if you, as a manager, are going to obtain the maximum benefit from your computer you must understand what it is doing. You must understand the simple accounting cycle and the possible variations of this cycle that you will learn later in this text, such as, for example, the use of special-purpose

journals. The knowledge of this cycle that you have obtained so far from this text, and the knowledge you will acquire subsequently in the text, are essential for you to be able to relate to a computer accounting program intelligently. In a business situation, you will be expected to discuss with your accountant the design of an accounting system(s) that will provide the information you desire and/or need to manage your business. It is therefore essential for a manager to understand what a computer accounting program does and exactly how it processes financial transactions.

The Format of a Computerized General Ledger

We have been studying general ledger accounts using the "T" account format. Exhibit 4–10 presents a sample of a computerized general ledger. Although all computerized general ledgers are not the same in appearance, because the rules of accounting do not change for computerized systems, they all must contain the same information as the "T" account. For the sake of comparison, below the computerized general ledger is presented a "T" account containing the same information as the accounts receivable account shown in the computerized general ledger.

There are slight differences between the "T" account format and the computerized general ledger. For instance, in this computer-generated general ledger, the debits and credits are listed together in one column—the debits as plus amounts, and the credits as minus amounts. Therefore, the total of debits and the

GENERAL LEDGER
Page 1
June 30, 2008

Account No.	Description	Date	Ref.	Current	Balances
101	Cash				1,468.00
	Sale	06/02/08	001 GJ	500.00	
	Expense	06/03/08	001 GJ	-172.00	
				328.00	1,796.00
105	Accounts receivable				4,792.00
	Sale	06/03/08	001 GJ	750.00	
	Sale	06/04/08	001 GJ	500.00	
	Collection	06/09/08	002 GJ	-1,362.00	
				-112.00	4,680.00
108	Inventory				6,666.00
	Cost of sales	06/02/08	001 GJ	-180.00	
	Cost of sales	06/03/08	001 GJ	-280.00	
	Cost of sales	06/04/08	001 GJ	-200.00	
	Purchased inventory	06/12/08	002 GJ	1,349.00	
				689.00	7,355.00

Accounts receivable			**No. 105**		
Bal.	5/31/08	4,792.00	6/9/08 GJ2	1,362.00
	6/3/08 GJ1	750.00		
	6/4/08 GJ1	500.00		
Totals		6,042.00		1,362.00
Bal.	6/30/08	4,680.00		

Exhibit 4–10 Comparison of a computer-generated general ledger and a "T" account.

total of credits do not appear, as they do in the "T" account. In other computer-generated general ledgers, the debits and credits are listed in separate columns. In that format, the totals of debits and credits would appear.

But such slight differences do not affect the basic similarity between the manual and computer-generated general ledger formats. All general ledgers, whether computer-generated or not, must contain at least the following information, which is: a beginning balance, the debits and credits to each account, the dates they occurred, the journal and page from which they were posted, and an ending balance.

This computer-generated general ledger contains postings of individual transactions. Later, when we study special-purpose journals, you will learn that entire groups of transactions can be posted in one single entry and on one date. Usually these entries represent page totals from special-purpose journals. The detailed listing of all the transactions included in such an entry would be found in the special-purpose journal from which it was posted. In that case, a business would probably enter in the general ledger the date of the latest transaction, or the date of the end of the accounting period being posted in addition to the journal and the page from which the total was posted.

Accounting books in manual systems were usually loose-leaf, and an entire page was dedicated to each general ledger account so that new pages could be added when the preceding page was full. As Exhibit 4–10 demonstrates, in a computerized system the computer prints the general ledger accounts in a continuous fashion, occupying only a portion of a page for each account, often printing several accounts on each page. It does not have to dedicate an entire page to each account because the original printout is discarded and a new one is prepared every time additional entries are posted to the computerized ledger.

SOME KEY TERMS INTRODUCED IN THIS CHAPTER

1. **Account classification system.** A convention for numbering accounts according to their location on the financial statements. The most commonly used account classification system assigns numbers in the 100 range to assets, in the 200 range to liabilities, in the 300 range to equity accounts, in the 400 range to revenue accounts, in the 500 range to cost of sales accounts, and in the 600 range to expense accounts.
2. **Chart of accounts.** A listing of all the accounts in a business in numerical order after they have been assigned numbers according to the account classification system used. *See* account classification system.
3. **General journal.** *See* journal.
4. **General ledger.** The accounting book of final entry, as opposed to the journals, which are the books of initial entry. It includes all the accounts in an accounting system. It is to this set of accounts that transaction data initially entered in the journals is ultimately posted. *See* journal, and also posting.
5. **GIGO.** This is an acronym for "garbage in, garbage out," which means that if you enter erroneous information into a computer it will give you erroneous information back.
6. **Indenting.** Whenever credits are entered in a general journal the name of these accounts must be indented, that is written a reasonable distance to the right of and away from the left-hand margin of the journal. This is done to differentiate them from the names of accounts being debited.

7. **Journal.** An accounting record book of initial entry where transactions are entered in chronological order (as they occur). Transactions are posted from here to the general ledger. Besides the general journal there are other journals called special-purpose journals designed for recording specific kinds of transactions more efficiently. Transactions should only be entered in one journal, whether it is the general journal or a special-purpose journal.

8. **Online accounting system.** A computer-based accounting system that updates all the financial records and financial statements as each transaction is recorded.

9. **Point-of-sales accounting system.** An accounting system that not only updates all financial records as each transaction is recorded, but also records sales transactions as they occur at the location (point) where the sale is made.

10. **Posting.** The process of transferring transaction data initially entered in the general journal, or special purpose journals, to their corresponding general ledger accounts.

11. **"T" account.** A general ledger account format used for educational purposes because of the ease with which it can be created—it is basically a matter of crossing two lines in the form of a "T." Nevertheless, this account contains all the same data as a general ledger account under any other format.

QUESTIONS

1. What is a trial balance?
2. Why is the general journal called a book of original entry?
3. May a journal entry have more credits than debits? Explain.
4. In what order are accounts listed on the chart of accounts?
5. In what sequence are journal entries entered in a journal?
6. What is posting?
7. What is the function of the general ledger?
8. What is a "T" account?
9. If the trial balance of the general ledger is in balance can we be assured that there were no errors or omissions in our work? Explain.
10. What is a chart of accounts and why is it a useful device?
11. Should you underline an open balance in a general ledger account?
12. When you post to the general ledger, what two pieces of information should you write next to each posting entry?
13. Do you always need a "total" line in a "T" account?
14. If a trial balance does not balance, what are the eight types of errors that may cause it to be out of balance?
15. Do computerized accounting programs help avoid any of these error sources? If so, how do they help avoid them?
16. What does it mean when we say that the trial balance is in balance?
17. What does GIGO mean, and what are its broad implications?
18. What are some ways that computerized accounting programs facilitate the accounting process?
19. Using computerized accounting systems does not relieve the manager of responsibility for being thoroughly familiar with the accounting process. Discuss.

EXERCISES

1. **(a)** Analyze the following transactions of the Rustic Hotel in terms of values exchanged and debits and credits.
   (b) Prepare a general journal on a sheet of paper and journalize these transactions.

   Feb. 15   The Rustic Hotel purchases $4,561 worth of food and beverages on account.
   18   The hotel's sales for the week amount to $6,457, of which $2,344 are on open account.
   20   The hotel collects $3,789 on open accounts.
   21   The hotel pays its creditors $3,672.
   25   The hotel buys an oven for $5,600. It pays $1,600 in cash plus two notes payable of $2,000 each. One is due at the current year end, the other at the following year end.

   (c) Is there sufficient information to determine the balance in accounts receivable and accounts payable? If not, what information is lacking? Are the accounts receivable and accounts payable of the hotel increasing or decreasing?
2. **(a)** Create a chart of accounts and "T" accounts for the following accounts of Roger Jones' Restaurant: Roger Jones' capital, inventory–food, cash, equipment, rent expense, sales, cost of food sold, prepaid expenses, accounts payable, utilities expense.
   (b) Analyze the following transactions and post them directly to the above "T" accounts.
   1. Roger Jones, a sole proprietor, invested $4,000 worth of food and $20,000 cash in his new restaurant.
   2. The restaurant purchased equipment worth $5,000.
   3. The restaurant paid the current month's rent ($1,000) and the final month's rent ($1,000) on a one-year lease at the beginning of the month.
   4. The restaurant recorded the week's cash sales amounting to $6,338. It used $2,446 worth of food and beverages in making these sales.
   5. The restaurant received an electricity invoice in the amount of $1,432.
   (c) What step of the accounting cycle has been omitted? When is it useful to post in this fashion?
3. Prepare a chart of accounts for the following accounts:

Accounts payable	Land	Sales
Accounts receivable	Mortgates payable	Utilities expense
Buildings	Notes payable	Withdrawals
Cash—Rotunda Bank	Bob Gray's capital	Cost of sales
Cash—Wilmont Bank	Payroll expense	Equipment
Prepaid expenses	Inventory	Rent expense

4. **(a)** Calculate the balance in the following accounts payable account on each of the dates that activity was recorded in the account.

Accounts Payable   **No. 202**

6/4	2,341	Beginning bal.	6,823
6/10	2,871	6/7	3,688
6/18	3,289	6/15	6,889
6/26	3,142	6/23	8,934

(b) What can be said about the company on the basis of the changes in this account balance?

5. **(a)** Prepare a chart of accounts and a trial balance of the following "T" accounts.

(b) Determine the balance in the accounts receivable account.

Accounts Payable	Accounts Receivable	Cash
5,347		8,972

Inventories	Property Under Construction	Building
3,446	12,691	30,000

Partner A's Capital	Partner B's Capital	Prepaid Expenses
30,000	30,000	1,277

Withdrawals Partner A	Withdrawals Partner B	Sales
1,000	1,000	15,000

Rent Expense	Payroll Expense	Utilities Expense
2,000	4,370	1,454

Land	Notes Payable	Equipment
10,000	10,000	5,000

Cost of Food Sold
5,431

Note: The balance of the accounts receivable "T" account was omitted from the above presentation.

6. Prepare a trial balance for the general ledger accounts below. Does it balance? Find the two mistakes in the following journal entries and their related general ledger accounts. Begin by checking the balances of the general ledger accounts, then use the other techniques learned in this chapter.

<table>
<tr><td colspan="6" align="center">General Journal   **Page 78**</td></tr>
<tr><th colspan="2">Date
2007</th><th>Description</th><th>Ref.</th><th>Dr</th><th>Cr</th></tr>
<tr><td>July 27</td><td colspan="2">Accounts payable</td><td></td><td>23,456</td><td></td></tr>
<tr><td></td><td colspan="2">Cleaning expense</td><td></td><td>4,821</td><td></td></tr>
<tr><td></td><td colspan="2" align="center">Cash</td><td></td><td></td><td>28,277</td></tr>
<tr><td></td><td colspan="2">Paid cleaning company for current and previous services</td><td></td><td></td><td></td></tr>
<tr><td>29</td><td colspan="2">Cash</td><td></td><td>3,491</td><td></td></tr>
<tr><td></td><td colspan="2" align="center">Accounts Receivable</td><td></td><td></td><td>3,491</td></tr>
<tr><td></td><td colspan="2">Collected an accounts receivable</td><td></td><td></td><td></td></tr>
<tr><td>29</td><td colspan="2">Accounts Receivable</td><td></td><td>7,416</td><td></td></tr>
<tr><td></td><td colspan="2">Cash</td><td></td><td>4,952</td><td></td></tr>
<tr><td></td><td colspan="2" align="center">Sales</td><td></td><td></td><td>12,341</td></tr>
<tr><td></td><td colspan="2">Record cash and credit sales</td><td></td><td></td><td></td></tr>
<tr><td>29</td><td colspan="2">Cost of sales</td><td></td><td>5,174</td><td></td></tr>
<tr><td></td><td colspan="2" align="center">Inventory</td><td></td><td></td><td>5,174</td></tr>
<tr><td></td><td colspan="2">Record cost of sales</td><td></td><td></td><td></td></tr>
<tr><td>30</td><td colspan="2">Equipment</td><td></td><td>15,000</td><td></td></tr>
<tr><td></td><td colspan="2" align="center">Notes payable</td><td></td><td></td><td>10,000</td></tr>
<tr><td></td><td colspan="2" align="center">Cash</td><td></td><td></td><td>5,000</td></tr>
<tr><td></td><td colspan="2">Bought equipment in exchange for 6 month note payable and cash</td><td></td><td></td><td></td></tr>
</table>

Cash   No. 101

Bal.	7/25	98,659	7/27 GJ 78	28,277
	7/29 GJ78	3,491	7/30 GJ 78	5,000
	7/29 GJ79	4,952		
Totals		107,102		33,277
Bal.	7/31	73,825		

Isabel's capital   No. 304

Bal.	7/25	500,000
Bal.	7/31	500,000

Accounts Receivable   No. 105

Bal.	7/25	137,105	7/29 GJ 78	3,491
	7/26 GJ77	19,358		
	7/29 GJ78	7,416		
Totals		163,879		3,491
Bal.	7/31	160,388		

Notes payable   No. 242

Bal.	7/25	20,000
	7/26 GJ77	11,000
	7/30 GJ78	10,000
Bal.	7/31	41,000

Equipment   No. 143

Bal.	7/25	50,000
	7/30 GJ78	15,000
Bal.	7/31	65,000

Accounts payable   No. 201

7/27 GJ78	23,456	Bal.	7/25	73,467
			7/26 GJ77	3,591
Totals	23,456			77,058
		Bal.	7/31	53,602

Building				No. 140
Bal. 7/25	300,000			
Bal. 7/31	300,000			

Inventory				No. 116
Bal. 7/25	13,467	7/29 GJ78	5,174
7/26 GJ77	49,362		
Totals	62,829		5,174
Bal. 7/31	57,655		

Payroll expense				No. 601
Bal. 7/25	28,455			
7/26 GJ77	3,782			
Bal. 7/31	32,237			

Sales				No. 401
		Bal. 7/25	142,559
		7/26 GJ77	4,277
		7/29 GJ78	12,341
		Bal. 7/31	156,177

Cost of sales				No. 501
Bal. 7/25	41,266			
7/29 GJ78	5,174			
Bal. 7/31	46,440			

Cleaning expense				No. 609
Bal. 7/25	13,467			
7/27 GJ78	4,821			
Bal. 7/31	18,288			

7. For the following transactions entered in the general journal briefly describe the transaction that has taken place. In the Ref. column write in a reasonable account number based on the chart of accounts presented in this chapter.

Date 2012	Description	Ref.	Debit	Credit
15-Mar	Accounts receivable		2,000	
	Cash		1,000	
	Sales			3,000
15-Mar	Cost of Sales		665	
	Inventory–food			665
17-Mar	Equipment		5,000	
	Notes payable			5,000
19-Mar	Inventory–food		1,000	
	Accounts payable			1,000
22-Mar	Cleaning services		700	
	Accounts payable			700
22-Mar	Salaries & wages		750	
	Cash			750
27-Mar	Cash		500	
	Accounts receivable			500
30-Mar	Accounts payable		800	
	Cash			800

SHORT PROBLEMS

1. Find the six mistakes in the following three journal entries and in their related general ledger accounts. When the errors have been corrected, the trial balance totals should be $973,467.

General Journal   **Page 25**

Date 2009	Description	Ref.	Dr	Cr
August 3	Cash	101	600,000	
	Stove	146	25,000	
	Jack's capital	305		620,000
	Owner makes additional $625,000 investment in business			
9	Building	148	300,000	
	Equipment	147	100,000	
	Cash	101		210,000
	Mortgage payable	260		190,000
	Business buys building and equipment			
15	Inventory		50,000	
	Accounts payable	301		50,000
	Business buys inventory on credit			

Cash   **No. 101**

Bal.	7/31	105,000	8/9	GJ25	210,000
	8/3	600,000			
Totals		705,000			200,000
Bal.	8/15	505,000			

Jack's capital   **No. 305**

			Bal.	7/31	100,000
				8/3	620,000
			Bal.	8/15	720,000

Stove   **No. 146**

			Bal.	7/31	0
				8/3 GJ25	25,000
			Bal.	8/15	25,000

Mortgage payable   **No. 260**

			Bal.	7/31	–0–
				8/15 GJ25	190,000
			Bal.	8/15	190,000

Equipment   **No. 147**

Bal.	7/31	0			
	8/9 GJ25	100,000			
	8/15 GJ25	50,000			
Bal.	8/15	150,000			

Accounts payable   **No. 301**

			Bal.	7/31	13,467
				8/15 GJ25	5,000
			Bal.	8/15	18,467

Building   **No. 148**

Bal.	7/31	0			
	8/9 GJ25	300,000			
Bal.	8/15	300,000			

Inventory   **No. 102**

Bal.	7/31	8,467			
	8/15 GJ25	50,000			
Bal.	8/15	58,467			

2. You were hired as the manager of the Secret Corner restaurant on April 1, 2008. The restaurant's accountant was dismissed before you arrived and you are being asked to record the restaurant's transactions and prepare a trial balance during the first week of April until a new accountant can be hired. The restaurant is a very small operation and serves sandwiches and soft drinks only. It was formed as a corporation. The general ledger balances as of March 31, 2008 are presented on the next page, but the balance in the common stock account is missing.

Transactions:

April 2   The electricity invoice for $600 was received and recorded but not paid.

April 3   The $1,000 rent for the month of April was paid. You decide not to use a prepaid rent account because you will not be preparing a financial statement until the end of the month.

April 5   Payroll in the amount of $900 was paid.

Cash			No. 101
Bal. 3/31	55,945		

Common stock			No. 320

Inventory–Food & Beverage			No. 112
Bal. 3/31	10,000		

Accounts payable			No. 201
		Bal. 3/31	2,345

Sales			No. 401
		Bal. 3/31	102,000

Cost of Sales			No. 501
Bal. 3/31	35,700		

Payroll			No. 601
Bal. 3/31	13,000		

Advertising			No. 623
Bal. 3/31	4,600		

Utilities			No. 674
Bal. 3/31	2,100		

Rent			No. 682
Bal. 3/31	3,000		

April 7   Sales are all cash sales and amounted to $6,000 for the week.
April 7   Cost of sales for the above sales amounted to $2,000.

Instructions:

(a) Fill in the correct balance as of March 31 in the common stock account.

(b) Journalize the above transactions.

(c) Copy the above "T" accounts to a worksheet, post the journal entries to the appropriate "T" accounts, and calculate a balance as of April 7, 2008.

(d) Prepare a trial balance as of April 7, 2008.

3. The French Taste Company is opening the Crepe Shop in partnership with a local resident, Suzette Pierre, in July of 2009. The following transactions took place before you were hired. You are told to establish an accounting system and record these transactions. The partnership is called the Crepe Shop.

July 1   Suzette Pierre and the French Taste Company each deposited $50,000 in the Crepe Shop's bank account as their initial investment.

   2   The partnership signed a $440,000 mortgage note payable to the French Taste Company. It is an interest-free loan from the French Taste Company to the Crepe Shop. The principal of the loan won't begin to be repaid until August 2010. This note covers the purchase of land worth $100,000, a building worth $200,000, equipment worth $95,000 and inventory worth $45,000 needed to operate the Crepe Shop.

   8   A deposit of $300 was given to the power company and of $50 to the water company.

   16   Sales for the period amounted to $30,000. They are all cash sales.

   16   The cost of food and beverages used in making these sales is $10,000.

   17   Salaries were paid in the amount of $4,236.

   18   The water and electricity invoices were received, amounting to $160 and $772, respectively.

   19    $896 was paid by the partnership to its creditors.

   20   A full year's property insurance policy was purchased for $4,800, and a six month liability insurance policy was purchased for $1,200, both for cash.

   28   Each partner took $4,000 cash from the partnership as a withdrawal of part of the profits.

Instructions:

(a) Using the chart of accounts in Exhibit 4–5 as a guide, prepare a new chart of accounts. Add any new accounts you require and omit those that are not needed.

(b) Prepare a general journal and enter the above transactions in the general journal. Be sure to provide a short description of each transaction.

(c) In the Ref. column of the general journal enter the account number of the general ledger account to which each amount would be posted.

4. Perform the following steps for the general journal of the ABC Snack Shop presented below:

   1. Write a brief description for each journal entry.

   2. Based on the chart of accounts presented in Exhibit 4–5 create a chart of accounts for these journal entries.

   3. Prepare a general ledger with a "T" account for each account on your chart of accounts. Be sure to number the "T" accounts.

   4. Then post the following journal entries, and as you post be sure to enter, in the general journal Ref. column, the corresponding general ledger account number to which you are posting.

   5. Finally, prepare a trial balance of this general ledger as of October 30, 2011.

Date 2011	Description	Ref.	Debit	Credit
4-Oct	Cash		40,000	
	Equipment		40,000	
	Marisabel's capital			40,000
	Eugene's capital			40,000
7-Oct	Land		80,000	
	Building		190,000	
	Equipment		30,000	
	Cash			50,000
	Mortgage payable			250,000
12-Oct	Utility deposits		800	
	Cash			800
16-Oct	Inventory–food		30,000	
	Accounts payable			30,000
17-Oct	Cash		25,000	
	Accounts receivable		5,000	
	Sales–food & beverage			30,000
20-Oct	Salaries & wages		5,000	
	Cash			5,000
23-Oct	Cash		1,000	
	Accounts receivable			1,000
26-Oct	Accounts payable		5,000	
	Cash			5,000
29-Oct	Advertising		1,200	
	Accounts payable			1,200
30-Oct	Marisabel's withdrawals		2,000	
	Eugene's withdrawals		2,000	
	Cash			4,000

LONG PROBLEMS

1. The Wholey Donut Company is opening a new take-out donut shop in partnership with a local resident, John Smith, in June of 2007. The following transactions took place before you were hired. You are told to establish an accounting system and record these transactions. The partnership is called the Wholey-Smith partnership.

June 1   John Smith and the Wholey Donut Company each deposited $30,000 in the Wholey Donut partnership's bank account as their initial investment.

     2   The partnership signed a $480,000 mortgage note payable to the Wholey Donut Company. It is payable $24,000 per year plus 10% interest. This note covers the purchase of the land and building to be used by the partnership. Similar land in that location recently sold for $50,000.

     4   The partnership purchased kitchen supplies for cash in the amount of $2,352.

     5   Donuts and beverages were purchased on credit from the Wholey Donut Company for $21,876.

     8   A deposit of $600 was given to the power company and of $100 to the water company.

     16   Sales for the period amounted to $25,368. They are all cash sales.

     16   The cost of food and beverages used in making these sales is $9,237.

     17   Salaries were paid in the amount of $6,328.

     18   The water and electricity invoices were received, amounting to $96 and $772, respectively.

     19    $896 was paid by the partnership to its creditors.

     21   A full year's insurance policy was purchased for $4,800 cash.

     23   Newspaper publicity was paid for in the amount of $2,000 for the month of June.

     28   Each partner withdrew $2,500 from the partnership.

     30   A monthly mortgage payment of $2,000 was made against the principal of the mortgage. One month's interest on the mortgage note was also paid.

Instructions:

(a) Journalize the above transactions.

(b) Using the chart of accounts in Exhibit 4–5 as a guide, prepare a new chart of accounts. Add any new accounts you require and omit those that are not needed.

(c) Prepare the necessary "T" accounts and post the transactions. Be sure to number the "T" accounts according to the chart of accounts.

(d) Prepare a trial balance as of June 30, 2007.

2. The Lockwood Motel Corporation was organized on October 1, 2008 with the objective of buying some land and an unused building to be converted into a motel. The following transactions took place during the first month, October 2008:

Oct. 1   The Lockwood Motel Corporation sold shares of $500 par common stock to Mr. Lockwood for $250,000 cash.

     2   The corporation borrowed $50,000 from a bank against a note payable at 12% interest (APR).

     3   The corporation purchased land and a building at a total cost of $500,000. Similar land was selling for $150,000. Of this amount $100,000 was paid in cash and a $400,000 mortgage note payable bearing 12% interest was signed for the balance.

6   The cost of remodeling the building for motel use was $105,000. Of this amount $65,000 was paid in cash. The balance of the remodeling services was received on account.

8    $1,000 was paid for advertising in the month of October.

10   A $4,800 insurance policy was purchased to provide coverage for the entire year.

12   Lodging accommodations were provided for the employees of a corporation who attended a local convention. The corporation was invoiced $6,000.

15   Cash room sales were $25,000.

16   Salaries were paid in the amount of $2,000.

18   A $300 water invoice was received and paid.

20   A $1,000 principal payment was made on the mortgage note payable and a $5,000 principal payment was made on the bank note payable. Interest on the bank note was $590 and the mortgage note was $2,236. The interest amounts were paid in addition to the principal payments.

25   The electricity invoice of $1,300 was received.

27   A full year's property taxes were paid in advance. They amounted to $3,600.

31   Cash sales for the second half of the month were $30,000.

Instructions:

(a) Journalize the above transactions.

(b) Using Exhibit 4–5 as a guide, prepare a new chart of accounts. Add any new accounts you require and omit those that are not needed.

(c) Prepare the necessary "T" accounts and post these transactions. Be sure to number the "T" accounts according to the chart of accounts.

(d) Prepare a trial balance as of October 31, 2008.

3. Alouette Restaurant was organized by Luis Debayle Pallais in Miami, Florida. He formed a corporation to protect himself against personal liability. The following transactions took place during the corporation's first month in existence, the month of August, 2008.

Aug. 1   The Alouette Restaurant sold 200 shares of $1,000 par common stock to Luis for $200,000.

2   The corporation borrowed $100,000 from a bank in the form of a note payable.

5   A one-year lease contract was signed for a locale. Rent is $2,000 per month. First and final months' rent were paid upon signing.

8   Equipment was purchased for $160,000; $100,000 was paid in cash and a $60,000 worth of food and beverages was purchased, half on account and half for each.

10    $15,000 worth of food and beverages was purchased, half on account and half for cash.

15   Salaries were paid in the amount of $3,000.

17    $2,000 was paid for advertising during the month of August.

19    $6,000 of accounts payable were paid.

22    $9,000 was invoiced to a local business for catering services rendered.

22   Food and beverages consumed in the above catering services amounted to $4,500.

24   A water invoice for $100 was received and paid.

25   An electricity invoice for $1,200 was received but not paid.

27    $6,000 was collected on accounts receivable.

28    $2,400 was paid for insurance coverage throughout the entire fiscal year, beginning August 1, 2008.

31 Cash sales for the month amounted to $27,000.

31 $9,000 worth of food and beverages was consumed in making the month's cash sales.

Instructions:

(a) Journalize the above transactions.

(b) Using Exhibit 4–5 as a guide, prepare a new chart of accounts. Add any new accounts you require and omit those that are not needed.

(c) Prepare the necessary "T" accounts and post these transactions. Be sure to number the "T" accounts according to the chart of accounts.

(d) Prepare a trial balance as of August 31, 2008.

4. The accountant of the One Way Travel Agency is having trouble balancing the first month's trial balance. He brings the agency's trial balance and general ledger (shown below) to you, the manager of the travel agency, and requests your help. Point out to your accountant the errors he has made and indicate how to correct them.

ONE WAY TRAVEL AGENCY
Trial Balance
At January 31, 2007

	Dr	Cr
Cash	15,153.13	
Accounts receivable	21,777.29	
Commissions receivable	1,089.17	
Equipment	1,341.00	
Utility deposits	1,000.00	
Accounts payable–trade		1,374.24
Accounts payable–airlines		15,100.26
Notes payable		5,000.00
Owners' equity		20,000.00
Commission revenue		1,847.21
Payroll expense	500.00	
Supplies expense	142.12	
Advertising		265.13
Rent	800.00	
Telephone	18.70	
Utilities expense	362.17	
Totals	43,183.58	43,586.84

General Ledger

Cash

1/1	20,000.00	1/3	1,000.00
1/12	5,000.00	1/14	265.13
1/16	15,100.26	1/19	21,777.29
1/29	758.04	1/24	81.05
		1/25	1,341.00
		1/29	500.00
Totals	40,858.30		24,964.47
Bal.	15,893.83		

Accounts Receivable

1/19	21,777.29	
Totals	21,777.29	
Bal.	21,777.29	

Commissions Receivable

1/18	758.04	1/29	758.04
1/22	1,089.17		
Totals	1,847.21		758.04
Bal.	1,089.17		

Equipment			Utility Deposits		
1/25	1,341.00		1/3	1,000.00	
Totals	1,341.00		Totals	1,000.00	
Bal.	1,341.00		Bal.	1,000.00	

Accounts Payable–Trade			Accounts Payable–Airlines		
		1/10	61.07		
		1/27	326.17		
		1/28	800.00		
		1/31	187.00		
		Totals	1,374.24		
		Bal.	1,374.24		

(right side Accounts Payable–Airlines)

1/16	15,100.26
Totals	15,100.26
Bal.	15,100.26

Notes Payable			Owners' Equity		
		1/12	5,000.00		
		Totals	5,000.00		
		Bal.	5,000.00		

(Owners' Equity)

1/1	20,000.00
Totals	20,000.00
Bal.	20,000.00

Commission Revenue			Payroll Expense		
		1/18	758.04	1/29	500.00
		1/22	1,089.17	Totals	500.00
		Totals	1,847.21	Bal.	500.00
		Bal.	1,847.21		

Supplies Expense			Advertising		
1/24	81.05				1/14	265.13
1/10	61.07				Totals	265.13
Totals	142.12				Bal.	265.13
Bal.	142.12					

Rent			Telephone		
1/28	800.00		1/31	187.00	
Totals	800.00		Totals	187.00	
Bal.	800.00		Bal.	187.00	

Utilities Expense		
1/27	326.17	
Totals	326.17	
Bal.	326.17	

5. The Restin Inn Motel, a sole proprietorship owned by Mr. Restin, has been in operation for a month. Mr. Restin has kept track of his transactions and wishes to know whether or not he earned a profit.

   (a) Record and summarize the transactions below in a way that will enable Mr. Restin to know what the financial position of Restin Inn is at month-end (March 31, 2008), and also to know the results of its operations during March.

   (b) Using the summarized information from (a), prepare a balance sheet as of March 31, 2008 and an income statement for the month ending March 31, 2008.

Mar. 1 Mr. Restin deposited $100,000 in Restin Inn's bank account as his initial investment.

2 Purchased land and building by giving a $20,000 down payment and signing a $180,000 mortgage note for the balance. The land was appraised at $300,000. The note is payable monthly over 20 years and 12% annual interest (APR) must be paid on the outstanding balance monthly.

4 Purchased equipment for $10,000 and furniture in the amount of $15,000, giving $5,000 cash and signing two notes payable of $10,000 each, payable at the end of the current year and the end of the following year.

6 Purchased cleaning supplies in the amount of $100 on account.

8 Purchased $200 worth of office supplies for cash.

10 Paid $500 for the required licenses and taxes.

15 Deposited $5,600 for cash room rentals and recorded $1,200 in rentals on open account.

15 Paid employees $1,300.

18 Paid $681 cash for water system repairs.

23 Purchased 1-year insurance coverage for $3,600 cash.

25 Ran an ad in newspaper. Cost $653 on credit.

27 Paid $500 to vendors on invoices due.

28 Collected $600 of amounts due to Restin Inn.

31 Received telephone invoice for $438.

31 Received and paid utility invoices in the total amount of $361.

31 Deposited $4,374 in cash receipts for room rentals and $341 in collections on account.

31 Paid employees $1,300.

31 Withdrew $2,500 for personal use.

31 Paid monthly mortgage installment: $750 for principal and $1,800 for interest.

Adjusting the Trial Balance: The Financial Statement Worksheet | **5**

The learning objectives of this chapter are:

- Introduce step 5 of the accounting cycle—adjusting the trial balance.
- Understand the role of the accrual basis of accounting in the adjusting process.
- Understand the need for, and purposes, of adjusting entries.
- Identify the major types of adjusting entries: prepayments, accruals, utilization of assets, unearned revenues, and bad debts.
- Make adjusting entries at the end of the accounting period.
- Prepare an adjusted trial balance.
- Use the financial statement worksheet to facilitate the completion of the adjusting process and the preparation of financial statements.

The first four steps of the accounting cycle were explained in Chapters 3 and 4. Thus, up to this point we have learned how to (1) identify and (2) record the inputs of the accounting system (the business transactions), (3) how to summarize their effect on the various general ledger accounts, and (4) how to verify the accuracy of these accounts by taking a trial balance of the general ledger and proving the equality of debit and credit balances.

After the business transactions have been journalized and posted and a trial balance prepared, the next step of the accounting cycle is to adjust the trial balance in order to update certain account balances.

Business transactions were recorded during the accounting period as they took place, and thus several accounts will require adjustment to reflect the passage of time. This will be needed in order to prepare financial statements in conformity with the accrual basis of accounting (proper matching of expenses against revenues during each accounting period). Many of the amounts listed on the trial balance will be included in the financial statements without change. The balance of cash, for instance, is usually transferred without modification to the financial statements. Conversely, other accounts will have to be adjusted to show their proper balance on the financial statements.

It is important to understand that typical adjusting entries are not caused by errors and will not be triggered by the issuing of source documents. Instead, they result from the analysis of the trial balance accounts, and in many cases judgment is involved in deciding on the particular adjusting entry to be recorded.

Ordinarily, an adjusting entry affects a balance sheet and an income statement account. Hence, failure to record the adjustment will result in an overstatement or understatement of revenues and/or expenses. Correspondingly, the results of operations reported by the hospitality firm and its financial condition will also be misreported.

Adjusting entries are prepared on the last day of the accounting period. They are journalized and posted in the same manner as original entries. After the adjusting entries have been recorded, an adjusted trial balance is taken to check on the accuracy of the ledger accounts before preparing the financial statements. Generally, most hospitality firms will use a financial statement worksheet as an orderly way of presenting all the pertinent information for the preparation of financial statements.

In this chapter, we commence with an analysis of the need for and purposes of adjusting entries. In our discussion we emphasize the significance of the proper application of the accrual concept of accounting in the adjustment process. Next, we divide the adjusting entries into five main types: prepayments, accruals (accrued expenses and accrued revenues), utilization of assets, unearned revenues, and bad debts.

Finally, we review the use of the financial statement worksheet as a tool for facilitating the preparation of formal financial statements. An extended illustration of a financial statement worksheet of a hospitality entity is examined using a step-by-step approach.

ADJUSTING ENTRIES: NEED AND PURPOSES

Accounting derives the proper amounts to be reported on the financial statements as the basis on which to make sound business decisions. In accomplishing this objective, we record and summarize the business transactions during each accounting period and take the trial balance of the general ledger to ascertain the equality of the value exchanges inherent to all business transactions. Yet, the analysis of the trial balance amounts might reveal that some accounts need to be adjusted so that they properly reflect the assets, liabilities, owners' equity, revenue, and expenses of the hospitality business as they should appear on the formal financial statements. Accordingly, the prime objective of adjusting entries is to update the trial balance accounts before the financial statements are prepared to reflect the passage of time from the day the transactions were first recorded to the last day of the accounting period.

Assume that a hotel room attendant earning $50 per day is paid for her five-day week each Friday. If the last day of the accounting period falls on a Tuesday, the appropriate expense for the preceding Monday and Tuesday would not be recognized as an expense of the current accounting period inasmuch as there was no evidence that a business transaction took place. Hence, an adjustment that records wage expenses of $100 is necessary in order to update the information to be reported on the financial statements. Likewise, the entry will also affect a balance sheet account, salaries payable (also referred to as accrued expenses), reflecting the hotel's liability for those wages.

We have already seen that the proper determination of net income on the income statement requires the consistent application of the accrual concept of accounting. That is, revenues are recognized when earned while expenses are recognized when incurred, regardless of when cash is received or paid out. Therefore, adjustments are needed when a transaction is recorded in one accounting period, but its recognition as revenue or expense, according to the accrual concept, belongs in another accounting period. The above example of unrecorded wage expenses clearly illustrates this point. Specifically, the recognition of the wage expense incurred belongs in the current accounting period even though the wage payment will be recorded in the subsequent period.

As previously noted, adjusting entries are journalized on the last day of the accounting period in the same way as are original journal entries. After adjusting entries are posted to the general ledger, the accounts will be ready for use in the preparation of financial statements. There are five basic types of adjustments:

1. Expenses paid in advance: prepayments
2. Unrecorded revenues and expenses: accruals
3. Utilization of assets: depreciation and inventory adjustments
4. Unearned revenue
5. Bad debts

PREPAYMENTS

Prepayments are items paid in advance that will benefit one or more accounting periods. As a result of acquiring a future value at the time of the payment, an asset is created that will be consumed in the operations of the hospitality business and hence become an expense.

The purpose of the prepaid adjustment is to recognize the expense by debiting the expired or used portion of the payment to the appropriate expense account while recording the decrease in the asset with a credit to the asset prepaid expenses. In this manner, the expense is recognized in the period of incurrence rather than in the period of payment.

The prepaid adjustment will result in the proper presentation of both the asset (prepaid expenses) and the expense on the financial statements. Specifically, the prepaid expense account will reflect the unexpired portion of the prepayment as of the last day of the accounting period, whereas the expense account will show the amount of the prepayment that was actually consumed (incurred) during the period.

Examples of prepayment adjustments are prepaid insurance, prepaid rent, and prepaid licenses. Let us consider the following example: On October 1, 2006, Benji's Place made a premium payment of $2,400 on a policy providing for two-year insurance coverage. When the premium is paid, an asset is created since the restaurant is acquiring future benefits in the form of insurance protection.

The general journal (GJ) entry to be recorded on the books of Benji's Place is as follows:

2006

Oct. 1   Prepaid Insurance   2,400
               Cash   2,400

In this entry, we debited the asset account (prepaid insurance) in order to record the purchase of an item having a future value to the restaurant, namely insurance coverage for a two-year period commencing October 1, 2006.

Assuming that Benji's Place completes its recording process on December 31, 2006, the following information will appear in the prepaid insurance account resulting from the above transaction:

Prepaid Insurance

Oct. 1		2,400
Bal.	Dec. 31	2,400

Thus, the unadjusted trial balance of Benji's Place for the year ended December 31, 2006 will show a debit balance of $2,400 in the account prepaid insurance. However, this balance is not correct, because it does not reflect the reduction of the prepayment arising from the consumption of insurance during the current accounting period. For this reason, an adjustment is required.

The adjusting entry will consist of recording the expired or used portion of the prepayment as an expense, $300 (2,400 divided by 24 months = 100/month × 3 months = 300), while reducing the original prepayment of $2,400 to its proper future value of $2,100 (2400 − 300) as of December 31, 2006. The required adjusting entry in general journal form follows:

<u>2006</u>

Dec. 31   Insurance Expense   300
                Prepaid Insurance   300

After posting the above adjusting entry to the appropriate accounts, the adjusted balances would be:

Prepaid Insurance				Insurance Expense		
Oct. 1	2,400	Adj.	300	Adj.	300	
Bal. Dec. 31	2,100			Bal. Dec. 31	300	

We can see how the adjusted balances of prepaid insurance and insurance expense will now reflect the proper values to be reported on the financial statements for the year 2006. Prepaid insurance will reflect the unexpired (or unused) portion of the prepayment on the balance sheet of Benji's Place as of December 31, 2006, that is, $2,100. (This amount represents 21 months' future value of the prepayment for the period beginning January 1, 2007 and ending September 30, 2008.) Likewise, the insurance expense to be reported on the income statement for the year ending December 31, 2006 will represent the portion of the insurance premium consumed during the current period, $300 (3 months commencing October 1, 2006 and ending December 31, 2006).

Accordingly, the asset (prepaid expenses) will reflect the future value of the prepayment on the balance sheet prepared as of the last day of the period, while the corresponding expense reported on the income statement will show the past value of the prepayment applicable to the current accounting period.

ACCRUALS

To properly recognize certain revenues earned or expenses incurred during the period, accrual adjustments may be required. The term accrual will denote the increase in a revenue or expense account during the accounting period not properly recognized in the normal recording process. There are two kinds of accruals: accrued expenses (unrecorded expenses) and accrued revenues (unrecorded revenues).

Accrued Expenses

Accrued expenses are expenses incurred during the current accounting period and not yet recorded, because they are generally not due to be paid until a future period. In the accrual basis of accounting, all expenses consumed during the period must be recognized in the period of incurrence. This is accomplished by recording the accrued expense adjustment, debiting the appropriate expense account and crediting the related liability account, reflecting the obligation to pay for the item(s) consumed.

Common examples of accrued expenses are accrued salaries and accrued interest. Also, some expenses incurred for which invoices have not yet been received are often recorded as accrued expenses by estimating the applicable expenses (for example, telephone, electricity, and water). The earlier case of the unrecorded wages of a hotel room attendant is an example of accrued salaries and wages. We shall now consider the following illustration of accrued interest.

On November 1, 2006, Tastee Restaurant borrowed $100,000 from the Fifth National Bank and signed a 90-day note bearing interest at the rate of 12 percent APR. The following entry would be recorded on November 1 for this transaction:

2006

Nov. 1   Cash   100,000
               Notes Payable   100,000

Assuming this was the only note on the books of the restaurant, the following balances would appear on the unadjusted trial balance for the calendar year ending December 31, 2006:

	Dr	Cr
Notes Payable		100,000
Interest Expense	0	

That is, the account interest expense would not reflect the cost of using the $100,000 for the months of November and December, 2006, since no payment was made during that period. Obviously, this is not correct inasmuch as interest expense accrues day by day and thus must be recognized as an expense regardless of payment. We shall record the cost incurred in using the $100,000 during the months of November and December 2006 by debiting interest expense in the amount of $2,000 (100,000 × 1% monthly interest = 1,000 × 2 months = 2,000). We then credit the corresponding liability account, accrued interest payable (or a similarly named account, such as interest payable or accrued expenses), to recognize the amount owed for interest on the note payable, which shall be paid in the near future. The adjusting entry to be recorded is

2006

Dec. 31   Interest Expense   2,000
                Accrued Interest Payable   2,000

After posting the above adjusting entry to the appropriate accounts, the following information will be reflected in the general ledger:

Accrued Interest Payable		Interest Expense	
Adj.	2,000	Adj.	2,000
Bal. Dec. 31	2,000	Bal. Dec. 31	2,000

In this manner, the interest expense account would show the actual expense incurred during the current period. This amount ($2,000) would be reported as an expense on the income statement, representing the cost incurred during the year ending December 31, 2006. Likewise, the accrued interest payable balance of

$2,000 would appear as a liability on the balance sheet, reflecting the restaurant's obligation for the interest incurred on the note as of the last day of the period (December 31, 2006).

Accrued Revenues

Accrued revenues are revenues earned in the current accounting period and not yet recorded. We have noted before that revenues are to be recognized at the time they are earned. Thus, an adjusting entry will be required in which we record the revenues earned and the related receivable, an asset account normally called accrued income receivable (or some other similar name selected by the company). The entry is made by debiting the accrued receivable account and crediting the revenue account.

Examples of accrued revenue are not so common as those of accrued expenses. In the hospitality industry, we can cite accrued interest on a note receivable, or other asset investment (for example, savings accounts), and unrecorded rent revenue. Let us consider the following illustration of accrued interest on a note receivable.

Assume that XYZ Hotel loans $10,000 to ABC Company on March 1, 2006 by signing a 60-day note bearing interest at 12 percent APR. This transaction would originally be recorded as follows:

<u>2006</u>

March 1	Notes Receivable	10,000	
	Cash		10,000

If XYZ Hotel closes its books on March 31, 2006, the interest earned during the month of March would not be reflected in the accounts to be reported on the financial statements. Thus, an adjusting entry is required on March 31, 2006 to record the interest earned during March in the amount of $100 (10,000 × 12% = 1200, 1200 divided by 12 months = 100), as follows:

<u>2006</u>

March 3	Accrued Interest Receivable	100	
	Interest Income		100

Thus, the accrued interest receivable will show an adjusted balance of $100. This will appear on the balance sheet as an asset since it reflects the revenue earned but not yet collected. At the same time, the interest income balance of $100 will appear on the income statement for the month ending March 31, 2006, representing the interest earned by XYZ Hotel during that period.

UTILIZATION OF ASSETS

Two main types of adjustments deal with the utilization or exhaustion of assets during the accounting period: depreciation or amortization of property and equipment, and inventory adjustments.

Depreciation and Amortization

With the exception of land, property and equipment (for example, buildings, autos, furniture, and equipment) have a limited useful life. Therefore, the future service potential of these assets will decline as they are used in the operations of the business. That is, the asset (property and equipment), through use, will become an expense that will be referred to as depreciation (in cases where the asset is not legally owned by the business we shall use the term amortization).

Depreciation entails the allocation of the cost of the asset to each accounting period it is expected to benefit. In this manner, depreciation will encompass the portion of the property and equipment that has expired during the accounting period and thus has become an expense used by the hospitality business in the production of revenues.

The depreciation adjusting entry is made by debiting depreciation expense, using an estimated value of the asset's expired cost during the current period. Instead of reflecting the decrease in the asset value by crediting the property and equipment, we shall credit a separate account called accumulated depreciation. This account will be considered a contra-asset account since it will be shown on the balance sheet as a reduction of the asset account property and equipment. Let us consider the following example as an illustration of depreciation adjustments.

On September 1, 2005, Best Hotel Corporation purchased furniture and equipment with an estimated useful life of 10 years for $61,000 cash. It is expected that the furniture and equipment will be worth $1,000 at the end of its 10-year estimated useful life (known as salvage or residual value). The following entry is made to record the original transaction:

2005

Sept. 1   Property and Equipment   61,000
           Cash   61,000

Assuming that Best Hotel Corporation closes its books on December 31, 2005, we shall have to make an adjustment to record the periodic decrease of the property and equipment during the four months ending December 31, 2005. There are several methods of estimating the amount of depreciation. We shall use the simplest method (straight-line) in recording the required depreciation adjustment. (A detailed treatment of other depreciation methods is given in Chapter 11.)

Using the straight-line method of depreciation, the adjusting entry will be:

2005

Dec. 31   Depreciation Expense   2,000
          Accumulated Depreciation—
             Furniture & Equipment   2,000

We estimate the amount of depreciation by spreading equally the cost of the asset (net of salvage value) over its estimated useful life. In other words, the annual depreciation expense is given by:

$$\frac{\text{cost} - \text{salvage value}}{\text{estimated useful life in years}} = \frac{61,000 - 1,000}{10 \text{ years}} = 6,000$$

Since we are recording the expense applicable to the four-month period ending December 31, 2005, we use monthly depreciation of $500 (6000 divided by 12 months), multiplied by four months: $4 \times 500 = \$2,000$:

Depreciation Expense		Accumulated Depreciation— Furniture and Equipment	
Adj. 2,000			Adj. 2,000
Bal. Dec. 31 2,000			Bal. Dec. 31 2,000

As can be seen, the depreciation expense account shows an adjusted balance of $2,000. This expense, which represents the consumption of the asset property and equipment during the current period, will be reported on the income statement. Similarly, the contra-asset account, accumulated depreciation—furniture and equipment, will appear on the balance sheet as a deduction from the asset property and equipment, as follows:

Property & Equipment	$61,000
Less: Accumulated Depreciation—Furniture & Equipment	2,000
	$59,000

In this manner, the original cost of the asset ($61,000) remains in the asset account reported on the balance sheet. The resulting amount of $59,000 (net of accumulated depreciation) is better known as net book value of the property and equipment.

The above procedure for recording depreciation is similarly followed in making amortization adjustments related to improvements on leased property. We shall cover this topic in Chapter 11.

Inventory Adjustments

There are two classes of inventories in a typical hospitality organization: (1) inventories held for sale (for example, food inventory), and (2) inventories used in the regular course of business (for example, housekeeping supplies inventory).

Inventories Held for Sale.   The balance of the food (or beverage) inventory accounts appearing in the trial balance of a hospitality firm includes the beginning inventory plus the purchases made during the period (known as items available for sale). Obviously, inventory items are used in making the sale. Nevertheless, the cost of these sales is normally not accounted for during the period. This will be done at the end of the period by making an adjusting entry encompassing the transfer of the cost of the inventory sold from the asset account (inventory) to an expense account (cost of sales).

For example, Simplicity Restaurants showed a $31,000 balance in its general ledger food inventory account on December 31, 2006:

Food Inventory

Bal. Jan. 1	2,000	
Feb. 3	4,000	
Apr. 15	5,000	
June 30	3,000	
Sept. 10	10,000	
Dec. 4	7,000	
Bal. Dec. 31	31,000	

The $31,000 balance represents a combination of the beginning inventory of $2,000 and five purchases of food inventory items made by the restaurant during the year (total $29,000). On December 31, 2006, the last day of the accounting period, a physical count of inventory items revealed that there was $4,000 of inventory in stock. Accordingly, an adjusting entry is required to record the utilization of inventory items in making the sales during the year 2006. In journal form, the entry is:

2006

Dec. 31   Cost of Food Sold   27,000
                   Food Inventory   27,000

We can see that the cost of inventory items used in making the 2006 food sales amounted to $27,000 (31,000 − 4,000) or the difference between the balance shown in the general ledger account and the actual inventory count on December 31. In other words, cost of food sold represents the following:

$$\underset{\text{of food sold}}{\text{Cost}} = \underset{\text{food inventory}}{\text{Beginning}} + \underset{\text{purchases}}{\text{Food}} - \underset{\text{food inventory}}{\text{Ending}}$$

$$27{,}000 \quad = \quad 2{,}000 \quad + \quad 29{,}000 \quad - \quad 4{,}000$$

At the same time, the food inventory account at the end of the period will show an adjusted balance of $4,000 that will appear on the balance sheet as an asset since it reflects the inventory items actually on hand on that date (as determined by the physical count). The topic of accounting for inventories held for sale will be covered in depth in Chapter 11.

Supplies Inventory.   As we already know, when supplies (for example, housekeeping supplies, office supplies) are purchased, their cost increases the asset account supplies, resulting in a debit to supplies inventory. As supplies are used in the normal course of business they become expenses. Nevertheless, the consumption of supplies during the period is not accounted for since it does not represent an original transaction. An adjustment recording the supplies used during the period (supplies expense) while reducing the supplies inventory account will be necessary on the last day of the accounting period.

For instance, Heat Travel Services, Incorporated purchased office supplies in the amount of $300 on May 1, 2005. This purchase will be recorded as follows:

2005

May   Office Supplies Inventory   300
                   Cash   300

If an additional purchase of $500 worth of office supplies is made on July 10 on account, a similar entry to record this transaction will be

2005

July 10   Office Supplies Inventory   500
                     Accounts Payable   500

At the end of the six-month period ending October 31, 2005, the account office supplies inventory shows:

Office Supplies Inventory		
May 1	300	
July 10	500	
Bal. Oct. 31	800	

If a count of office supplies on October 31, 2005 reveals that the total amount of supplies on hand is $200, an adjustment to record the consumption of $600 (800 − 200) of office supplies during the period is required. The adjustment will be:

<u>2005</u>

Oct. 31   Office Supplies Expense   600
                 Office Supplies Inventory   600

After posting this adjusting entry to the appropriate general ledger accounts, the office supplies inventory account will show an adjusted balance of $200 to be shown as an asset on the balance sheet of Heat Travel Services, Incorporated as of October 31, 2005. This amount represents the future value of the office supplies inventory on the very last day of the accounting period. Similarly, the office supplies expense has an adjusted balance of $600 to be reported on the income statement for the six-month period ending October 31, 2005, reflecting the consumption of office supplies during that period.

BAD DEBTS

When services are sold on credit, experience has shown that not all of the amount due from the customers (accounts receivable) will be collected. In this manner, a portion of the claims against the customers will prove to be uncollectible. The loss, or expense, resulting from the failure to collect all credit sales is known as bad debts expense. Following the conservatism concept of accounting, the carrying value of an asset should be reduced when there is evidence that cost cannot be recovered. Thus, the net carrying value of the asset accounts receivable will be decreased through the recognition of bad debts expense. This adjustment will involve the use of an estimate, such as a percentage of total sales or total accounts receivable, to be determined based on previous experience and other pertinent factors.

To illustrate, let us assume that the trial balance of Fabulous Inn at December 31, 2005 includes accounts receivable in the amount of $100,000. It is estimated that 3 percent of these accounts are uncollectible. An adjusting entry debiting bad debts expense $3,000 (3% $\times$ $100,000) and crediting a contra-asset account called allowance for doubtful accounts is made, as follows:

<u>2005</u>

Dec. 31   Bad Debts Expense   3,000
                 Allowance for Doubtful Accounts   3,000

This adjusting entry will result in the proper matching of bad debts expense with 2005 revenues. To this end, estimated uncollectible accounts arising from 2005 credit sales are recognized as expenses in that year. At the same time, the net carrying value of the asset, accounts receivable, is reduced by deducting an allowance for doubtful accounts from accounts receivable in the asset section of the balance sheet in the following manner:

Accounts Receivable	$100,000
Less: Allowance for Doubtful Accounts	3,000
	$ 97,000

We shall discuss accounts receivable and bad debts in greater depth in Chapter 12.

UNEARNED REVENUE

An unearned revenue (or deferred income) results when the hospitality firm receives payment for services prior to the time they are earned. The payment does not represent revenue based on the realization principle since it has not been earned as of yet. Instead, the acceptance of the advance payment increases cash and gives rise to a liability, known as unearned revenue, resulting from the hospitality company's obligation to render the specified services at some future time.

Let us assume, for instance, that on October 10, 2005, Xilo's Cruise Lines received $10,000 of customers' deposits to be used against future cruise reservations. The original entry to record this transaction is

2005

Oct. 10 Cash   10,000
                Customers' Deposits   10,000

Customers' deposits are a liability that reflects the obligation of Xilo's Cruise Lines to provide room services to the specific customers at a stipulated future date. Let us further assume that $6,000 of the customers' deposits recorded on October 10, 2005 were applied to December reservations. We must then record the following adjusting entry on December 31, 2005 (the last day of the accounting period) in order to transfer the $6,000 deposit from the unearned revenue liability to the revenue earned account (room sales):

2005

Dec. 31 Customers' Deposits   6,000
                Room Sales   6,000

Consequently, the earned portion of the customers' deposits for the year ended December 31, 2005 ($6,000) will be included as part of the room sales account on the 2005 income statement of Xilo's Cruise Lines. Similarly, the adjusted balance of the customers' deposit account shown below ($4,000) will appear on the liability section of the balance sheet prepared by Xilo's Cruise Lines as of December 31, 2005:

Customer's Deposits		
Adj. 6,000	Oct. 10	10,000
	Bal. Dec. 31	4,000

The $4,000 adjusted balance indicates the unearned portion of the customers' deposits that were received on October 10 as of the balance sheet date (December 31, 2005). When earned, at some future time, the customers' deposits will be recognized as revenue.

THE ADJUSTED TRIAL BALANCE

After adjustments are recorded in the journal and posted to the general ledger, we take another trial balance of the general ledger, which is termed an adjusted trial balance. The adjusted trial balance can be used as the basis to prepare formal financial statements since it contains the proper amounts of assets, liabilities, revenue, and expenses to be reported on the balance sheet and the income statement. Refer to Exhibit 5–1, which shows the adjusted trial balance of Mermaid Hotel for

MERMAID HOTEL
Adjusted Trial Balance
December 31, 2006
(in Thousands of Dollars)

	Debit	Credit
Cash	$120	
Accounts receivable	30	
Allowance for doubtful accounts		$ 5
Prepaid expenses	15	
Land	50	
Furniture and equipment	200	
Accumulated depreciation		60
Accounts payable		10
Notes payable		30
Mortgages payable		100
Accrued expenses		20
Customers' deposits		10
Ms. Mermaid, capital		100
Ms. Mermaid, withdrawals	10	
Room sales		200
Other income		20
Salaries and wages	60	
Utilities expense	30	
Depreciation expense	10	
Interest expense	10	
Other expenses	20	
	$555	$555

Exhibit 5–1   Adjusted trial balance—Mermaid Hotel.

the year ended December 31, 2006. As stated before, financial statements can be prepared from the adjusted trial balance shown in Exhibit 5–1. If this is done, the income statement is ordinarily prepared first, since the net income amount (revenue less expenses) is needed to complete the balance sheet's owners' equity section. An income statement for the year ended December 31, 2006 and a balance

MERMAID HOTEL
Income Statement
for the Year Ended December 31, 2006
(in Thousands of Dollars)

Revenues		
Room sales		$200
Other income		20
Total revenues		220
Expenses		
Salaries and wages	$ 60	
Utilities expense	30	
Depreciation expense	10	
Interest expense	10	
Other expenses	20	
Total expenses		130
Net income		$ 90

Exhibit 5–2   Income statement—Mermaid Hotel.

MERMAID HOTEL
Balance Sheet
December 31, 2006
(in Thousands of Dollars)

Assets			Liabilities & Owner's Equity	
Cash		$120	Liabilities	
Accounts receivable	30		Accounts payable	$ 10
Less: allowance for doubtful			Notes payable	30
accounts	5	25		
Prepaid expenses		15	Mortgages payable	100
Land		50	Accrued expenses	20
Furniture and equipment	200		Customers' deposits	10
Less: accumulated depreciation	60			
			Total liabilities	170
		140		
			Owner's equity	180
			Total liabilities and	
Total assets		$350	owner's equity	$350

Exhibit 5–3   Balance sheet—Mermaid Hotel.

sheet as of December 31, 2006, prepared from the adjusted trial balance of the Mermaid Hotel (Exhibit 5–1) are presented in Exhibits 5–2 and 5–3.

As we can see, the adjusted trial balance (Exhibit 5–1) has served as a basis for preparing the balance sheet and income statement of Mermaid Hotel as of December 31, 2006 and for the year then ended (Exhibits 5–2 and 5–3).

We shall now illustrate the use of the financial statement worksheet as a tool that will further facilitate the preparation of formal financial statements as well as the adjusting and closing entries (step 7 of the accounting cycle; to be discussed in Chapter 6).

THE FINANCIAL STATEMENT WORKSHEET

As already indicated, the financial statement worksheet does not replace the formal financial statements or journalizing and posting of adjusting and closing entries, but it is indeed an excellent device that brings together all the information necessary in the preparation of financial statements, resulting in a more timely completion of this task. It also serves as a point of reference to management in the decision-making process.

After the financial statement worksheet and the formal financial statements are completed, adjusting entries like the ones described earlier in this chapter must still be recorded in the general journal and posted to the general ledger, since the latter are the actual accounting records of the hospitality firm. The financial statement worksheet provides a convenient means of arranging the adjustment data and acts as a link between the accounting records and the formal statements while showing the net income or net loss for the period before formal financial statements are prepared.

The Worksheet Approach

The financial statement worksheet consists of a columnar sheet of paper that normally includes the following:

(1)
NAME OF COMPANY
Financial Statement Worksheet
Period Covered

Account No.	Account name	(2) Trial balance		(3) Adjustments		(4) Adjusted trial balance		(5) Income statement		(6) Balance sheet	
		Dr	Cr	Dr	Cr	Dr	Cr	Dr	Cr	Dr	Cr

Exhibit 5–4   Blank sheet of financial statement worksheet. (1) heading, (2) trial balance columns, (3) adjustments columns, (4) adjusted trial balance columns, (5) income statement columns, (6) balance sheet columns.

1. Heading (name of company, the term worksheet, and the period covered)
2. Trial balance (unadjusted) columns
3. Adjustment columns
4. Adjusted trial balance columns
5. Income statement columns
6. Balance sheet columns

Exhibit 5–4 is a blank financial statement worksheet, noting the various parts (numbered as above).

Preparing the Financial Statement Worksheet

There are six steps in preparing a worksheet for a hospitality firm:

1. Enter the heading on the worksheet and the headings for each of the five pairs of columns: trial balance, adjustments, adjusted trial balance, income statement, and balance sheet.
2. Place the unadjusted trial balance figures in the trial balance columns.
3. Enter the necessary adjusting entries in the adjustments columns.
4. Combine the unadjusted trial balance and the adjustments to produce the adjusted trial balance.
5. Extend all the amounts in the adjusted trial balance to the income statement or balance sheet columns.

6. Determine the net income or net loss for the period as the balancing amount in both financial statement columns. Enter the net income or net loss on the worksheet, total the financial statement columns, and double underline.

Illustrative Worksheet: Spencer's Restaurant

A step-by-step description of the worksheet of the Spencer's Restaurant follows.

Steps 1 and 2: Headings and Unadjusted Trial Balance. The worksheet for Spencer's Restaurant shown as Exhibit 5–5 includes the proper headings (step 1) and the trial balance before adjustments for the year ended July 31, 2005 (step 2).

Note that the information for the trial balance columns of the worksheet is obtained from the general ledger (step 4 of the accounting cycle). After placing the initial trial balance on the worksheet and ascertaining the equality of debit and credit balances in the general ledger, these totals are double-underlined as shown in Exhibit 5–5.

Steps 3 and 4: Adjustments and Adjusted Trial Balance. Adjustment information is entered in the adjustment columns on the worksheet (see Exhibit 5–6). An identification key letter is used to cross-reference the debit and the credit adjustments as they are entered in the adjustments columns.

The adjustments for Spencer's Restaurant are listed below:

1. To adjust for expired insurance, $7 (debit insurance expense, credit prepaid insurance)
2. To adjust for the cost of inventory used in making the sales during the period, $89 (debit cost of food sold, credit food inventory)

SPENCER'S RESTAURANT
Step 1 ⟶ Financial Statement Worksheet
for the Year Ended July 31, 2005
(in Round Dollars)

Account title	Acct. no.	Trial balance Debit	Trial balance Credit	Adjustments Debit	Adjustments Credit	Adjusted trial balance Debit	Adjusted trial balance Credit	Income statement Debit	Income statement Credit	Balance sheet Debit	Balance sheet Credit
Cash	101	100									
Accounts receivable	104	200									
Notes receivable	105	300									
Food inventory	120	110									
Prepaid insurance	130	12									
Furniture & equipment	160	220									
Accumulated depreciation	165		88								
Accounts payable	201		150								
Notes payable	202		100								
Spencer's, capital	301		502								
Spencer's, withdrawals	310	50									
Sales	401		300								
Other income	403		20								
Salaries & wages	503	100									
Interest expense	510	20									
Other operating expenses	515	48									
		1,160	1,160								

Step 2

Exhibit 5–5 Steps 1 and 2 of the financial statement worksheet for Spencer's Restaurant.

3. To adjust for annual depreciation of furniture and equipment, $22 (debit depreciation expense, credit accumulated depreciation)

4. To adjust for the accrued interest expense $5 (debit interest expense, credit accrued interest payable)

5. To adjust for accrued salaries, $7 (debit salaries and wages expense, credit accrued salaries payable)

6. To adjust for accrued interest income, $18 (debit accrued interest receivable, credit interest income)

These adjustments are recorded in the adjustments columns of the worksheet (step 3) in the same manner as they will be (or were) journalized. In the event that the accounts to be debited or credited are not listed in the beginning trial balance, additional accounts, as needed, are added at the bottom of the worksheet.

Next, the information in the trial balance and adjustments columns of the worksheet is combined for each account in order to determine the adjusted trial

SPENCER'S RESTAURANT
Step 1 ⟶ **Financial Statement Worksheet**
for the Year Ended July 31, 2005
(in Round Dollars)

Account title	Acct. no.	Trial balance Debit	Trial balance Credit	Adjustments Debit	Adjustments Credit	Adjusted trial balance Debit	Adjusted trial balance Credit	Income statement Debit	Income statement Credit	Balance sheet Debit	Balance sheet Credit
Cash	101	100				100					
Accounts receivable	104	200				200					
Notes receivable	105	300				300					
Food inventory	120	110			(b) 89	21					
Prepaid insurance	130	12			(a) 7	5					
Furniture & equipment	160	220				220					
Accumulated depreciation	165		88		(c) 22		110				
Accounts payable	201		150				150				
Notes payable	202		100				100				
Spencer's, capital	301		502				502				
Spencer's, withdrawals	310	50				50					
Sales	401		300				300				
Other income	403		20				20				
Salaries & wages	503	100		(e) 7		107					
Interest expense	510	20		(d) 5		25					
Other operating expenses	515	48				48					
		1,160	1,160								
			Step 2								
Insurance expense	505			(a) 7		7					
Cost of food sold	500			(b) 89		89					
Depreciation expense	506			(c) 22		22					
Accrued interest payable	208				(d) 5		5				
Accrued salaries payable	209				(e) 7		7				
Interest income	402				(f) 18		18				
Accrued interest receivable	110			(f) 18		18					
				148	148	1,212	1,212				
					Step 3		Step 4				

Exhibit 5–6   Steps 3 and 4 of the financial statement worksheet for Spencer's Restaurant.

balance amounts (step 4). In those accounts not affected by adjusting entries, the same balance appearing in the initial trial balance is transferred to the adjusted trial balance columns. If the account in the trial balance has a debit balance, the debit adjustments are added and the credit adjustments are subtracted in calculating its adjusted balance. Similarly, if the account in the trial balance has a credit balance, credit adjustments are added and debit adjustments are deducted in determining the proper adjusted balance.

After the adjusted trial balance is completed, we must once more ascertain the equality of value exchanges (debit balances = credit balances). When this is done, we double-underline the debit and credit columns of the adjusted trial balance. At this time, these balances reflect the proper amounts that will appear on the financial statements.

Steps 5 and 6: Completion of the Worksheet. As noted earlier, the adjusted trial balance contains all the information needed to prepare the financial statements. The next step in the preparation of the worksheet is to extend all the adjusted balance amounts to either the income statement or the balance sheet columns.

As shown in Exhibit 5–7, each item on the adjusted trial balance of Spencer's Restaurant is transferred to the appropriate financial statement column. Assets, liabilities, and owners' equity accounts are transferred to the balance sheet columns, whereas revenue and expense accounts are transferred to the income statement columns of the worksheet. For instance, the cash (asset) debit balance of $100 is extended to the debit column of the balance sheet; the salaries and wages expense debit balance of $107 is extended to the debit column of the income statement. Notice that accumulated depreciation is extended to the balance sheet credit column since it is a contra-asset account. To avoid making errors by overlooking accounts, it is best to extend the accounts line by line in strict sequence, beginning with cash, which is normally the first account listed.

Once all accounts from the adjusted trial balance are extended to the appropriate financial statement columns, the worksheet is completed by determining the net income or net loss for the period (step 6). The difference between the totals of the two income statement columns and the two balance sheet columns will represent the net income or net loss for the period. A net income is indicated if the sum of the income statement credit column (or revenues) is greater than the sum of the income statement debit column (or expenses). On the other hand, if the sum of the income statement debit column (or expenses) exceeds the sum of the income statement credit column (or revenues), a net loss has been incurred for the period. The net income or net loss is then entered in the column with the smaller totals. That is, net income will be added to the total of the income statement debit column and to the total of the balance sheet credit column. Conversely, a net loss will appear as an addition to the income statement credit column and to the balance sheet debit column totals.

Note that the financial statement worksheet of Spencer's Restaurant reports net income of $40 for the year ended July 31, 2005 in Exhibit 5–7. This amount was found by obtaining the difference between the totals of the debit and credit columns of the income statement and balance sheet. (Income statement difference: credit column $338 − debit column $298 = $40; balance sheet difference: debit column $914 − credit column $874 = $40.) As previously noted, net income is added to the debit column of the income statement and to the credit column of the balance sheet. Since the net income is a balancing figure, the totals of the debits and credits of the last four columns of the worksheet should be double-underlined as an indication that the completed worksheet is in balance.

SPENCER'S RESTAURANT
Step 1 ⟶ **Financial Statement Worksheet**
for the Year Ended July 31, 2005
(in Round Dollars)

Step 5

Account title	Acct. no.	Trial balance Debit	Trial balance Credit	Adjustments Debit	Adjustments Credit	Adjusted trial balance Debit	Adjusted trial balance Credit	Income statement Debit	Income statement Credit	Balance sheet Debit	Balance sheet Credit
Cash	101	100				100				100	
Accounts receivable	104	200				200				200	
Notes receivable	105	300				300				300	
Food inventory	120	110			(b) 89	21				21	
Prepaid insurance	130	12			(a) 7	5				5	
Furniture & equipment	160	220				220				220	
Accumulated depreciation	165		88		(c) 22		110				110
Accounts payable	201		150				150				150
Notes payable	202		100				100				100
Spencer's, capital	301		502				502				502
Spencer's, withdrawals	310	50				50				50	
Sales	401		300				300		300		
Other income	403		20				20		20		
Salaries & wages	503	100		(e) 7		107		107			
Interest expense	510	20		(d) 5		25		25			
Other operating expenses	515	48				48		48			
		1,160	1,160								

Step 2

Account title	Acct. no.	Trial balance Debit	Trial balance Credit	Adjustments Debit	Adjustments Credit	Adjusted trial balance Debit	Adjusted trial balance Credit	Income statement Debit	Income statement Credit	Balance sheet Debit	Balance sheet Credit
Insurance expense	505			(a) 7		7		7			
Cost of food sold	500			(b) 89		89		89			
Depreciation expense	506			(c) 22		22		22			
Accrued interest payable	208				(d) 5		5				5
Accrued salaries payable	209				(e) 7		7				7
Interest income	402				(f) 18		18		18		
Accrued interest receivable	110			(f) 18		18				18	
				148	148	1,212	1,212	298	338	914	874

Step 3 Step 4

Net income Step 6 ⟶ 40   40

338 338 914 914

Exhibit 5–7 Steps 5 and 6 of the financial statement worksheet for Spencer's Restaurant.

Advantages of the Financial Statement Worksheet Approach

In sum, the advantages of the financial statement worksheet approach to the preparation of financial statements of a hospitality organization are:

- It provides a check on the arithmetic accuracy of the overall accounting process.
- It can be used as a point of reference by record-keeping personnel.
- It eliminates the need for separate trial balances (both adjusted and unadjusted).
- It serves as a basis for the preparation of adjusting and closing entries (closing entries will be covered in Chapter 6).
- It may be used as a management tool in assessing a company's performance prior to the actual preparation of financial statements.
- It facilitates and speeds up the preparation of formal financial statements.

It is evident that the financial statement worksheet is an excellent aid to financial statement preparation. Once the worksheet is completed, all the information necessary to prepare formal financial statements is readily available. It will be rather simple, indeed, to prepare formal financial statements by referring to a completed worksheet in view of the fact that all the account balances have been sorted into income statement and balance sheet classifications. All that will be needed is to recast the worksheet information into more formal balance sheet and income statement formats. This will be illustrated in the following chapter.

SOME KEY TERMS INTRODUCED IN THIS CHAPTER

1. **Accruals.** *See* accrued expenses and accrued revenues.
2. **Accrued expenses.** Expenses incurred during the accounting period not yet recorded.
3. **Accrued revenues.** Revenues that were earned but not recognized in the accounts during the accounting period.
4. **Accumulated depreciation.** A contra-asset account used to accumulate the total depreciation recorded on property and equipment; deducted from the corresponding assets on the balance sheet.
5. **Adjusting entries.** Journal entries made on the last day of the accounting period in order to update the trial balance accounts before the financial statements are prepared.
6. **Adjusted trial balance.** A trial balance prepared after all adjusting entries were recorded in the general journal and posted to the general ledger.
7. **Allowance for doubtful accounts.** A contra-asset count that shows the estimated amount of accounts receivable that will not be collected; shown as a reduction from accounts receivable on the balance sheet.
8. **Amortization.** The write-off of the cost of an asset over its estimated useful life.
9. **Bad debts.** An estimate of the accounts receivable that are uncollectible.
10. **Deferred income.** *See* unearned revenue.
11. **Estimated useful life.** The period of time in which an asset will be of value to the firm.
12. **Expired insurance.** Portion of an insurance premium that has been incurred.
13. **Financial statement worksheet.** *See* worksheet.
14. **Straight-line depreciation.** A method of depreciation that allocates the cost of property and equipment evenly over the estimated useful life of the asset.
15. **Unadjusted trial balance.** A trial balance prepared before adjusting entries are reflected in the accounts.
16. **Unearned revenue.** Payments received in advance for services to be provided in the future. Examples include customers' deposits and unearned transportation revenue.
17. **Unexpired insurance.** Portion of the insurance premium that has not expired and thus it has a future value to the firm.
18. **Worksheet.** An accounting tool used to bring together all the information needed in the preparation of financial statements, adjusting entries, and closing entries; also called financial statement worksheet.

QUESTIONS

1. Why are adjusting entries needed at the end of the accounting period?
2. Explain how adjusting entries affect the determination of the net income for the accounting period.
3. Describe the five types of adjusting entries.

4. What is meant by unearned revenue? Give two examples of unearned revenue applicable to a hospitality firm.
5. What are prepayments? What original entry is made when expenses are paid in advance? What adjusting entry may be needed at the end of the accounting period?
6. What are accruals? Give two examples of two accrued expenses applicable to the hospitality industry.
7. What effect would the failure to make an adjusting entry for accrued salaries expense have on the net income for the period?
8. What is depreciation? Why are depreciation adjustments necessary?
9. Explain the purpose of using the accumulated depreciation account in recording depreciation adjustments. In what financial statement will this account appear?
10. Describe four advantages of the financial statement worksheet approach.
11. What is the purpose of the financial statement worksheet?
12. Does the financial statement worksheet eliminate the need for formal financial statements?
13. What is bad debts expense? Why does the conservatism principle require a bad debts adjustment?
14. Accumulated depreciation in the balance sheet credit column of the financial statement worksheet of Great Escape Inn is $10,000 larger than depreciation expense in the income statement debit column of the same worksheet. Explain how this is possible.
15. What is the purpose of using key letters or numbers in recording adjusting entries in the adjustments columns of a financial statement worksheet?
16. Is it possible to prepare adjusting and closing entries and complete financial statements without preparing a financial statement worksheet? Explain.

EXERCISES

1. An examination of the prepaid insurance account of Tank Restaurants shows a balance before adjustments of $9,600 as of October 31, 2006 (the end of the fiscal year). Prepare the required adjusting entries in the general journal under each of the following assumptions:
   (a) An examination of insurance policies reveals insurance that cost $4,000 has expired during the period.
   (b) An examination of insurance policies shows unexpired insurance of $6,400 as of October 31, 2006.
2. Travel Consultant, Inc., borrows $100,000 on October 31, 2006, from Haven National Bank for 90 days with interest payable at the time of repayment of the note at 12 percent APR. Prepare the required adjusting entry on December 31, 2006.
3. The balances of the following accounts, taken from the adjusted trial balance columns of the financial statement worksheet of RJ Inn for the year ending December 31, 2006, are presented in random order:

(a) Cash	$ 10	(i) Furniture and equipment	$90
(b) Cost of food sold	28	(j) Room sales	85
(c) Prepaid insurance	12	(k) Food sales	40
(d) Rent expense	7	(l) Accounts receivable	22
(e) Depreciation expense	10	(m) Insurance expense	16
(f) Salaries and wages	30	(n) RJ, withdrawals	12
(g) RJ, capital	100	(o) Other expenses	20
(h) Accumulated depreciation	20	(p) Accounts payable	12

Required:
Indicate to which column of the financial statement worksheet each account balance would be extended.

4. Use the information from Exercise 3 above to calculate the following:
   (a) Total assets
   (b) Total revenues
   (c) Total expenses
   (d) Net income for the year 2006
   (e) Total owner's equity, December 31, 2006.

5. On June 30, 2007, Best Restaurants purchased property and equipment with an estimated useful life of 10 years for $30,000. Its salvage value is estimated to be $1,000.
   (a) Record appropriate adjusting entries at December 31, 2007 and December 31, 2008 in the general journal. The company uses straight-line depreciation.
   (b) Determine the net book value of the property and equipment at December 31, 2008 and show proper presentation on the balance sheet as of that date.

SHORT PROBLEMS

1. Prepare adjusting entries in the general journal from the following information pertaining to the accounts of Perfect Place Inn as of November 30, 2006 (the end of its fiscal year):
   (a) The prepaid insurance account shows a balance of $120 representing the May 31, 2006 premium payment for one-year fire insurance coverage.
   (b) Furniture and equipment ($1,000) is being depreciated using the straight-line method and an estimated useful life of five years. (no salvage value). Annual depreciation has not been recorded.
   (c) Salaries and wages earned by employees for November 28, 29, and 30, have not been recorded. Weekly wages (five days) amount to $800.
   (d) Interest earned on a note receivable not yet collected is $50.
   (e) The customers' deposit account has a balance of $800 before adjustments. Of these deposits, $300 were earned during November 2006. The food inventory account reveals an unadjusted balance of $80. The correct amount of food inventory on hand is $30 on November 30, 2006.

2. Selected account balances were taken from the trial balance of Glowing Inn (before adjustments) for the year ended August 31, 2006.

Prepaid insurance	$ 240
Accumulated depreciation, building	50
Accumulated depreciation, furniture and equipment	10
Salaries and wages expense	102
Interest expense	60
Customers' deposits	20
Housekeeping supplies inventory	70
Building	500
Notes payable	200
Furniture and equipment	500

   (a) Record the necessary adjusting entries as of August 31, 2006 in the general journal using the following information:

1. The balance of prepaid insurance represents a two-year insurance policy purchased on June 1, 2006.
2. An inventory of housekeeping supplies revealed $10 on hand on August 31, 2006.
3. Depreciation on the building is calculated using the straight-line method and an estimated useful life of 30 years (no salvage value).
4. Depreciation on the furniture and equipment is calculated using the straight-line method and an estimated useful life of 10 years (no salvage value).
5. Customers' deposits represent advance payments received in July 2006 for August and September 2006 reservations. Of the deposits, $9 was used during August 2006.
6. Interest on the $200 note issued on June 1, 2006 has not been recorded. The annual interest rate is 15%.

(b) Determine the adjusted balances of the following accounts: prepaid insurance, customers' deposits, accumulated depreciation, building, interest expense, salaries and wages expense, and housekeeping supplies inventory.

3. Data pertaining to the accounts of Revelation Resorts for the month of February 2006 follow:
   1. A two-year fire insurance premium of $660 had been paid on December 1, 2005.
   2. A customer paid a $40 deposit on January 1, 2006 to be applied against a March 2006 reservation.
   3. The total daily payroll is $400 and employees are paid each Wednesday for all work done during the preceding week. February 28 falls on a Friday.
   4. The resort has furniture and equipment that cost $5,000 and has an estimated life of 10 years (no salvage value). The monthly depreciation has not been recorded.
   5. Rent of $2,800 for the month of February 2006 will be paid on March 1, 2006.
   6. Included in the room sales account are advance payments of $450 for services to be rendered in March 2006.
   7. The office supplies inventory account has an unadjusted balance of $1,300. Office supplies on hand were $1,120 on February 28, 2006.
   8. The balance of the notes payable account ($10,000) represents a 14 percent interest-bearing note dated January 1, 2006 and due July 1, 2006.

   Required:
   (a) Prepare adjusting entries in the general journal on February 28, 2006.
   (b) Explain the effect on net income of not making each adjusting entry.

LONG PROBLEMS

1. The following transactions were engaged in by Dolphin Travel Services (a proprietorship) during its first month of operation in 2005:

   Oct. 1 Mr. David Dolphin invested $150,000 to start a new business under the name Dolphin Travel Services.
   2 Borrowed $100,000 from the Fourth National Bank to be repaid in 90 days (12 percent APR).
   5 October office rent is paid, $1,000.
   6 Purchased furniture and equipment on account, $50,000.

8 Paid cash for supplies, $800.
10 Sales commissions received in cash, $20,000.
15 Paid salaries and wages, $2,000.
20 Paid $1,200 for a one-year general insurance coverage.
21 Paid $20,000 toward the furniture and equipment purchase of October 6.
24 Paid salaries and wages, $2,500.
28 Sales commissions: $25,000 in cash, $28,000 on account.

Required:
(a) Enter the October transactions in the general journal.
(b) Post the journal entries to general ledger "T" accounts and determine account balances.
(c) Set up a 10-column financial statement worksheet.
(d) Take a trial balance of the general ledger using the first two money columns of the worksheet.
(e) Complete the adjustments columns of the financial statement worksheet using the following adjustment information:
  1. Salaries and wages incurred, but not yet paid, as of October 31, 2005: $400.
  2. Record the expired insurance for the month of October 2005.
  3. Record accrued interest for the month of October.
  4. Use straight-line depreciation and a 10-year estimated useful life in recording depreciation.
  5. Commissions earned, not yet recorded, $5,000.
  6. Supplies inventory on hand at October 31, 2005, $200.
(f) Complete the financial statement worksheet, determining the amount of net income or net loss of Dolphin Travel Services for the month of October, 2005.
(g) Prepare an income statement of Dolphin Travel Services for the month ended October 31, 2005, and a balance sheet as of October 31, 2005.
2. The account balances (in thousands of dollars) in the general ledger of On Board Travel Agency on July 31, 2005 (the end of its fiscal year), before adjustments, were as follows:

Debit balances		Credit balances	
Cash	$ 30	Accumulated depreciation	$ 80
Accounts receivable	158	Notes payable	100
Notes receivable	20	Accounts payable	120
Furniture and fixtures	300	Aly Seat—capital	100
Inventories	20	Sales	382
Prepaid insurance	14	Other income	20
Salaries expense	120		
Interest expense	60		
Other expenses	80		
	$802		$802

The data for the adjustments are as follows:
1. The prepaid insurance balance represents an entry made on May 31, 2005 for the cost of a one-year policy expiring on May 31, 2006.
2. Interest on the $100,000 note payable issued on June 30, 2005 is due to be paid on September 30, 2005 at a 12 percent annual rate of interest.

3. Inventories at July 31, 2005, $7,000.
4. Furniture and fixtures are being depreciated using the straight-line method and an estimated useful life of five years (no salvage value). Annual depreciation has not been recorded.
5. Salaries for the last two days of the period ended July 31, 2005 have not been recorded, $1,000.

Required:
(a) Record adjusting entries in the general journal.
(b) Post adjusting entries, adding other "T" accounts as necessary.
(c) Prepare an adjusted trial balance as of July 31, 2005.
(d) Prepare in good form a balance sheet as of July 31, 2005, a statement of owner's capital, and an income statement for the year ended July 31, 2005.

3. The general ledger of Jolly Restaurant on December 31, 2006, shows the following accounts and balances (presented in random order):

Cash	$ 5,000
Accounts receivable	2,000
Furniture and equipment	14,000
Accumulated depreciation	2,000
Accounts payable	4,000
Prepaid insurance	1,200
JJ, capital	8,000
JJ, withdrawals	2,000
Salaries and wages expense	6,000
Sales	20,000
Notes payable	4,000
Advertising expense	1,500
Other operating expenses	4,000
Housekeeping supplies inventory	1,800
Interest expense	500

The adjustment data for the year 2006 are as follows:
1. The balance in the prepaid insurance account represents a one-year insurance policy purchased on September 1, 2006.
2. An inventory of housekeeping supplies showed $1,100 worth of supplies used during the year.
3. The furniture and equipment is depreciated using the straight-line method and a five-year estimated useful life (salvage value $500).
4. Interest on a six-month note ($4,000) dated August 1, 2006 and bearing interest at the rate of 15% per year, has not been recorded.
5. Salaries and wages for the five-day week ended Friday, January 2, 2007, $200, will be paid on that day.

Required:
(a) Prepare a complete financial statement worksheet for the year ended December 31, 2006, entering the adjustments directly on the worksheet.
(b) Prepare a balance sheet, income statement, and statement of owner's equity as of and for the year ending December 31, 2006.

4. The following account balances in random order have been extracted from the general ledger of FRB Suites as of December 31, 2006.

Account title	Acct. no.	Trial balance		Adjustments		Adjusted trial balance		Income statement		Balance sheet	
		Dr	Cr	Dr	Cr	Dr	Cr	Dr	Cr	Dr	Cr
Accounts payable	201		1,000								
Accounts receivable	110	3,000									
Accumulated depreciation	175		200								
Accrued interest payable	215										
Cash	103	1,000									
Common stock	310		1,000								
Depreciation expense	598										
Insurance expense	595										
Interest expense	596										
Furniture and fixtures	170	1,000									
Prepaid insurance	132	600									
Notes payable	202		1,000								
Sundry expenses	572	100									
Salaries expense	500	400									
Room sales	400		2,000								
Other income	402		400								
Utilities expense	580	200									
Supplies expense	515										
Supplies inventory	120	300									
Retained earnings	315		1,000								
		6,600	6,600								

Required:

(a) Use the data provided below to adjust the trial balance for the year-ended December 31, 2006.

(b) Complete the financial statement worksheet determining the net income or (loss) for the year 2006.

Adjustment data:

1. Supplies inventory physical count at December 31, 2006, $200.
2. Note payable was issued on October 1,2006, bearing interest at 12 percent APR, due January 2, 2007.
3. Furniture and fixtures are depreciated using the straight-line method over a 10-year estimated useful life.
4. Prepaid insurance represents the premium, paid June 1, 2006, for one-year coverage.

Completing the Accounting Cycle 6

The learning objectives of this chapter are:

- To complete the accounting cycle.
- To illustrate the use of the financial statement worksheet in preparing formal financial statements.
- To understand the need and purposes of closing entries.
- To review the last step of the accounting cycle—closing the books.
- To record and post closing entries.
- To prepare a post-closing trial balance.
- To provide an overview of the optional procedure of reversing entries.
- To highlight the main differences between closing procedures of sole proprietorships, partnerships, and corporations.
- To present a flowchart of all the steps of the accounting cycle for review purposes.

In Chapter 5, we explained how the financial statement worksheet helps organize the accounting data needed to produce the output (or end product) of the accounting system—information to management in the form of financial statements. Usually, the remaining steps in the accounting cycle can be completed in a timely fashion using the financial statement worksheet as a point of reference. The completed worksheet will provide the information required to prepare the formal income statement and balance sheet. Management and other financial statement users in appraising the past performance of the hospitality business and in making economic decisions regarding the future of the firm will then use these statements. Moreover, the financial statement worksheet will also be used to complete the final step of the accounting cycle—closing the books. This last step is needed to make the accounting records ready for the next accounting period by transferring the net income (or net loss) of the period to the owner(s) of the hospitality firm.

In this chapter we first illustrate the use of the financial statement worksheet in the preparation of formal financial statements—step 6 of the accounting cycle. The financial statement worksheet of Spencer's Restaurant (see Exhibits 5–2 to 5–7) is used as the basis to prepare the balance sheet, statement of owner's equity, and income statement of the restaurant as of and for the year ended July 31, 2010.

Next, the seventh and last step of the accounting cycle, closing the books, is reviewed. In this regard, we explain the need and purposes of closing entries, setting forth the main differences between nominal and real accounts. An in-depth coverage of each of the four closing entries will be presented. Also, a post-closing trial balance is prepared as a means to check, one more time, the accuracy of the general ledger.

Once closing procedures are completed, we consider an optional additional procedure known as reversing entries. These entries are journalized at the beginning of each accounting period in order to facilitate the recording of certain income and expense transactions taking place during the period. Then, the main differences and similarities between certain procedures used by proprietorships (and partnerships) and those applicable to corporations are highlighted. Finally, a flowchart of all the steps in the accounting cycle is included for review purposes.

PREPARATION OF FINANCIAL STATEMENTS: STEP 6 OF THE ACCOUNTING CYCLE

As noted earlier, after the financial statement worksheet is completed, all of the information needed to prepare the financial statements is readily available. Nonetheless, the data must be rearranged into a more formal financial statement presentation.

Two basic financial statements are prepared using the financial statement columns of the worksheet: (1) the income statement and (2) the balance sheet. In addition, many hospitality firms prepare a separate statement of owners' equity or capital (statement of retained earnings for a corporation) using data from the worksheet. Exhibit 5–7, the worksheet of Spencer's Restaurant for the year ended July 31, 2010, is used as the basis to prepare formal financial statements for the restaurant.

Income Statement Preparation

The income statement for the period is normally prepared first. All of the information needed to prepare the income statement of Spencer's Restaurant for the year ended July 31, 2010 is found in the income statement columns of the completed worksheet (Exhibit 5–7). The credit column lists the individual revenue accounts, totaling $338, whereas the debit column contains the individual expenses, a total amount of $298.

The income statement for Spencer's Restaurant for the year ended July 31, 2010 is given in Exhibit 6–1.

This simple format income statement consists of four sections:

1. Statement heading (name of company, name of statement, and period covered)
2. Revenue section
3. Expense section
4. Net income (or net loss) amount

Statement of Owner's Equity Preparation

Once the income statement is done, the next statement that is normally prepared is the statement of owners' equity. Adding the net income of the period to the beginning capital, and subtracting the withdrawals completes the statement for the period. The resulting amount will represent the ending capital and will also appear on the balance sheet as an indication of the owner's equity in the business on the last day of the accounting period.

(1)
SPENCER'S RESTAURANT
Income Statement
for the Year Ended July 31, 2010

Revenues (2)		
Sales		$300
Other income		20
Interest income		18
Total revenues		338
Expenses (3)		
Salaries and wages expenses	$107	
Insurance expense	7	
Cost of food sold	89	
Interest expense	25	
Depreciation expense	22	
Other operating expenses	48	
Total expenses		298
Net income (4)		$40

Exhibit 6–1   Spencer's Restaurant income statement. (1) Statement heading (name of company, name of statement, and period covered); (2) revenue section; (3) expense section; (4) net income (or net loss) amount.

The information needed for the beginning capital amount and for the withdrawals made during the period is generally found in the balance sheet columns of the financial statement worksheet. However, if additional investments were made by the owner(s) during the current accounting period, it becomes necessary to refer to the owner's capital account in the general ledger to determine the actual amounts invested, which must be added to the beginning capital in preparing the statement of owner's equity.

The net income for the period is the balancing number on the income statement and balance sheet columns of the worksheet, and it is also the bottom figure on the first basic financial statement (the income statement). As noted before, we add the net income to the beginning balance of owner's capital on the statement of owner's equity. Conversely, we deduct a net loss from the beginning capital balance, if applicable.

The formal statement of owner's equity of Spencer's Restaurant for the year ended July 31, 2010 is given in Exhibit 6–2.

Balance Sheet Preparation

The information necessary to prepare the balance sheet is found in the balance sheet columns of the worksheet. The balance sheet debit column contains all the asset accounts to be included on the balance sheet. Similarly, the balance sheet credit column contains the liabilities of the company and the owners' equity accounts. It also includes the contra-asset accounts (e.g., accumulated depreciation) to be deducted from the corresponding assets on the formal balance sheet.

A simple form of the balance sheet usually consists of:

- Statement heading (name of company, name of statement, and statement date)
- Asset section

SPENCER'S RESTAURANT
Statement of Owner's Equity
for the Year Ended July 31, 2010

Beginning balance	$502
Add: Net income for the period	40
	542
Less: Withdrawals	50
Ending balance	$492

Exhibit 6–2 Spencer's Restaurant statement of owner's equity.

- Liability section
- Owners' equity (owner's capital ending balance)

As previously indicated, the balance sheet is based on the fundamental accounting equation and thus follows the premise of equality inherent in the double-entry accounting system, namely, that assets are equal to liabilities plus owner's equity. The balance sheet of Spencer's Restaurant as of July 31, 2010, is shown in Exhibit 6–3.

We can see that the financial statement worksheet debit column total of $914 (Exhibit 5–7) does not agree with the total assets on the formal balance sheet ($754). The worksheet debit column includes the withdrawals account ($50), which is not an asset account. Furthermore, the accumulated depreciation (shown in the credit column of the worksheet) was deducted from the asset account furniture and equipment ($110) on the balance sheet.

SPENCER'S RESTAURANT
Balance Sheet
July 31, 2010

Assets

Cash		$100
Accounts receivable		200
Notes receivable		300
Accrued interest receivable		18
Food inventory		21
Prepaid insurance		5
Furniture and equipment	$220	
Less: Accumulated depreciation	110	110
Total assets		$754

Liabilities & Owner's Equity

Liabilities

Accounts payable	$150
Notes payable	100
Accrued interest	5
Accrued salaries	7
Total liabilities	262
Owner's Equity	492
Total liabilities & owner's equity	$754

Exhibit 6–3 Spencer's Restaurant balance sheet.

The reconciliation of the total amount in the debit column of the worksheet and the total assets on the balance sheet follows:

Balance sheet worksheet debit column		$914
Less: Withdrawals	50	
Accumulated depreciation	110	160
Total assets on balance sheet		$754

The above illustrations of the financial statements of Spencer's Restaurant are examples of simple format financial statements. As we progress, we shall see that there are several alternatives for presenting financial and operating data on the financial statements. Chapters 9 and 10 present an in-depth coverage of the presentation of financial statements in the hospitality industry.

CLOSING THE BOOKS: STEP 7 OF THE ACCOUNTING CYCLE

After the financial statements are completed, the last step of the accounting cycle is the closing procedures needed to prepare the general ledger for the next accounting period. As stated in Chapter 2, revenues belong to the owner(s) whereas expenses must be absorbed by the owner(s). The closing process will credit the owners with their share of revenues while debiting the owners with the expenses they must absorb, thereby increasing owners' equity with the revenues of the period and decreasing owners' equity with the expenses of the period.

Based on the foregoing, we shall call revenues and expenses temporary (or nominal) accounts. Their balances will be closed or cleared at the end of each accounting period inasmuch as revenue and expenses are established as subdivisions of owners' equity during each accounting period in order to determine the periodic net income (or net loss). However, once the output of the accounting system has been produced (financial statements) these temporary accounts have served their purpose and will be closed by reducing them to zero. In this manner, revenues and expenses will have a fresh start at the beginning of each new accounting period.

Balance sheet accounts, on the other hand, are referred to as permanent (or real) accounts. They will not be closed at the end of the period. Rather, the ending balances of assets, liabilities, owners' equity, and contra-asset accounts (such as accumulated depreciation) will be carried forward to the next accounting period.

The three main objectives of closing the books can be summarized as follows:

1. To close temporary accounts, reducing their balance to zero.
2. To transfer the net income (or net loss) to the appropriate owners' equity account.
3. To make the general ledger ready for the next accounting period.

Closing Process

As a practical matter, after the financial statements are prepared, the adjusting entries which are shown on the worksheet are posted to the general ledger in order to bring it into agreement with the financial statements. Once the general ledger accounts reflect the proper adjusted balances, we are ready to close the revenue and expense accounts, transferring the net income (or net loss) of the period to the owner(s) of the hospitality organization. The closing entries are first recorded in the general journal and then posted to the general ledger.

In lieu of transferring each revenue and expense account directly to the owners' capital account, the income summary account is created as a means of simplifying the closing procedures. This account will, in turn, be closed by transferring its balance to the appropriate owners' equity account. We shall again refer to the completed financial statement worksheet as a basis to complete the closing process. The actual procedures for closing the books consist of four entries:

1. Close all revenue accounts to income summary.
2. Close all expense accounts to income summary.
3. Close the income summary account to the appropriate owner(s) equity account.
4. Close the withdrawals(s) account to the capital(s) account (only applicable to proprietorships and partnerships).

The closing entries will be reviewed using the Spencer's Restaurant worksheet for the year ended July 31, 2010 (Exhibit 5–7) as a point of reference.

Entry No. 1: Closing the Revenue Accounts

Since all the revenue accounts have a normal credit balance, we need to debit all revenue accounts appearing in the income statement credit column of the financial statement worksheet to bring their balance to zero. At the same time, we credit the income summary account for the total of all revenue account balances as reflected in the income statement credit column of the worksheet.

The first closing entry for Spencer's Restaurant is shown below:

<u>2010</u>

July 31	Sales	300	
	Interest income	18	
	Other income	20	
	Income summary		338
	To close revenue accounts.		

After posting the above entry to the general ledger, the accounts will show the following:

Sales			
Closing 1	300	Bal. July 31	300

Other Income			
Closing 1	20	Bal. July 31	20

Interest income			
Closing 1	18	Bal. July 31	18

Income Summary		
	Closing 1	338

Note that the double-ruled lines in the revenue accounts indicate that the debits and credits are equal and the account has a zero balance. Also note that the amount of the period's revenue ($338) has been transferred to the credit side of the income summary account.

Entry No. 2: Closing the Expense Accounts

The second closing entry will reduce all expense accounts to a zero balance by transferring them to the income summary account. Since the expense accounts all have debit balances, they will have to be credited to obtain a zero balance. The income summary account is debited for the total of all the expenses.

The information for closing expenses is found in the debit column of the worksheet. The expense accounts are closed in the order in which they appear on the worksheet. After transferring the total of all the expense accounts to income summary, the debit side of this account will include all expenses. The second closing entry for Spencer's Restaurant is:

<u>2010</u>

July 31	Income Summary	298	
	Salaries and wages		107
	Insurance expense		7
	Cost of food sold		89
	Interest expense		25
	Depreciation expense		22
	Other operating expense		48
	To close the expense accounts.		

After posting the first two closing entries to the general ledger, the balance of the income summary account will represent the net income (or net loss) of the period since its credit side includes the total revenues (closing entry No. 1) and the debit side includes the total expenses (closing entry No. 2). We have already seen that the excess of revenues over expenses is the net income of the period.

The income summary account for Spencer's Restaurant appears below:

Income Summary			
Closing 2	298	Closing 1	338

Thus, the income summary account has a credit balance of $40 (338 − 298), which is the net income of Spencer's Restaurant for the year ended July 31, 2010.

Entry No. 3: Closing the Income Summary Account

After the first two closing entries are recorded and posted to the general ledger, all the revenue and expense accounts have zero balances, and the income summary account has a balance equal to the net income or loss for the accounting period.

The third closing entry will transfer the balance of the income summary account to the appropriate owner's equity account. As a result of this, the capital account will increase with the net income of the period or decrease with a net loss. After revenues and expenses are closed, the income summary has served its purpose and is closed to the capital account. The third closing entry for Spencer's Restaurant follows:

<u>2010</u>

July 31	Income summary	40	
	Spencer's, capital		40
	To close the income summary account.		

In "T" account form, the income summary and the capital account of Spencer's Restaurant will reflect the following:

Income Summary

Closing 2	298	Closing 1	338
Closing 3	40		
	338		338

Spencer's, Capital

	July 31 Bal.	502
	Closing 3	40

Note that after the first three closing entries are recorded and posted, the capital account shows an increase of $40, resulting from the transfer of net income from the income summary account to Spencer's capital. Similarly, the income summary account has no balance.

Entry No. 4: Closing the Owner's Withdrawals

The last closing entry completes the closing process by transferring the owner's withdrawals account balance to the capital account. The withdrawals account is considered a nominal account, and thus it is temporary in nature. It remains open during each period in order to account for the amounts withdrawn by the owner(s). The withdrawals account, however, is closed at the end of the period by crediting it (since it has a normal debit balance) and debiting the owner's capital account. The last closing entry for Spencer's Restaurant is:

2010

July	Spencer's, capital	50	
	Spencer's, withdrawals		50
	To close the withdrawals account.		

The effects of the above entry in the capital and withdrawals accounts are shown below:

Spencer's, Capital

Closing 4	50	Bal. July 31	502
		Closing 3	40
	50		542
		Bal.	492

Spencer's, Withdrawals

July 31 Bal.	50	Closing 4	50

After all closing entries are recorded and posted, the balance of the capital account will be in agreement with the owner's equity balance shown on the balance sheet (see Exhibit 6–3). The balance will include the amount of capital at the beginning of the period plus additional investments (if applicable) made during the period, net income addition or net loss deduction, and withdrawal deductions. To facilitate review of the closing process, Exhibit 6–4 summarizes the effect of the four closing entries described in the preceding pages.

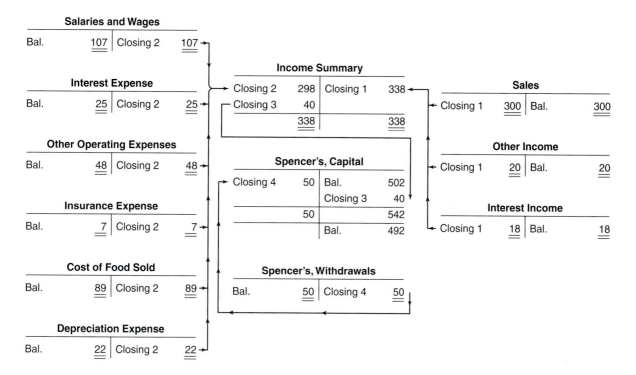

Exhibit 6–4 Spencer's Restaurant closing procedures for the year ended July 31, 2010.

THE POST-CLOSING TRIAL BALANCE

After the closing process has been completed, a new trial balance is prepared in order to check the equality of the debit and credit balances found in the general ledger.

The post-closing trial balance will only include real accounts (balance sheet accounts) since only those will remain open at the end of the closing process. The nominal (or temporary) accounts would have no balance and thus would not appear on the post-closing trial balance. The post-closing trial balance will therefore serve as a final check on the equality of the accounts, and it will ascertain that the ledger is in balance to begin a new accounting period.

The post-closing trial balance of Spencer's Restaurant as of July 31, 2010, is presented in Exhibit 6–5. Note that no revenue or expense accounts are listed and that the Spencer's, capital account has been increased by the periodic net income as a result of the closing process.

REVERSING ENTRIES: AN OPTIONAL PROCEDURE

An optional procedure often used in practice is to record reversing entries of accrual adjustments on the first day of each accounting period. The main purpose of reversing entries is to simplify the recording of payments and receipts of accruals by allowing these transactions to be entered on the books in a routine fashion. In recording reversing entries, we reverse the debits and credits used in the accrual adjusting entries.

To illustrate, we refer to a two-year note payable of $1,000 (issued on July 1, 2010, bearing annual interest at the rate of 12 percent) on the books of TCI Hotel.

SPENCER'S RESTAURANT
Post-closing Trial Balance
July 31, 2010

	Dr	Cr
Cash	$100	
Accounts receivable	200	
Notes receivable	300	
Accrued interest receivable	18	
Food inventory	21	
Prepaid insurance	5	
Furniture and equipment	220	
Accumulated depreciation		$110
Accrued interest		5
Accrued salaries		7
Notes payable		100
Accounts payable		150
Spencer's capital		492
	$864	$864

Exhibit 6–5   Spencer's Restaurant post-closing trial balance.

The interest is payable annually on June 30. On December 31, 2010, the following adjusting entry was recorded to accrue interest from July 1 to December 31, 2010 (12% × 1,000 = 120 ÷ 2 = 60).

<u>2010</u>

Dec. 31 Interest expense   60
            Accrued interest payable   60
        To record six-months' interest

On January 1, 2011 (the first day of the new accounting period), we record the following entry in the general journal:

<u>2011</u>

Jan. 1   Accrued interest payable   60
          Interest expense   60
        To reverse accrual.

On June 30, 2011, the interest payment is recorded in a routine manner as follows:

<u>2011</u>

June 30 Interest expense   120
           Cash   120
        To record payment of 12% interest.

After posting the above entries to the general ledger, the interest expense account would reflect the actual expense for the period commencing January 1, 2011 and ending June 30, 2011, as follows:

Accrued Interest Payable		**Interest Expense**	
2011	**2010**	**2011**	**2011**
Jan. 1 Reversing <u>60</u>	Dec. 31 Balance <u>60</u>	June 30 120	Jan. 1 Reversing 60
		Dec. 31 Balance 60	

PROCEDURES APPLICABLE TO A CORPORATION

The accounting process for a corporation is basically the same as for sole proprietorship (or partnership), which has been the subject of our in-depth review in the last few chapters. Nonetheless, there are some differences:

- Corporations will have one additional accrual adjustment, namely, the accrual of income taxes. This will result from the fact that corporations are subject to taxation of their income, whereas partnerships and proprietorships do not pay a separate income tax. The accrual will entail a debit to income taxes expense and a credit to income taxes payable.

- Corporations do not have withdrawal accounts since shareholders are normally not allowed to take money and/or property out of the business for personal use. However, a comparable transaction for a corporation would be the recording of dividends paid to shareholders, which are debited to dividends and credited to cash. Dividends will be considered a contra-equity account (in the same manner as withdrawals) and will be closed to the appropriate equity account during the closing process (i.e., retained earnings).

- The closing process of corporations is very much the same as has been illustrated in this chapter for Spencer's Restaurant (a sole proprietorship), but the retained earnings account is used to transfer net income to owners' equity in the case of corporations.

We consider the following closing entries of Dynasty Hotels on October 31, 2011 (the end of its fiscal year) to illustrate the closing procedures applicable to corporations.

Entry No. 1

    2011

Oct. 31	Room sales	80,000	
	Food sales	35,000	
	Beverage sales	18,000	
	Other income	5,000	
	Income summary		138,000
	To close revenue accounts.		

Entry No. 2

    2011

Oct. 31	Income summary	121,000	
	Salaries and wages		55,000
	Cost of sales		25,000
	Supplies expense		15,000
	Depreciation expense		8,000
	Other expenses		3,000
	Income tax expense		15,000
	To close expense accounts.		

Entry No. 3

2011			
Oct. 31	Income summary	17,000	
	Retained earnings		17,000
	To close the income summary account.		

Entry No. 4

2011			
Oct. 31	Retained earnings	4,000	
	Dividends		4,000
	To close the dividends account.		

The effect of the above entries on the general ledger accounts is presented below:

Income Summary			
Closing 2	121,000	Closing 1	138,000
Closing 3	17,000		
	138,000		138,000

Retained Earnings			
Closing 4	4,000	Bal.	3,000
Closing 3			17,000
	4,000		20,000
		Bal.	16,000

Dividends			
Bal.	4,000	Closing 4	4,000

It is apparent that the closing of revenue and expense accounts is exactly the same for corporations, partnerships, and proprietorships (closing entries No. 1 and No. 2). The transfer of net income to owners' equity is essentially the same for corporations (closing entry No. 3), except for the use of the retained earnings account. As far as closing entry No. 4 is concerned, some corporations will omit this entry altogether by recording the dividends as a direct reduction of retained earnings, as we shall describe in Chapter 12.

THE ACCOUNTING CYCLE: FLOWCHART

In this chapter and the three preceding ones, the accounting cycle has been subjected to an in-depth review. We conclude this chapter with a flowchart showing all the steps of the accounting cycle (Exhibit 6–6).

SOME KEY TERMS INTRODUCED IN THIS CHAPTER

1. **Closing entries.** Journal entries made at the end of each accounting period to clear revenue and expense accounts, transferring the period's net income to the appropriate owners' equity account.
2. **Closing the books.** Step 7 of the accounting cycle.
3. **Income summary.** A temporary account into which revenue and expense accounts are closed at the end of the accounting period.
4. **Nominal accounts.** *See* temporary accounts.
5. **Permanent account.** *See* real accounts.
6. **Post-closing trial balance.** A trial balance prepared after closing entries are recorded in the general ledger.

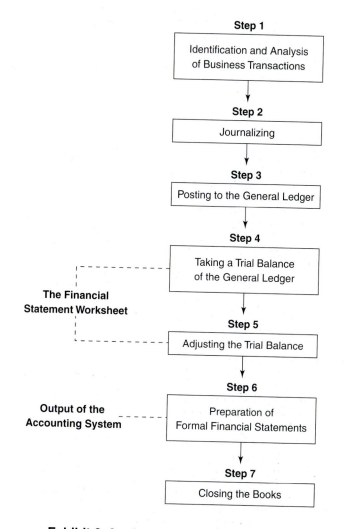

Exhibit 6–6 Accounting cycle flowchart.

7. **Real accounts.** Balance sheet accounts. They are not closed at the end of the accounting period.

8. **Reversing entries.** Journal entries that reverse the adjusting entries pertaining to accruals, thereby permitting the routine recording of subsequent related receipts and payments. This is an optional procedure.

9. **Temporary account.** The revenue, expense, income summary, dividend, and withdrawal accounts which are closed at the end of each accounting period.

QUESTIONS

1. How is the financial statement worksheet used to prepare formal financial statements?

2. What is the primary objective of an income statement? List the main sections of a simple-form income statement.

3. Is the financial statement worksheet a substitute for formal financial statements? Discuss.

4. What are the main elements of a statement of owners' equity?
5. What are the principal reconciling items between the balance sheet debit column of the financial statement worksheet and the total assets on the balance sheet?
6. Distinguish between adjusting and closing entries.
7. What are the major objectives of closing entries?
8. What are real accounts? What are nominal accounts? List three examples of each.
9. Describe the four steps needed to complete closing procedures. What is the purpose of the income summary account?
10. What is the purpose of a post-closing trial balance?
11. What is the purpose of reversing entries? What type of adjusting entries are normally reversed?
12. Distinguish between closing procedures for partnerships and corporations.
13. List all the steps in the accounting cycle.

EXERCISES

1. Indicate the effect on net income of extending the following accounts on a financial statement worksheet:
   (a) Prepaid rent to the income statement credit column
   (b) Accumulated depreciation to the income statement credit column
   (c) Insurance expense to the balance sheet debit column
   (d) Accrued salaries payable to the income statement credit column
   (e) Common stock to the balance sheet credit column
2. The R Hotel Corporation uses the following accounts for its accounting system. For each item, indicate whether the account appears on the balance sheet or the income statement, and also indicate the accounts that would be closed at the end of the accounting period:
   (a) Rooms salaries
   (b) Accrued interest payable
   (c) Cash
   (d) Mortgages payable
   (e) Accounts receivable
   (f) Interest income
   (g) Common stock
   (h) Depreciation expense
   (i) Income tax expense
   (j) Food sales
   (k) Income tax payable
   (l) Accrued interest receivable
   (m) Unearned revenue
   (n) Prepaid expenses
3. Which of the following accounts will not have a balance in a post-closing trial balance?
   (a) Withdrawals
   (b) Prepaid rent
   (c) Land
   (d) Accounts receivable
   (e) Room sales
   (f) Rent expense
   (g) Cash
   (h) Common stock

   (i) Accumulated depreciation
   (j) Interest expense
  (k) Customers' deposits
   (l) Cost of food sold
  (m) Retained earnings
  (n) Prepaid expenses

SHORT PROBLEMS

1. Consider the following data for A Hotel Corporation as of and for the year ended December 31, 2010:

• Accounts receivable	$ 2,000
• Cash	1,000
• Retained earnings, end of period	20,000
• Total liabilities	118,000
• Room sales	100,000
• Total expenses	140,000
• Common stock	150,000
• Property and equipment, at cost	300,000
• Food sales	50,000
• Other income	5,000
• Prepaid expenses	2,000
• Short-term investments	3,000
• Accumulated depreciation	50,000
• Inventories	10,000
• Long-term investments	20,000

   Compute the following amounts:
   (a) Total assets
   (b) Total shareholders' equity
   (c) Net income for the period
   (d) Retained earnings, beginning of period (assume no dividends were declared during the period)

2. Using the data from problem 1 above, prepare:
   (a) Closing entries in general journal form.
   (b) A post-closing trial balance as of the end of the period.

3. Consider the following data included in the adjusted trial balance of Proven Travel Company on November 30, 2010.

	Dr	Cr
Salaries expense	30,000	
Accrued salaries payable		1,000

   Required:
   (a) Record the appropriate reversing entry in the general journal on December 1, 2010.
   (b) Record payment of $5,000 salaries in the general journal on December 4, 2010.

LONG PROBLEMS

1. Consider the following account balances from the income statement columns of the financial statement worksheet of M&B Restaurant for the year ended December 31, 2008.

	Dr	Cr
Food sales		100,000
Beverage sales		40,500
Other income		1,000
Rent expense	10,000	
Salaries and wages	65,000	
Supplies expense	10,000	
Insurance expense	10,500	
Depreciation and amortization	5,000	
Other operating expenses	2,500	
Interest expense	2,500	
	105,500	141,500

(a) Prepare the income statement of M&B Restaurant for the year ended December 31, 2008.

(b) Record closing entries in the GJ.

2. Following are the financial statement columns of the October 2007 worksheet of Aquarius Place.

	Income statement		Balance sheet	
	Dr	**Cr**	**Dr**	**Cr**
Cash			6,000	
Accounts receivable			5,000	
Accrued interest receivable			1,000	
Inventories			6,000	
Land			50,000	
Building			100,000	
Furniture and equipment			30,000	
Accumulated depreciation				50,000
Deferred charges			2,000	
Accounts payable				10,000
Notes payable				20,000
Mortgages payable				60,000
Accrued expenses				8,000
A. Aquarius, capital				10,000
Sales		150,000		
Other income		10,000		
Salaries and wages	60,000			
Interest expense	3,000			
Depreciation and amortization	5,000			
Other expenses	50,000			
	118,000	160,000	200,000	158,000

Required:

(a) Prepare an income statement for the month of October 2007.

(b) Prepare a statement of owner's equity for the month ended October 31, 2007 (additional investments by Mr. Aquarius during October 2007 amounted to $4,000).

(c) Prepare a balance sheet as of October 31, 2007.

(d) Prepare closing entries in GJ form.

(e) Prepare a post-closing trial balance as of October 31, 2007.

(f) What account balances will be carried forward to November 1, 2007 for (1) building, (2) accrued expenses, (3) sales, (4) salaries and wages, (5) accrued interest receivable, (6) mortgages payable, and (7) A. Aquarius, capital?

3. The income statement and balance sheet columns of the financial statement worksheet of An Important Restaurant Corp., for the year ended July 31, 2008 follows:

	Income Statement		Balance sheet	
	Dr	Cr	Dr	Cr
Cash			3,000	
Accounts receivable			5,000	
Accounts payable				1,000
Income taxes payable				650
Interest expense	200			
Salaries and wages	1,300			
Property and equipment			10,000	
Accumulated depreciation				2,000
Common stock				5,700
Retained earnings				8,000
Income tax expense	650			
Other expenses	500			
Sales		3,000		
Other income		300		
	2,650	3,300	18,000	17,350

(a) Prepare an income statement, a statement of retained earnings, and a balance sheet as of July 31, 2008 and for the year then ended.
(b) Record closing entries in the GJ.
(c) Open "T" accounts for each account listed on the financial statement worksheet. Post closing entries to the "T" accounts.
(c) Prepare a post-closing trial balance.

4. The account balances in the ledger of Lively Inn on February 29, 2008 (the end of its fiscal year), were as follows:

Debit Balances		**Credit Balances**	
Cash	$ 300	Accumulated depreciation	$ 55
Accounts receivable	225	Notes payable	100
Food inventory	140	Accounts payable	120
Furniture and fixtures	200	Common stock	200
Supplies inventory	10	Retained earnings 2/28/07	300
Prepaid insurance	50	Room sales	200
Salaries expense	100	Food sales	80
Interest expense	50	Beverage sales	50
Payroll tax expense	10		
Other expenses	20		
	$1,105		$1,105

The data for the adjustments are as follows:
1. Cost of food sold, $100.
2. Interest accrued on notes payable, $20.
3. Supplies inventory February 29, $5.
4. Salaries incurred during February, but not paid to employees, $20.
5. Expired insurance not recorded, $10.
6. Depreciation for the year, $20.

Required:

(a) Set up simple "T" accounts with the balances given above.

(b) Record adjusting entries in the general journal.

(c) Post adjusting entries, adding other "T" accounts as necessary.

(d) Prepare a balance sheet and an income statement sheet as of and for the period ended February 29, 2008.

(e) Journalize closing entries.

(f) Post closing entries to the general ledger "T" accounts.

(g) Prepare a post-closing trial balance as of February 29, 2008.

(h) Record reversing entries in the general journal on March 1, 2008.

Special-Purpose Journals and Subsidiary Ledgers | 7

The learning objectives of this chapter are:

- To understand how special-purpose journals accelerate and facilitate the recording of the most common transactions, and help management find initial entries more quickly.
- To know that the four most commonly used special-purpose journals are: a) the sales journal, b) the cash receipts journal, c) the purchases journal, and d) the cash disbursements journal.
- To know how to enter transactions in the four most commonly used special-purpose journals.
- To understand how subsidiary ledgers provide detailed management information not provided by general ledger accounts, and know the meaning of a control account.
- To know how to post and use subsidiary ledgers, and how to prepare a subsidiary ledger schedule.
- To become familiar with the cashier's daily report.
- To understand that hotels usually have at least two subsidiary accounts receivable ledgers: a) the guest ledger, and b) the city ledger.
- To have a cursory understanding of a night auditor's duties and of the daily transcript, the special-purpose journal he or she prepares.
- To become aware of some other special-purpose journals used solely in the hospitality industry.

In previous chapters we have learned that the general journal is the accounting book of original entry used to record transactions initially in the accounting system. However, it is practical to use the general journal as the sole book of original entry only when there are few transactions to record, as in the case of the sample problems included in a book of this nature. When the number of transactions increases to the level encountered in even a small hospitality entity, introducing and processing transactions in the accounting system through the general journal becomes cumbersome, unnecessarily time-consuming, and makes it more difficult to access this information later. To facilitate the introduction, processing, and accessing of numerous transactions of a similar nature, other journals, called special-purpose journals, should be used. These journals are designed to accelerate steps 2 and 3 of the accounting cycle—journalizing and posting. They, as well as subsidiary ledgers, also facilitate management access to this information at a later time.

The organization of financial data and its presentation in the form of financial statements is only one of the objectives of accounting. An equally important objective is to record the initial transaction data in a form that enables management to access it easily and efficiently. To achieve this latter objective, special-purpose journals must be used to record similar transactions together in one book of initial entry, and subsidiary ledgers must be used to enable management to know the composition of certain general ledger accounts. If management needs to investigate whether or not a sales entry was correctly made, looking for it in a special-purpose sales journal, where only sales entries are recorded, is faster and more efficient than looking in a general journal, where all kinds of different entries must be sifted through in addition to the sales entries. Thus, special-purpose journals help management access information in the books of initial entry—the journals.

Subsidiary ledgers, on the other hand, provide management with detailed information concerning data recorded in the book of final entry—the general ledger. For example, the accounts receivable general ledger account tells management how much is owed the company in total. But it does not tell management who owes the company money, nor how much is owed by each customer. A subsidiary accounts receivable ledger must be maintained in order to have access to such detailed information. The same applies to the accounts payable general ledger account. It tells management the total amount that the company owes to others, but a subsidiary ledger is required to inform management how much is owed to each supplier and service provider. In fact, any general ledger account may have a related subsidiary ledger. The property and equipment accounts usually have a subsidiary ledger indicating the cost and related charges for each item of property or equipment. The accrued expenses and the prepaid expenses accounts also have subsidiary ledgers indicating which specific expenses have been accrued or prepaid, and how much.

This chapter first explains the disadvantages of using a general ledger when recording many transactions of a similar nature, and it explains the advantages of using special-purpose journals for this purpose. Next we explain the use of the four basic special-purpose journals: 1) the sales journal, 2) the cash receipts journal, 3) the purchases journal, and 4) the cash disbursements journal. Then, the format and use of the accounts receivable and accounts payable subsidiary ledgers are explained, along with their relationship to their general ledger control accounts and the preparation of subsidiary ledger schedules. After this, a brief overview of some additional hotel accounting records and journals is given, including the night auditor's duties. Finally, the chapter concludes with a discussion of how automated accounting systems impact the accounting process.

DISADVANTAGES OF USING THE GENERAL JOURNAL TO RECORD NUMEROUS TRANSACTIONS OF A SIMILAR NATURE

Businesses make thousands, or more, sales transactions daily. All of these transactions have in common the fact that they require a debit to a cash account or to an accounts receivable account. They also share the characteristic that they require a credit to a sales account, of which there may be one, or many (room sales, food sales, beverage sales, etc). To demonstrate how cumbersome it is to post similar transactions through the general journal the process of recording and posting a list of sales transactions through the general journal is shown in Exhibit 7–1.

Date	Description	Dr	Cr
March 2	Accounts receivable–Mary Tum	450	
	Room sales		450
2	Cash	230	
	Room sales		230
2	Accounts receivable–Mary Tum	37	
	Telephone sales		37
2	Accounts receivable–Paul Tanbel	340	
	Food sales		340
2	Accounts receivable–Kim Stuben	760	
	Room sales		760
2	Cash	58	
	Beverage sales		58
2	Accounts receivable–Stu Pundel	23	
	Telephone sales		23
2	Accounts receivable–Si Hong	480	
	Room sales		480
2	Cash	125	
	Food sales		125
2	Cash	94	
	Beverage sales		94
2	Accounts receivable–Mina Valua	210	
	Food sales		210
2	Accounts receivable– Si Hog	10	
	Telephone sales		10

Accounts Receivable

3/2/XX	450
3/2/XX	37
3/2/XX	340
3/2/XX	760
3/2/XX	23
3/2/XX	480
3/2/XX	210
3/2/XX	10
Bal.	2,310

Cash

3/2/XX	230
3/2/XX	58
3/2/XX	125
3/2/XX	94
Bal.	507

Room Sales

450	3/2/XX
230	3/2/XX
760	3/2/XX
480	3/2/XX

Food Sales

340	3/2/XX
125	3/2/XX
210	3/2/XX

Beverage Sales

| 58 | 3/2/XX |
| 94 | 3/2/XX |

Telephone Sales

37	3/2/XX
23	3/2/XX
10	3/2/XX

NOTE: **For the sake of brevity and because they are repetitive, the transaction descriptions above have been omitted.**

Exhibit 7–1 Example of recording and posting numerous similar transactions through the general journal.

This is a recording of several sales transactions through the general journal. As is evident from the above, the disadvantages of recording and posting repetitive transactions in this manner are the following:

1. The names of the accounts must be written over and over again, once for each entry, a time-consuming process.
2. The individual entry amounts must be posted to their respective general ledger accounts one by one, another time-consuming process.
3. Because of this repetitive copying, there is a much greater opportunity for making mistakes.

ADVANTAGES OF USING SPECIAL-PURPOSE JOURNALS

Compare this procedure to the recording and posting of the above same sales transactions using the simplified *sales journal* in Exhibit 7–2.

The advantages of using the special-purpose sales journal are mostly obvious, and are listed below. These advantages are identified by the corresponding numbers in Exhibit 7–2.

1. Account names do not have to be repeated for each entry. Each entry is simply made in the appropriately headed account column, thus saving a considerable amount of time.
2. Individual entries are not posted to their general ledger accounts. Only the totals for the entire period are posted, thus again saving time.
3. The possibility of errors is diminished because account names and amounts are not posted individually, thus eliminating repetition.
4. The use of special-purpose journals allows a firm to train employees in one particular type of entry, thereby accelerating entry speed, and also reducing the probability of errors.
5. Information is more readily available because it is recorded in a more compact and understandable form, both in the special-purpose journals and in the general ledger.

Explanation of the Five Basic Special-Purpose Journals

As explained earlier, special-purpose journals are designed for the specific purpose of recording only one type of frequently recurring business transaction. More than 95 percent of all business transactions are either sales, cash receipts, purchases, cash disbursements, or payroll transactions. Since these types of transactions tend to recur so frequently, they provide a natural basis for grouping accounts in the different types of special-purpose journals. The following is a list of the most commonly used special-purpose journals and their abbreviations:

- Sales journal (SJ)
- Cash receipts journal (CR)
- Purchases journal (PJ)
- Cash disbursements journal (CD)
- Payroll journal (PRJ)

The sales journal is used to record only sales transactions. Although sales may be made on a cash basis or on credit terms, the sales journal that we shall use in this text records all sales transactions, both cash and credit, in separate

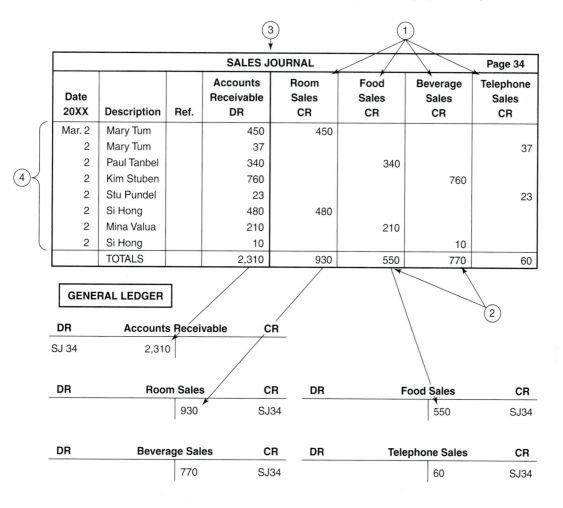

Exhibit 7–2 Example of recording and posting numerous similar transactions through the special-purpose sales journal.

columns, but they are both posted as debits to the general ledger accounts receivable account. In the case of cash sales, the total cash received is carried over to the cash receipts journal, from where it is posted to the general ledger as a credit to the accounts receivable account, thus offsetting the debit that was made to the accounts receivable account for cash sales in the sales journal. This allows all sales transactions to be recorded in the sales journal and all cash transactions to be recorded in the cash receipts journal. This will be explained with an example later in this chapter.

Without such a procedure, credit sales would have to be recorded in the sales journal and cash sales in a separate journal, the cash receipts journal. This would eliminate one of the advantages of the special-purpose journals, namely, the compact recording of accounting information in one single journal for each type of transaction. The sales journal allows the manager to have a comprehensive record of the company's sales and related information in one single journal. When the manager needs to look up information concerning a particular sale, the manager needs to look in one journal only. This represents a considerable saving of time.

The cash receipts journal is used to record all cash receipts, be they from cash sales, from collections on previous credit sales, from additional cash investments by the owners, from the sale of property and equipment, or from loan proceeds received.

The purchases journal is used to record all purchases on account. This includes purchases of both assets and services.

The cash disbursements journal is used to record all cash payments and discounts for prompt payment. Payments for cash purchases, payments on account, and loan repayments are all recorded in the cash disbursements journal.

The payroll journal is used to record payroll information. This journal is discussed fully in Chapter 8.

The general journal is still used to record transactions not recorded in any of the other journals. It is also used to record adjusting entries, closing entries, and correcting entries. Since entries of these types affect various accounts and are infrequently made, the flexibility provided by the general journal is ideal for this purpose.

THE SALES JOURNAL

Up to now we have been recording credit sales by making one of the following entries:

January 3, 20XX	Accounts receivable	1,000	
	Sales (rooms, food, etc.)		1,000
	To record a $1,000 credit sale		

or

January 3, 20XX	Cash	1,000	
	Sales (rooms, food, etc.)		1,000
	To record a $1,000 cash sale		

The sales journal facilitates the recording of transaction dates, transaction description, and debits to accounts receivable or cash. It does this by providing four columns to the left in the journal. The first column is used to record the transaction date, the next one to write a brief description reminding us of the nature of the sale, or to whom the sale was made, and the next two columns to record amounts received for cash sales (headed: Cash), or to record values received for credit sales (headed: Accounts receivable).

In the hospitality industry, there are many types of sales. There may be room sales, food sales, beverage sales, tennis club sales, telephone sales, etc. Many states also have a sales tax. Therefore, the sales journal must facilitate the recording of credits to the various sales accounts, and to the sales tax payable account. It does this by providing columns to the right in the sales journal, each column bearing the name of a particular type of sale.

Exhibit 7–3 presents a sales journal similar to the sales journal shown previously in this chapter. Look at this sales journal to identify the columns mentioned in the above two paragraphs. It is evident that it contains some columns on the right side of the journal that were not included in the simplified sample sales journal shown earlier in this chapter. These columns are for recording "sundry" sales, sales that are infrequent. A hotel may generate many different types of sales, some of which might occur very seldom. Thus, swimming pool items, golf items, and tennis items might be considered sundry sales if such sales do not take

FAIRVIEW HOTEL
Sales Journal

Date 20XX	Description	Ref.	Accounts Receivable DR	Room Sales CR	Food Sales CR	Beverage Sales CR	Telephone Sales CR	Sundry Sales				Sales tax Payable CR
								Account	No.	Ref.	Amount CR	
	TOTALS											

Exhibit 7–3 Example of a sales journal.

place on a repetitive basis. The account names for these sales, as well as the account numbers and amounts would be entered in the appropriate columns within the sundry section of the sales journal. The Ref. column (abbreviation for reference) in the sundry section of the sales journal is used to enter a check mark to indicate that a particular line of the sundry columns has been posted to its corresponding general ledger account. The first Ref. column, on the left side of the sales journal, will be explained when we discuss subsidiary ledgers.

We will now proceed to record the following five sales transactions in the sales journal to demonstrate how this special purpose journal functions. By following the entries for these sales, the reader should be able to understand its purpose and function more fully. For comparison's sake, these transactions will first be recorded as if they were being entered in a general journal. Then they will appear as recorded in the sales journal. Remember that transactions are never recorded in two journals. These entries are being shown in two journals for comparison purposes only. If an entry is recorded through the sales journal, the same entry should *not* be recorded in any other journal.

Five Sales Recorded Through the General Journal

March 28, 20XX	Accounts Receivable (Milton Corp.)	848	
	Room Sales		800
	Sales Tax Payable		48
March 29, 20XX	Accounts Receivable (Jon Ronstatt)	532	
	Food Sales		500
	Sales Tax Payable		32
March 29, 20XX	Accounts Receivable (Marie Caron)	53	
	Pool Sales		50
	Sales Tax Payable		3
March 30, 20XX	Cash	75	
	Pro Shop Sales		70
	Sales Tax Payable		5
March 30, 20XX	Accounts Receivable (Luka Font)	106	
	Food Sales		100
	Sales Tax Payable		6

Exhibit 7–4 presents these same five sales as they would appear when recorded through the sales journal.

Recording Transactions in the Sales Journal

The following steps are required to record a sale in the sales journal:

1. Enter the date of the transaction in the date column; the year should be entered in small digits under the word "date," and the month and day of the first transaction on the same line as the transaction. For subsequent transactions on the same page, only the day's date need be entered.
2. Enter the name of the client and/or invoice number in the description column.
3. Enter the debit to accounts receivable in the accounts receivable column. As explained below, this column will be posted as a debit to accounts receivable. Enter the corresponding credits to the sales and sales tax payable accounts in their appropriate credit columns. For infrequent sales, the name of the sales account is written in the sundry account column, the account number in the sundry No. column and the amount of the credit in the sundry

FAIRVIEW HOTEL
Sales Journal

Page 12

Date 20XX	Description	Ref.	Accounts Receivable DR	Room Sales CR	Food Sales CR	Beverage Sales CR	Telephone Sales CR	Sundry sales Account	No.	Ref.	Amount CR	Sales tax Payable CR
Mar. 28	Milton Corp.	✓	848	800								48
29	Jon Ronstatt	✓	532		500							32
30	Marie Caron	✓	53					Pool sales	# 408	✓	50	3
30	Cash sales	✓	75					Pro Shop	# 415	✓	70	5
30	Luka Font	✓	106		100							6
	TOTALS		1,614	800	600						120	94
			(105)	(401)	(403)						(232)	

Accounts Receivable   No. 105

3/31/XX	SJ12	1,614
3/31/XX	Bal.	1,614

Food Sales   No. 403

3/31/XX	SJ12	600
3/31/XX	Bal.	600

Room Sales   No. 401

3/31/XX	SJ12	800
3/31/XX	Bal.	800

Pool Sales   No. 408

3/31/XX	SJ12	50
3/31/XX	Bal.	50

Pro Shop   No. 401

3/31/XX	SJ12	70
3/31/XX	Bal.	70

Sales Tax Payable   No. 232

3/31/XX	SJ12	94
3/31/XX	Bal.	94

Exhibit 7–4   Example of a filled in sales journal and related general ledger accounts.

amount column. The sundry Ref. column is given a check when the amount is posted to the general ledger.

Journalizing Cash Sales in the Sales Journal

Cash sales from the various hotel departments are recorded in a manner similar to credit sales, as outlined in steps 1 to 3, except that the phrase "cash sales" is entered in the description column and no posting is made to the accounts receivable subsidiary ledger.

Crossfooting a Special-Purpose Journal

The general rule that debits must equal credits when preparing a journal entry still applies when using special-purpose journals. Therefore, the totals of the debit column must equal the totals of the credit columns. When this verification is made it is called "crossfooting" the columns (adding them across). If the total debits equal the total credits, it only means that equal amounts of debits and credits have been recorded. It does not, however, preclude the possibility of having entered a debit or a credit in the wrong account. Therefore, if an error is encountered later in the accounting process it may be necessary to verify that all entries in the journals were made to the correct accounts.

Posting from a Special-Purpose Journal

As stated earlier, one of the advantages of a special purpose journal is that by posting only the totals of entire columns, or even pages, of entries this process can be reduced to a single step for every account. Otherwise it would be necessary to post the hundreds, or more, individual entries included in each total. The posting steps are as follows:

1. Total each column.
2. Crossfoot the columns (including the sundry amount column), and make necessary corrections.
3. Post the totals from each column to its corresponding general ledger account—except for the sundry amount column. As amounts are posted, the date and the page number of the special purpose journal where the total amount is located should be written next to the posted amount.
4. The total of the sundry amount column is not posted because each individual line can contain a different type of sale. Therefore, these lines must be posted individually. After a line is posted, a checkmark should be made in the sundry Ref. column to indicate that the amount has been posted (see Exhibit 7–4).
5. As column totals are posted, the number of the account to which the total was posted should be entered in parentheses beneath the column total.
6. Calculate the new balance in each general ledger account as it is posted.

Posting to the Subsidiary Ledgers

When a general ledger account has a related subsidiary ledger (to be explained later in this chapter) then transactions must be posted twice from a special-purpose journal:

1. First the totals are posted to their respective general ledger accounts as explained above, and then
2. Each entry is posted a second time to its respective subsidiary ledger, as will be explained later.

Both the sales journal and the purchases journal have their respective subsidiary ledgers, called the accounts receivable and accounts payable subsidiary ledgers. Management must not only know the total balance in the accounts receivable and accounts payable accounts but must also know who owes the business and to whom the business owes on an individual basis. This information is provided by subsidiary ledgers.

When a special-purpose journal has one or more related subsidiary ledgers, a second Ref. column, in addition to the Ref. column in the sundry section of the special-purpose journals, is required. In all the special-purpose journals discussed in detail in this chapter, this column can be found on the left side of each journal. This column is used to make a checkmark indicating that each individual line has been posted to a subsidiary ledger.

Subsidiary ledgers may be posted at the same time that the general ledger account is posted; or they may be posted on an ongoing basis, as they occur. The latter may be a better approach because it is important for management to know the balances in the individual subsidiary ledger accounts at all times.

Again, it should be noted that the Ref. column discussed above is different from the Ref. column in the sundry section of the special purpose journals. The Ref. column in the sundry section is used to make a checkmark indicating that the amount on that line has been posted to a general ledger account (as opposed to a subsidiary ledger account).

Balances Brought Forward

For the sake of simplicity, the special-purpose journals shown in this chapter cover only a few transactions. Therefore there are no "balances brought forward" from previous pages. But if there were more than one page in a special-purpose journal, then the first line of that journal would be used to write the totals brought forward from each account on the previous page of the journal. In this case, in the description column, the words: "Balance brought forward" would be written.

Incorrect Balance in the Accounts Receivable Account

At this point in the posting process, the accounts receivable account contains an incorrect balance because both cash sales and credit sales have been posted as debits to the accounts receivable account. In fact, we should only have debited the accounts receivable account for credit sales. However, as explained earlier, if we only recorded credit sales in the sales journal, we would not have a single compact journal containing all the business' sales.

In order to correct this situation, we need to proceed to understand the function and operation of the cash receipts journal.

THE CASH RECEIPTS JOURNAL

The cash receipts journal is used to record all cash that is received by the hospitality entity. Therefore the debit column will be dedicated to the cash account (in contrast to the sales journal, which has two debit columns, the cash receipts journal only has one debit column). The usual sources of cash are cash sales and collections on credit sales. But a business may also receive cash from loan proceeds, the sale of property and equipment, or from the owners' investment. However, these latter three sources are rather infrequently used. This affects the structure of the cash receipts journal. Because these latter sources of cash are infrequent, they will be recorded in a sundry column like that used in the sales journal, and the only credit columns dedicated to a single account will be the columns for recording credits to the accounts receivable account produced by cash sales and collections on credit sales.

Making entries to a cash receipts journal, and posting from one, is done in the same way as in the sales journal, except, of course, different accounts are affected, as suggested above.

The cash receipts journal has the usual date, description, and Ref. columns. After the Ref. column come the cash in bank column, for recording debits to the cash account, two accounts receivable columns, and a sundry column. The first accounts receivable column is used to record credits to accounts receivable for cash sales. The other is used to record credits to accounts receivable for payments made on credit sales. As stated earlier, the sundry columns are used to record receipts of an infrequent nature, such as those from loan proceeds, refunds, the sale of property and equipment, or owners' investment. In Exhibit 7–5 the reader can see a sample cash receipts journal.

Transactions Recorded in the Cash Receipts Journal

The following is a description of the transactions that are recorded in the cash receipts journal:

1. Office supplies worth $125 were returned to a supplier and a refund was received.

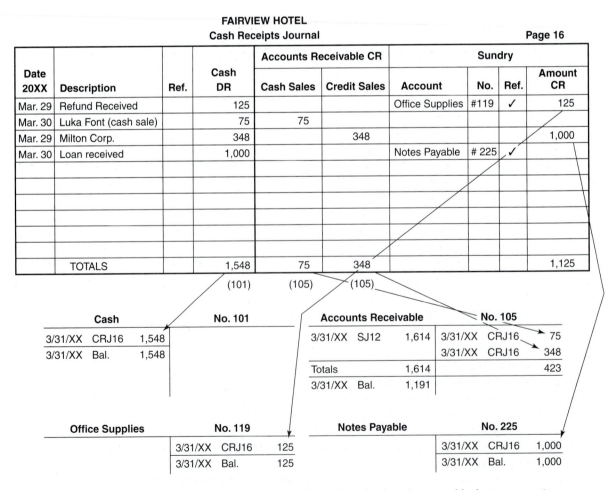

Exhibit 7–5 Example of a cash receipts journal and related general ledger accounts.

2. A $75 cash sale was made to Luka Font (see sales journal page in Exhibit 7–4).

3. Milton Corporation paid $348 on their account (an $848 credit sale was made to this corporation (see sales journal page in Exhibit 7–4).

4. The $1,000 proceeds from a loan were received.

Journalizing and Posting in the Cash Receipts Journal

These two steps are performed in the cash receipts journal in much the same way described for the sales journal. Therefore, they will not be discussed here. The reader can review these steps by referring back to the related discussion with regard to the sales journal.

Correcting the Balance in the Accounts Receivable Account

As you will recall, it was stated earlier that, because both cash sales and credit sales were recorded by debiting the accounts receivable account through the sales journal, the balance in the accounts receivable account was overstated by the amount of cash sales. Now, however, through the cash receipts journal, we have posted the cash sales as a credit to accounts receivable. This credit offsets the previous debit to accounts receivable for cash sales made through the sales journal, leaving the correct balance in the accounts receivable account. This can be verified as follows:

1. Credit sales recorded in the sales journal = $ 1,539

2. Payments on credit sales recorded in the cash receipts journal = 348

Balance in accounts receivable account should be (and is) = $ 1,191

THE PURCHASES JOURNAL

The purchases journal serves to record all purchases on account (credit purchases). A purchases journal is shown in Exhibit 7–6 along with some related general ledger accounts. Since the transactions entered in the purchases journal are quite self-explanatory, no explanation of these transactions is provided here.

The following should be noted about this journal:

1. It contains the usual date, description, and Ref. columns.

2. It contains the usual set of sundry columns to make entries into accounts not frequently used.

3. It is different from the sales journal and cash receipts journal in that the leftmost money column, the accounts payable column, is a credit column, not a debit column, as was the case with the above-mentioned journals. This is because accounts payable is a liability account and therefore increases with credits. Thus, the balancing entries in the columns to the right of the accounts payable column will be debit entries, the opposite of what is the case with the sales journal and cash receipts journal.

4. Because most purchases in an established business are made on credit terms, they will end up being recorded in the purchases journal. Those few purchases that are made on cash terms will be recorded in the last of the four journals, which we will discuss later in this chapter—the cash disbursements journal. Because so few purchases are cash purchases, recording these purchases through the cash disbursements journal, instead of in the purchases journal with a credit to accounts payable, is not considered a

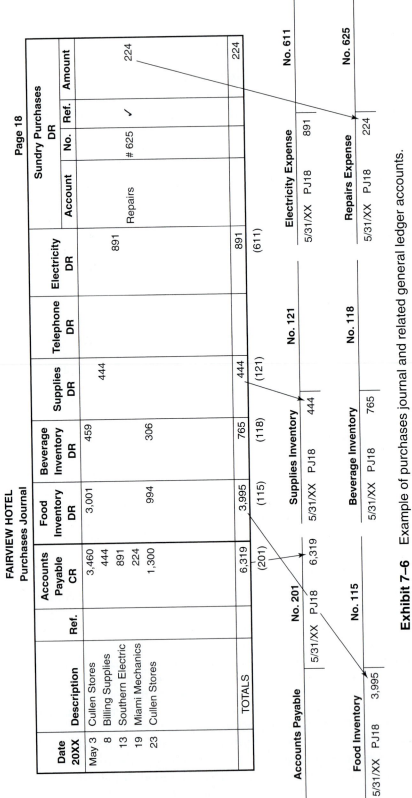

Exhibit 7-6 Example of purchases journal and related general ledger accounts.

significant departure from our stated goal of compact recording of data. Of course, if it is desired to record all purchases, even cash purchases, as a credit to accounts payable through the purchases journal, then an offsetting debit entry will have to be made to the accounts payable account through the cash disbursements journal. This is similar to the procedure used to record cash sales through the sales journal.

Journalizing in the Purchases Journal

The following steps are required to record entries in the purchases journal:

1. Enter the date of the transaction in the date column of the purchases journal in the usual manner.
2. Enter the name of the supplier and invoice number or account number in the description column.
3. Enter the credit to accounts payable in the accounts payable column and the corresponding debits in the appropriate expense or purchase account columns. Use the sundry column to record entries in the less frequently used accounts, following the same procedure specified for journalizing sundry items in the sales journal.

Posting to the General Ledger

After all entries for the accounting period have been made in the purchases journal, the general ledger accounts are posted by following the steps previously explained for posting to the general ledger from the sales journal (substituting purchases journal for sales journal).

THE CASH DISBURSEMENTS JOURNAL

The cash disbursements journal is used to record all cash payments. Since payments are usually made by check, it is often called the check register. Included in this journal are payments on account (payments for services or goods we previously received on credit and were recorded in the accounts payable account), cash purchases, purchases of assets, and loan repayments. A cash disbursements journal is shown in Exhibit 7–7.

The specific transactions recorded in this sample cash disbursements journal are the following:

June 2   Fairview Hotel pays the $1,300 invoice due to Cullen Stores within the 10-day discount period (the related purchase was recorded in the purchases journal).

June 9   A $125 cash purchase of food inventory is made.

June 14   A loan of $5,000 is repaid to Florida Bank.

June 18   The electricity bill of $891 is paid. The invoice from the power company had previously been recorded as an account payable. The power company did not offer any discount for early payment.

June 24   The $224 invoice due Miami Mechanics was paid. Either this company offered no purchase discount for early payment, or, if it did, Fairview Hotel decided not take the discount. The related purchase in May was recorded in the purchases journal.

June 28   An oven is purchased from Cook's Sales for cash.

June 29   The $444 invoice due Billing Supplies was paid. No discount was taken because Billing Supplies does not offer a prompt payment discount.

FAIRVIEW HOTEL
Cash Disbursements Journal

Page 23

Date 20XX	Description	Ref.	Check Number	Cash in Bank CR	Purchase Discounts CR	Accounts Payable DR	Food Inventory DR	Supplies DR	Sundry DR Account	Sundry DR No.	Sundry DR Ref.	Sundry DR Amount
June 2	Cullen Stores		3456	1,274	26	1,300						
9	Dario Purveyors		3457	125			125					
14	Florida Bank		3458	5,000					Notes Payable	# 264	✓	5,000
18	Southern Electric		3459	891		891						
24	Miami Mechanics		3460	224		224						
28	Cook's Sales		3461	3,000					Equipment	#168	✓	3,000
29	Billing Supplies		3462	444		444						
	TOTALS			10,958	26	2,859	125					8,000
				(101)	(503)	(201)	(120)					

Cash   No. 101

6/30/XX	CDJ23	10,958	

Accounts Payable   No. 201

6/30/XX	CDJ23	2,859	

Notes Payable   No. 264

6/30/XX	CDJ23	5,000	

Purchase Discounts   No. 503

6/30/XX	CDJ23	26	

Food Inventory   No. 201

6/30/XX	CDJ23	125	

Equipment   No. 168

6/30/XX	CDJ23	3,000	

Exhibit 7–7   Example of cash disbursements journal and related general ledger accounts.

PURCHASE DISCOUNTS

Before proceeding to point out some important aspects of this journal, it is necessary to discuss purchase discounts. Some suppliers motivate their customers to pay their invoices before they are due. When offered by a supplier, these credit terms are stated on an invoice as follows: 2/10, Net 30. This means that if the invoice is paid within 10 days the customer can deduct 2 percent from the invoice amount and only pay the difference, 98 percent of the invoice amount. If the invoice is not paid within 10 days, then the full amount of the invoice must be paid within 30 days, or the customer risks losing the supplier's credit privileges.

In the case of our sample cash disbursements journal, there is an original invoice amount of $1,300 due to Cullen Stores on which the purchaser (Fairview Hotel) is entitled to a 2 percent discount. Therefore, the check is written in the amount of $1,274, instead of $1,300. This is calculated as follows:

Original Invoice amount	$1,300
2 % Purchase Discount	26
Net Amount of Check	$1,274

The $1,274 is entered in the cash in bank column to reduce the cash in bank (a credit to the cash account), the $26 discount is entered in the purchases discount column to reduce cost of sales (a credit to cost of sales), and a debit for $1,300 is entered in the accounts payable column to reduce accounts payable by the full amount of the invoice.

Highlights of the Cash Disbursements Journal

The following should be noted about this journal:

1. It contains the usual date, description, and Ref. columns.
2. To the right of the Ref. column it contains a check number column to record the number of the check with which payment is being made.
3. It contains the usual set of sundry columns to make entries into accounts not frequently used.
4. It is different from the sales journal and cash receipts journal in that the leftmost money column, the cash column, is a credit column, not a debit column, as was the case with the above mentioned journals. This is because payments reduce the cash account, and since it is an asset account it is reduced with credits. Thus, the balancing entries in the columns to the right of the cash column will be debit entries, the opposite of what is the case with the sales journal and cash receipts journal. These columns can record debits to expenses or assets, which increase these two types of accounts, or they can record debits to liability accounts, which reduce these accounts.
5. The cash disbursements journal also has a second credit column on the left side, titled "purchase discounts." As explained earlier, this column is used to record a discount taken for payment of an invoice within a specified discount period.
6. To the right of the cash and purchase discounts credit columns, and before the sundry columns, the cash disbursements journal usually has several columns to record the most frequently made cash purchases. As usual, these columns bear the title of the account that is affected by entries in each column. There should be as many columns as there are types of accounts used to record frequent cash purchases.

Journalizing in the Cash Disbursements Journal

The steps required to record entries in the cash disbursements journal are listed below:

1. Enter the date of the transaction in the date column of the cash disbursements journal in the usual manner.
2. Enter the name of the check payee (recipient) in the description column. The supplier's account number might be entered for payments on account, as well as the invoice number.
3. Enter the number of the check in the check number column.
4. Enter the credit to the cash account for the amount of the check.
5. If paying on account and entitled to a discount, then enter the amount of the discount in the discount column.
6. If paying on account, enter a debit in the accounts payable column for the full invoice amount, whether the purchase discount is taken or not. For any other type of payment, enter debits in the appropriate account columns. Use the sundry columns to record entries in the less frequently used accounts, using the procedure described in step 3 of the section "Recording Transactions in the Sales Journal."

Posting to the General Ledger

After all entries for the accounting period have been made in the cash disbursements journal, the general ledger accounts are posted by following the steps previously explained for posting to the general ledger from the sales journal (substituting cash disbursements journal for sales journal).

SUBSIDIARY LEDGERS

In the sales journal shown in Exhibit 7–4, it should be noted that the names of the customers were entered in the Description column. But only the total debit to accounts receivable was posted to the general ledger accounts receivable account. This means that this account will inform management concerning the total amount owed to the Fairview Hotel, but it won't give management the details of who owes the hotel, and how much each individual customer owes. This is, for obvious reasons, very important management information.

In order to have a detail of the individual customers' balances, the hotel must create a subsidiary ledger for accounts receivable. This ledger will consist of ledger pages identical to general ledger pages, which, for our learning purposes, will be in the "T" account format. These individual customer subsidiary ledger pages will contain an exact replica of all the charges and payments entered in the general ledger account, except that they will not be lumped together in one total, they will be posted separately to each individual customer's "T" account.

After posting from the sales journal and from the cash receipts journal to the accounts receivable general ledger account as shown in Exhibit 7–4 and 7–5, this account appears as follows:

Accounts Receivable			No. 105		
3/31/XX	SJ12	1,614	3/31/XX	CRJ16	75
			3/31/XX	CRJ16	348
Totals		1,614			423
3/31/XX	Bal.	1,191			

It has a balance of $1,191. In order to create a subsidiary ledger for the above accounts receivable general ledger account, it is necessary to enter all the sales from the sales journal and all the payments from the cash receipts journal in individual customer subsidiary ledger accounts. This is usually done at the time that the general ledger is posted. The subsidiary ledger pages for the above accounts receivable general ledger account are shown in Exhibit 7–8.

By reviewing the accounts receivable subsidiary ledger presented in Exhibit 7–8 it is now possible to easily determine which customers still owe the Fairview Hotel, and how much each customer owes. Jon Ronstatt owes $532, Marie Caron owes $53, Milton Corporation owes $500, and Luka Font owes $106.

Subsidiary Ledger Schedules and Control Accounts

In Exhibit 7–8 a subsidiary ledger schedule is evident beneath the subsidiary ledger accounts. This schedule enables management to determine whether or not it has accounted for all the subsidiary ledgers related to a particular general ledger account and to determine if they have been posted correctly. If the total of the balances of the subsidiary ledger accounts equals the balance in the related general ledger account, then it is more likely that all the subsidiary ledgers have

FAIRVIEW HOTEL
ACCOUNTS RECEIVABLE SUBSIDIARY LEDGER

Jon Ronstatt			No. 105.1		
3/29/XX	SJ12	532			
3/31/XX	Bal.	532			

Marie Caron			No. 105.2		
3/30/XX	SJ12	53			
3/31/XX	Bal.	53			

Milton Corportation			No. 105.3		
3/28/XX	SJ12	848	3/29/XX CRJ16		348
3/31/XS	Bal.	500			

Luka Font			No. 105.4		
3/28/XX	SJ12	75	3/30/XX CRJ16		75
3/28/XX	SJ12	106			
Totals		181			75
3/31/XX	Bal.	106			

FAIRVIEW HOTEL
ACCOUNTS RECEIVABLE SUBSIDIARY LEDGER SCHEDULE

At March 31, 20XX

Subsidiary Ledger Account No.	Customer Name	Amount Due
105.1	Jon Ronstatt	$532
105.2	Marie Caron	53
105.3	Milton Corporation	500
10.5.4	Luka Font	106
	Subsidiary Ledger Total	$1,191

NOTE: The total of the subsidiary ledger schedule should equal the balance in the related general ledger account. That these two amounts do agree can be verified for this example by comparing the above $1,191 total with the $1,191 balance in the accounts receivable general ledger account which appears in Exhibit 7–5.

Exhibit 7–8 Example of accounts receivable subsidiary ledger and subsidiary ledger schedule.

been accounted for and posted correctly. Of course a mistake could have been made in posting both to the general ledger account and to the subsidiary ledger accounts, but it is much less likely that such an identical and duplicate error would be made.

Because the above comparison with the general ledger account indicates to management that all subsidiary ledgers have been accounted for and posted to correctly, the general ledger account is called the control account when a related subsidiary ledger exists.

Highlights of Subsidiary Ledgers and Subsidiary Ledger Schedules

The following should be noted about subsidiary ledgers and subsidiary ledger schedules:

1. The subsidiary ledger is posted on an ongoing basis to its related general ledger control account.
2. Some subsidiary ledgers, such as the accounts receivable and accounts payable subsidiary ledgers, are posted from two journals. For example, the above accounts receivable subsidiary ledger accounts receive their debit entries from the sales journal and their credit entries from the cash receipts journal.
3. The subsidiary ledger accounts have numbers relating them to their general ledger control account. In the case of the subsidiary ledger shown in Exhibit 7–8, the control account is the accounts receivable account, whose number in Exhibit 7–4 and 7–5 is shown as #105. The subsidiary ledger accounts therefore have numbers beginning with 105.
4. In the above subsidiary ledger, the individual account balances have been calculated as of the end of the month of March. With the use of online computer systems, however, these balances are now calculated and maintained on a daily basis.

Guest Ledger and City Ledger

In this text, we have been using the "T" account format to represent subsidiary ledger accounts. Hotels, however, have a special format for their accounts receivable subsidiary ledgers. Each individual customer has a "folio" page to show the activity in that customer's account. The folio page contains the same information as the "T" account format, but it is organized in a different manner. Exhibit 7–9 presents an example of a typical folio page used by a hotel along with an explanation of the different parts of the folio page to enable the reader to verify that it contains all the information contained in a "T" account.

Another unique aspect of hotel accounting must be mentioned at this point: Hotels maintain more than one accounts receivable subsidiary ledger. This means that more than one subsidiary ledger schedule must be prepared. But the totals of all the subsidiary ledger schedules should still equal the total in the accounts receivable control account. The two most important accounts receivable subsidiary ledger schedules are:

1. The guest ledger, and
2. The city ledger.

The guest ledger includes all the folios of guests who are still at the hotel and who will have to pay their bills before they leave the hotel. The city ledger includes all the folios of guests who enjoy extended credit privileges with the hotel. They will not have to pay their bills before they leave. Corporations are most

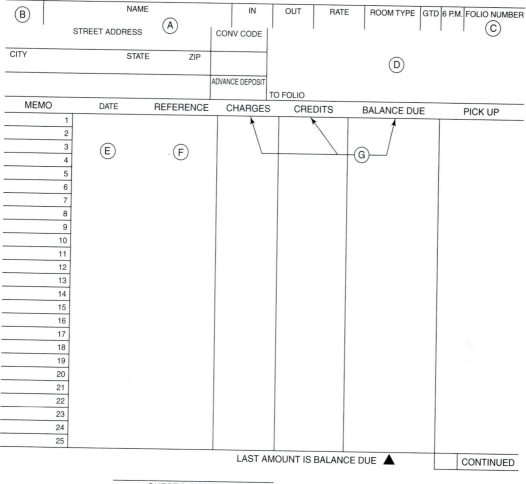

Description of an Accounts Receivable Subsidiary Ledger Account

An accounts receivable subsidiary ledger account consists of the seven parts listed below. They are identified by encircled letters as indicated below.

(A) The name and address of the client.
(B) The client's account number.
(C) The subsidiary ledger page number, if the client's ledger has more than one page.
(D) The authorized credit terms.
(E) A column for the transaction date.
(F) A description column for indicating the type of sale (for example, room, or food and beverage).
(G) One or more columns for entering the (1) balance brought forward (if any)

Exhibit 7–9 Example of accounts receivable subsidiary ledger folio.

likely to have city ledger accounts, although some individuals who are frequent patrons of a hotel can also be granted such privileges. The credit card company accounts are all city ledger accounts. When a guest pays with a credit card, the balance of his guest ledger folio is transferred to the city ledger folio of the credit card company whose card the guest uses. In addition to the above two ledgers, hotels may maintain a "delinquent" ledger for all delinquent accounts.

With regard to the subsidiary ledger presented in Exhibit 7–8, let us assume that Milton Corporation and Marie Caron both enjoy extended credit privileges at the Fairview Hotel. If this were the case, then the subsidiary ledger schedules for the city ledger and the guest ledger would appear as follows:

Guest Ledger Schedule	
(Must pay before leaving hotel)	
Jon Ronstatt	532
Luka Font	106
Guest Ledger Total	638

City Ledger Schedule	
(Will be invoiced after leaving hotel)	
Milton Corporation	500
Marie Caron	53
City Ledger Total	553

Again, the total of the two subsidiary ledger schedules must equal the balance in their related accounts receivable control account, as shown below:

Guest Ledger Total	$ 638
City Ledger Total	553
Accounts Receivable General Ledger Control Account Balance	$1,191

When a Guest Pays with a Credit Card

When a customer pays with a credit card the amount is charged to the account of the credit card company. In the case of hotels, the balance in the guest ledger folio for the individual guest is transferred to the city ledger folio card of the credit card company. The credit card company's folio is in the city ledger subsidiary ledger because they are not guests at the hotel.

When a credit card company charges a business a commission for accepting the credit card as payment, a convenience for the customers of the business, this commission is deducted by the credit card company when paying the business what it owes on behalf of its cardholders. Thus, if a credit card company owes a hotel $100,000 and charges a 1 percent commission, the credit card company would only pay the hotel $99,000. The hotel would record receipt of this payment as follows:

	Dr	Cr
Cash	99,000	
Commission Expense	1,000	
Accounts Receivable		100,000

CASHIER'S DAILY REPORT AND OTHER FREQUENTLY USED JOURNALS

So far in this chapter we have explained the basic journals used by a hospitality entity. However, each entity tends to have its own version of these journals and its own procedures for collecting and transferring data from the different departments to the general ledger and subsidiary ledgers. To that end, the additional accounting records shown in Exhibit 7–10 are frequently used in the hospitality industry. Of particular importance is the cashier's daily report, a record of daily receipts used by the various department cashiers in a hospitality entity to

FAIRVIEW HOTEL

Front Office Cash Receipts and Cash Disbursements Journal

Cashier: Mary James				Watch: 4:00 PM–12:00 PM			Date: 4/1/09			

				Receipts			Disbursements			
					Accounts receivable				Accounts receivable	
Acct no.	Room no.	Guest	Ref.	Cash 101 Dr	Guest 104 Cr	City 104 Cr	Cash 101 Cr	Paid for:	Guest 104 Dr	City 104 Dr
3231	42	John Allan					100	Cash advance		100
3232	101	Bill Tenor		292	292					
3231	42	John Allan		406		406				
		Totals		698	292	406	100			100

Cashier's Daily Report

Department: Restaurant   **Cashier:** F. Williams

Date: 4/2/09   **Time:** 1:00 AM to 12:00 PM

Sales
Guest vouchers	$ 560
Credit cards	320
Cash	2,342
Total sales receipts	$3,222
Currency	1,361
Checks	981
Guest vouchers	560
Credit card vouchers	320
Total enclosed	$3,222
(over) under	0
Total	$3,222

City Journal

Description	Room no.	Rooms	Restaurant	Other Description	Amount	Advances
Mary Penn	361	160	53	Tennis Club	150	200

Transfer Journal

Name and address	Room	Guest acct.	Guest ledger Dr	Guest ledger Cr	City ledger Dr	City ledger Cr	Delinquent ledger Dr	Delinquent ledger Cr
John Mobley	346	36912		1,248	1,248			
Sandra Potts						469	469	

Exhibit 7–10   Example of cashier's daily report and other special-purpose journals.

(1) reconcile sales with receipts, and (2) provide the necessary cash sales information for recording in the cash receipts journal. For example, the $2,342 in cash sales receipts shown on the cashier's daily report in Exhibit 7–10 would subsequently be recorded in a cash receipts journal, such as that shown in Exhibit 7–5.

Because such a large percentage of the accounting activity of a hotel is related to the rooms department, in many hotels the front office has a separate cash receipts and cash disbursements journal, such as the one shown in Exhibit 7–10, called the front office cash receipts and cash disbursements journal. Exhibit 7–11 shows one way cash receipts information may flow to the general ledger and accounts receivable subsidiary ledger when such a journal is used in addition to the summary cash receipts journal.

Notice that the accounts receivable subsidiary ledger must be posted directly from the front office cash receipts and cash disbursements journal, when one exists, because it is used to record receipts on an individual client basis. The summary cash receipts journal will only contain column totals transferred to it from the front office cash receipts and cash disbursements journal.

The right half of the front office cash receipts and cash disbursements journal is used to record cash advances or disbursements such as COD deliveries made on behalf of guests. In Exhibit 7–10 we see that John Allan received a $100 cash advance.

Column totals are transcribed in the usual manner to the summary cash receipts journal for subsequent transfer to the general ledger accounts receivable control account in the general ledger. Since this journal is submitted to the accounting office daily, the entire page is dated rather than each line.

The city journal is used by the front desk to record charges that will subsequently be transferred to individual city ledger cards. It is used in those cases when the city ledger is maintained by the central accounting office or when there is no time at the front desk for posting charges to individual city ledger accounts. It is also submitted to the accounting office daily, and so the entire sheet is dated, rather than each line.

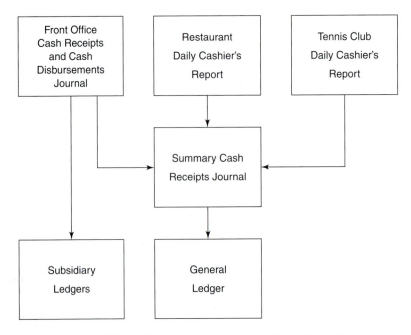

Exhibit 7–11 Flow of hotel cash receipts information when more than one cash receipts journal is used.

The transfer journal (shown in Exhibit 7–10) is used to record transfers of charges between two guests or to transfer guests from the guest ledger to the city ledger and vice versa. It is also used to transfer a guest to other ledgers that may be in use, such as the delinquent ledger for overdue accounts. This journal helps the night auditor verify that all transfers have been made on the subsidiary ledger.

NIGHT AUDITOR'S DUTIES

The primary duty of the night auditor is to verify that all guest charges and payments are posted to clients' accounts, i.e., the accounts receivable subsidiary ledger. To do this, the night auditor prepares a special schedule called the daily transcript, an example of which is presented in Exhibit 7–12.

Before preparing the daily transcript the night auditor takes the following steps:

1. The night auditor reconciles the total guest charge sales and credit card sales, as reported on the departmental cashiers' daily reports, with the total of the guest charge vouchers and credit card vouchers received from each department.
2. The night auditor verifies that all vouchers have been posted to the appropriate clients' accounts receivable subsidiary ledgers.
3. The night auditor posts the appropriate daily room charge to each client's subsidiary ledger account based on the daily room reports shown in Exhibit 7–13.

After the above preliminary verification, the night auditor is ready to prepare the daily transcript using information posted to each individual subsidiary ledger account. In the first two columns, the room number and the guest's account number are entered. The previous day's balance on each individual ledger account is then entered in the balance brought forward column, and all of the current day's charges from the various departments in the appropriate columns to the right. Any cash advance given to the client is entered in the cash advances column. Charges transferred to the client from another account are entered in the first transfers column. The total of departmental charges, advances, and transfers-in is thus entered in the total charges column. Client payments, allowances, and charges transferred out of the client's account are entered in the appropriate credit columns. The new account balance is then calculated by subtracting the credits from the total charges, and it is entered in the balance forward column on the far right.

Toward the bottom of the transcript is a line titled "city." This line is used to record all entries from the city journal when one is in use. Since these charges have not been transcribed to individual city ledger accounts, they must be recorded as totals directly from the current day's city journal.

As final verification that all charges and credits have been posted to clients' accounts, the night auditor totals all the columns of the transcript. The totals for each department column must equal the total of vouchers sent by that department according to the cashier's daily report. Also, the total in the balance forward column must equal the total of all the individual subsidiary ledger accounts balances. The verification is completed by crossfooting (adding across) the column totals to determine that the balance brought forward column total, plus the day's

SAMPLE HOTEL

Daily Transcript

Date: August 5, 2006

| Room no. | Guest acct. | Bal. brought forward | Room | Restaurant | Bar | Snack bar | Cash advances | Transfers in | Total charges | Credits | | | | Bal. forward |
										Cash	Allowances	Transfers out	
48	3468	1,234	120	58	35		100		313	500	20		1,027
77	3469	361	80			8			88	120			329
65	3471	2,671	180	127	160	15	200		667	1,000	100		2,238
91	3473	98	80		10				105				203
100	3474	667	80	25	15				120				787
Subtotal		5,031	540	210	220	23	300		1,293	1,620	120		4,584
City		12,432	1,347	326	279	162	500		2,614	1,273	312		13,461
Totals		17,463	1,887	536	499	185	800		3,907	2,893	432		18,045

Exhibit 7-12 Sample hotel daily transcript.

Daily Rooms Report

Date: _____

Room no.	Guest acct. no.	Number of occupants	Room rate	Sales tax	Room no.	Guest acct. no.	Number of occupants	Room rate	Sales tax
101					161				
102					162				
103					163				
104					164				
105					165				
106					166				
107					167				
108					168				

Housekeeper's Report

Date: _____

Room no.	Status	Room no.	Status	Room no.	Status
101		131		161	
102		132		162	
103		133		163	
104		134		164	
105		135		165	
106		136		166	
107		137		167	

Exhibit 7–13 Room reports used by the night auditor. The daily rooms report is prepared by the night desk clerk and the housekeeper prepares the housekeeper's report. After updating the daily rooms report for late arrivals, the night auditor compares the daily report with the housekeeper's report to verify that every room reported as occupied is included in the daily rooms report. He or she then posts the room rate and sales tax shown on the daily rooms report to each client's ledger.

charge totals, less the day's credit totals, equals the balance forward column total on the daily transcript.

After preparing the daily transcript, the night auditor sends the following items to the central accounting office:

- The daily transcript
- The rooms report and housekeeper's report
- The transfer journal
- The city journal (if central accounting is responsible for posting the city ledger)
- Departmental cashiers' reports, with all vouchers and cash register tapes; and a summary of the front office cash receipts and cash disbursements journal
- All accounts of guests who have checked out and paid

Aside from preparing the daily transcript, the night auditor may have other duties such as:

- Preparing the daily report of operations—a summary sheet of all the hotels sales and receipts of the month to date, including the calculation of statistics such as average room rate or percentage occupancy
- Posting all charges from the city journal to the city ledger
- Helping the front desk clerk catch up with any reports that have not been prepared
- Preparing new account cards for guests that have been at the hotel seven days
- Notifying the credit department of unpaid balances overdue more than a certain number of days, any unusually large charges, or accounts with balances in excess of a specified limit

COMPUTERS AND THE TRADITIONAL ACCOUNTING PROCESS

Computers greatly accelerate the traditional accounting process mainly because:

1. Amounts need be entered only once in a computer, and the computer performs all the required accounting steps. No manual posting, totaling, preparing trial balances, etc. are required.
2. Certain computers, called point-of-sale computers, enable sales clerks to record transaction information at the very moment that a sale is made, reducing the number of accounting clerks required to copy and record information from sales invoices after the fact (after a sale is made).

However, a computer must still perform all the steps of the accounting cycle. Computers merely perform them faster. They still prepare journals, a general ledger, subsidiary ledgers, trial balances, and financial statements. Therefore, it is still essential for a manager to understand and be familiar with the accounting process as it is explained in this text. Otherwise managers will not know what their computers are doing with the raw input data, nor will they know what information can be obtained from the raw accounting data that might be useful to their management function.

As is illustrated in Exhibit 7–14, a computer system has three stages: (1) input, (2) processing, and (3) output. These stages can be subdivided into five segments as follows:

Input
1. Instructions must be entered initially, telling the computer what to do with the data that it will process.
2. Any previously processed data (e.g., the previous month's general ledger) that are going to be modified by new data (checks, invoices, or journal entries) must be entered in the computer.
3. New data (checks, invoices, or journal entries) must be entered.

Processing
4. The computer must merge the new data with the previous data and process it as instructed.

Output
5. The computer must generate the processed data.

As stated earlier, a computer acts like a very fast accounting clerk, but it is totally ignorant concerning accounting. Because of its processing speed, a

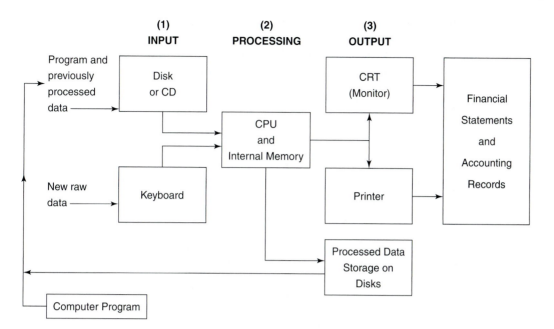

Exhibit 7-14   The basic elements of a computer system.

computerized accounting system provides financial statements and other accounting reports on a more timely basis for use in the managerial decision-making process. However, it cannot make decisions. Management must still decide what and how information will be processed. Management must still make decisions, such as what depreciation methods will be used, which inventory valuation method will be used, which expenditures will be considered expenses and which will be capitalized as assets, etc. Therefore, it is just as important as ever for managers to understand the intricacies of the accounting process because the correctness of information they input into their computers depends on their knowledge of this process, and on their knowledge of what information the accounting process is capable of providing for them.

SOME KEY TERMS INTRODUCED IN THIS CHAPTER

1. **Accounts payable subsidiary ledger.** All the individual accounts containing transactions and balance due to each supplier of a business. The total of these individual account balances should equal the balance in the accounts payable general ledger account.
2. **Cash disbursements journal.** A special-purpose journal used to record cash disbursements.
3. **Cash receipts journal.** A special-purpose journal used to record cash receipts.
4. **City ledger.** A subsidiary ledger related to the accounts receivable general ledger account used by hotels to record the individual account activity of guests who have left the hotel and enjoy extended credit privileges. The total of the balances in the city ledger plus the total of the balances in the guest ledger should equal the balance in the accounts receivable general ledger account. (*See also* Guest ledger.)
5. **Control account.** Another name for a general ledger account when it has a related subsidiary ledger. The total of the subsidiary ledger schedule should equal the balance in its related general ledger account when all subsidiary ledgers are included. Therefore the general ledger account balance is called

the "controlling" balance that indicates to management that all subsidiary ledgers have been accounted for.

6. **Guest ledger.** A subsidiary ledger related to the accounts receivable general ledger account used by hotels to record the individual account activity of guests who are still at the hotel. The total of the balances in the city ledger plus the total of the balances in the guest ledger should equal the balance in the accounts receivable general ledger account. (*See also* City ledger.)

7. **Purchases journal.** A special-purpose journal used to record purchases.

8. **Sales journal.** A special-purpose journal used to record all sales, both cash and credit sales.

9. **Special-purpose journal.** A journal with columns dedicated to individual accounts, used to: a) simplify initial entry of similar types of transactions, b) reduce the possibility of committing errors as a result of posting totals, instead of individual transactions, to the general ledger, and c) facilitate the finding and review of initial transaction entries.

10. **Subsidiary ledger.** A second set of ledger accounts, maintained in addition to the general ledger accounts, for the purpose of providing the detailed breakdown of general ledger account balances into subaccounts required by management to make management decisions. (*See also* Guest ledger and City ledger.)

11. **Subsidiary ledger schedule.** A list of all the subsidiary ledger account balances, whose total should equal the balance in the related general ledger control account. (*See also* Control account.)

QUESTIONS

1. Why are special-purpose journals used in accounting?
2. Besides the general journal, what are the five most commonly used special-purpose journals, and why are they divided into these five types?
3. Which journal is used to record purchases on credit? Cash purchases?
4. What is another name for the cash disbursements journal? Explain.
5. When special-purpose journals are used, what is the general journal used for?
6. In what journal would the proceeds of a loan be recorded? The proceeds from the sale of property or equipment? The proceeds from the sale of services for cash?
7. What is the purpose of the sundry columns in the special-purpose journals?
8. What is a control account? What is a subsidiary ledger schedule?
9. What is the function of the two Ref. columns in the special-purpose journals?
10. What is the function of subsidiary ledgers in general? The accounts receivable subsidiary ledger? The accounts payable subsidiary ledger?
11. What is the function of the cashier's daily report?
12. Who prepares the daily transcript? Why is the daily transcript prepared?
13. What are the three stages in a computer system? Describe them.
14. Why is it important to understand the accounting process in detail now that computers perform most of the accounting functions?

EXERCISES

1. State in which journal(s) each of the following transactions would be recorded.
   (a) Purchased a grill costing $1,000 on 60 days credit.
   (b) Paid wages of $789 to an employee.

(c) Recorded a closing entry.
(d) Made a $500 credit sale.
(e) Made an $800 cash sale.
(f) Collected $350 on account.
(g) Accrued $250 of electricity expense.
(h) Purchased $2,000 worth of inventory for cash.
(i) Paid a $670 supplier's invoice that was due.
(j) Received the proceeds of a $5,000 loan from the bank.

2. Below are presented one page each from the Rigor Restaurant's sales journal and cash receipts journal. Prepare the necessary general ledger and subsidiary ledger accounts using the "T" account format. Number the subsidiary ledger accounts in numerical sequence beginning with 1. Then post from the sales journal and cash receipts journal to the general ledger and accounts receivable subsidiary ledger accounts performing all required posting steps.

Sales Journal Page 2

Date 2000	Description	Ref.	Accounts receivable No. 104	Food sales No. 401	Beverage sales No. 402	Sundry			
						Account	No.	Ref.	Amount
Jan. 2	Joe Rosol		754	260	454	Souvenirs	403		40
2	Mary Brown		152	97	55				
2	Williams, Inc.		1,589	889	433	Souvenirs	403		267
2	Cash sales		8,247	6,121	1,746	Candy machines	404		380
5	Cash sales		6,322	4,810	1,512				

Cash Receipts Journal Page 3

Date 2000	Description	Ref.	Cash in bank No. 101	Accounts receivable Cash sales No. 104	Accounts receivable Credit sales No. 104	Account	No.	Ref.	Amount
Jan. 2	Sold oven		1,000			Equipment	142		1,000
2	Bank loan		30,000			Notes payable	205		30,000
2	Cash sales		8,247	8,247					
5	Payment—Joe Rosol		200		200				
5	Payment—Williams, Inc.		1,000		1,000				
5	Cash sales		6,322	6,322					

3. Answer the following questions based on the cash disbursements journal below:
   (a) Describe each of the transactions recorded in the journal.
   (b) What do the amounts recorded on the line described as "balance brought forward" represent?
   (c) What do the checks in the first Ref. column signify? What do the checks in the sundry Ref. column signify?
   (d) What do the numbers in brackets beneath each column total signify?

Cash Disbursements Journal   Page 3

Date 2001	Description	Check No.	Cash No. 101	Purchase discounts No. 502	Ref.	Accounts payable No. 201	Sundry			
							Account	No.	Ref.	Amount
Jan. 31	Balance brought forward		112,302	3,672		108,403				7,571
31	Brown's suppliers	363	883	18	✓	901				
31	Local National Bank	364	10,000				Notes payable	205	✓	10,000
31	Laurel Food Purveyors	365	2,381	49	✓	2,430				
31	Kill-All Fumigators	366	622		✓	622				
31	National Electric Equipment	367	2,446				Equipment	142	✓	2,446
31	Powerful Electric Co.	368	1,089		✓	1,089				
31	City of Miami	369	362				Licenses	612	✓	362
	Totals		130,085	3,739		113,445				20,379
			(101)	(502)		(201)				

(e) What is the most likely reason that separate columns were not provided for the notes payable account, the equipment account, and the licenses account?

(f) How would you crossfoot this journal? What is the purpose of cross-footing a journal?

4. (a) From the following transactions select those that should be posted to the general ledger accounts payable and purchase discount accounts in the general ledger and its subsidiary ledger accounts. Prepare general ledger and subsidiary ledger "T" accounts, post them directly and calculate the balance for each account. Do *not* journalize them.

June 1 Purchased $1,000 worth of food on 2/10, net 30 credit terms from Brown's Suppliers.

2 Purchased a refrigerator for $2,500 cash from All-Electronics, Inc.

3 Purchased $562 worth of office supplies from Pencil Worth Office Supplies on account. Terms are 5/15, net 60.

4 Purchased $1,824 worth of beverages from Bubbling Brook Beverage purveyors on 2/20, net 45 credit terms.

10 Paid the appropriate amount to settle the outstanding balance due Brown's Suppliers for the June 1 purchase, taking the discount into consideration.

16 Received invoice for $85 from the Kleen-Kline Garbage Pick-up Company, terms are net 15 days.

20 Paid the appropriate amount to reduce the balance due Bubbling Brook Beverage purveyors to one-half the current balance. (Take the discount into consideration.)

21 Paid $300 to Pencil Worth Office Supplies on account.

25 Paid $50 for a part-time secretary who worked today on a contract basis.

(b) Prepare a subsidiary ledger schedule. What is the control account for the accounts payable subsidiary ledger? Does your subsidiary ledger schedule balance with its control account?

5. Answer the following questions concerning the daily transcript presented on the next page:

   (a) Describe the function of each column in the daily transcript.

   (b) What is the function of the line labeled city?

   (c) What is the purpose of the daily transcript?

Daily Transcript   April 3, 2001

| Room no. | Guest account | Balance brought forward | Room | Restaurant | Cash advances | Transfers in | Total charges | Credits | | | |
								Cash	Allowances	Transfers out	Balance forward
61	489	235	120	44	100	10	274				509
44	492	462	60				60	50			472
102	493	581	90	23			113	70		10	614
38	510	329	60				60				389
Subtotal		1,607	330	67	100	10	507	120		10	1,984
City		1,340	540	252	50		842	300			1,882
Total		2,947	870	319	150	10	1,349	420		10	3,866

6. Post the following transactions of the Newcastle Hotel during April of the year 20XX to the following general ledger accounts:

   • Room sales account
   • Food sales account
   • Accounts receivable account
   • Cash account

Further Instructions:

When posting, record ALL sales, both cash and credit, as if they were cash sales, and then record the cash sales a second time, as credits to accounts receivable and debits to the cash account. This is to help you understand how sales are posted from the special purpose sales journal, and how ultimately the accounts receivable account ends up with the correct balance, despite the fact that cash sales are debited to this account as if they were credit sales.

   Before beginning to post, calculate mathematically what the correct balance in the accounts receivable account should be on April 30, 20XX. Then compare this balance to the balance you have in the accounts receivable general ledger account after posting the following transactions.

Year is 20XX

April 1   Generated $5,000 of cash room sales and $3,000 credit sales.
April 4   Generated $3,300 of cash food sales and $1,800 credit sales.
April 18   Collected $1,200 on previous credit sales.
April 23   Generated $6,700 of cash room sales and $2,300 credit sales.
April 30   Collected $800 on previous credit sales.

7. What is the principle duty of the night auditor?

   (a) Prepare employee payrolls

   (b) Take reservations

   (c) Collect cash from the restaurant

   (d) Verify that all transactions have been posted correctly to each customer's account.

8. The Old Post Road Hotel only generates room sales and uses a special-purpose sales journal with two accounts receivable columns, one for recording cash sales and one for recording credit sales. It generates 80 room sales per day (including both cash and credit sales). Which of the following are true? More than one may be true.
   (a) The number of transactions to be journalized each month would be greatly reduced.
   (b) The total in the two accounts receivable columns would be debited to the accounts receivable account.
   (c) The number of postings to the general ledger sales account would be reduced by one-half.
   (d) It would post three amounts to the general ledger and 80 amounts to the accounts receivable subsidiary ledger.

9. Which of the following statements about computer-based accounting systems is false? More than one may be false.
   (a) Some computer systems allow sales transactions to be entered into the accounting system at the same time the sale is made.
   (b) Computers can perform all the steps of the accounting cycle by themselves automatically after transactions are recorded, and they do it faster than humans.
   (c) The concepts of special-purpose journals and subsidiary ledgers do not apply to compuer-based accounting systems.
   (d) It is not necessary to post manually when there is a computer based accounting system.
   (e) All of the above.

10. Which of the following steps are not required to record a credit sale in the sales journal? Exclude steps required for posting to the ledgers. More than one step may be excludable.
    (a) Enter the date of the transaction.
    (b) Enter the name of the customer.
    (c) Enter a check mark in the first Ref. column.
    (d) Enter the sales amount in the accounts receivable column.
    (e) Enter the sales amount in the sales column.
    (f) Enter a check mark in the second Ref. column.

11. The purchases journal serves to record (Answer True or False):
    (a) Cash purchases
    (b) Guest charges
    (c) Purchases on account
    (d) Payments for previous credit purchases
    (e) All of the above

SHORT PROBLEMS

1. The Overview Inn had the following sales and receipts during the month of June 20XX. (Add 6 percent sales tax to all sales and round sales tax amounts to the nearest dollar.)

   Year is 20XX

   June 5   Bill Comet spent three days at the motel and paid $200 for his room, $90 for food, $100 for beverages. He also spent $80 at the gift shop (record gift shop sales in the sundry columns).

   8   Marta Perez enjoyed extended credit privileges and left the following open balance in her account: $500 for her room, $225 for

food, and $97 for beverages. She also bought some sun screen at the pool shop (record in sundry columns) for $10.

9 The proceeds of a $20,000 note payable were received.

12 Roberto Calas checked out and paid his bill at the hotel as follows: room $250, food $180, and beverages $95.

19 Paul Gotley incurred the following charges at the motel and paid with an American Sponsor credit card: room $640, food $455, and beverages $166.

20–29 The inn was closed.

30 Cash sales for the month were food $3,800, beverages $2,600, souvenir shop $1,700, and pool shop $1,000.

30 Marta Perez paid $500 on account.

30 The American Sponsor credit card company paid Paul Gotley's bill. The card company does not charge the establishment for its services, and so the full amount of the bill was collected by the inn.

Note: Don't forget to add the 6 percent sales tax to all sales transactions.

(a) Prepare a sales journal and cash receipts journal similar to those in Exhibits 7–4 and 7–5 and journalize these transactions. Be sure to include sundry columns when preparing your journals. Assume there are no balances brought forward in either journal.

(b) Assign account numbers to your accounts using the chart of accounts in chapter 4 as a guide.

(c) Prepare the required general ledger and subsidiary ledger accounts in "T" account format. Assume beginning account balances are zero.

(d) Post from the journals to the general ledger and subsidiary ledger accounts, performing all required posting steps. Number the subsidiary ledger accounts by using the number that you give the related general ledger control account and adding a "1", "2", "3", etc., separated by a hyphen, after the control account number (e.g., if you give the general ledger accounts receivable account the number "107", then the first subsidiary ledger account number should be "107–1").

(e) Prepare an accounts receivable subsidiary ledger schedule and verify that it balances with its related control account.

2. The Never Late Airline made the following purchases and payments during the month of August 20XX:

Year is 20XX

August 1 Purchased fuel worth $4,000 on 2/10, net 30 credit terms from Fast Fuel, Inc.

5 Purchased beverages worth $1,300 on 2/30, net 60 credit terms from the Sweetwater Corporation.

8 Purchased Office supplies worth $900 on credit from the Merser Company.

10 Paid the appropriate amount due for fuel purchases made August 1 from Fast Fuel, Inc. (Take the appropriate discount into consideration.)

15 Purchased a cooler for $4,000 cash from the Everkool Company.

18 Received an invoice from the Contract Cleaning Company for $2,000, but did not pay it immediately.

19 Received electricity invoice for $400 from the All Electric Co. but did not pay it immediately.

(a) Prepare a purchases journal and cash disbursements journal similar to those in Exhibits 7–6 and 7–7 and journalize these transactions. Be sure to include sundry columns. Assume there are no balances brought forward in either journal.

(b) Assign account numbers to your accounts using the chart of accounts in Chapter 4 as a guide.

(c) Prepare the required general ledger and subsidiary ledger accounts in "T" account format. Assume the cash account has an ending balance of $30,000 on July 31, 20XX.

(d) Post from the journals to the general ledger and subsidiary ledger accounts, performing all required posting steps. Number the subsidiary ledger accounts by using the number that you give the related general ledger control account and adding a "1", "2", "3", etc., separated by a hyphen, after the control account number (e.g., if you give the general ledger accounts payable account the number "201", then the first subsidiary ledger account number should be "201–1").

(e) Prepare an accounts payable subsidiary ledger schedule and verify that it balances with its related general ledger control account.

LONG PROBLEMS

1. The Tranquil Inn Motel had the following sales and receipts during the month of April 2002. (Add 5 percent sales tax to all sales and round sales tax amounts to the nearest dollar.)

April 4   John Brown spent three days at the motel and paid $240 for his room, $120 for food, $40 for beverages. He also spent $40 at the souvenir shop (record souvenir shop sales in the sundry columns).

6   Marilyn Roberts enjoyed extended credit privileges and left the following open balance in her account: $580 for her room, $324 for food, and $77 for beverages. She also bought some tennis balls at the pro shop (record in sundry columns) for $15.

7   Cash sales for the week were food $1,892, beverages $767, gift shop $387, and pro shop $124.

8   The proceeds of a $10,000 loan were received.

10   Jim Konklin paid his bill at the hotel as follows: room $341, food $161, and beverages $65.

11   The Walton Co. enjoyed extended credit privileges at the motel and held a small convention there. It accumulated the following balance in it's account: rooms $2,640, food $1,980, and beverages $992.

14   Cash sales for the week were food $2,361, beverages $1,824, souvenir shop $823, and pro shop $361.

17   Robert Magnuson incurred the following charges at the motel and paid with a credit card: room $340, food $121, and beverages $66.

18–27   The motel was closed.

28   Marilyn Roberts paid $300 on account.

29   The credit card company paid Robert Magnuson's bill. The card company does not charge the establishment for its services, and so the full amount of the bill was collected by the motel.

30   Cash sales for the last week in April were food $873, beverages $431, souvenir shop $162, and pro shop $91.

30   William Joseph has been at the hotel seven days, will pay cash upon departure, and has incurred the following charges: room

$560, food $310, and beverages $112. It is hotel policy to invoice guests who do not enjoy extended credit privileges every seven days.

(a) Prepare a sales journal and cash receipts journal similar to those in Exhibits 7–4 and 7–5 and journalize these transactions. Be sure to include sundry columns when preparing your journals.

(b) Assign account numbers to your accounts using the chart of accounts in Chapter 4 as a guide.

(c) Prepare the required general ledger and subsidiary ledger accounts in "T" account format. Assume beginning account balances are zero.

(d) Post from the journals to the general ledger and subsidiary ledger accounts, performing all required posting steps. Number the subsidiary ledger accounts in numerical sequence beginning with 1.

(e) Prepare an accounts receivable subsidiary ledger schedule and verify that it balances.

2. The Fun-and-Sun Tour Bus Line made the following purchases and payments during the month of November.

Nov. 1 Purchased food worth $1,348 on 2/10, net 30 credit terms from Trusting Food, Inc.

　　 5 Purchased beverages worth $894 on 2/30, net 60 credit terms from the Drink-All Corporation.

　　 8 Purchased cleaning supplies for $779 cash, from the Quick-Kleen Company.

　　 10 Paid the appropriate amount due for food purchases made November 1 from Trusting Food, Inc.

　　 15 Purchased a freezer for $2,361 cash from U-Kool-It Company.

　　 18 Paid November rent of $2,000 to Solid State Real Estate Company.

　　 19 Received water invoice for $400 from the Eversweet Water Co. but did not pay it immediately. The invoice covers the period from the November 1 to November 15.

　　 21 Received and paid the fuel invoice for $1,872 from Growler Gas Company.

　　 25 Purchased kitchen equipment worth $1,312 on 2/10, net 45 terms from the Havital Company (record in sundry columns).

　　 28 Paid the appropriate amount to reduce the outstanding balance with the Drink-All Corporation to half the current balance. Take discount into consideration.

(a) Prepare a purchases journal and cash disbursements journal similar to those in Exhibits 7–6 and 7–7 and journalize these transactions. Be sure to include sundry columns.

(b) Assign account numbers to your accounts using the chart of accounts in Chapter 4 as a guide.

(c) Prepare the required general ledger and subsidiary ledger accounts in "T" account format. Assume beginning account balances are zero.

(d) Post from the journals to the general ledger and subsidiary ledger accounts, performing all required posting steps. Number the subsidiary ledger accounts in numerical sequence beginning with 1.

(e) Prepare an accounts payable subsidiary ledger schedule and verify that it balances.

3. The Lofty Pines Hotel (located next to a lake) had the following sales and cash receipts during the month of July. (Add 5% sales tax to all sales and round sales tax amounts to the nearest dollar.)

July 5 Peter Gordner spent five days at the hotel. He enjoyed extended credit privileges, and so he charged the following to his account: room $750, food $342, and beverages $134.

7 Cash sales at the hotel for the week were food $6,671, beverages $3,642, candy machines $1,012, and boat rentals $892 (record candy machines and boat rentals in the sundry columns).

9 John Karstens stayed at the hotel four days and paid for the following upon departure: room $500, food $205, and beverages $106.

11 The hotel sold an old piece of kitchen equipment for $1,000 cash.

12 Peter Gordner paid $500 on his account.

14 Cash sales for the week were room $5,581, food $2,877, beverages $1,431, candy machines $984, and boat rentals $651.

18 Barbara Rushmont stayed at the hotel and incurred the following charges: room $640, food $112, and beverages $55. She paid with a credit card.

20 The hotel borrowed $10,000, for which it signed a note payable to the bank.

21 Charles McMoor enjoyed extended credit privileges at the hotel and left the following charges open on his account when he departed: room $1,340, food $742, and beverages $464.

28 Cash sales for the week were food $3,456, beverages $1,448, candy machines $631, and boat rentals $346.

30 Charles McMoor paid $1,000 on his account.

30 It is hotel policy to invoice every seven days those guests who do not enjoy extended credit privileges. Joanne Barlot, a transient guest, was invoiced for the following, since it was her seventh day at the hotel: room $1,050, food $544, and beverages $378.

(a) Prepare a sales journal and cash receipts journal similar to those in Exhibits 7–4 and 7–5 and journalize these transactions. Be sure to include sundry columns.

(b) Assign account numbers to your accounts using the chart of accounts in Chapter 4 as a guide.

(c) Prepare the required general ledger and subsidiary ledger accounts in "T" account format. Assume beginning account balances are zero.

(d) Post from the journals to the general ledger and subsidiary ledger accounts, performing all required posting steps. Number the subsidiary ledger accounts in numerical sequence beginning with 1.

(e) Prepare an accounts receivable subsidiary ledger schedule and verify that it balances.

4. The Wait-less Fast Food Diet Restaurant made the following purchases and payments during the month of May:

May 4 Purchased food worth $2,560 on 5/10, net 45 credit terms from Fed-Up Foods Co.

6 Purchased cleaning supplies from Sanitary Mary, Inc. for $560 cash.

10 Purchased some tables from the All-Restaurant Co. for $1,200 cash (record in sundry columns).

14 Paid the appropriate amount to reduce the balance due Fed-Up Foods Co. by half. Take the discount into consideration.

15 Paid $5,000 of notes payable that were due to First Bank (record in sundry columns).

17 Received and paid the electricity invoice for the first 15 days of May to All-Electric Co. It amounted to $996.

18 Purchased $1,450 worth of food and $560 worth of beverages from the International Food Supply, Co. on 2/10, net 30 credit terms.

20 Paid the appropriate amount to reduce the remaining balance in the Fed-Up Foods Co. account by half. No discount may be taken since the discount period has expired.

25 Received the water invoices for the first 20 days of the month from the City Water Co. but did not pay it. The amount is $344.

28 Paid the appropriate amount to reduce the balance in the International Food Supply Co. by half. Remember you are paying within the discount period.

(a) Prepare a purchases journal and cash disbursements journal similar to those in Exhibits 7–6 and 7–7 and journalize these transactions. Be sure to include sundry columns.

(b) Assign account numbers to your accounts using the chart of accounts in Chapter 4 as a guide.

(c) Prepare the required general ledger and subsidiary ledger accounts in "T" account format. Assume all beginning account balances are zero, except for the notes payable account, which has a beginning balance of $10,000.

(d) Post from the journals to the general ledger and subsidiary ledger accounts, performing all required posting steps. Number the subsidiary ledger accounts in numerical sequence beginning with 1.

(e) Prepare an accounts payable subsidiary ledger schedule and verify that it balances.

5. Using the format presented in Exhibit 7.12, prepare a daily transcript for a 10-room hotel, the Overnite Inn, on September 5, 2003, based on the information in the daily rooms report and housekeeper's report below. All guests are transient (do not enjoy extended credit privileges).

Daily Rooms Report — Date: September 5, 2003

Room no.	Guest account	Number of occupants	Room rate	Sales tax
1		0		
2	3467	1	$50	$2.50
3		0		
4		0		
5	3469	2	$70*	$3.50
6	3471	1	$50	$2.50
7	3470	1	$40	$2.00
8		0		
9		0		
10	3468	1	$40	$2.00

*Double occupancy rate

Housekeeper's Report — Date: September 5, 2003

Room	Status	Room	Status
1	Unoccupied	6	Occupied
2	Occupied	7	Occupied
3	Unoccupied	8	Unoccupied
4	Unoccupied	9	Unoccupied
5	Occupied	10	Occupied

The night auditor received the following signed guest vouchers with the cashier's report from the restaurant and bar:

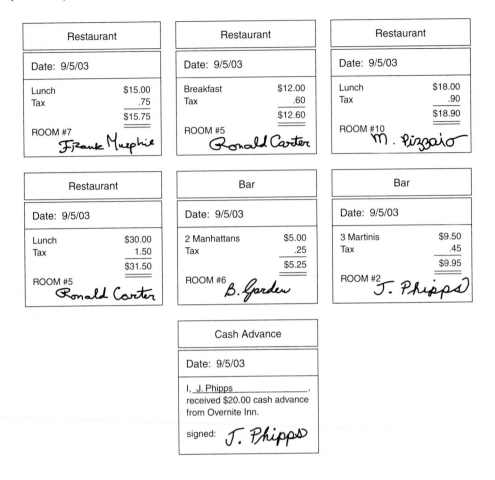

Restaurant	
Date: 9/5/03	
Lunch	$15.00
Tax	.75
	$15.75
ROOM #7 *Frank Murphie*	

Restaurant	
Date: 9/5/03	
Breakfast	$12.00
Tax	.60
	$12.60
ROOM #5 *Ronald Carter*	

Restaurant	
Date: 9/5/03	
Lunch	$18.00
Tax	.90
	$18.90
ROOM #10 *M. Pizzaio*	

Restaurant	
Date: 9/5/03	
Lunch	$30.00
Tax	1.50
	$31.50
ROOM #5 *Ronald Carter*	

Bar	
Date: 9/5/03	
2 Manhattans	$5.00
Tax	.25
	$5.25
ROOM #6 *B. Garden*	

Bar	
Date: 9/5/03	
3 Martinis	$9.50
Tax	.45
	$9.95
ROOM #2 *J. Phipps*	

Cash Advance
Date: 9/5/03
I, _J. Phipps_ , received $20.00 cash advance from Overnite Inn.
signed: *J. Phipps*

In addition to the above, you are given the following information:

(a)

Guest account no.	Account balance at 9/4/03
3467	0
3468	$ 89
3469	$798
3470	$115
3471	$ 65

(b) Upon reviewing his subsidiary ledger card you notice that guest number 3469 paid $700 on his account today.

(c) You also notice that yesterday a $15 bar invoice was posted erroneously to guest account number 3469 whereas it should have been posted to guest account number 3470. Use the transfer columns to make the correction.

(d) Guest number 3471 was charged a $70 room rate yesterday by mistake. The current room rate is $50. Use the allowances column to make the correction.

(e) Mr. J. Phipps' account is number 3467.

Payroll Accounting | 8

The learning objectives of this chapter are:

- To understand the basic concepts and terminology relating to the payment and recording of a payroll.
- To understand the various types of payroll deductions and employer payroll taxes.
- To understand the responsibilities of the employer with regard to reporting and paying federal and state payroll taxes.
- To know how to use the special-purpose payroll journal and how to post to the general ledger and subsidiary payroll ledgers.
- To understand the responsibilities of the employer with regard to the calculation of payroll amounts in the context of the wage-hour law, the tip credit, and the related additional tax reporting requirements.
- To understand the difference in recording pay to an employee and an independent contractor.
- To understand the importance of controlling salaries and wages, and to learn some review techniques for controlling this expense category.
- To understand a few aspects of Canadian payroll tax law.

The sale of services, a labor-intensive endeavor, is the major source of revenue in the hospitality industry. It is only logical, therefore, that, with the exception of cost-of-sales expense in restaurants, payroll and related expenses be the major expense category in the typical hospitality entity. In the United States, it can vary between 20 and 35 percent of every dollar of revenue. Knowledge of payroll accounting and control methods is consequently of primary importance to industry management.

In this chapter, certain basic concepts and terms relating to payrolls are explained first, along with the procedures for calculating and recording payroll deductions and employer payroll taxes. After this, there is a brief explanation of Canadian payroll tax procedures and the differences in recording pay to independent contractors. This is followed by an explanation of the use of the payroll journal and employee subsidiary ledgers, as well as the process of accruing a payroll. The last three sections of the chapter include a summary of the wage-hour law's impact on the hospitality industry, a brief explanation of IRS tip reporting requirements, and a discussion of some procedures for controlling salaries and wages.

SALARIES AND WAGES

We have previously learned that the expense account for recording payrolls is called "salaries and wages." Salaried employees are usually paid a fixed amount regardless of the number of hours worked. Wages are paid to employees whose pay is based on the number of hours they work. Their hourly rate is multiplied by the number of hours worked to obtain the amount of wages paid. Thus an employee who worked 40 hours and was paid $7 per hour would have earned $280.

Previously, in this text, salaries and wages have been recorded by an entry such as the following:

	Dr	Cr
Salaries and Wages	280	
Cash		280
To record a $280 payroll payment		

Amounts Withheld from Salaries and Wages

This simple form of recording salaries and wages does not take into account the fact that an employer needs to make certain deductions from an employee's gross pay for one or more of the following reasons:

- Certain taxes due by an employee must be withheld by the employer for later remittance to the federal or state governments, and
- An employee may voluntarily authorize the employer to withhold certain amounts for subsequent remittance to savings plans, medical insurance companies, pension plans, or as union dues, loan repayments or charitable contributions.

As a consequence of these deductions, a distinction must be made between an employee's gross pay and net pay, the net pay being the amount actually received by an employee after all deductions have been made.

Taxes Owed by Employees: Withheld by Employer

The first type of deduction listed above involves some or all of the following types of taxes:

- Prepayments on income taxes that an employee may owe to the federal, state, or city governments at the end of the calendar year
- Payments of the social security tax owed by an employee to the federal government
- Payments of the medicare tax owed by an employee to the federal government

Withheld Income Taxes

Cities and states, as well as the federal government, may levy income taxes. In this text, we will limit ourselves to discussing the withholding of U.S. federal income taxes only, along with a brief overview of Canadian payroll tax law. However, the procedure for recording the withholding of other income tax amounts is similar to that for recording the withholding of federal income taxes.

The Current Tax Payments Act of 1943, which is part of the Internal Revenue Code (IRC) requires employers to withhold from an employee's gross salaries and wages an amount to be applied against that employee's potential income tax liability at the end of the year. This deduction is called "withheld income tax." The amount of tax withheld is based on estimated amounts obtained from tables included in a pamphlet titled "Circular E—Employer's Withholding Tax Guide" published by the Internal Revenue Service (IRS). Because employees have different deduction amounts and may have other sources of income, at the end of the calendar year an employee may either owe more money to the IRS, or may be due a refund of part or all the income taxes withheld. Additional taxes due are paid and refunds are claimed when an employee files his or her own personal tax return at year-end.

Using Circular E

A sample of two half-pages from the 1998 Circular E is presented in Exhibit 8–1. It should be noted that there are different tables in the Circular E for weekly, bi-weekly, semi-monthly, monthly, and daily pay periods. Each of the above categories is subdivided into tables for single and for married employees because the effective tax rates of single and married employees may be different. The half-pages we have chosen to include here correspond to weekly pay for employees who are married and weekly pay for single employees.

The first step in using Circular E is to determine whether or not an employee is married or single and the pay date frequency. This indicates what table to use. Once you have determined the appropriate table you must find the employee's pay in the two left-most columns which specify weekly pay ranges. To the right of these columns you will note that there are 11 columns, one headed 0 and ten headed from 1 to 10. These columns indicate the number of withholding allowances that an employee claims. The more withholding allowances an employee claims, the less tax will be withheld. An employee indicates how many allowances he or she can claim by preparing a W-4 form, which every employee must sign and give to their employer when they are hired or when any information on the previous form has changed. In general, an employee can claim one allowance for him or herself, one for a spouse, if married, and one for each dependant. Because the IRS definition of "dependent" can be extensive, we will limit ourselves here to stating that children are usually dependents, and, for purposes of solving problems in this text, you may assume that they are.

Social Security and Medicare Taxes

The Federal Insurance Contributions Act (FICA) of 1935 provides for workers to receive monthly pension payments upon reaching the designated retirement age. In 1965, the medicare program, providing certain medical insurance coverage, was added to the benefits receivable by retirees. Both of these programs are funded by taxes collected under FICA.

To fund these benefits, as of 2003, employers must withhold 6.2 percent of employees' gross salaries and wages as a social security tax and 1.45 percent of the employees' gross salaries and wages as a medicare tax. There is a maximum salaries and wages amount (the base amount) above which the social security tax is not payable. This changes annually, as is evident in Exhibit 8–2. The maximum tax rates in this exhibit are obtained by multiplying the rate percent by the base amount.

There is no maximum ceiling for salaries and wages with regard to the medicare tax. All salaries and wages, no matter how much they may be, are subject to the 1.45 percent medicare tax.

SINGLE Persons—WEEKLY Payroll Period

(For Wages Paid in 1998)

If the wages are—		And the number of withholding allowances claims is—										
At least	But less than	0	1	2	3	4	5	6	7	8	9	10
		The amount of income tax to be withheld is—										
300	310	38	30	23	15	7	0	0	0	0	0	0
310	320	40	32	24	16	8	1	0	0	0	0	0
320	330	41	33	26	18	10	2	0	0	0	0	0
330	340	43	35	27	19	11	4	0	0	0	0	0
340	350	44	36	29	21	13	5	0	0	0	0	0
350	360	46	38	30	22	14	7	0	0	0	0	0
360	370	47	39	32	24	16	8	0	0	0	0	0
370	380	49	41	33	25	17	10	2	0	0	0	0
380	390	50	42	35	27	19	11	3	0	0	0	0
390	400	52	44	36	28	20	13	5	0	0	0	0
400	410	53	45	38	30	22	14	6	0	0	0	0
410	420	55	47	39	31	23	16	8	0	0	0	0
420	430	56	48	41	33	25	17	9	2	0	0	0
430	440	58	50	42	34	26	19	11	3	0	0	0
440	450	59	51	44	36	28	20	12	5	0	0	0
450	460	61	53	45	37	29	22	14	6	0	0	0
460	470	62	54	47	39	31	23	15	8	0	0	0
470	480	64	56	48	40	32	25	17	9	1	0	0
480	490	65	57	50	42	34	26	18	11	3	0	0
490	500	67	59	51	43	35	28	20	12	4	0	0
500	510	68	60	53	45	37	29	21	14	6	0	0
510	520	70	62	54	46	38	31	23	15	7	0	0
520	530	72	63	56	48	40	32	24	17	9	1	0
530	540	75	65	57	49	41	34	26	18	10	3	0
540	550	78	66	59	51	43	35	27	20	12	4	0
550	560	81	68	60	52	44	37	29	21	13	6	0
560	570	83	69	62	54	46	38	30	23	15	7	0
570	580	86	72	63	55	47	40	32	24	16	9	1
580	590	89	74	65	57	49	41	33	26	18	10	2
590	600	92	77	66	58	50	43	35	27	19	12	4

Page 36

MARRIED Persons—WEEKLY Payroll Period

(For Wages Paid in 1998)

If the wages are—		And the number of withholding allowances claims is—										
At least	But less than	0	1	2	3	4	5	6	7	8	9	10
		The amount of income tax to be withheld is—										
1,140	1,150	185	171	156	142	127	114	106	99	91	83	75
1,150	1,160	188	173	159	144	130	116	108	100	92	85	77
1,160	1,170	191	176	162	147	133	118	109	102	94	86	78
1,170	1,180	194	179	164	150	135	121	111	103	95	88	80
1,180	1,190	196	182	167	153	138	124	112	105	97	89	81
1,190	1,200	199	185	170	156	141	126	114	106	98	91	83
1,200	1,210	202	187	173	158	144	129	115	108	100	92	84
1,210	1,220	205	190	176	161	147	132	117	109	101	94	86
1,220	1,230	208	193	178	164	149	135	120	111	103	95	87
1,230	1,240	210	196	181	167	152	138	123	112	104	97	89
1,240	1,250	213	199	184	170	155	140	126	114	106	98	90
1,250	1,260	216	201	187	172	158	143	129	115	107	100	92
1,260	1,270	219	204	190	175	161	146	131	117	109	101	93
1,270	1,280	222	207	192	178	163	149	134	120	110	103	95
1,280	1,290	224	210	195	181	166	152	137	123	112	104	96
1,290	1,300	227	213	198	184	169	154	140	125	113	106	98
1,300	1,310	230	215	201	186	172	157	143	128	115	107	99
1,310	1,320	233	218	204	189	175	160	145	131	116	109	101
1,320	1,330	236	221	206	192	177	163	148	134	119	110	102
1,330	1,340	238	224	209	195	180	166	151	137	122	112	104
1,340	1,350	241	227	212	198	183	168	154	139	125	113	105
1,350	1,360	244	229	215	200	186	171	157	142	128	115	107
1,360	1,370	247	232	218	203	189	174	159	145	130	116	108
1,370	1,380	250	235	220	206	191	177	162	148	133	119	110
1,380	1,390	252	238	223	209	194	180	165	151	136	121	111

| $1,390 and over | Use Table 1(b) for a MARRIED person on page 34. Also see the instructions on page 32. |

Page 39

Exhibit 8–1   Sample page excerpts from IRS Circular E.

Year	Rate %	Base amount	Maximum tax	
			Employer	Employee
1996	6.2	$62,700	$3,887.40	$3,887.40
1997	6.2	$65,400	$4,054.80	$4,054.80
1998	6.2	$68,400	$4,240.80	$4,240.80
1999	6.2	$72,600	$4,501.20	$4,501.20
2000	6.2	$76,200	$4,724.40	$4,724.40
2001	6.2	$80,400	$4.984.80	$4.984.80

Exhibit 8–2   Social Security tax rate and base amounts.

JOURNALIZING SALARIES AND WAGES, WITHHELD TAXES AND VOLUNTARY PAYROLL DEDUCTIONS

Since amounts deducted from an employee's pay must be remitted by the employer to the federal and local governments and to the organizations administering the various voluntary deduction amounts, all payroll deductions are recorded as liabilities of the employer. The employer is merely acting as collection agent for the various organizations and has no right to keep the funds. An example of a payroll journal entry to record the salary of a hypothetical employee, John Adams, and the assumptions upon which it is based, is given in Exhibit 8–3.

John Adams must pay social security tax only on $100 of this week's earnings because he has already earned $68,300 in the current year (1998), and the maximum pay subject to social security tax is $68,400 in 1998 (see Exhibit 8–2).

Employer Taxes and Workers' Compensation Insurance

In addition to the taxes levied on employees and deducted from their pay, the employer is responsible for certain payroll-related federal and state taxes and insurance payments, which constitute an additional expense for the employer. These additional employer expenses may be divided into three categories:

Assumptions

John Adams
Marital status:	married
Withholding allowances:	five
Voluntary deduction:	union dues = $20
Pay frequency:	weekly
Cumulative pay received up to last payroll in 1998:	$68,300
Amount of current week's pay:	$1,370

Journal Entry

	Dr	Cr
Salaries & wages expense	$1,370.00	
Withheld income tax payable		$ 177.00
Social security tax payable (6.2% × 100.00)		6.20
Medicare tax payable (1.45% × $1,370.00)		19.87
Union dues payable		20.00
Cash		1,146.93

To record John Adam's weekly salary

Exhibit 8–3   Sample payroll entry.

1. Social security and medicare taxes
2. Federal and state unemployment taxes
3. Workers' compensation insurance

The employer is required to pay a social security and medicare tax equal in amount to that paid by the employee, 6.2 percent of gross salaries and wages in 2002 for social security, and 1.45 percent of gross salaries and wages for medicare. The one exception to this—tip income—is discussed later in this chapter.

Additionally, the Federal Unemployment Tax Act (FUTA) imposed a tax on the employer to fund the establishment and administration of employment offices throughout the United States. In 2003, the tax rate was 6.2 percent of gross salaries and wages, up to maximum salaries and wages per employee of $7,000 per year. Thus, if an employee earns $7,100 in any year the employer does not owe the FUTA tax on the $100 paid to the employer above the maximum $7,000 amount. Since all states have a similar unemployment tax (the SUTA tax), the federal government allows part of the state tax to be applied as a credit against the federal unemployment tax if an employer pays the SUTA tax on a timely basis. This reduces the effective rate of federal unemployment tax down to .8 percent (6.20% − 5.40% = .8%). Because the federal unemployment tax is an employer expense, no payroll deduction is made for it. This also means that a separate journal entry is required to record this employer payroll tax as well as other payroll taxes levied on the employer.

As of this writing, most states have levied an unemployment tax on employers of which the proceeds are used to pay a weekly subsidy (unemployment compensation benefits) to employees who were laid-off because of downsizing or other valid cause. Employees who quit their job voluntarily, or are fired for good cause, may not collect state unemployment benefits. The rates for this tax vary according to an employer's turnover experience. The initial rate assigned to a company by all states is 2.7 percent of gross salaries and wages up to maximum salaries and wages, per employee, of $7,000, the same maximum applicable to the FUTA tax. In 2003, in Florida, companies with low employee turnover could have the rate reduced as low as .01 percent and companies with high employee turnover could have it increased to as high as 5.4 percent. Thus, an employer who has lower employee turnover and receives a state unemployment tax rate of less than 2.7 percent will pay less total unemployment taxes, and an employer with high turnover and a state tax rate above 2.7 percent will pay more total unemployment taxes. This can be seen more clearly in Exhibit 8–4. Like the FUTA tax,

	Employee turnover		
	Low	**Average**	**High**
Gross salaries and wages (Consists of 3 employees' pay—none of whom have cumulative annual earnings above $7,000):	$10,000	$10,000	$10,000
State unemployment tax rate:	1%	2.7%	4.5%
State unemployment tax:	$100	$270	$450
Federal unemployment tax rate (6.2% less 5.4%):	0.8%	0.8%	0.8%
Federal unemployment tax:	$80	$80	$80
Total unemployment tax:	$180	$350	$530

Exhibit 8–4 Calculation of federal and state unemployment taxes.

the SUTA tax is also recorded through a journal entry other than through the payroll entry presented in Exhibit 8–3.

Every state requires employers to carry some form of workers' compensation insurance. In some cases, the state administers the fund, and in others, private insurance companies sell the coverage. The purpose of this insurance is to reimburse workers for injury or death incurred while at work. This insurance constitutes an employer expense. The premium is usually paid at the beginning of the year and is adjusted by an additional payment or a refund at year-end depending on the employer's experience factor. The amount paid varies from state to state and is based on gross salaries and wages, subject to an upper limit and to the degree of risk in each employment category. Since payment is made before the coverage is actually used, workers' compensation payments are usually debited to a prepaid workers' compensation account.

Journalizing Employer Payroll Taxes and Workers' Compensation Insurance

The employer's portion of the social security and medicare taxes, as well as the federal and state unemployment taxes and workers' compensation insurance are charged to their individual expense accounts. The corresponding credit entries are made to their respective current liability account and prepaid workers' compensation account. The employer's payroll tax entries are usually made in the general journal. A sample of both a payroll entry and an employer's payroll tax entry is presented in Exhibit 8–5.

The employer must pay FUTA and SUTA on only $200 of Charles Markworth's gross wages this week because the other $100 are in excess of the $7,000 maximum earnings subject to these taxes.

Employer Payroll Tax Reporting Requirements

Both the federal and state governments require the employer to report and pay payroll taxes and withheld income taxes periodically. Each employer must obtain an employer identification number by filing form SS-4 with the IRS. This employer identification number must be entered in all payroll tax forms sent to the IRS. Sole proprietorships, partnerships, and corporations must all obtain employer identification numbers whether or not they have any employees, since the number is also used to relate income tax information to a business entity.

IRS form 941 is used to report social security and medicare taxes due to the federal government, both those due by the employee and those due by the employer. It must be submitted by the employer to the IRS no later than one month after the end of each calendar quarter, i.e., by April 30, July 31, October 31, and January 31. IRS form 940 is used to report the FUTA tax to the federal government. It must be postmarked no later than January 31 of the year following the reporting year. The SUTA tax forms are designed by each state because this is a state-imposed tax. Like the federal form 941 these forms must be submitted quarterly, and must be postmarked no later than one month after the end of the corresponding quarter. In Florida the name of the SUTA tax form is UCT-6. Federal payroll taxes are deposited in local banks accompanied by depositary receipts obtainable from the IRS, or, after a business attains a certain size, they must be transferred to the IRS electronically. State payroll taxes are mailed to the state revenue office.

The timing of the payment of payroll taxes is subject to many different and often complex rules and conditions, depending on the amount that is owed, which in turn usually depends upon the size of the payroll. A full explanation of these is not appropriate for a text of this nature. This information is readily obtainable from the IRS and state revenue offices.

Assumptions

Charles Markworth

Marital status:	single
Withholding allowances:	one
Voluntary deduction:	Health Insurance = $30
Pay frequency:	weekly
Cumulative pay received up to last payroll in 1998:	$6,800
Amount of current week's pay:	$300
Workers' compensation insurance expired:	$15
State unemployment tax rate:	2.7%

Payroll Journal Entry

	Dr	Cr
Salaries & wages expense	$300.00	
Withheld income tax payable		$ 30.00
Social security tax payable (6.2% × 300.00)		18.60
Medicare tax payable (1.45% × $300.00)		4.35
Health insurance payable		30.00
Cash		217.05

Employer's Payroll Tax Journal Entry

	Dr	Cr
Social security tax expense (6.2% × $300)	$18.60	
Medicare tax (1.45% × $300)	4.35	
FUTA tax expense (0.8% × $200)		
($7,000 − $6,800 = $200)	1.60	
SUTA tax expense (0.027 × $200)	5.40	
Workers' compensation insurance expense	15.00	
Social security tax payable		$18.60
Medicare tax payable		4.35
FUTA payable		1.60
SUTA payable		5.40
Prepaid workers' compensation		15.00

Exhibit 8–5   Journal entries to record Charles Markworth's payroll check and his employer's payroll tax expense.

At year-end, the employer is responsible for reporting to each individual employee the total amount of earnings, social security and medicare taxes withheld, and federal and local income taxes withheld. This is done by providing each employee with a W-2 form, which must be distributed to employees no later than January 31 of the following year. The employer must also send a copy of each W-2 to the Social Security Administration (SSA) along with form W-3, which contains a summary total for each of the categories reported on the W-2 tax forms. Form W-3 is due on the last day of February.

CANADIAN PAYROLL TAX PROCEDURES

Canadian law is somewhat more complex than that of the United States. Because of this, only a few major points of Canadian payroll tax law will be briefly covered.

In Canada, the federal government collects both federal and provincial income taxes, except in Quebec, where the process is reversed. The province of

Quebec collects the federal and provincial income taxes. It is the only province where two separate income tax returns must be filed.

Form TD1: Personal Tax Credits Return

This form is the equivalent of the U.S. form W-4 and is prepared by employees to inform their employers of the number of tax credits (called withholding allowances in the United States) they are entitled to receive. By filling in form TD1 each employee can determine their claim code, which varies from 0 to 10. This claim code is then used in calculating withholding amounts in the Payroll Deduction Tables.

Payroll Deduction Tables

These are booklets, similar to Circular E in the United States, printed for each province to reflect that province's income tax rates and containing the withholding percentages for the six (seven in some provinces) Canadian payroll tax withholdings. These tables have eleven columns corresponding to the eleven claim codes determined by the calculations performed on form TD1. The higher the claim code the lower the amount of withholding required for each type of tax.

Payroll Tax Withholdings

Under Canadian law, there are four withholding amounts, corresponding to an equivalent number of taxes, as described below. Two of these taxes, the federal and provincial income taxes, are combined into one withholding, reducing the number of different withholding tables included in the payroll deduction tables booklet to the following three:

- Canada pension plan
- Employment insurance
- Federal income tax and provincial income tax

Of these, the income taxes are payable only by employees and the remaining two taxes are paid by both employer and employee. The pension plan withholding for the employee is matched by the employer, but in the case of employment insurance, the employer pays 1.4 times the employee's amount. In contrast to the United States, rates are not differentiated for different employer lay-off experiences.

Other Payroll Taxes

In addition to the above four withholdings (counting federal and provincial income taxes separately) there are two, and in some provinces three, additional taxes:

- Medical insurance
- Workers' compensation
- Various taxes that go under the names of Health and Welfare, or Health and Education

In some provinces, medical insurance is paid by both employee and employer in varying percentages depending upon the province, or according to a union contract. In other provinces, the medical insurance tax is included in the income tax withholding amounts.

INDEPENDENT CONTRACTOR

Sometimes it is necessary to hire personnel on an independent contract basis. Such persons work for several business entities without becoming the exclusive employee of any one of them. Examples of this type of worker are temporary help, musicians or entertainers, and cleaning people. The employer is not responsible for deducting employee payroll taxes and does not incur liability for employer's payroll taxes when hiring workers on an independent contract basis. Certain requirements of the IRS must be complied with in order to classify a worker as an independent contractor. Because of their complexity, IRS regulations concerning this matter must be considered in-depth before deciding that a business does not have to withhold and pay payroll taxes on a worker.

RECORDING THE PAYROLL

As is the case with regard to all other procedures for recording accounting information the payroll recording procedure must not only record all data accurately but must also give management access to the recorded data in a meaningful manner that will help management make good decisions. Also, the procedure must provide a trail by which management can trace recorded data in a logical manner to find any recording errors. To meet these requirements an effective payroll recording system consists of the following three elements:

1. Adequate source documents containing the basic information needed to calculate salaries and wages due
2. A payroll journal to record payroll information compactly and efficiently
3. Employee subsidiary ledgers to provide detailed payroll data concerning each employee

Adequate Source Documents

Every employer should have an employee file, which should contain, as a minimum, the employee's application, employment contract and any amendments thereto, any voluntary payroll deduction authorizations, and the W-4 form. The contract should specify the employee's salary, if salaried, or hourly wage rate. It should also specify the overtime pay rate, number of days sick leave allowed, holidays allowed, and employee benefits such as pension and insurance plans.

Additionally, for wage-earning employees, a record of hours worked and, in the case of overtime hours, an authorization slip (see Exhibit 8–6) is recommended. A supervisor's authorization is important to control overtime hours, which are paid at a higher rate. The record of hours worked may be maintained manually by a supervisor, but a commonly used record of time worked is the clock punch time card. This card, plus any overtime authorization slip, is turned in to the accounting department weekly and serves as the basis for determining the weekly gross wage amount.

The Payroll Journal

After the employee's gross earnings have been determined, the necessary payroll information is recorded in the payroll journal, also called the payroll register. The payroll journal is a special-purpose journal designed to:

- Facilitate the process of recording and posting payroll information
- Accumulate information for preparing payroll tax reports
- Record all payroll information compactly in one journal

```
┌─────────────────────────────────────────┐
│           Overtime Authorization          │
├─────────────────────────────────────────┤
│ Employee Name: _____   │
│                                           │
│ Date overtime to be worked: _____    │
│                                           │
│ _____    _____      │
│ Date signed          Supervisor           │
└─────────────────────────────────────────┘
```

Exhibit 8–6 Employee overtime record form.

A sample payroll journal is shown in Exhibit 8–7 along with its related general ledger accounts. The journal includes a date column, a column for the name of the employee being paid, and the usual Ref. column, where a check is made to indicate that the appropriate employee's individual subsidiary ledger account has been updated with the current payroll information.

The expense distribution columns are used to record the employee's gross pay as an expense (debit) of the department where he or she works. There is a sundry column for recording the salaries and wages of employees in minor departments. After the expense distribution columns come the deductions columns for recording payroll tax deductions and other employee-authorized deductions. Since these must be paid by the employer to third parties, they are recorded as liabilities (credits) on the employer's balance sheet. Finally, to the far right is the net pay column for recording the amount of pay actually received by the employee.

The payroll shown in Exhibit 8–7 was paid in cash. A check was drawn for the total amount in the net pay column and each employee's net pay amount was placed in an envelope along with a pay slip. The pay slip contains all the necessary information to enable an employee to verify that the net pay has been properly calculated. When a payroll is paid by check, an additional column is added to the payroll journal for entering the check number. In this case, the pay slip is usually an integral part of the payroll check.

Employee Subsidiary Ledger

The employee subsidiary ledger contains a detailed breakdown per employee of all information contained in the general ledger payroll expense accounts and payroll-related liability accounts. This detailed information:

- Helps management verify that it has followed correct payroll procedures
- Provides employee information during the year if requested, and at year-end on form W-2
- Helps management prepare payroll tax reports to the IRS and the local governments

A sample employee subsidiary ledger is shown in Exhibit 8–8. A subsidiary ledger contains all required information for calculating employee's pay. It also contains a detailed record of an employee's payment dates, gross salary or wages, payroll deductions, and net pay. If the employee were paid by check it would also contain a record of the paycheck numbers.

Each employee subsidiary ledger is usually totaled quarterly. A subsidiary ledger schedule (a total of all the individual subsidiary ledger balances) is then prepared to verify the balances in the general ledger departmental salaries and wages accounts as well as other information to be presented on the quarterly

Payroll Journal

Date 2002	Employee	Ref.	Rooms #606 DR	Food #607 DR	Administrative and General #608 DR	Sundry Account	No.	Ref.	Amount	Withheld Federal Income Tax No. 230 CR	Social Security Tax No. 233 CR	Medicare Tax No. 235 CR	Savings Plan No. 237 CR	Medical Insurance No. 239 CR	Net Pay Cash Acct. No. 101 CR
Oct.															
14	Michelle Brandon	✓		200						16	12	3		20	149
14	Michael Carver	✓			1000					80	62	15	100	40	703
14	Juan Gonzalez	✓	700							65	43	10	50	60	472
14	Barbara Norden	✓	200							23	12	3		20	142
14	Maria Perez	✓			2000					120	124	29	150	60	1517
14	Paul Lejeune	✓				Pool	609	✓	500	50	31	7		40	372
14	Hangbo Kim	✓	300							41	19	4	10	20	206
14	Pik Wei Lam	✓		300						26	19	4		40	211
			1200	500	3000				500	421	322	75	310	300	3772
			(606)	(607)	(608)					(230)	(233)	(235)	(237)	(239)	(101)

Partial General Ledger

Cash   No. 101

10/13/02	Bal.	10,000	10/14/02	PRJ-11	3,772
10/14/02	Bal.	6,228			

Withheld Federal Income Tax Payable   No. 230

10/13/02	Bal.	8,750
10/14/02	PRJ-11	421
10/14/02	Bal.	9,171

Social Security Tax Payable   No. 233

10/13/02	Bal.	6,622
10/14/02	PRJ-11	322
10/14/02	Bal.	6,944

Medicare Tax Payable   No. 235

10/13/02	Bal.	1,549
10/14/02	PRJ-11	75
10/14/02	Bal.	1,624

Due to Savings Plan Fund   No. 237

10/13/02	Bal.	2,550
10/14/02	PRJ-11	310
10/14/02	Bal.	2,860

Rooms Salaries & Wages   No. 606

10/13/02	Bal.	30,000
10/14/02	PRJ-11	1,200
10/14/02	Bal.	31,200

Food Salaries & Wages   No. 607

10/13/02	Bal.	13,000
10/14/02	PRJ-11	500
10/14/02	Bal.	13,500

Administrative & General Salaries & Wages   No. 608

10/13/02	Bal.	62,000
10/14/02	PRJ-11	3,000
10/14/02	Bal.	65,000

Pool Salaries & Wages   No. 609

10/13/02	Bal.	7,000
10/14/02	PRJ-11	500
10/14/02	Bal.	7,500

Exhibit 8–7   Sample payroll journal.

Michelle Brandon's Subsidiary Ledger

Name: Michelle Brandon
      1325 S.W. 16 Ave.
      Miami, Florida 33111

Social Security No.: 999-99-9999
Birthdate: March 10, 1978
Other Deductions: Med. Ins. $20/week
Number of Allowances: 2

Marital Status: Married
Regular Rate: $5.00

Overtime Rate: $7.50

Payroll Date	Hours Worked		Gross Earnings	Withhold Federal Income Tax	Social Security Tax	Medicare Tax	Other Deductions		Net Pay
	Regular	Overtime					Savings Plan	Medical Insurance	
10/07/02	40	2	215	18	13	3		20	161
10/14/02	40		200	16	12	3		20	149

Exhibit 8–8 Michelle Brandon's partial subsidiary ledger. There are no entries prior to October 7, 1998, nor totals for the previous quarters because the October 7, 2002 pay period was this employee's first with the company. Refer to the payroll journal in Exhibit 8–7 to ascertain the source of the October 14, 2002 payroll data.

197

payroll tax reports to the local and federal governments. Having quarterly totals also facilitates the preparation of W-2 forms at year end, since only four amounts need be added to verify annual totals.

Journalizing a Payroll and Posting to the Employee Subsidiary Ledger

The steps for recording a payroll are as follows:

1. Enter the date on which the payroll period ends in the date column.
2. Enter the name of the employee in the Employee column.
3. Enter the amount of the employee's gross salary or wages in the column for the department to which it will be charged. If it is to be charged to a department with few employees it should be entered in the sundry columns by entering the name of the account, the account number, and the amount.
4. The amount of withheld federal income tax to be deducted is obtained from IRS Circular E based on the employee's W-4 information and is entered in the column marked accordingly.
5. The social security and medicare tax to be deducted is calculated on the employee's gross salary or wage amount and is entered in the social security and medicare tax columns.
6. Any voluntary deductions, such as those listed earlier in the chapter, would be entered in their appropriate columns. In this example two voluntary deductions are available—a savings plan and medical insurance.
7. All of the deduction amounts are subtracted from the employee's gross salary or wages, and the net pay amount is entered in the net pay column.
8. Enter the above information on each employee's subsidiary ledger and make a check in the Ref. column appearing immediately after the employee's name.

Posting to the General Ledger

After the payroll is complete, the information is posted to the general ledger as follows:

1. Total the various columns in the payroll journal, including the miscellaneous amount column.
2. Add the totals across (crossfoot) to determine that the total of all the debit columns equals the total of all the credit columns.
3. Post the column totals to their general ledger accounts, except for the sundry column.
4. Below each account column total in the payroll journal enter the number of the general ledger account to which it was posted.
5. Post each amount in the sundry column to its general ledger account individually and make a check in the sundry Ref. column next to each posted amount.

PAYROLL ACCRUAL

When a firm's accounting period cut-off date does not coincide with the end of a payroll period, an accrual entry must be made to record the partial pay period that falls within the current accounting period. For example, if a business' accounting period ends on a Thursday, April 30, and it pays its next payroll on Friday, May 1, then all the salaries and wages since the previous Friday, April 24,

Assumptions

Department:	Rooms
Payroll period ends:	January 2
Accounting period ends:	December 31
Days in work week:	7 days
Payroll amount:	$700.00
Withheld income tax for pay period:	$ 70.00
Social security tax for pay period:	43.40
Medicare tax for pay period:	$ 10.15
Savings plan deduction for pay period:	$ 35.00
Federal unemployment tax for pay period:	$ 5.60
State unemployment tax for pay period:	$ 18.90

Accrual Entry

	Dr	Cr
Employee's salaries		
Room's salaries and wages	500.00	
Accrued salaries and wages payable		500.00
Employer's payroll taxes		
Social security tax expense	31.00	
Medicare tax expense	7.25	
Federal unemployment tax expense	4.00	
State unemployment tax expense	13.50	
Social security tax payable		31.00
Medicare tax payable		7.25
Federal unemployment taxes payable		4.00
State unemployment taxes payable		13.50

To accrue five-sevenths of the seven-day pay period ending January 2

Exhibit 8–9   Sample accrual entry.

will not be recorded until the day after the accounting books are closed, on May 1. As a result this expense will be recorded in the following accounting period.

In order to record the payroll for the six days since the last pay date (Friday, April 24), which will not be recorded in April through the normal accounting process, it is necessary to make an accrual entry for these six days' payroll. To do this, the normal expense accounts are debited. But instead of crediting the cash account, the appropriate accrued expenses payable accounts are credited.

This accrual entry must not include accruals for withheld taxes nor amounts corresponding to voluntary employee deductions since these do not become a liability of the firm until the payroll is actually paid. A sample accrual entry, along with the assumptions upon which it is based, is presented in Exhibit 8–9.

COMPUTERS IN PAYROLL ACCOUNTING

A computerized payroll system makes all payroll calculations, prints out employees' checks, prints payroll tax checks to the government, and updates the general ledger and employees' subsidiary ledgers automatically. It also prints out all required government reporting forms. It can do this because it contains the following information in its memory:

- A list of salaried employees and their salary amounts
- The hourly rate and overtime rate of wage earning employees

- All required and voluntary deductions
- Employee payroll tax rates
- The department to which each employee's salary is to be charged

Only the hours worked by each employee and any changes in employee salaries, wages, or deductions need to be entered in the computer before it prints out all required payroll documents.

Some computerized payroll systems, called after-the-fact payroll systems, are not programmed to print checks or to calculate deductions and net pay amount. All payroll information must be calculated manually and entered into the computer. The computer system will then prepare a payroll journal and individual employee subsidiary ledgers and will print out the necessary information for preparing government payroll tax reports. Some after-the-fact systems will also print out all government reports in the proper format and will print W-2 and W-3 forms at year end.

IMPACT OF THE WAGE-HOUR LAW ON PAYROLL ACCOUNTING

Commonly known as the wage-hour law, the Fair Labor Standard Act was passed by Congress in 1938. It was not made applicable to hotels and restaurants until 1967, when food and beverage establishments having sales of at least $250,000 were brought under the Act. Effective December 31, 1981, this limit has been increased to $362,000. The wage-hour law is a complicated and intricate act including more than 20 amendments or additions. Its impact on the hospitality industry is felt mainly through the following provisions:

- It establishes the tip credit.
- It establishes a minimum hourly wage.
- It establishes (as of this writing) the minimum overtime pay rate as one and one half times the basic hourly rate and specifies that any hours over 40 worked during a week must be paid at the overtime rate. It also provides tests to determine which employees are exempt from the minimum wage and minimum overtime rate.
- It defines employer record-keeping requirements.

We have already discussed the effect of overtime and overtime rates on payroll accounting. In this section, we explain the tip credit and its relationship to the minimum wage, and briefly review how properly maintained payroll records aid in complying with the record keeping requirements of the Act.

The Tip Credit

The tip credit, which has great impact on the hospitality industry because of its large number of tip-earning employees, was instituted by The Fair Labor Standard Act on January 1, 1980. As of this writing, this provision of the Act allows an employer to consider, as part of the employee's minimum wage, a certain amount of the tips received and kept by an employee who earns more than $30 a month in tips. These tips, used to fulfill the minimum wage requirements are called "tips deemed wages." An employer may apply up to $3.02/hour of an employee's tip income against the employer's minimum wage payment requirement, which is currently $5.15 per hour. Employees may be paid an hourly wage as low as $2.13 ($5.15 − $3.02) if they actually earn and keep tips equivalent to at least

$3.02/hour. The total of the minimum $2.13 of direct wages paid by an employer plus the tips earned by a tip-earning employee may never be less than the minimum wage of $5.15.

Although the tip credit provision is quite clear in its intent, it has secondary implications with regard to payroll accounting procedures and related record-keeping requirements. These requirements of the wage-hour law are rather far-ranging. The most pertinent requirements for a hospitality firm are that records in the following areas be maintained accurately for each employee and preserved by an employer for at least two years (and in some cases three years):

- Actual time worked
- Overtime paid
- Employees compensated with board, lodging, or other facility
- Employees exempt from the law
- Tipped employees

In order to avoid violating tip credit provisions, separate records of wages, tips deemed wages, and tips must also be maintained. This separation is made most easily on the payroll journal and employee subsidiary ledgers by adding additional columns for tips and tips deemed wages, thus allowing ready verification of the fact that the minimum wage requirement has been met. The separate recording in the payroll journal and employee subsidiary ledgers of wages, tips deemed wages, and tips also facilitates compliance with payroll tax reporting requirements for tips, which, as we shall see in the following section, are different than those for salaries and wages.

Reporting Tip Income

Not only do tips constitute a significant form of remuneration in the hospitality industry, but they also entail more complex IRS reporting requirements. All employees who earn $20 or more per month in tips while working for one employer must report these tips to their employer by the tenth day of the following month on IRS form 4070—Employee's Report of Tips to Employer—shown in Exhibit 8–10. A subsidiary form, 4070A, is used by an employee to record daily tip income, but is not submitted to the employer (see Exhibit 8–11).

Although he or she does not report tips less than $20 per month to the employer, employees are still responsible for reporting these tips on their year-end tax return.

Form **4070** (Rev. March 1975) Department of the Treasury Internal Revenue Service	Employee's Report of Tips to Employer	Social Security Number
Employee's name and address		Tips received directly from customers . $
Employer's name and address		Tips received on charge receipts . . $
Month or shorter period in which tips were received		
from _____ , 19 ___ , to _____ , 19 ___		Total tips . $
Signature		Date

Exhibit 8–10 IRS Form 4070—Employee's Report of Tips to Employer.

Employee's Daily Record of Tips

Employer's name

Month		Year	
Date	Tips received directly from customers	Tips received on charge receipts	
1	$	$	
2			
3			
4			
5			
6			
7			
8			
9			
10			
11			
12			
13			
14			
15			
16			
Sub-totals	$	$	

(Continued on back)   Form 4070A   (Rev. 3–75)

Exhibit 8–11   Form 4070A—Employee's Daily Record of Tips.

Employers must know the amount of tips earned by each employee because they are required by the IRS to deduct the employee's social security and medicare tax and income tax withholding from the employee's wages. This requirement applies to all tips, both those deemed wages and those not deemed wages. If the employee's gross wages are insufficient to cover all required tax deductions, the employer must report this undeducted amount to the IRS at year end on form W-2. It must be understood of course that social security taxes are withheld from the employee's wages and tips, and additionally are payable as a tax to the employer, only up to the maximum earnings subject to the social security tax (this limit was $80,400 in 2001). There is no earnings limit for the medicare tax, all wages and tips are subject to this tax no matter how large they may be.

	Reported tips deemed wages	Reported tips not deemed wages
Employee social security tax and withheld income tax deduction required	Yes	Yes
Employer liable for FICA taxes (Social Security and Medicare)	Yes	Yes

Tip-Reporting Requirement in TEFRA

An additional tip-reporting requirement incorporated in the Tax and Equity Fiscal Responsibility Act (TEFRA) applies to establishments that serve food or beverage, employ 10 or more employees, and are not fast-food or carry-out establishments. Every employer falling under the Act and whose employees, as a group, are not reporting tips equivalent to at least 8 percent of the establishment's gross receipts must allocate additional tip income to its employees in order to achieve this required 8 percent level.

These allocated tips are called imputed tips. Allocation may be made by negotiation with each employee, according to hours worked, or by a direct method such as the server's name on checks or receipts. No withheld income tax, social security tax, or medicare tax must be deducted from an employee's wages for imputed tips, nor is an employer liable for its social security and medicare tax on imputed tips—the employer must merely report them to the IRS at year-end. Employees, of course, must include these imputed tips as part of their earnings on their personal income tax return at year-end.

A certain amount of relief from the 8 percent requirement may be available on an individual establishment basis if an employer believes that tips actually received are less than 8 percent of gross sales. In this case, the employer may request from the IRS a reduction to the actual percentage, but never less than 5 percent. The merits of each individual request determine whether or not it is granted.

CONTROLLING SALARIES AND WAGES EXPENSE

Because salaries and wages are such a significant part of hospitality industry expenses, it is of primary importance to control them effectively. A twofold approach to this problem is the most effective and consists of (1) adequate planning, and (2) implementation of certain measures, called internal control procedures, to minimize the possibility of willful or involuntary errors in executing payroll functions.

Adequate planning of personnel needs is important because it avoids waste through overstaffing. This is accomplished by defining job tasks and employee productivity, and by preparing estimates of future sales in order to tailor the workforce to a firm's actual needs more closely.

Internal control procedures involve the separation of responsibility for the following payroll functions:

- Control of personnel files
- Preparation of the payroll
- Paying employees
- Recording payroll information
- Reconciling the payroll bank account

By dividing responsibility for these functions among different employees, the probability of discovering errors or fraud increases since the employees involved in the payroll function will be reviewing each other's work. Also, certain established procedures may be used to increase internal control:

- Require two signatures on important documents such as checks or when making changes in personnel file documents
- Use card punch time clocks to help assure that the correct time is entered on the card

- Rotate payroll personnel; rotated personnel have a better chance to discover errors previously undetected
- Require a supervisor's written authorization of overtime hours

In addition, properly designed management reports enable management to detect unusual changes in a payroll-related account. Showing payroll-related accounts in as much detail as possible facilitates the detection of small changes in accounting balances. Similarly, showing the percentage relationship of the various payroll expenses to sales or to some other logical standard of reference facilitates detection of small changes in amounts. Showing comparison amounts for previous periods also makes unusual variations stand out.

However, even the most elaborately designed internal control system can be overcome with time if there is collusion among employees. Frequent management review of payroll functions is therefore necessary. This review should not only determine that current internal control procedures are being carried out effectively but should also include a review of the procedures themselves in case changes in the accounting system may have made some procedures obsolete.

SOME KEY TERMS INTRODUCED IN THIS CHAPTER

1. **Accrued payroll.** When a business closes its accounting books on a day other than a payday, the payroll expense since the last pay period up to the closing date is not included in the closed out period. To correct this error the payroll for these days must be accrued, that is entered in the general journal through an accrual adjusting entry.
2. **After-the-fact payroll.** A computerized payroll system that does not print checks nor calculate pay amounts. The payroll data must be entered into the program after-the-fact. The program then proceeds to summarize the data and prepare W-2, W-3 and other payroll related forms for submission to the appropriate government agencies.
3. **Base amount.** The amount of salaries or wages that is subject to the social security tax. Any salaries and wages greater than the base rate paid out in any one year are not subject to this tax.
4. **Circular E.** A publication of the Internal Revenue Service that is also called the "Employer's Withholding Tax Guide," which contains tables and instructions indicating how employers are to withhold taxes due by their employees.
5. **Depositary receipts.** An IRS form that is submitted by employers to banks whenever they deposit federal taxes that they owe as employers, as well as taxes that have been withheld from their employees.
6. **Employee subsidiary ledger.** The subsidiary ledger that contains all the employee's personal pay data on a cumulative basis throughout the year, such as gross pay, net pay, and all withholding amounts.
7. **Employer identification number.** *See* Form SS-4.
8. **Fair labor standards act.** Law passed in 1938 which, among other things, establishes the tip credit, minimum wage, minimum overtime pay and employer record-keeping requirements.
9. **Federal Insurance Contributions Act (FICA).** The law which initially established the social security system and was later expanded to include medicare.
10. **FICA.** *See* Federal Insurance Contributions Act (FICA).
11. **Form SS-4.** The IRS form used by employers to request an employer identification number (EIN) from the IRS. This number is used whenever the

employer makes a payment, submits a tax form, or communicates with the Internal Revenue Service in any way.

12. **Form UCT-6.** The form, used in the state of Florida, for employers to report and submit their state unemployment tax payments. Other states have similar forms, but with different names.

13. **Form W-2.** The IRS form used by employers to communicate to their employees their total earnings, and withheld tax amounts annually.

14. **Form W-3.** The IRS form used by employers to summarize the data contained on all the W-2 forms they prepare. It serves as a control to enable employers to verify that they have sent all required W-2 forms and to enable the social security service to verify that it has received all W-2 forms included in form W-3.

15. **Form W-4.** The IRS form used by employees to communicate personal information to their employers, for example marital status and withholding allowances, that employers need to properly withhold taxes from the employee's pay.

16. **Form 940.** An IRS form used to report annually to the IRS the amount of FUTA tax paid during the year.

17. **Form 941.** The IRS form used by employers to report quarterly to the IRS the amount of withheld income tax, plus employer and employee portions of the social security and medicare taxes.

18. **Forms 4070 and 4070A.** Forms designed by the IRS to facilitate tip reporting. Form 4070A is to be used by tip earning employees to keep track of tips received. Form 4070 is used to report tips to an employer.

19. **FUTA tax.** The federal unemployment tax, proceeds of which are used to gather unemployment statistics throughout the United States.

20. **Gross pay.** The total amount of pay that an employee earns. This amount is the pay before deducting all payroll taxes and any voluntary deductions requested by an employee.

21. **Imputed tips.** *See* TEFRA

22. **Income tax.** Tax on the income generated by a business or individual.

23. **Independent contractor.** A worker who works for various employers and usually works under his or her own supervision and using his or her own equipment. The full definition, however, is quite complex. The advantage of hiring a worker as an independent contractor is that the employer is not responsible for paying employer payroll taxes on their pay, nor for withholding payroll taxes from their pay.

24. **Internal Revenue Code.** The tax law created by congress to authorize the taxation of individuals and businesses.

25. **Internal Revenue Service.** The government agency created by Congress to collect taxes and otherwise enforce the Internal Revenue Code.

26. **Medicare tax.** A tax imposed by the federal government on both employers and employees, used to help retired employees cover their medical expenses.

27. **Net pay.** The amount of an employee's gross pay that he or she receives after all payroll taxes and any voluntary amounts have been deducted.

28. **Overtime rate.** The hourly pay rate which employers are obliged by the Fair Labor Standards Act to pay hourly employees when they work more than 40 hours per week, currently one and one half times the regular hourly rate.

29. **Payroll journal.** The special-purpose journal designed specifically for recording the payment of payrolls. When a payroll is recorded in a payroll journal it should not be recorded in the general journal. The employer's payroll taxes are, however, still recorded in the general journal.

30. **Salary.** Remuneration received by an employee who is not compensated on an hourly basis.

31. **Social security tax.** A tax imposed by the federal government on both employers and employees, used to pay retirement benefits to employees.
32. **SUTA tax.** The state unemployment tax, proceeds of which are used to pay unemployment benefits to workers who have been laid off from their jobs.
33. **TEFRA.** The Tax Equity and Fiscal Responsibility Act passed in 1982. This law is designed to minimize employee under reporting of tips. One of its provisions creates "imputed tips"—a minimum level of tips required to be reported to the IRS by certain types of employers of tip earning employees.
34. **Tip credit.** The Fair Labor Standards Act allows employers to consider up to $3.02 of employees tips as part of the minimum wage of $5.15. This is called the tip credit.
35. **Tips deemed wages.** The amount of tips that an employer can count as part of the minimum wage paid to their tip earning employees—currently $3.02. *See also* Tip credit.
36. **Voluntary deduction.** This is a deduction from his or her pay that an employee voluntarily requests the employer to make and remit to specific entities, such as medical insurance plans, savings plans or unions.
37. **Wages.** Remuneration of an employee based on an hourly rate, multiplied by the number of hours worked.
38. **Wage-Hour Law.** This is a popular name for the Fair Labor Standards Act passed in 1938. *See* Fair Labor Standards Act.
39. **Withheld income tax.** The withholding of part of an employee's salaries or wages by an employer as an advance payment of the employee's income tax. Withheld income tax amounts are remitted to the Internal Revenue Service by the employer.
40. **Withholding allowance.** A withholding allowance enables an employee to automatically deduct a specific amount on his or her tax return thereby reducing the income tax they must pay. This deduction amount increases from year to year based on inflation.
41. **Workers' compensation insurance.** An insurance policy, required by all states, that employers must buy in order to protect their employees from any harm they may suffer while on the job.

QUESTIONS

1. On average, what percentage of every revenue dollar is used to pay salaries and wages and related expenses in the hospitality industry?
2. What are three deductions an employer may make from employees' earnings?
3. Excluding workers' compensation insurance, what taxes must an employer pay on the earnings of its employees?
4. How are deductions from an employee's pay recorded on the books of the employer? How are the employer's payroll taxes recorded on the employer's books?
5. What is the difference between an employee and an independent contractor? Describe the differences in the procedure involved in paying each.
6. What is the function of the following IRS forms? (a) W-4 (b) W-2 and W-3 (c) 941 (d) 940 (e) SS-4
7. How often must an employer file form 941? form 940? How often must an employer pay social security, medicare taxes and withheld income taxes to the federal government? Federal unemployment taxes?
8. What payroll functions should not be performed by the same person in order to maximize internal control?

9. Besides internal control procedures, what other procedures are there for controlling payroll and related expenses?
10. When should payroll and related expenses be accrued?
11. What is the tip credit? What is the maximum amount of the tip credit?
12. What law governs overtime hours, the overtime rate, and the tip credit?
13. What are imputed tips? What law created imputed tips? What type of employers must report imputed tips?
14. What act requires an employer to report imputed tips and how is the amount of imputed tips determined?
15. Must an employer pay FICA tax on reported tips that are not deemed wages? On imputed tips? On tips deemed wages?
16. Where would you look (1) If you wanted to know how much one of your employees was paid up to the previous pay period? (2) If you wanted to know how much income tax was withheld from an employee during the year?
17. Where would you look if you want to know how much your entire payroll was last week?
18. What payroll records might you want to see in order to verify whether or not a mistake was made in paying a wage-earning employee?

EXERCISES

1. Based on the page from Circular E provided in this text (Exhibit 8–1) specify the dollar amount to be withheld from the pay of each of the following employees:
   (a) Maria Rivera is single and earned $440 this week. She takes care of her mother who is considered to be her dependent for tax purposes.
   (b) John Matthews is married and has two children. His weekly pay is $1,280.
   (c) Rousseau Etienne is married and has three children. His weekly pay is $1,245.
2. The Funway Travel Agency's fiscal year ends September 30, 1998, a Friday. The company's payroll cut-off date is Wednesday, September 28, 1998, in order to give the company time to prepare the payroll by Friday, the company's payday. The following information is available concerning the Funway Travel Agency.
   - Average daily gross payroll, $700
   - Average daily withheld income taxes, $100
   - Social security tax for 1998 on maximum earnings per Exhibit 8.2, 6.2%
   - Medicare tax for 1998, 1.45%
   - State unemployment tax base rate on maximum earnings of $7,000, 2.7%
   - Funway Travel Agency's state unemployment tax experience rate, 4%
   - Federal unemployment tax rate is 6.2%, less 5.4% if SUTA tax is paid on time. Assume timely payment of SUTA tax
   - No employee had cumulative gross earnings in excess of $6,000
   - Ignore workers' compensation insurance
   - Round amounts to nearest dollar
   (a) Does the Funway Travel Agency need to accrue any payroll or payroll taxes before closing its books on September 30?
   (b) If so, prepare the accrual entry.
3. The Stamfort Hotel pays its bellhops less than the minimum wage, whenever reported tips are sufficient to allow it to do so. The following wage and tip information is provided concerning John Willing, a hotel bellhop,

for the week ended November 21, 1998 (round amounts to nearest dollar):
- Hours worked during the week, 40 hours
- Tips earned and reported during the week, $120
- His hourly wage is $8.00 per hour. His employer takes advantage of the tip credit
- John Willing's cumulative gross earnings (wages plus tips) through November 14, 1998, $60,000
- Social Security tax rate, 6.2% on maximum earnings, per Exhibit 8–2.
- Medicare tax rate, 1.45%
- Withheld income taxes per Circular E (Exhibit 8–1); John Willing is single
- State unemployment tax base rate is 2.7% on maximum earnings of $7,000
- Federal unemployment tax rate is 6.2%, less 5.4% if employer pays SUTA tax on time. Assume timely payment of SUTA tax
- Ignore workers' compensation insurance

(a) Calculate John Willing's hourly tip earnings. How much does the Stamfort hotel have to pay him in order to comply with the Fair Labor Standards Act based on John Willing's hourly tip earnings?

(b) Show the journal entry to record John Willing's wages, tips deemed wages, and payroll taxes, as well as his employer's payroll tax liabilities.

SHORT PROBLEMS

1. For the following employees, based on the 1998 base pay shown in Exhibit 8–2, as well as on any pertinent information concerning the medicare tax, FUTA and SUTA given in this chapter, determine:
   - the amount of social security tax that must be withheld from their pay,
   - the amount of social security tax that their employer must pay,
   - the amount of medicare tax that must be withheld from their pay,
   - the amount of medicare tax that their employer must pay,
   - the amount of FUTA and SUTA that must be withheld from their pay,
   - the amount of FUTA and SUTA that their employer must pay.

   (a) Jose Pacheco earned $68,400 up to the previous pay period. During the current period he will earn $3,000.

   (b) Tone Rettedal earned $68,000 up to the previous pay period. During the current pay period she will be paid $2,000.

   (c) Hang Bok Kim earned $35,000 up to the previous pay period. During the current pay period she will earn $500.

   (d) Roseanne Winarto earned $6,500 up to the previous pay period. During the current pay period she will be paid $700.

   (e) Kiyoaki Yanase earned $5,000 up to the previous pay period. During this pay period he will be paid $1,800.

2. Melisa Forthright works for the Glendale Restaurant. She is married with no children, but does not claim her husband as a deduction, so she just has one withholding allowance. Melisa Forthright was paid for the week ended September 12, 1998 as follows:

   Assumptions:
   - Cumulative gross earnings as of September 5, 1998, $67,400
   - No state income tax
   - Ignore worker's compensation insurance
   - Medicare tax rate, 1.45%
   - State unemployment tax base rate on maximum earnings of $7,000, 2.7%

- Federal unemployment tax rate is 6.2% less 5.4% if state unemployment taxes are paid on time
- Social security tax rate for 1998 on maximum earnings, 6.2%

Pay data:
- Gross salary, $1,370
- Federal income tax withheld, $250
- Weekly deduction for union dues, $100

3. The Welcome Home Hotel paid John Wilson for the week ended August 10, 1998, as follows. John Wilson is married and has one child:
- Gross salary, $1,380
- Federal income tax withheld, see Circular E (Exhibit 8–1)
- State income tax withheld, $50
- Weekly deduction for savings account, $100
- Deduction for medical insurance with Helpful Medical Co., $75
- Cumulative gross earnings as of August 3, 1998, $67,000
- Social security tax rate for 1998 on maximum earnings, 6.2% (see Exhibit 8–2)
- Medicare tax rate for 1998 on earnings, 1.45%
- State unemployment tax base rate on maximum earnings of $7,000, 2.7%
- Federal unemployment tax rate is 6.2% less 5.4% if employer pays SUTA tax on time. Assume timely payment of SUTA tax
- Ignore workers' compensation insurance

(a) Based on the specific deduction amounts and payroll tax rates indicated above, as well as any additional information given, show the journal entry or entries required to record John Wilson's pay and the hotel's payroll tax obligations. Round amounts to nearest dollar.

(b) What payroll record would indicate to the hotel the amount of John Wilson's cumulative earnings to date?

4. The following information is given concerning Cirila Mathews, an airline stewardess apprentice (round amounts to nearest dollar):
- Hours worked, 60 hours
- Hourly wage, $5.00
- No special agreement was made with her employer concerning her overtime rate
- Authorized weekly deduction for union dues, $10
- Cumulative earnings to February 7, 1998, $6,000
- Withheld income tax information should be obtained from Exhibit 8–1; Cirila is single
- Social security tax rate for 1998 is 6.2% on maximum earnings per Exhibit 8–2
- State unemployment tax base rate on maximum earnings of $7,000, 2.7%
- The airline's state unemployment tax experience rate, 2%
- Federal unemployment tax rate is 6.2%, less 5.4% if employer pays SUTA tax on time; assume timely payment of SUTA tax
- Ignore workers' compensation insurance

(a) Calculate the journal entry or entries required to record her pay for the week ended February 14, 1998.

(b) What payroll record would indicate to her employer the amount of Cirila Mathews' cumulative earnings to date?

LONG PROBLEMS

1. Based on the following information for the Sleepy Hollow Hotel, perform the following steps. Round amounts to nearest dollar.

Employee	Motel department	Pay rate	Hours worked	Cumulative earnings through Oct. 8, 1998	Married	Dependents	Deductions	
							Save-it plan	Safety Medical, Inc.
C. LaRoux	Rooms	$22/hr	50	$68,000	Yes	3	$60	$100
P. Vanegas	Restaurant	$7.50/hr	40	6,800	No	1	30	60
Ji-Ling Cho	Restaurant	$6/hr	50	9,000	No	2	40	70

(a) Prepare and journalize a payroll journal for the week ended October 15, 1998. Use Exhibit 8–1 to obtain correct withheld income tax amounts. No special agreement concerning the overtime rate was reached with the employees. The company pays by check and the last payroll check number used was 3672. Social security tax is 6.2% in 1998. See Exhibit 8–2 for maximum earnings subject to social security tax in 1998. Medicare tax is 1.45%.

(b) Prepare subsidiary ledgers for each employee and post to them from the payroll journal, using all required posting steps.

(c) Prepare a general journal and record any payroll-related entries that should be recorded in this journal. The state unemployment tax base rate is 2.7% on maximum earnings of $7,000; the company's state unemployment tax experience rate is 4%; the federal unemployment tax rate is 6.2%, less 5.4% if SUTA tax is paid on time. Assume SUTA is paid on a timely basis.

(d) Prepare general ledger "T" accounts and post to them from the payroll journal and general journal. Assume beginning balances are zero.

2. Use the following information from the Princely Palate Restaurant to execute the instructions listed below (round amounts to nearest dollar):

Employee	Motel department	Pay rate	Hours worked	Cumulative earnings through Oct. 8, 1998	Married	Dependents	Deductions		
							Save-it plan	Union dues	State income tax
Yu-Wi Fong	Restaurant	$24/hr	50	$70,000	Yes	3	$70	$150	$60
Britt Houg	Kitchen	$29/hr	40	68,100	Yes	0	40	90	22
Carlos Rivera	Kitchen	$6/hr	50	9,000	No	2	50	80	15
Saul Levy	Restaurant	$8/hr	40	6,800	No	0	50	60	16
Yashi Kagawa	Bar	$5.50/hr	60	6,000	No	7	60	70	16

(a) Prepare and journalize a payroll journal for the week ended November 28, 1998. Use Exhibit 8–1 to obtain the correct withheld income tax amounts. No special agreement regarding overtime rates was reached with the employees. The company pays its payroll in cash. Social security tax is 6.2% in 1998. See Exhibit 8–2 for maximum earnings subject to social security tax in 1998. The medicare tax is 1.45%.

(b) Prepare subsidiary ledgers for the first three employees and post to them from the payroll journal using all required posting steps.

(c) Prepare a general journal and record any payroll related entries that should be recorded in this journal. The state unemployment tax base rate is 2.7% on maximum earnings of $7,000. The company's state unemployment tax experience rate is 2%. The federal unemployment tax rate is 6.2%, less 5.4% if the SUTA tax is paid on time. Assume timely payment of the SUTA tax.

(d) Prepare general ledger "T" accounts and post to them from the payroll journal and general journal. Assume beginning balances are zero.

3. Based on the following information for the week ended October 15, 1998, execute the instructions (a) to (c). (Use 1998 social security tax information from Exhibit 8–2 and income tax withholding information from Exhibit 8–1.) the medicare tax rate is 1.45%.

Employee's name	Giovanni Tromba	Werner Von Horn	Torgay Gensing
Department	Rooms	Coffee Shop	Coffee Shop
Total hours worked	60	50	40
Hourly rate	$18/hr	$6/hr	$7.5/hr
Married	Yes	No	No
Dependents	0	0	1
Union dues	$90	$70	$50
Savings plan	$70	$50	$30
Cumulative year-to-date earnings (1988)	$69,000	$24,000	$6,800
State unemployment tax rate	2.7%	2.7%	2.7%
Federal unemployment tax rate (6.2%–5.4%)	0.8%	0.8%	0.8%

(a) Prepare a weekly payroll journal for the company. The information is for the week ended October 15, 1998. The company pays in cash.

(b) Prepare the journal entry to record salaries and wages expense. In what journal is this entry made?

(c) Prepare the journal entry to record payroll tax expense. In what journal is this entry made?

4. Answer the following questions based on the information given. (Use the 6.2% social security tax rate, the 1.45% medicare tax rate, and assume none of the employees will have earned the maximum subject to the social security tax unless otherwise noted.) Round amounts to nearest cents:

(a) John Smith worked 40 regular hours in one week and reported average weekly tips of $50. What is the minimum hourly wage his employer must pay him?

(b) William Martin worked 30 regular hours in a week and reported average weekly tips of $100. What is the minimum hourly wage his employer must pay him?

(c) Mary Zufa worked 30 regular hours in a week. She was paid wages of $75 and reported tips of $80. What amount does her employer have to withhold in employee FICA tax and how much employer's FICA tax is the employer liable for?

(d) Karl Rogan worked 40 regular hours in a week. He earned $80.40 in wages and reported $115.00 in average weekly tips. His employer also imputed tips amounting to $20 (under a negotiated agreement) because reported tips did not amount to 8% of the food and beverage establishment's gross sales. The establishment had more than 10 tip-earning employees and was considered an elegant restaurant. What amount does his employer have to withhold in employee FICA tax and how much employer's FICA tax must the employer pay?

(e) Paul Walters has earned $68,400 in wages and tips not deemed wages (see Exhibit 8–2) in 1998. His employer has paid him $55,100 in wages. If Paul Walters is paid $200 this week for 40 hours of work and reports $180 in tips, how much FICA tax must his employer withhold from Paul's wages and reported tips? Must the employer withhold income tax from Paul's wages and reported tips? How much FICA tax is the employer liable for?

(f) Marlene Johnston has earned $68,400 in wages, tips deemed wages, and tips not deemed wages (see Exhibit 8–2) in 1998. Her employer has paid her $50,000 in wages and she has earned $6,000 in tips deemed wages during the current year. Her employer paid Marlene $85 in wages and she reported $160 in tips during the current week in which she worked 25 hours. How much FICA tax must the employer withhold from Marlene's wages, tips deemed wages, and tips not deemed wages? Must the employer withhold income taxes from Marlene's wages, tips deemed wages, and tips not deemed wages? How much FICA tax is the employer liable for?

(g) Myrtle Fox has earned $6,900 in 1998. She was paid $300 in weekly wages during the current week. Her employer has a state unemployment tax base rate of 2.7% and an experience rate of 4%, payable on the first $7,000 of wages paid. The federal unemployment tax rate is 3.5%, also payable on the first $7,000 of wages paid, less any necessary adjustment for the appropriate state unemployment tax rate. How much state unemployment tax must her employer pay? How much federal unemployment tax? How much unemployment tax must Myrtle pay?

FINANCIAL STATEMENTS II

The Balance Sheet | 9

The learning objectives of this chapter are:

- To explain the purposes and contents of a classified balance sheet.
- To distinguish between the account and the report formats in preparing a balance sheet.
- To classify assets and liabilities into acceptable categories.
- To prepare a classified balance sheet in good form.
- To understand the statement of retained earnings as a supplementary statement to the balance sheet.
- To review the major contents of the balance sheet of a publicly held company in the hospitality industry.

Financial statements and other accounting reports are the end product of the accounting system. As a final product, the financial statements communicate information to hospitality management and to other users, which will serve as a basis upon which to make rational decisions concerning the future of the hospitality firm.

Hospitality management, as well as creditors, investors, and other users of accounting information are concerned with the analysis and interpretation of the data included in the financial statements. However, before they are ready to understand and use the accounting information effectively, they must be armed with a good understanding of how financial statements are prepared. In achieving this basic accounting understanding, in previous chapters, an in-depth review of how hospitality business transactions are processed through the accounting system was made. This involved identifying the value exchanges, recording them, transferring the recorded entries to a book of final entry (the general ledger), adjusting the account balances at the end of the period by using the financial statement worksheet, and finally preparing the financial statements with the completed worksheet serving as a point of reference.

In previous chapters, we also learned to prepare simple form financial statements. Starting with this chapter, we discuss in greater depth the preparation of formal financial statements. In this chapter, we will emphasize the review of the balance sheet. In Chapter 10, we examine the income statement based on the Uniform System of Accounts for the Lodging Industry presentation.

In addition to the balance sheet and the income statement, a third basic financial statement is required for a complete financial statement presentation: the statement of cash flow. We explained the basic objectives of this third basic financial statement in Chapter 1, but we do not include an in-depth coverage of it because it is befitting to discuss this topic in more advanced textbooks.

This chapter first explains the main objectives for preparing a formal balance sheet, and then describes the scope and content of a properly classified balance sheet. In doing so, an analysis of the major categories of accounts included in a balance sheet of a publicly held company in the hospitality industry is included. We also explain the statement of retained earnings as a supporting statement to the balance sheet and the two balance sheet formats: the account form and the report form, illustrating the main differences in arranging balance sheet items.

THE BALANCE SHEET: SCOPE AND OBJECTIVES

The balance sheet is a status report, that is, it reflects the financial position of a company at a point in time. That is why it is sometimes called "statement of financial position." The balance sheet tells the readers what resources the hospitality firm owns and where these resources came from. The financial position of the hospitality firm is shown by listing the assets (resources owned by the business), its liabilities (creditors' claims), and the equity of the owners of the firm as of a specific date known as the "balance sheet date."

We have seen how the balance sheet is an expanded version of the fundamental accounting equation, and thus expresses the dual-aspect concept of accounting. It follows that the sum of assets shown on the balance sheet must always equal the sum of liabilities plus owners' equity. Up to this point, we have learned to prepare a simple form balance sheet. This format was acceptable for obtaining a good understanding of a balance sheet, its relationship to the income statement, and the duality aspect of how business transactions always affect the different elements of the balance sheet (i.e., every transaction can be expressed in terms of its balance sheet effect).

However, the main objective for preparing a balance sheet is to provide users with useful and reliable information concerning the financial position of the hospitality firm as of the balance sheet date. In achieving this prime objective, the assets, liabilities, and owners' equity are classified into account categories.

CLASSIFIED BALANCE SHEET

There is, indeed, a certain degree of flexibility in classifying assets, liabilities, and owners' equity accounts. Thus, not every hotel, restaurant, airline, cruise line, or travel agency will make the same balance sheet classifications. Nonetheless, we shall examine an acceptable version of a classified balance sheet for a hospitality firm, keeping in mind that other classifications are equally acceptable. A detailed review of the individual balance sheet categories will be included. (Refer to Exhibit 9–1 to aid in understanding the following discussion material.)

ASSETS

Assets are resources or properties owned by the hospitality organization and represent future values owned by the business. A more formal definition of assets is included in the Statement of Financial Concepts No. 3 issued by the Financial Accounting Standards Board (FASB): "Assets are probable future economic benefits obtained or controlled by a particular entity as a result of past transactions or events."

HOSPITALITY SAMPLE FIRM, INC.
Balance Sheet
December 31, 2000
(in thousands of dollars)

Assets

Current assets

Cash	4,080
Short-term investments	600
Accounts receivable, less allowance for doubtful accounts of $20	2,060
Inventories	2,200
Prepaid expenses	1,300
Total current assets	10,240

Property and equipment

Land	16,800
Buildings	73,000
Furniture and equipment	20,100
Total property and equipment	109,900
Less accumulated depreciation	14,100
Net property and equipment	95,800

Other assets

Preopening expenses	2,850
Investments in Subsidiary Co.	10,200
Total other assets	13,050
Total assets	$119,090

Liabilities and Shareholders' Equity

Current liabilities

Current portion of long-term debt	$3,000
Accounts payable	1,400
Income taxes payable	200
Accrued expenses	1,800
Total current liabilities	6,400

Long-term liabilities

Long-term debt, less current installments included above	88,000
Notes payable due 2005	12,000
Total long-term liabilities	100,000
Deferred taxes	4,800

Shareholders' equity

Common stock	1,650
Additional paid-in capital	4,100
Retained earnings	2,140
Total shareholders' equity	7,890
Total liabilities & shareholders' equity	$119,090

Exhibit 9–1   Balance sheet for Hospitality Sample Firm, Inc.

The key points included in this definition are:

- Probable future economic benefits
- Controlled by the organization
- Resulting from past transactions or events

The first key point of this definition (probably future economic benefits) addresses the issue of reasonable expectation. That is, based on the available evidence we can expect a future benefit to the organization that should eventually result in an increase in cash inflows. The second key element of an asset (control feature) relates to the ability of the firm to obtain the future economic benefit as well as give others access to it. The third key element of an asset (past transactions or events) refers to the fact that the transactions giving rise to the future benefit controlled by the firm have already occurred.

Cost is the proper basis to account for assets on the balance sheet, except when there is convincing evidence that cost cannot be recovered, in which case we use the lower of cost or market (replacement value) following the conservatism concept of accounting.

Classification of Assets

For balance sheet purposes, assets are customarily classified into three general categories: current assets, property and equipment, and other assets. However, we already indicated that there is a high degree of flexibility in practice, both in terms of terminology and presentation of specific asset items, especially in the property and equipment and other assets classifications. We shall examine several acceptable alternative presentations throughout this book.

The asset classifications are listed on the balance sheet in their order of liquidity or expected conversion into cash. Thus, current assets are always listed first since they include the most liquid assets.

Current Assets.   Current assets consist of cash and other assets that are reasonably expected to be converted into cash or consumed by the hospitality firm within one year from the balance sheet date, the normal operating cycle of the business. The typical current assets of a hospitality firm include cash, short-term investments, receivables (notes and accounts receivable), inventories, and prepaid expenses. "Deferred income taxes—Current" (representing the tax effects of temporary differences in the bases of current assets and current liabilities for financial and income tax reporting purposes) might also be included under current assets.

Cash.   Since cash is the ultimate measure of liquidity, it is always the first current asset listed on the balance sheet. Cash includes actual currency as well as any type of negotiable instruments that are readily convertible into money. Hence, cash items for an ordinary hotel or restaurant include checking accounts in banks, savings accounts, certificates of deposit, sales drafts signed by credit card customers, and cash on hand (house banks, for example). In all cases, we are referring to unrestricted funds, which are funds that can be used at the firm's discretion at any time.

Short-Term Investments.   Short-term investments, also called marketable securities are investments that can readily be resold whenever cash is needed by the hospitality organization. They include stock investments in other corporations as well as bond investments. Since these investments are intended as a ready source of cash, they are highly liquid, and thus are listed on the balance sheet following cash.

FASB Statement No. 115, "Accounting for Certain Investments in Debt and Equity Securities," requires that stock or debt securities purchased for short-term profit potential be adjusted to current market value with holding gains or losses reported on the income statement.

Accounts Receivable.   Accounts receivable represent amounts due from customers of the hospitality organization for services rendered on credit. These accounts are expected to be realized in cash within one year from the balance sheet date, and thus are listed on the balance sheet as current assets.

As explained in Chapter 7, in a hotel operation there are two principal sets of accounts receivable maintained by the organization: the guest ledger and the city ledger. The guest ledger covers accounts from customers currently registered at the hotel, while the city ledger reflects credit charges by authorized persons or companies who are not registered guests. Both city and guest ledger amounts are combined in the presentation of accounts receivable on the balance sheet.

The amount of accounts receivable is largely dependent on the credit policies of the hospitality firm. It is important to recognize that the faster accounts receivable are converted into cash, the better the financial condition of a company. Moreover, older accounts receivable represent a very difficult management problem. It follows that the establishment of a proper policy covering the extension of credit and the collection of accounts is of utmost importance to a hospitality service company.

Notes Receivable. Short-term notes receivable represent amounts due to the hospitality organization evidenced by a formal written promise to pay the specified amount of money within the normal operating cycle of one year. These notes are usually interest-bearing.

Allowance for Doubtful Accounts. Experience has shown that not all receivables can be collected in full. Consequently, we must provide for possible losses on accounts and notes receivable in order to conform to GAAP. Such provision is included as a direct reduction of the receivables on the balance sheet using the account "allowance for doubtful accounts" (see Exhibit 9–1).

The allowance for doubtful accounts is a contra-asset account since it is shown as a direct reduction of an asset account, notes receivable or accounts receivable.

The amount of the provision for doubtful accounts is based upon historical experience, industry averages, specific appraisal of individual accounts, or other accepted methods. It should represent the portion of accounts and notes receivable estimated to be uncollectible.

Inventories. Inventories consist of merchandise and supplies essential to the conduct of the business. In the hospitality service industry, inventories usually consist of food, beverages, and supplies. As a rule, the hospitality service companies are not inventory intensive, that is, inventories represent a very small fraction of the total assets of the enterprise. Nevertheless, proper inventory control management is an extremely important consideration to many segments of the hospitality industry, especially the foodservice business, because of the perishable nature of food inventory.

Disclosure of the basis for valuing inventories must be stated either on the face of the balance sheet or in an appended footnote. Following GAAP, inventories are valued at the lower of cost or market. A detailed coverage of methods of determining inventory cost is given in Chapter 11.

Prepaid Expenses. Prepaid expenses represent advance payments made by the hospitality firm for benefits expected to be received within one year from the balance sheet date. Typical expenses subject to prepayment in the hospitality industry include insurance, licenses, property taxes, and rent.

Prepaid expenses are included under current assets because they are expected to be consumed by the business within one year from the balance sheet date. They will not be converted into cash but if not paid in advance, they would require the use of current assets during the operating cycle. Therefore, prepaid expenses will become expenses when consumed.

Property and Equipment. Property and equipment comprise long-lived assets (with a useful life in excess of one year) used in the production of revenue. Some common items included under property and equipment in a hospitality company balance sheet are land, building and building improvements, furniture fixtures and equipment, transportation equipment, and improvements to leased property (leasehold improvements). These assets are usually listed on the balance sheet according to their degree of permanence. However, there is no uniformity in the way hospitality companies do this.

All property and equipment, with the exception of land, have a limited useful life, and thus we allocate the cost of these assets over their estimated useful life in accordance with GAAP. (We have already noted that this allocation process is referred to as depreciation.) The property and equipment are then shown on the balance sheet at net book value, which is cost less accumulated depreciation.

Accumulated Depreciation. The accumulated depreciation represents the total amount of the property and equipment that have been depreciated from the time of purchase to the balance sheet date. It is a contra-asset account, appearing as a deduction from the total cost of the property and equipment on the balance sheet.

Other Assets. Other items having a probable future economic benefit to the hospitality firm that do not fit the criteria of current assets or property and equipment should either be listed separately or grouped under the general category "other assets." Some examples of "other assets" are deferred charges, cash surrender value of life insurance, long-term investments, security deposits, long-term receivables, and intangible assets (goodwill, trademarks, franchises). Cash balances that are restricted to the acquisition of property and equipment or payment of obligations could also be included in this classification.

There is no uniform way to present other assets on the balance sheet. Some hospitality firms may show, for example, investments and advances to affiliates and others as a separate heading following total current assets. Conversely, other firms may include these long-term investments under other assets or as a separate category following property and equipment.

Long-Term Investments. Long-term investments comprise investments in securities of other corporations, which are either (1) not readily marketable, or (2) not intended as a ready source of cash, and include investments in affiliated companies made for control purposes. In such cases, any amounts due from these affiliates for cash advances are combined with the corresponding investment account on the balance sheet.

A common type of long-term investment for control purposes is the establishment of a parent-subsidiary relationship whereby the parent company has the ability to exert influence or legal control over the subsidiary by virtue of owning more than 50 percent of the outstanding shares of stock of the subsidiary company.

Deferred Charges. Deferred charges (also referred to as deferred expenses) represent long-term prepayments for expenditures that are expected to benefit several future periods. In the hospitality industry we find such items as organization costs, prepaid financing costs, and prepaid advertising included under deferred charges.

Cash Surrender Value of Officers' Life Insurance. The cash surrender value of officers' life insurance refers to the cash value accumulated up to the balance sheet date on the life insurance policies covering the lives of certain officers and other key members of the hospitality organization. Since it is not the company's intention to cancel or surrender the insurance policy in the normal course of business, this long-term future value is shown under other assets on the balance sheet.

Intangible Assets. Intangible assets are assets with no physical existence possessing rights that are of future value to the hospitality firm. All intangible assets are charged to operations (expensed) through the process of amortization, which involves the systematic recording of periodic charges to operations over the estimated useful life of the respective asset, not to exceed forty years. Consequently, intangible assets are shown on the balance sheet net of accumulated amortization.

Goodwill, franchises, trademarks, and patents are examples of intangible assets. Goodwill relates to the excess of the purchase price over the appraised value of net assets of a purchased company. Goodwill can be purchased, not built into a business, and thus it can be recorded only in connection with the acquisition of a business. It reflects the combination of intangible factors such as location, management expertise, and reputation, relating to the purchased firm's ability to realize high returns to its owners in the future.

Franchises refer to the legal right granted by a business to render or produce specific services or products. This right is normally stated in a franchise agreement that defines the geographical area as well as other terms of the franchise relationship. Examples of hospitality companies that operate as franchises are McDonald's, Burger King, Wendy's, and Dunkin Donuts. The cost of obtaining the franchise is shown on the balance sheet net of amortization over the duration of the franchise.

LIABILITIES

Liabilities are outsiders' claims against the company's resources (assets). They represent obligations to creditors of the firm. More formally, liabilities are probable future sacrifices of economic benefits arising from present obligations of a particular entity to transfer assets or provide services to other entities in the future as a result of past transactions or events. Three key points are included in the preceding definition:

1. Current duty or responsibility to other entities to be settled through the probable future transfer of assets or providing services
2. Obligation or future sacrifice of economic benefits
3. Arising from transactions that have already occurred

It is evident that the existence of a legally enforceable claim is not a prerequisite for an obligation to be included as a liability as long as the transfer of assets or services is otherwise probable.

Classification of Liabilities

Liabilities are customarily classified into two categories: current liabilities and long-term liabilities. In theory, liabilities should be listed in their probable order of liquidation, that is, those that are expected to be paid first are shown first, those expected to be paid next are shown next, and so on. As a practical matter, however, in many instances there is no particular sequence in which individual current liability and long-term liability items appear in the balance sheet. In all cases, current liabilities are shown first.

Current Liabilities. Current liabilities are obligations that are expected to be paid, or settled otherwise, within one year from the balance sheet date, the normal operating cycle. Such obligations normally require the use of current assets or the creation of other current liabilities. Some common current liabilities in the hospitality industry are accounts payable, short-term notes payable, current portion of long-term debt, income taxes payable, accrued expenses, and unearned revenue. Deferred income taxes—current (representing the tax effects of temporary differences between the bases of current assets and current liabilities for financial and tax reporting purposes) could also be included in this classification.

Short-Term Notes Payable. Short-term notes payable are formal written promises made by the hospitality firm to pay money to creditors within one year from the balance sheet date. A note payable may be given to secure an extension of time in which to pay an accounts payable or may arise when the company borrows money from a bank or other financial institution for business use. Normally, in a bank loan, the bank collects interest when the loan is repaid. However the interest due as of the balance sheet date is not shown under notes payable, only the principal due on the note. The interest due, if any, will be shown on a separate line under accrued interest or will be combined with other accrued expenses.

Current Portion of Long-Term Debt. The current portion of long-term debt is the portion of a mortgage or other long-term obligations due to be paid within one year from the balance sheet date. Since it represents an amount owed within one year from the balance sheet date, it is deducted from the total long-term debt and shown as a current liability.

Income Taxes Payable. Income taxes payable comprise the amount of federal and state income taxes still owed to the government as of the balance sheet date.

Accrued Expenses. Accrued expenses represent expenses incurred during the accounting period but not yet paid or recorded. The typical expenses that are subject to accrual include salaries, interest, and payroll taxes.

Unearned Revenue. Unearned revenue reflects revenues received or billed in advance of the performance of the service. In this case a future service is owed the customer instead of cash, and thus the hospitality firm is indicating that such services are forthcoming.

Customer deposits received by a hotel as deposits on room reservations represent unearned revenue since the hotel will not recognize these amounts as revenue until actually earned, when the customers receive the service. Similarly, the unearned portion of rentals or transportation revenues received will be included with unearned revenue or listed under a separate listing as a current liability.

Long-Term Liabilities. Long-term liabilities are those obligations due after one year from the balance sheet date. Typical long-term liabilities in the hospitality industry are mortgages payable, bonds payable, and notes payable.

Mortgages Payable. Mortgages payable represent promissory notes secured by a claim against real property, normally land and buildings. It has been a major source of cash traditionally used in financing several segments of the hospitality industry, especially lodging. As previously stated, any portion of the mortgage due within one year from the balance sheet will be shown as a current liability. Furthermore, additional disclosures of interest rate, maturity date, etc., will be included as a note to the financial statements.

Bonds Payable. Bonds are long-term obligations that normally require semiannual interest payments and that can be issued or sold at face value, at a discount (below face value), or at a premium (above face value) subject to all conditions stated on a bond indenture.

According to APB opinion No. 21, when bonds are sold at a premium, the current carrying value of bonds payable shown on the balance sheet will include the amount of the premium. Likewise, if bonds are sold at a discount, the amount of the discount will be subtracted from bonds payable on the balance sheet. The amount of the bond discount or bond premium will then be amortized (written off) over the life of the bond. The amortization of bond discount will result in an increase of interest expense, whereas the amortization of bond premium will reduce interest expense.

Long-Term Notes Payable.   Notes payable, included under long-term liabilities, represent promissory notes due to be paid over periods extending beyond one year from the balance sheet date.

Other Liabilities.   There are some items that do not clearly fit the criteria to be considered either current or long-term liabilities. Since they typically represent long-term obligations of the hospitality firm arising from the operation of the business, many firms show them on a separate line right after long-term liabilities. Examples of those items, at times referred to as other liabilities, include deferred income taxes, minority interest, and pension obligations.

Deferred taxes represent the timing difference caused by using different accounting methods for tax- and financial-reporting purposes. The most significant timing difference to a hospitality firm relates to the use of an accelerated method of depreciation for tax purposes while using straight-line depreciation for financial statement reporting purposes. This will cause tax expense on the income statement to be higher than taxes actually payable as stated on the tax return form. The difference is called deferred tax. Under FASB Statement No. 109 companies need to recognize tax liabilities for all temporary differences when there is expectation that the difference will be offset in future accounting periods. Other timing differences include those arising from capitalized interest during the construction period.

OWNERS' EQUITY

As previously noted, the title used in referring to the owners' equity on the balance sheet depends on the particular legal form of organization used by the hospitality firm. In all cases, however, the owners' equity section of the balance sheet will represent the difference between the total assets and the total liabilities, reflecting the equity interest of the owner(s) of the organization.

We shall focus our attention on the corporate form of legal organization, the predominant legal form of organization in the United States and in many other countries. Hence, we shall review the main items of the shareholders' equity (or stockholders' equity), the term used in referring to the owners' equity of a corporation. Additional coverage of corporation accounting is included in Chapter 12.

Shareholders' equity is the residual ownership interest in the assets of an entity that remains after deducting its liabilities. It is divided into two basic parts: (1) contributed capital and (2) retained earnings.

Contributed Capital

The contributed-capital accounts reflect the shareholders' contributions to the firm through the issuance of capital stock. The contributed-capital accounts include common stock, preferred stock, and additional paid-in capital.

Common Stock

Common stock represents the ownership rights given by a corporation and formalized by the issuance of shares of common stock. If the corporate charter only authorizes one type of capital stock, it is common stock. Therefore, common shareholders are considered the owners of the corporation.

The amount shown on the corporate balance sheet for common stock represents either the par value or the stated value of the issued shares of common stock.

Preferred Stock

Preferred stock is a special type of stock that some corporations have been given authorization to issue by their board of directors. Preferred shareholders have priority over common shareholders in distribution of assets in the event of liquidation, dividends, and other specified areas.

Additional Paid-In Capital

Additional paid-in capital reflects the amount received from shareholders in excess of the par value or stated value of the issued shares of both common and preferred stock. Traditionally, paid-in additional capital was referred to as capital surplus. But, the use of this term has been discontinued as a result of the misleading implications of the word "surplus."

Retained Earnings

The amount of retained earnings represents the cumulative net income of the hospitality firm since its formation, net of any amounts paid out to shareholders in the form of dividends. Retained earnings should not be confused with cash or any other asset. The earnings retained by the business may have been invested into the business for many different purposes, including the purchase of new kitchen equipment, expansion (opening new restaurants or hotels), and renovation of hotel rooms.

The importance to users of financial statements of understanding the changes in retained earnings between two balance sheet dates is the major reason why the amount of retained earnings that appears on the balance sheet is supplemented by a separate statement of changes in retained earnings.

STATEMENT OF RETAINED EARNINGS

The statement of retained earnings includes the detail of the changes occurring in the retained earnings balance from the beginning to the end of the period. There are two main elements that explain the changes in retained earnings between two balance sheet dates: (1) net income or net loss, and (2) dividends. The net income or net loss for the period, as shown on the income statement, is added to/or deducted from the beginning balance of retained earnings. From this total, dividends declared during the period are deducted, resulting in the ending balance of retained earnings to be shown on the shareholders' equity section of the corporate balance sheet.

From the foregoing it is apparent that retained earnings is the link between the balance sheet and the income statement in that the net income from the income statement is added to the beginning balance of retained earnings in the determination of the ending balance of retained earnings. The resulting amount is shown on the balance sheet net of dividends. An illustrative statement of retained earnings is given in Exhibit 9–2.

ABC INNS
Statement of Retained Earnings
for the Year Ended December 31, 2000

Balance, December 31, 1999	$10,000
Add: Net income for the year	6,000
Total	16,000
Less: Dividends	2,000
Balance, December 31, 2000	$14,000

Exhibit 9–2 Statement of retained earnings for ABC Inns.

BALANCE SHEET FORMATS

As previously stated, there is a great degree of flexibility in the presentation of individual items on the balance sheet. Yet, at all times the balance sheet is seen as an expression of the fundamental accounting equation (assets = liabilities + owners' equity).

There are two basic balance sheet formats: the account form and the report form. In the account form, the assets are listed on the left-hand side, and the equities (liabilities and owners' equity) are listed on the right-hand side. The report form of the balance sheet, on the other hand, lists assets at the top of the page and equities below assets. This format is widely used for external reporting purposes. An example of the report form was the balance sheet included as Exhibit 9–1.

ILLUSTRATIVE BALANCE SHEET: WENDY'S INTERNATIONAL

We now examine the balance sheet presentation of an actual firm in the hospitality industry: Wendy's International, Inc. and Subsidiaries (see Exhibit 9–3). It is important, however, to recognize that not all hospitality firms adhere to this format; on the contrary, each firm's balance sheet should be modified to meet individual requirements. However, the balance sheet of a hotel, restaurant, cruise operation or airline company will not differ materially from that of other companies inside or outside the hospitality industry.

The following comments will serve to review major items associated with the Wendy's International balance sheet (see Exhibit 9–3), thereby facilitating the understanding of this format in light of what this chapter has covered:

1. There are two comparative balance sheets in this format: the current year and the preceding year balance sheets. The latter is included for comparative purposes.

2. Footnotes (or notes to the financial statements) are considered an integral part of the financial statements. They include additional detail about several balance sheet items (i.e., property and equipment, net) which are being summarized on the balance sheet.

3. Asset classifications include current assets, property and equipment, and other assets. In addition, cost in excess of net assets acquired and deferred income taxes are listed separately.

4. Property and equipment items include land, buildings, leasehold improvements, restaurant equipment, other equipment and capital leases. Except for land, all property and equipment is subject to depreciation or amortization. A detailed review of depreciation and amortization is included in Chapter 11.

5. Other assets include the long-term portion of notes receivable, pre-opening costs and capitalized software development costs. As previously stated, other assets listed separately are deferred income taxes and cost in excess of net assets acquired, which is also referred to as goodwill. It arises when a company acquires another company and pays more than what the company is worth due to intangible factors such as talented management and a good location. Intangible assets such as franchise fees are amortized over their respective useful lives by writing them off as expenses.

6. Current liabilities consist of accounts and drafts payable, accrued expenses, current portion of long-term debt, and amounts due to company's officers.

Consolidated Balance Sheet   **December 28, 1997 and December 29, 1996**

(Dollars in thousands)	1997	1996
Assets		
Current assets		
Cash and cash equivalents	$ 234,262	$ 218,956
Accounts receivable, net	66,755	53,250
Notes receivable, net	13,897	11,003
Deferred income taxes	31,007	15,760
Inventories and other	35,633	37,994
	381,554	336,963
Property and equipment, net	1,265,500	1,207,944
Notes receivable, net	178,681	118,994
Goodwill, net	51,346	51,636
Deferred income taxes	15,117	12,938
Other assets	49,482	52,959
	$1,941,680	$1,781,434
Liabilities and Shareholders' Equity		
Current liabilities		
Accounts payable	$ 107,157	$ 108,629
Accrued expenses		
Salaries and wages	31,377	24,741
Taxes	21,615	18,502
Insurance	30,899	30,337
Other	14,415	18,874
Current portion of long-term obligations	7,151	6,681
	212,614	207,764
Long-term obligations		
Term debt	205,872	197,622
Capital leases	43,891	44,206
	249,763	241,828
Deferred income taxes	81,017	62,956
Other long-term liabilities	14,052	12,114
Commitments and contingencies		
Company-obligated mandatorily redeemable preferred securities of subsidiary Wendy's Financing I, holding solely Wendy's Convertible Debentures	200,000	200,000
Shareholders' equity		
Preferred stock, authorized: 250,000 shares		
Common stock, $.10 stated value per share, authorized: 200,000,000 shares		
Issued: 115,946,000 and 113,148,000 shares, respectively	11,595	11,315
Capital in excess of stated value	353,327	312,570
Retained earnings	839,215	740,311
Translation adjustments and other	(18,191)	(5,712)
	1,185,946	1,058,484
Treasury stock, at cost: 129,000 shares	(1,712)	(1,712)
	1,184,234	1,056,772
	$1,941,680	$1,781,434

Exhibit 9–3 Wendy's consolidated balance sheet.

7. Long-term liabilities, referred to as long-term obligations, represent the portion of the long-term debt due after one year from the balance sheet date. As noted earlier, the principal forms of long-term debt in the hospitality industry are mortgages, bonds, notes payable, and capital leases. An appropriate description of the type of long-term debt, the interest rate, maturity date, and other pertinent data is normally disclosed in a note to the financial statements.

8. As indicated earlier in this chapter, other liabilities are listed separately before shareholders' equity. In this presentation it includes deferred income taxes arising from timing differences in the recognition of income tax expense for financial statement and tax purposes.

9. Commitments and contingencies give recognition to items not included on the balance sheet but disclosed on the notes to the financial statements. Commitments are claims that may occur upon the future performance under a contract, such as a long-term purchase agreement with a supplier. Similarly, contingencies are existing conditions involving uncertainty as to their ultimate effect; their resolution being dependent upon specific future events. Examples of contingencies include lawsuits and tax examinations.

10. Shareholders' equity incorporates the two types of capital stock described before: preferred stock and common stock. Although a separate heading is not included for contributed capital accounts (preferred stock, common stock, and capital in excess of stated value—also known as additional paid-in capital), they are all listed before retained earnings.

11. Unrealized loss on investments represent the reduction in the market value of the investment not resulting from a sale transaction. Translation adjustments are gains or losses from foreign currency translations. Both of these items are included in shareholders' equity.

12. An additional item, treasury stock was deducted from the shareholders' equity section for it represents a contra-equity account. Treasury stock consists of shares of capital stock reacquired by the corporation, but not formally canceled. Further discussion of treasury stock appears in Chapter 12.

SOME KEY TERMS INTRODUCED IN THIS CHAPTER

1. **Account form.** A form of a balance sheet in which the assets are listed on the left-hand side and the liabilities and owners equity on the right-hand side.

2. **Additional paid-in capital.** The portion of paid-in capital that exceeds the par value (or stated value) of issued shares of both common and preferred stock. It is also called capital in excess of par (or stated value).

3. **Annual report.** A yearly report for stockholders and other interested parties prepared by management.

4. **Bonds payable.** Long-term obligations normally requiring semiannual interest payments that can be issued or sold at par (or face value), at a discount (below par) or at a premium (above par) subject to the conditions stated on a bond indenture.

5. **Cash surrender value of officers' life insurance.** The cash value accumulated up to the balance sheet date on the life insurance policies covering the lives of certain officers and other key members of an organization.

6. **Commitments.** Claims that may occur upon the future performance under a contract, such as a lease or a purchase agreement.

7. **Common stock.** The ownership rights given by a corporation evidenced by the issuance of shares of common stock.

8. **Contingencies.** Existing conditions involving uncertainty as to their ultimate effect; their resolution is dependent upon specific future events. Examples include lawsuits and tax examinations.

9. **Current assets.** Cash or other assets that can be converted into cash or consumed by the business within one year from the balance sheet date, the normal operating cycle.

10. **Current liabilities.** Obligations that are expected to be paid, or settled otherwise within one year from the balance sheet date, the normal operating cycle.

11. **Current portion of long-term debt.** The portion of a mortgage or other long-term obligations due to be paid within one year from the balance sheet date.

12. **Deferred charges or deferred expenses.** Long-term prepayments recorded as assets and written off in future periods.

13. **Franchises.** Legal right granted by an organization to render or produce specific services or products.

14. **Goodwill.** An intangible asset reflecting the purchase price over the appraised value of the net assets acquired.

15. **Intangible assets.** Long-term assets that have no physical existence but have a value based on legal privileges or rights that have been acquired at a cost to a firm.

16. **Long-term investments.** Investments in securities of other corporations that are not readily marketable or intended as a ready source of cash.

17. **Long-term liabilities.** Obligations that are expected to be paid, or otherwise settled, after one year from the balance sheet date. Examples include mortgages and bonds payable.

18. **Marketable securities (or short-term investments).** Investments in short-term securities (e.g., bonds, stocks) that can be readily converted into cash.

19. **Preferred stock.** A class of capital stock that possesses certain preferences over common stock in earnings distributions and in the event of liquidation of a corporation.

20. **Property and equipment.** Long-term assets used in the production of revenues (also known as fixed assets). Examples include land, buildings, furniture, kitchen equipment, leasehold improvements and construction in progress.

21. **Report form.** A form of a balance sheet under which assets are listed at the top of the page and the liabilities and owners' equity underneath assets.

22. **Retained earnings.** The cumulative earnings of a firm since its formation, net of any amounts paid out to shareholders in the form of dividends.

23. **Shareholders' equity (or stockholders' equity).** The owners' equity section of a corporate balance sheet.

24. **Statement of retained earnings.** A statement summarizing the changes in retained earnings during the period.

25. **Treasury stock.** Shares of outstanding stock that have been reacquired by the issuing corporation.

QUESTIONS

1. What is the primary purpose of a balance sheet?
2. What is a classified balance sheet? Discuss the significance of account classifications in the preparation of a balance sheet.
3. Explain how the account form of a balance sheet differs from the report form.
4. What is the basis for classifying assets on the balance sheet?

5. What are the common categories of assets?
6. What are current assets? Give three examples.
7. Distinguish between current and long-term liabilities. Give three examples of each.
8. What is a contra-asset account? How should such accounts be shown on the balance sheet? Give two examples.
9. What are non-current assets? Give two examples.
10. What is property and equipment? Give four examples.
11. What are intangible assets? Give three examples.
12. Distinguish between common stock and retained earnings.
13. Review the main differences between the owners' equity section of a sole proprietorship and that of a corporation.
14. What are deferred income taxes? Discuss.
15. What is the cash surrender value of officer's life insurance?
16. Distinguish between short-term and long-term investments.

EXERCISES

1. Classify the items listed below, using the following classification scheme:
   (a) Current assets (CA)
   (b) Property and equipment (PE)
   (c) Other assets (OA)
   (d) Current liabilities (CL)
   (e) Long-term liabilities (LTL)
   (f) Owners equity (OE)
   (g) Revenues (R)
   (h) Expenses (E)
       1. Note payable due in three years
       2. Prepaid licenses
       3. Beverage inventory
       4. Franchise fee revenue
       5. Rent incurred
       6. Accumulated depreciation
       7. RJ, capital
       8. RJ, withdrawals
       9. Salaries payable
       10. Accrued rent
       11. Cash
       12. Accounts receivable
       13. Interest incurred
       14. Building
       15. Goodwill
       16. Taxes incurred
       17. Rent earned
       18. Customers' deposits
2. Which of the following would be classified as a current asset?
   (a) Accounts receivable.
   (b) Short-term investments.
   (c) Supplies inventory.
   (d) All of the above.
   (e) None of the above.
3. Consider the following account balances of Magnum Inn, as of December 31, 2000:

Accounts payable	$ 2,000	Income taxes payable	$ 100
Accounts receivable	4,000	Food inventory	1,000
Accrued interest payable	200	Furniture and equipment	3,000
Accrued wages	100	Land	5,000
Accumulated depreciation—building	1,000	Mortgages payable (current portion)	100
Accumulated depreciation—furniture & equip.	100	Mortgages payable (non-current portion)	14,000
Allowance for doubtful accounts	10	Prepaid insurance	100
Building	20,000	Retained earnings	?
Cash	1,000	Security deposits	200
Common stock	15,000	Treasury stock	100
Deferred charges	200	Unearned revenue	200

Required:

(a) Determine total current assets.
(b) Determine total current liabilities.
(c) Determine total assets.
(d) Determine the net book value of property and equipment.
(e) Determine total shareholders' equity.

4. Indicate the classification of each of the accounts in column 1 by inserting the correct letter from column 2.

Column 1
(1) Certificates of deposit
(2) Notes receivable
(3) Construction-in-progress
(4) Deferred expenses
(5) Paid-in additional capital
(6) Preferred stock
(7) Cash surrender value of life insurance
(8) Land
(9) Accumulated depreciation
(10) Bonds payable
(11) Accrued interest payable
(12) Beverage inventory
(13) Interest receivable
(14) Deferred income taxes
(15) Rent paid in advance
(16) Unearned rent
(17) Allowance for doubtful accounts

Column 2
(a) Property and equipment
(b) Intangible assets
(c) Current assets
(d) Contra-assets
(e) Shareholders' equity
(f) Current liabilities
(g) Long-term liabilities
(h) Other assets
(i) Other liabilities

5. Classify the following items as: Current assets (CA), Investments (I), Property and equipment (PE), Other assets (OA), Current liabilities (CL), Long-term liabilities (LTL), Stakeholders' equity (SE) and other (O).
(a) Land
(b) Goodwill
(c) Additional paid-in capital
(d) Cash
(e) Unearned income
(f) Current portion of long-term debt
(g) Investments in subsidiaries
(h) Income taxes payable
(i) Prepaid expenses
(j) Minority interest
(k) Accrued payroll

(l) Marketable securities
(m) Preferred stock
(n) Treasury stock
(o) China, glassware, silver, linen and uniforms
(p) Accounts payable
(q) Accounts receivable
(r) Deferred charges
(s) Inventories

SHORT PROBLEMS

1. A recent annual report for Hilton Hotels reported the following balance sheet data (in millions of dollars):

	1997	1996
Land	$ 763	$ 712
Buildings and leasehold improvements	4,162	3,823
Riverboats	53	128
Furniture and equipment	942	891
Property held for sale or development	39	40
Construction-in-progress	196	106
	6,155	5,700
Less accumulated depreciation	1,161	1,002
	$4,994	$4,698

Required:
(a) What is the original cost of the furniture and equipment held by Hilton at the end of 1996? Explain answer.
(b) Were riverboats acquired or sold in 1997?

2. Consider the following information taken from the records of Tim's Travel Services at the end of the year ended December 31, 2004:

Marketable securities	$10,000
Cash	30,000
Prepaid insurance	3,000
Accounts receivable	10,000
Inventories	1,000

Required:
Complete the current asset section of a properly classified balance sheet in proper form.

3. Consider the following information from the records of Alonzo's Restaurant at the end of the year ended December 31, 1999:

Current Portion of Mortgages payable	$ 30,000
Accounts payable	10,000
Income taxes payable	3,000
Accrued interest payable	2,000
Bonds payable	40,000
Mortgages payable (net of current installments)	120,000
Notes payable due in year 2000	20,000

Required:

Complete the current and the long-term liability sections of a properly classified balance sheet in proper form.

4. Indicate the effect of the transactions listed below on each of the following: Current Assets (CA), Current Liabilities (CL), Total Assets (TA), and total Shareholders' Equity (SE).

	CA	CL	TA	SE
A. Sales on credit.				
B. Purchase of equipment on account.				
C. Collection on accounts receivable.				
D. Purchase of long-term investment for cash.				

LONG PROBLEMS

1. Prepare a properly classified balance sheet of Baker's Heaven Restaurant, Inc. as of December 31, 2002 using the data given below:

Cash	$ 22,600	Furniture & equipment	$30,000
Accounts receivable	25,500	Goodwill	10,000
Marketable securities	20,500	Accumulated depreciation	35,000
Accounts payable	30,000	Allowance for doubtful accounts	1,000
Food inventory	7,500	Additional paid-in capital	20,000
Common stock	100,000	Retained earnings 12/31/2001	23,200
Beverage inventory	9,200	Accrued salaries	3,000
Income taxes payable	5,200	Notes payable (due in 2005)	80,000
Prepaid expenses	5,100	Net income for the year 2002	10,200
Land	50,000	Dividends declared in 2002	7,200
Building	120,000		

2. Consider the following data for Dan's Services as of September 30, 2003.

____	1. Accounts payable	$12,000
____	2. Accounts receivable	10,000
____	3. Allowance for doubtful accounts	1,000
____	4. Accrued expenses	2,000
____	5. Accumulated depreciation	15,000
____	6. Equipment	90,000
____	7. Inventories	3,000
____	8. Cash	5,000
____	9. Short-term investments	8,000
____	10. Long-term investments	3,000
____	11. Current portion of mortgages payable	8,000
____	12. Common stock	30,000
____	13. Mortgages payable, net of current portion	55,000
____	14. Additional paid-in capital	20,000
____	15. Goodwill	3,000
____	16. Retained earnings	?

Account Descriptions

(a) Long-term assets used in operations
(b) The most liquid of all assets
(c) Stocks or bonds of other companies held for the purpose of exercising control
(d) An accumulation of the sum of the expense since the asset was acquired

(e) Monies due from customers arising from the sale or service rendered
(f) Monies due to vendors for purchases made on credit
(g) Installments due within one year from the balance sheet date
(h) Undistributed earnings of the corporation
(i) Estimate of the accounts that may not be collected
(j) Installments due after one year from the balance sheet date
(k) Excess of purchase price over appraised value of the net assets acquired in the purchase of a firm
(l) Monies due because expenses are incurred in a different period than when the cash outlay occurs
(m) Goods on hand held for sale or consumption in the normal course of business
(n) The capital stock of the residual owners
(o) Excess over legal par paid at the time of issuance of the stock
(p) Stocks and bonds of other corporations readily converted into cash

Required:

1. Match each account to the proper account description by placing the appropriate letter before the account name.
2. Prepare a classified balance sheet in good form.
3. Using the information provided below, prepare a properly classified balance sheet of Bayview Hotels as of November 30, 2003 and a statement of retained earnings for the year ending November 30, 2003.

BAYVIEW HOTELS, INC.
Adjusted Trial Balance
November 30, 2003

Debit balances		Credit balances	
Cash	$ 6,000	Accumulated depreciation	$ 6,000
Short-term investments	10,000	Notes payable	
Notes receivable		(short-term)	20,000
(due 1/2/09)	13,000	Accounts payable	8,000
Accounts receivable	4,000	Allowance for doubtful	
Inventories	6,000	accounts	2,000
Prepaid expenses	2,000	Customers deposits	1,000
Furniture and equipment	40,000	Common stock	30,000
China, glassware, and uniforms	2,000	Additional paid-in capital	2,000
Franchises	6,000	Retained earnings	15,000
Long-term receivables	8,000	Sales	120,000
Treasury stock	9,000		
Departmental expenses	40,000		
General and administrative expenses	56,000		
Interest expense	2,000		
	$204,000		$204,000

Additional Information

(a) Income taxes for the year ended November 30, 2003 have not been recorded. Income tax rate, 30%.
(b) Dividends declared during the fiscal year 2003 were $5,000. They were already deducted from retained earnings.

4. Selected data on Speedy Air Lines, Inc., for the year ended October 31, 2007, appear below:

Dividends	$ 24,000	Maintenance supplies inventory	$38,000
Current maturities	15,300	Cash	10,000
of long-term debt		Short-term investments	28,000
Accounts payable	160,000	Long-term investments	30,000
Accounts receivable	280,000	Accrued expenses	60,000
Deferred income taxes	330,000	Unearned transportation revenues	20,000
Long-term debt	157,000	Income taxes payable	3,300
Flight equipment	2,300,000	Notes payable (short-term)	80,000
Ground property and equipment	370,000	Additional paid-in capital	90,000
Accumulated depreciation	1,200,000	Retained earnings	?
Prepaid expenses	10,500	Allowance for doubtful accounts	8,000
Common stock	60,000		
Preferred stock	10,000		

Required:

(a) Prepare a properly classified balance sheet as of October 31, 2007.

(b) Prepare a statement of retained earnings for the year ended October 31, 2007 (retained earnings balance October 31, 2006, $829,200).

The Statement of Income | 10

The learning objectives of this chapter are:

- To explain the purposes and contents of an income statement.
- To distinguish between the single-step and the multi-step formats in preparing an income statement.
- To contrast hospitality industry income statements to those of commercial firms.
- To review the major objectives of the Uniform System of Accounts for the Lodging Industry.
- To review the major sections of the statement of income based on the ninth revised edition of the Uniform System of Accounts for the Lodging Industry.
- To prepare a statement of income based on the ninth revised edition of the Uniform System of Accounts for the Lodging Industry format.
- To understand the accounting treatment and presentation of special items in the income statement.
- To understand the use of departmental income statement schedules.
- To review the major contents of the income statement of a publicly held company in the hospitality industry.

The statement of income—the second basic financial statement—is a statement of flow, reflecting the results of operations of the hospitality firm for a particular period of time (a month, a quarter, or a year).

The statement of income (also known as the income statement or statement of operations) indicates whether management has achieved its primary objective of securing an acceptable level of earnings for the owners of the hospitality organization. This is done by showing the revenues earned by the firm during a specific accounting period, the expenses associated with earning these revenues, and the resulting net income or net loss for the period reported.

The information concerning profit-oriented activities is of utmost importance to all parties interested in the hospitality firm. Yet, different kinds of information are needed for internal and external purposes. Internally, hospitality management requires the determination of income or loss by department or segment of the business in addition to the performance of the company as a whole. In this manner, the income statement represents a yardstick of operating performance as well as management's report card. External users, on the other hand, do not require the same amount of detail concerning revenues and expenses, and thus the income statement will not be as elaborate as the report prepared for internal purposes.

As stated in previous chapters, the balance sheet presentation for a hotel, restaurant, club, or any other segment of the hospitality service industries will not differ materially from that of other commercial firms, whether the statement is prepared for internal or external use. However, the income statement presentation involves a different approach, especially if it is prepared for management purposes. For instance, the operations of a hotel might include room rentals, sales of food and beverages, telecommunications, and therefore it tends to be highly departmentalized. As a result, hotel management must be apprised of the individual performance of all major revenue-producing departments or activities in order to conduct an effective operational analysis as the basis for making sound decisions concerning the future of the business. Through the development of the Uniform System of Accounts for the Lodging Industry (USAL), this specific need for information has been effectively addressed.

In this chapter, we first give a general overview of the statement of income by describing its major components. Moreover, the relationship between the balance sheet and the income statement is reviewed. A clear contrast between a hospitality income statement and that of manufacturing and merchandising firms is also presented. Then, the chapter examines the USAL, the most comprehensive hospitality industry system. A discussion of the various sections of the long-form income statement based on the ninth revised edition of USAL approved by the American Hotel and Motel Association and currently considered the acceptable accounting manual for the lodging industry is included. The remainder of the chapter deals with the accounting treatment and presentation of special items in the income statement and the review of the income statement of Hilton Hotels Corporation and Subsidiaries.

STATEMENT OF INCOME

As already indicated the statement of income shows the results of hospitality business operations over a period of time. Revenues and expense accounts are set up to describe the various aspects of the firms' operations, with the difference in these accounts representing either net income or net loss.

The heading of an income statement should include the following:

- Name of the hospitality firm
- The title of the statement (statement of income, income statement or statement of operations)
- Time period covered by the statement

It is important to recognize that the issue date of the statement, e.g., December 31, 2010, is not sufficient; we must also indicate its time period, i.e., whether the statement refers to the month ended December 31, 2010 or the year ended December 31, 2010. A properly headed income statement might include the information "For the Month ended December 31, 2010."

There are two general formats for income statements: (1) single-step and (2) multistep. With the single-step format, all revenues and gains (such as other income) are first totaled; total expenses and costs are then deducted from total revenues to arrive at the income before income taxes. Finally, income taxes are deducted in determining the amount of net income for the period. In this manner, we arrive at net income in one step. By contrast, the multistep income statement

MONIQUE TRAVEL AGENCY
Income Statement
for the Year Ended December 31, 2000

Revenues		
Commissions		$25,000
Other income		5,000
		30,000
Expenses		
Salaries and wages	$5,000	
Supplies	2,000	
Administrative and general	3,500	
Marketing	1,500	
Interest	1,000	
Depreciation	2,000	
Other	1,000	
		16,000
Income before income taxes		14,000
Income taxes		5,000
Net income		$ 9,000

Exhibit 10–1   Income statement for Monique Travel Agency.

arrives at net income in various steps, providing for more detailed information about operations. Exhibit 10–1 gives an example of a single-step income statement, normally used for external reporting purposes. Note that income taxes are the last expense appearing on the income statement because it is based on the amount of income before income taxes.

INCOME STATEMENT COMPONENTS: REVENUES, EXPENSES, GAINS AND LOSSES

The basic components of an income statement are revenues, expenses, gains, and losses. All these elements can be combined in different ways to obtain several measures of enterprise performance. While the resulting net income (or net loss) is the final measure of operating performance, several intermediate components can be utilized to evaluate operating results. Intermediate components in a hotel income statement include such items as operated departmental income and income before interest, depreciation, amortization and income taxes (EBITDA). Other operations in the hospitality industry might include gross profit (or gross margin) or operating income.

Revenues

Revenues have been defined as the inflows of cash or other properties in exchange for goods and services. A more formal definition of revenues is: Revenues are inflows or other enhancements of assets of an entity or settlements of its liabilities (or a combination of both) during a period from delivering or producing goods, rendering services, or other activities that constitute the entity's ongoing major or central operations.

Revenue results in an increase in equity attributable to the normal operations of the organization. Generally, revenues encompass all income-producing activities of the hospitality firm resulting from sales of products, services, or commissions. In a restaurant, for example, the major sources of revenue are food and beverage sales. A hotel organization might have room sales, food and beverage sales, and casino sales. Other sources of revenue that may apply to segments of the hospitality industry include interest income, franchise fees, management fees, and dividend income.

Recognition of revenue is an area of major concern inasmuch as early recognition of revenue not only has a major effect on the determination of net income, but also produces a corresponding increase in equity. In accordance with the realization concept of accounting, revenue is to be recognized at the time it is earned, which generally occurs when goods are sold or services are rendered. Revenue is to be measured by the cash received plus the fair market value of any other asset or assets received.

Expenses

Expenses are goods or services consumed in the regular operations of a business by virtue of the process of earning revenues. Expenses are outflows or other consumption of assets or incurrences of liabilities (or a combination of both) during a period from delivering or producing goods, rendering services, or carrying out other activities that constitute the entity's ongoing major or central operations.

As we have already seen, properly matching expenses against revenues during each accounting period is a crucial objective in the preparation of an income statement. In recognizing expenses, what is important is when the expense is incurred, not when payment is made. We recognize salaries and wages expenses, for instance, in the period the employees actually work for the organization, regardless of when the cash is paid out. The transactions and events that give rise to expenses can take many different forms: cost of goods sold, salaries and wages, rent, interest, depreciation, and so on.

Gains and Losses

Gains are defined as increases in equity (net assets) from peripheral or incidental transactions of an entity and from all other transactions and other events and circumstances affecting the entity during a period except those that result from revenues or investments by owners. Losses, on the other hand, are decreases in equity (net assets) from peripheral or incidental transactions of an entity and from all other transactions and other events and circumstances affecting the entity during a period except those that result from expenses or distributions to owners. Simply stated, gains and losses are increases (or decreases) in equity resulting from transactions not related to the entity's main operations. They are thus considered secondary activities. Examples include losses related to assessments of fines or damages by courts.

RELATIONSHIP OF THE INCOME STATEMENT TO THE BALANCE SHEET

A clear relationship exists between the first two basic financial statements that must be recognized throughout our income statement review. As discussed in Chapter 9, the amount of net income (or net loss) reported on the income statement is added to (or subtracted from) the beginning balance of retained earnings in determining the ending balance of retained earnings shown in the equity section of the balance sheet, net of earnings distributions in the form of dividends. Consequently, the net income reported on the income statement, together with

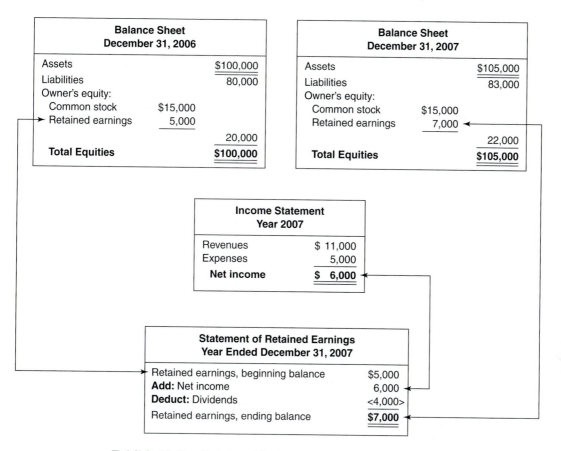

Exhibit 10–2   Relationship between financial statements.

the dividends declared during the period, generally serves to explain the change in retained earnings between balance sheets prepared at the beginning and at the end of the accounting period. To illustrate this relationship, we review the example shown as Exhibit 10–2. As can be seen the earnings for the year 2007 ($6,000), together with the dividends declared during that year ($4,000), explain the change in retained earnings between the beginning (2006) and ending (2007) balance sheets, establishing a clear link between the balance sheet and the income statement.

CONTRAST OF A HOSPITALITY INCOME STATEMENT WITH OTHER COMMERCIAL ENTERPRISES' INCOME STATEMENTS

A typical hospitality firm earns revenue by offering various services to the public. A hotel offers accommodation services; a country club offers its members the use of its pool, tennis courts, and other facilities; a restaurant offers its customers a dining experience.

Alternatively, a merchandising or manufacturing firm earns revenue by selling goods. If these firms are unable to sell the goods, they can be inventoried and marketed in the future. Consequently, the most significant expense a typical commercial company incurs is the cost of the merchandise it sells (cost of goods sold or manufactured). Traditionally, the cost of goods sold has been directly deducted from revenue in arriving at the gross profit from sales (often called gross margin). A summarized format of an income statement for a commercial firm is as follows:

Sales	$xx
Less: Cost of sales	xx
Gross profit	xx
Less: Operating expenses	xx
Income before income taxes	xx
Income taxes	xx
Net income	$xx

This format clearly focuses on the importance of gross profit from sales in the evaluation of the overall profitability of a manufacturing or merchandising firm. By contrast, hospitality firms' operations are largely departmentalized, denoting the significance of the various services provided to customers. Indeed, unsold room nights can not be placed on the shelf as inventory. This unique feature of a great number of hospitality firms requires the classification of both revenue and expenses on the income statement according to the different activities of the business. As a result, relating expenses attributable to specific revenue-producing activities becomes an effective management tool in the evaluation of departmental performance. While other commercial firms rely on gross profit from sales as a basic measure of profitability, hospitality companies emphasize the determination of departmental income in the evaluation of operating performance. The basic structure of a hospitality firm income statement is summarized below:

Departmental Revenue	$xx
Less: Departmental expenses	xx
Departmental Income	xx
Less: Indirect expenses	xx
Income before income taxes	xx
Income taxes	xx
Net income	$xx

This format places emphasis on the determination of departmental income, from which indirect expenses are deducted to arrive at income before income taxes. The term "indirect expenses" implies that these are expenses not directly related to specific revenue-producing activities or departments. Indirect expenses include both operating and nonoperating items.

Another unique feature of hospitality industry income statements is the great significance of labor costs to the industry. While the cost of sales is normally the major expense for manufacturing and merchandising companies, payroll costs represents the principal expense category for hospitality firms as a result of the labor-intensive nature of the industry. In fact, for many hospitality firms payroll costs are well over one-third of total revenues.

Moreover, fixed expenses (e.g., depreciation and interest) are also considered very important in the evaluation of a hospitality firm's operating results, denoting the capital-intensive nature of the industry. These fixed costs do not vary in direct proportion with changes in sales and are treated as indirect expenses in the formal income statement.

All of the aforementioned operating characteristics of hospitality industry companies have been taken into account in the development of USAL, an all-inclusive format that embraces nearly all the major sources of hospitality service revenues.

THE UNIFORM SYSTEM OF ACCOUNTS FOR THE LODGING INDUSTRY: DEVELOPMENT AND MAIN PURPOSES

The Hotel Association of New York City with the prime objective of providing a uniform classification, organization, and presentation of financial information developed the Uniform System of Accounts for the Lodging Industry (USAL) in 1923. This created a "common language" in the reporting of financial statements within the lodging industry. The USAL (previously known as the Uniform System of Accounts for Hotels) was approved by the American Hotel and Motel Association and has been updated on several occasions in order to keep it current. The latest revision (ninth edition), published in 1996, included a number of changes needed for the financial statements to conform to new pronouncements of the FASB and industry practices.

The USAL has served as the guiding light in the formulation of other uniform systems in the hospitality service industries. These systems include, among others, the Uniform System of Accounts for Restaurants, supported by the National Restaurant Association, and the Uniform System of Accounts for Clubs, sponsored by the Club Managers Association. We have selected the USAL for review since it incorporates most revenue-producing activities included in all the other systems.

Through the development of a uniform presentation of financial statements, the following objectives are achieved by using a uniform system of accounts:

- Facilitates comparability between financial statements of hospitality firms. It is possible to compare a firm's current performance not only with that of previous years but also with similar operations of the same segment of the industry

- Enables the efficient flow of managerial information by showing the operating results of each major revenue-producing unit or department, thereby providing a basis for analyzing and evaluating departmental performance

- Recognizes the need for and importance of a proper system of responsibility accounting. The specific grouping of revenue and expense items permits the evaluation of the individual(s) responsible for a particular unit

- Provides a convenient and effective accounting system, which can be used by any operation within the applicable segment of the hospitality industry; this includes a standardized format of organizing, classifying, and preparing financial statements

- Simplifies the development of regional, national, and worldwide industry statistics in the hospitality industry; these can be utilized as a measure of operating performance by individual firms searching for operational problem areas in need of managerial attention by allowing each firm to compare itself to comparable regional firms

In sum, the USAL provides a convenient and efficient method of presenting the results of operations of specific segments of the industry. As indicated before, the USAL has become the generally accepted manual for reporting lodging industry operating results. This system is, indeed, an excellent tool that gives high priority to management's need for information upon which to base operating judgments. Further, the USAL is fairly flexible and can be easily adapted to suit the needs of individual operations. It is important to recognize, however, that the USAL is not mandatory.

We now discuss the income statement presentation of the USAL; a format that is best suited for managerial purposes. Supporting departmental schedules are prepared for all revenue and expenses included in the summary statement of income, thereby providing detailed information to lodging managers.

REVIEW OF THE SUMMARY STATEMENT OF INCOME

The summary income statement (previously known as long-form income statement) based on the USAL is designed for internal management use, in line with the major objectives discussed earlier. It summarizes the results of operations of the hotel in more detail than is contained in the traditional short-form income statement prepared for external purposes. The arrangement of revenue and expense items reported on this format makes possible the effective measurement of all major revenue-producing activities of the hotel operation.

The basic structure of the long-form income statement is shown in Exhibit 10–3. Section I contains all revenue-producing activities of the hotel. Expenses directly attributable to these revenue-producing departments are charged against the appropriate unit. Deducting departmental expenses from departmental revenues then makes the determination of departmental income. This departmental income serves as a basis on which to evaluate departmental performance.

In Section II undistributed operating expenses are deducted from total departmental income in determining income after undistributed operating expenses (previously known as income before fixed charges), a measure of the overall efficiency of the entire operation. The undistributed operating expenses are incurred for the benefit of the whole organization and therefore are not allocated to specific departments. For instance, the salary of the general manager is assumed to be incurred for the benefit of the entire organization, and not for the benefit of a particular department.

Section III consists of fixed charges deducted in arriving at income before income taxes. These fixed expenses are the capital costs of the hotel inasmuch as they are a function of the cost of the property and thus are beyond the control of operating management. As a result, fixed expenses are not taken into account in the evaluation of the overall operating performance, which is measured by income after undistributed operating expenses. Finally, income taxes are deducted from income before income taxes in determining the net income (or net loss) for the period, commonly referred to as the "bottom line." Theoretically, many of the indirect costs (undistributed operating expenses and fixed expenses) could be allocated to operated departments. For instance, marketing expenses can be allocated on the basis of departmental revenues. Likewise, utility costs could be apportioned on the basis of space occupied or meter readings. Other basis of apportioning indirect costs to operated departments might be total departmental payroll, number of persons employed in each department, and total department earnings.

Section I	
Operated departments	
Departmental revenue	$xx
Less: Departmental expenses	xx
Operated departmental income	xx
Section II	
Less: Undistributed operating expenses	xx
Income after undistributed operating expenses	xx
Section III	
Less: Fixed charges	xx
Income before income taxes	xx
Less: Income taxes	xx
Net income	$xx

Exhibit 10–3 Basic structure of the summary income statement.

Nevertheless, allocation of indirect expenses is not considered a reliable and precise procedure because it is not possible to assign costs to the various operating departments on a logical and accurate basis at all times. As a result, departmental earnings may vary depending on the particular basis of allocation used. Hence, a large number of hotel operations do not allocate indirect costs to operated departments. Instead, they take the position that indirect expenses are incurred on behalf of the business as a whole.

The in-depth review of the summary income statement following USAL focuses on the analysis of the three major sections and the individual captions of the statement. Refer to the summary statement of income of Perfect Inn presented as Exhibit 10–4.

PERFECT INN
Summary Statement of Income
for the Year Ended December 31, 2010
in Thousands of Dollars

	Net Revenues	Cost of Sales	Payroll & Related Expenses	Other Expenses	Income (Loss)
Operated Departments					
Rooms	$1,523		$395	$80	$1,048
Food	626	208	218	67	133
Beverage	230	62	65	23	80
Telecommunications	50	45	15	5	(15)
Rentals and other income	5				5
Total operated departments	$2,434	315	693	175	1,251
Undistributed Operating Expenses					
Administrative & general			48	25	
Marketing			33	34	
Information systems			20	12	
Human resources			22	5	
Transportation			13	8	
Property operation & maintenance			32	49	
Utility costs			4	88	
Total undistributed operating expenses			172	221	393
Income after undistributed operating expenses	$2,434	$315	$865	$396	858
Rent, property taxes and insurance					201
Income before interest, depreciation and income taxes					657
Income expense					110
Income before depreciation and income taxes					547
Depreciation expense					150
Income before income taxes					397
Income taxes					139
Net income					$258

Exhibit 10–4 Perfect Inn, summary statement of income for the year ended December 31, 2010.

Section I: Operated Departments

The prime objective of Section I is to segregate all revenues and expenses applicable to each revenue-producing activity of the hotel in order to determine the departmental income (or loss). (This should also serve as a basis for evaluating each department head's performance.) While each major revenue producing department (or activity) of the operation will be shown on a separate line on the statement, minor revenue-producing departments and other miscellaneous sources are combined into one heading.

In order to facilitate the determination of departmental income, the USAL format has five working columns: (1) net revenues, (2) cost of sales, (3) payroll and related expenses, (4) other expenses, and (5) income or (loss).

The net revenue column (1) includes the total revenues derived by each individual unit from sales, net of allowances for rebates and overcharge adjustments. Column (2), (3), and (4) consist of three summarized expense categories charged to specific departments of the company. Column (5) then represents the resulting departmental income (or loss). Thus, the determination of each department's income (or loss) becomes a fairly simple mechanical calculation, as follows:

A	−	B		=	C
(1)	(2)	(3)	(4)		(5)
Net Revenues	Cost of Sales	Payroll and Related Exp.	Other Expenses		Income (Loss)

In other words, departmental income (5) is the excess of departmental revenue (1) over departmental expenses (2, 3, and 4). If departmental expenses exceed departmental revenues, the resulting figure will be a departmental loss. The above relationships can be expressed (as illustrated above) using the equation

$$C = A - B$$

where C is departmental income, B the departmental expenses (cost of sales, payroll and related expenses, and other expenses), and A the departmental net revenue. In the case of a departmental loss (that is, for B greater than A)

$$D = B - A$$

where D is departmental loss (indicated by brackets in the statement).

We now discuss some of the individual units included under operated departments, commencing with the rooms department. Reference should be made to the summary statement of income (Exhibit 10-4) throughout our discussion.

Rooms Department. Room's revenue is generally the major source of income for a lodging operation, and so it is listed first on the long-form income statement. A supporting schedule contains additional information concerning the composition of the rooms department heading, which is summarized on the formal statement.

Rooms revenue is classified into transient and permanent, depending on whether or not the guest has established residency in the hotel for an extended period. The net revenue of the rooms department consists of total rooms revenues less allowances given in the form of adjustments for rebates and overcharges.

The expenses directly attributable to the rooms department are broken down in the income statement into two categories: (1) payroll and related expenses and (2) other expenses. Cost of sales does not apply to the rooms department, since room rentals do not involve the sale of goods, only of services. Therefore, the determination of room's departmental income or loss consists of:

$$\underset{(1)}{\underset{\text{net revenues}}{\text{rooms}}} - \underset{(3 \text{ and } 4)}{\underset{\text{departmental expenses}}{\text{rooms}}} = \underset{(5)}{\underset{\text{departmental income}}{\text{rooms}}}$$

$$\$1,523,000 \quad - \quad (395,000 + 80,000) \quad = \quad \$1,048,000$$

If rooms departmental expenses exceed net revenue; there will be a departmental loss:

$$\underset{(3 \text{ and } 4)}{\underset{\text{departmental expenses}}{\text{rooms}}} - \underset{(1)}{\underset{\text{net revenues}}{\text{rooms}}} = \underset{(5)}{\underset{\text{departmental loss}}{\text{rooms}}}$$

Because the rooms department is mainly concerned with service activity, payroll and related expenses representing the cost of staffing the rooms department of the hotel is the major expense category. Not only are salaries and wages included here, but also payroll taxes and employee benefits applicable to employees of the rooms department such as the front office manager, room clerks, maids, house-keepers, doorpersons, and bellpersons and porters.

Other expenses attributable to the rooms department are grouped together in the income statement and are itemized on schedule 1. These expenses relate primarily to the materials used in making up the rooms (laundry and cleaning supplies, linen, guest supplies), contract services, travel agent commissions for obtaining room business, telecommunications, complimentary guest services and the cost of reservation service.

Food Department. Food revenue includes sale of food, coffee, tea, milk, and soft drinks. It may be classified by the type of operation from which it is generated, such as restaurant, coffee shop, banquets, room service and others. As a result of the close ties between the food and beverage departments, which are generally under the responsibility of one department head, previous editions of the USAL recommended one combined heading for food and beverage operations on the income statement. Nonetheless, this was reversed in the ninth revised edition.

The food departmental schedule 2 (see Exhibit 10–5) of Perfect Inn provides the necessary information with respect to revenue and expense categories of the food department. The calculation of food departmental income entails the deduction of three expense categories (cost of sales, payroll and related expenses, and other expenses) from the net departmental revenue:

$$\underset{(5)}{\underset{\substack{\text{income}}}{\text{food departmental}}} = \underset{(1)}{\text{food net revenue}} - \underset{(2, 3, \text{ and } 4)}{\underset{\text{expenses}}{\text{food departmental}}}$$

$$\$133,000 \quad = \quad \$626,000 \quad - (\$208,000 + 218,000 + 67,000)$$

A departmental (loss) occurs when food expenses exceed food revenues.

A major cost in the food department is cost of sales, representing the raw materials used in the preparation of meals served to guests and furnished for employee meals. As shown by departmental schedule 2 (Exhibit 10–5), the calculation of net cost of food sold first requires the deduction of the cost of employee meals from the total cost of food consumed by guests and employees. The cost of

PERFECT INN
Food Departmental Schedule
Schedule 2

Total revenue	$629
Allowance	3
Net revenue	626
Cost of sales	
Cost of food	217
Less: Cost of employee meals	9
Total cost of food sold	208
Gross profit on sales	418
Expenses:	
Salaries and wages	200
Employee benefits	18
Total payroll and related expenses	218
Other expenses:	
China, glassware, silver and linen	15
Laundry and dry cleaning	3
Operating supplies	25
Training	4
Licenses	12
Other	8
Total other expenses	67
Total expenses	493
Departmental income (loss)	$133

Exhibit 10–5   Perfect Inn—food departmental schedule.

employee meals will in turn be charged against the respective departments whose employees are served (it is included as a payroll and related expense).

The cost of food sold is deducted from the food net revenue in arriving at the gross profit from the sale of food (also referred to as gross margin), which is considered an important measure of profitability, insofar as it reflects the earnings available to cover all the other operating costs of the department.

Another significant expense category in the food department is the payroll and related expenses, that is, the cost of staffing the food operation: salaries and wages, payroll taxes, and employee benefits provided to cooks, chefs, dishwashers, waiters, cashiers, and so on. It also includes any expense associated with leased labor.

Other operating expenses applicable to the food operation are the cost of items used in serving the guests (china, glassware, silver and linen) and the cost of utility items (cleaning supplies, paper supplies, kitchen fuel, and guest supplies).

Beverage Department.   Beverage revenues includes the revenues generated from the sale of alcoholic beverages and drinks. It may be classified by type of operation from which it is generated such as restaurant, lounges, mini-bars, and so on. It also includes revenues generated from the sale of snacks and cigarettes sold in various beverages facilities.

The calculation of beverage departmental income involves the deduction of beverage departmental expenses (cost of sales, payroll and related expenses and other expenses) from beverages net departmental revenues.

The cost of beverages sold includes the cost of wines, liquors, beers, mineral waters, syrups and other items that are used in the preparation of mixed drinks. Payroll and related expenses include cost of staffing the beverage operation: salaries and wages, payroll taxes, and employee benefits provided to beverage purchasers, stewards, bartenders, and so on. Other operating expenses applicable to the beverage operation are china, glassware, silver and linen, contract services, licenses, uniforms and so on.

Casino Department. Acknowledging the significance of casino operations, a fast growing segment of the hospitality industry, the seventh edition of the USAL (published in 1977) included a separate line for a casino department on its long-form income statement format. The casino schedule was dropped in the eighth edition published in 1987 upon recognition that for most operations with a casino, gaming (not rooms revenue) is the primary source of revenue. The ninth revised edition, however, recommended to include a casino department for those properties that have a casino, but is not the primary source of revenue.

When applicable, the calculation of casino departmental income involves the deduction of departmental expenses (payroll and related expenses, and other expenses) from net departmental revenues. Payroll and related expenses, the major cost of the casino operation, are the salaries and wages, payroll taxes, and employee benefits attributable to employees exclusively engaged in the generation of casino revenues, such as managers, florin, casino cashiers, hosts, and runners. A second major group of costs in the casino department (listed under other expenses) relates to complimentary travel, rooms, and food and beverage provided to casino patrons. Other casino operating costs are cleaning expenses, gaming taxes and license fees, contract services, credit and collection and uniforms.

Telecommunications. Telecommunications department (previously known as telephone department) includes revenues derived from the use of telecommunication facilities by guests including local and long-distance calls, facsimile services, modem services, and other telecommunication services used by guests. It should not include any amounts of telecommunication services used by management or other departments of the hotel. The calculation of the telecommunications departmental income or loss is made as follows:

$$
\begin{array}{ccc}
\text{telecommunication} & \text{telecommunication} & \text{telecommunication} \\
\text{net revenues} \quad - & \text{expenses} \quad = & \text{income (loss)} \\
(1) & (2, 3 \text{ and } 4) & (5) \\[4pt]
\$50{,}000 & -(45{,}000 + 15{,}000 + 5{,}000) = & (\$15{,}000)
\end{array}
$$

Telecommunication expenses include cost of sales, payroll and related expenses, and other expenses. The cost of sales, also known as cost of calls, includes the total amounts billed by the telecommunication companies for long-distance and local calls through the switchboard. Payroll and related expenses include the salaries and wages, the payroll taxes, and the benefits of the telecommunications manager, telephone operators, supervisors and technicians. Other expenses include contract services, the cost of uniforms for employees of telecommunication department and the cost of printing service manuals and telecommunication vouchers.

Other Operated Departments. As stated earlier, the summary statement of income format of the USAL is rather flexible and can be adapted to meet the reporting needs of individual lodging companies. In this regard, other major revenue-producing departments of the operation are listed separately on the statement of income, when applicable, and refer to departments operated by the hotel, as opposed to similar services operated by others under rental or concession arrangements; for example, health center, guest laundry, golf course, tennis, newsstand, swimming pool, garage and parking and gift/apparel shop departments.

Other operated departments are treated in the same way as the major departments. The departmental income or loss is determined by deducting the pertinent departmental expenses (cost of sales, payroll and related expenses, and other expenses) from the departmental net revenue. A separate departmental schedule should be prepared for each operated unit or department.

Rentals and Other Income.   Rentals and other income includes all revenue-producing activities of the company not listed as part of a specific operated department: rental income, interest income, dividend income, and the like. Since rentals and other income is part of the operated-departments section of the statement of income, it is taken into consideration in the calculation of total departmental income or loss, but because these revenue sources do not constitute an actual operated department, any related expenses are treated as a direct reduction from the revenue generated. Consequently, the net rentals and other income figure, shown in column 1 of the statement, is carried over to the departmental income column 5, as shown in the following example:

	(1) Net revenue	(2)	(3)	(4)	(5) Income (loss)
Rentals and other income	$5,000		no amounts		$5,000

Major sources of revenue reported as rentals and other income, include revenue generated from the rental of space within the property, commissions received from others for services, such as automobile rentals, taxicab, garage and parking, cash discounts for early payment to vendors, interest earned on cash investments, bank deposits, and from other sources. It is important to recognize that some of the items listed under rentals and other income might not clearly fit the description of operating income. A typical example is interest income, normally included after operating income on income statements prepared for most commercial entities. Hence, in certain situations where contractual agreements state that interest income should not be included in operating income, it should be reported separately, as a line item below income after undistributed operating expenses.

Departmental Income (Loss).   We have already seen that departmental income or loss is determined by deducting from total departmental net revenue the sum of departmental expenses (cost of sales, payroll and related expenses, and other expenses).

The operated-department income reflects the total income generated by all revenue-producing departments and activities of the operation. The overall profitability of the operation will depend on whether the total contribution of the operated departments covers all other operating costs as well as the fixed expenses of the organization. We shall now examine the second section of the long-form income statement, the undistributed operating expenses.

Section II: Undistributed Operating Expenses

The undistributed operating expenses are considered the overhead expenses of a hotel; that is, they are incurred for the benefit of the overall organization and hence are not allocated to any specific department, since it is not possible or practical to do so.

The undistributed operating expenses include the following groupings of expenses: (1) administrative and general, (2) human resources, (3) information systems, (4) security, (5) marketing, (6) franchise fees, (7) transportation, (8) property operation and maintenance, and (9) utility costs. Since all these items represent operating expenses, no amounts will appear under the columns net revenue or cost of sales on the income statement based on the USAL. Franchise fees used to be part of marketing in previous editions, yet in the ninth revised edition of USAL franchise fees are listed separately.

Administrative and General Expenses. Administrative and general expenses include costs of a general nature that relate to all departments in such a way that they are not assigned to any one department. That is, administrative and general expenses benefit the entire operation and are broken down into two categories on the income statement: payroll and related expenses and other expenses.

Salaries and wages, payroll taxes, and employee benefits associated with the employment of the general manager, accounting office personnel, and other administrative employees are part of administrative and general payroll and related expenses inasmuch as these expenses provide general benefit to all units. Likewise, a departmental schedule includes detailed information concerning the composition of other expenses, such as professional fees, bad debts, printing, stationery and postage, and dues and subscriptions.

Marketing. Marketing encompasses all costs incurred by the organization with the prime objective of obtaining and retaining customers. Included here are the salaries, wages, and other payroll-related expenses associated with employees working toward the marketing effort, namely, sales managers, advertising managers and staff, research analysts, and public relations managers and staff.

Marketing expenses are broken down by the different activities of the marketing function: sales, advertising, merchandising, public relations and other selling and promotional expenses. In addition to payroll costs, other marketing expenses are aimed at the creation of customers' perception of hotel services. They include travel and entertainment, printing, radio and television fees, and trade show expenses.

Franchise fees are reported as a separate line item under undistributed operating expenses. The feeling was that the distribution throughout the statement of income of the fees charged by franchisers made uniform presentation difficult. Conversely, the reporting of franchise fees as a separate line item facilitates comparability.

Property Operation and Maintenance, and Utility Costs. Property operation and maintenance, and utility costs are two separate line items associated with the operation and maintenance of the property. They include operation of the heating, refrigeration, air conditioning, and other mechanical systems in the hotel.

Like in the case of other undistributed operating costs, property, operation, maintenance, and utility costs are broken down into payroll costs and other costs. Payroll and related expenses relate to personnel such as the chief engineer and assistants, plumbers, electricians, and elevator mechanics. Other expenses include the cost of materials used in repairing buildings, furniture, fixtures and equipment, painting and decorating supplies, and heating and other utility costs.

Income after Undistributed Operating Expenses. Income after undistributed operating expenses (previously known as income before fixed charges, or house profit), is regarded as the best measure of overall managerial efficiency inasmuch as all revenues and expenses that are under the responsibility and control of operating management are considered in its calculation. That is why bonuses are often based on the amount of income after undistributed operating expenses, considered a good way to evaluate managerial performance and operating success.

Income after undistributed operating expenses represents the amount of income after deducting the total undistributed operating expenses (sum of payroll and related expenses, and other expenses on the income statement) from total operated department income. The remaining expenses, not yet recognized, are mainly capital costs. They are unrelated to operating performance, being a function of the cost of the property. As a result, they do not affect the determination of income after undistributed operating expenses.

Section III: Fixed Charges

Fixed charges are, in effect, the capital costs of the hospitality organization. By reason of the capital-intensive nature of the hospitality industry (especially the lodging segment), fixed charges represent very significant expenses on the income statement. Approximately thirty cents of each revenue dollar is needed to cover fixed costs.

Because fixed expenses are a function of investment and financing decisions made by top management, they are considered nonoperating, noncontrollable costs (not under the direct control of operating management). Thus, they are not taken into consideration in the evaluation of operating performance, as measured by income after undistributed operating expenses.

The fixed expenses are rent, property taxes, fire and general insurance, depreciation, amortization, and interest expense. The amount remaining after deducting each of the fixed expenses from income after undistributed operating expenses is called income before income taxes. When applicable, management fees and gain or loss on sale of property are deducted (or added to) income after undistributed operating expenses.

In previous editions, general insurance (i.e., premiums relating to liability, fidelity and theft coverage) were included under undistributed operating expenses under the premise that it was under the control of operating management. Currently, however, especially in the case of managed operations, the owner controls general insurance costs. Therefore, they are included under rent, property taxes, and insurance.

Income before Income Taxes

The resulting figure, after accounting for the gain or loss from sale of property as outlined above, is referred to as income before income taxes and includes all revenues earned net of all expenses incurred, except for income taxes, during the accounting period. Finally, the provision for income taxes is calculated on the basis of income before income taxes.

Income taxes, the last expense reported on a corporate income statement, reflects the portion of the corporate earnings paid and/or due to be paid to the government in compliance with the rules and regulations of the IRS and other government agencies responsible for the collection of income taxes. Since federal and state income tax laws have been designed with different objectives in mind than GAAP, it is not unusual that the financial statement treatment of certain transactions will differ from their tax treatment. A typical example is the difference between book and tax depreciation.

In all such cases, there is a need to account for the effects of timing differences between accounting or book income (on the financial statements) and taxable income (on the tax return). This results in deferred income tax, which simply represents the accumulated value of postponed taxes, that is, the total amount of taxes the hospitality firm defers by using tax treatments resulting in lower taxable income than the book income (income before income taxes) shown on the income statement. In addition, there is a need to segregate on the income statement the amount of income taxes currently payable (current income tax) and the amount deferred (deferred income tax), if applicable.

For the sake of simplicity, we shall use 40 and 50 percent as the corporate income tax rate in most of the examples and problems throughout this book. However, the actual corporate tax rate as of this writing is 35 percent.

As previously noted, the summary statement of income (based on the USAL) of Perfect Inn for the year ended December 31, 2010 should prove useful in reviewing the major sections of the long-form income statement outlined in the preceding pages.

SPECIAL INCOME STATEMENT ITEMS

In addition to reporting revenues earned and expenses incurred during the accounting period, the income statement includes (if applicable) special items such as: gains and losses from discontinued operations, extraordinary gains and losses, and cumulative effect of change in accounting principles.

Extraordinary Items

Gains and losses of an unusual and nonrecurring nature are reported near the bottom of the income statement, net of their income tax effect. In this manner, financial statement users can evaluate the company's performance without taking into consideration extraordinary items that are not expected to happen again.

Extraordinary items are events and transactions that are distinguished by their unusual nature and by the infrequency of their occurrence. Events that serve as clear examples of extraordinary items are fire losses or other major natural disasters causing property damage to lodging establishments, restaurants, or travel service firms (e.g., losses from tornadoes, hurricanes, earthquakes, and the like). If material, the extraordinary item (net of the corresponding income tax effect) is deducted from income before extraordinary items on the income statement. Additionally, appropriate disclosure of specific details concerning extraordinary items is required. This is normally part of the notes to the financial statements.

Prior-Period Adjustments

When an item is treated as a correction of earnings applicable to a prior period, an adjustment to the beginning balance of retained earnings is necessary. The prior-period adjustments frequently involve the correction of a material error associated with the financial statements of a prior period.

Prior-period adjustments, which are very rare, are excluded in the determination of the current period's net income inasmuch as they do not relate to the business activities of the current period. Instead, an adjustment to the accumulated earnings of prior periods is made through a charge or credit to the opening balance of retained earnings.

Examples of prior-period adjustments include the material understatement of the income tax provision of a prior period and settlements of significant amounts resulting from litigation or similar claims directly related to prior periods.

Discontinued Operations

Gains and losses from the disposal of a segment of a hospitality business should be reported separately from continued operations on the statement of income. In addition, the results of the discontinued operations of a segment of a hospitality business that has been sold, abandoned, or otherwise disposed of (but still operating), together with the gain or loss on the sale, are shown on the income statement under discontinued operations.

The phrase "a segment of a business" refers to a portion of the company that represents a major line of business or class of customer. For instance, when a hospitality chain operates restaurants and hotels, the company has two segments of its business. If it sells the restaurant division while continuing to operate the hotel division, operating results of the restaurants disposed of, together with the gain or loss on the sale, are reported as a discontinued operation on the statement of income.

There are two primary reasons for segregating the results of continuing operations from those of discontinued operations:

1. To provide useful information needed for evaluating the impact of discontinued operations on the business organization.
2. To enable the financial statement users to base future projections on income from continuing operations.

Cumulative Effect of a Change in Accounting Principle

When a hospitality firm changes from one accounting principle to another, such as changes in depreciation or inventory valuation methods, it needs to report the effect of the accounting change in a special section of the statement of income. The section usually appears after extraordinary items.

Financial statement users need to know what cumulative effect the accounting change would have had on net income of prior years in order to facilitate comparability between accounting periods. Accordingly, GAAP requires companies to disclose (in a footnote) the difference between the net income actually reported and the net income that the company would have reported if it had used the new method consistently.

COMPREHENSIVE INCOME

In June 1997, the Financial Accounting Standards Board (FASB) enacted Statement number 130, Reporting Comprehensive Income. Under the provisions of this statement, comprehensive income must be displayed in a financial statement in the period in which it is recognized. The term "comprehensive income" is defined as the change in equity of a business firm during a period from transactions and other events resulting from non-owner sources. It includes all changes in equity except those resulting from owners' investments and distribution to owners.

According to Statement 130, comprehensive income has two components: net income and other comprehensive income. No changes were made on items included under net income. Other comprehensive income includes foreign currency translation adjustments and unrealized gains and losses on investments in debt and equity securities.

The requirement to report comprehensive income in a financial statement can be satisfied in one of three ways:

- The one-statement approach: reports comprehensive income below net income in the Income Statement
- The two-statement approach: reconciles net income to comprehensive income in a separate Statement of Comprehensive Income
- The statement of changes in equity approach: reports comprehensive income as a component of the total change in equity for the period in a separate Statement of Shareholders' Equity

ILLUSTRATIVE INCOME STATEMENT:
HILTON HOTELS CORPORATION AND SUBSIDIARIES

We now examine the income statement presentation of an actual firm in the hospitality industry: Hilton Hotels Corporation and Subsidiaries (see Exhibit 10–6). The following comments will serve to review major items associated with the Consolidated Statement of Income of Hilton Hotels and Subsidiaries (Hilton), thereby facilitating the understanding of this format in light of what this chapter has covered:

1. The consolidated statements of Hilton are presented in comparative form for the years 1996, 1995, and 1994. In contrast to the balance sheet, three years of comparative data are required.
2. Footnotes (or notes to the consolidated financial statement) are considered an integral part of the financial statements. They include additional detail about revenue, expenses and other income statement items.
3. Hilton uses a modified single-step format in the preparation of the income statement.

Consolidated Statements of Income (in millions, except per share amounts)	Year Ended December 31, 1996	1995	1994
Revenue			
Rooms	$1,734	1,562	1,445
Food and beverage	857	782	738
Casino	857	791	729
Franchise fees	43	39	37
Other	449	381	352
	3,940	3,555	3,301
Expenses			
Rooms	508	484	462
Food and beverage	674	625	601
Casino	466	400	344
Other expenses, including remittances to owners	1,911	1,659	1,580
Corporate expense	52	32	28
	3,611	3,200	3,015
Operating Income	329	355	286
Interest and dividend income	38	35	22
Interest expense	(88)	(93)	(87)
Interest expense, net, from equity investments	(12)	(17)	(12)
Income Before Income Taxes and Minority Interest	267	280	209
Provision for income taxes	106	102	85
Minority interest, net	5	5	2
Income Before Extraordinary Item	156	173	122
Extraordinary loss on extinguishment of debt, net of tax benefit of 552	(74)	—	—
Net Income	$ 82	173	122
Earnings Per Share			
Income before extraordinary item	$ .79	.89	.63
Extraordinary loss	(.38)	—	—
Net Income Per Share	$ .41	.89	.63

Exhibit 10–6   Hilton Hotels Corporation and subsidiaries, consolidated statements of income for the years 1994, 1995, and 1996.

4. Operating costs and expenses are deducted from operating revenues in arriving at operating income.

5. The most significant source of revenue is derived from hotel room sales which includes the consolidated results of company-owned and leased properties. Casino gaming revenue includes the results of operations under Hilton, Bally and Flamingo brands as well partially owned casinos in Australia and other foreign markets.

6. The operating income contribution from the properties acquired in the Bally merger on December 18, 1996 was not significant to 1996 results.

7. Minority interest primarily results from the consolidation of a partially owned New Orleans Hilton Riverside and Towers.

8. Provision for income taxes represents the expense for federal and state income taxes on Hilton's corporate income.

9. Extraordinary items reflect the costs and expenses incurred in connection with the extinguishment of debt. The extraordinary loss totaled $74 million in 1996, net of a tax benefit of $52 million.

10. Earnings per share is computed by dividing net income before and after extraordinary item by the weighted average of common shares and common share equivalents outstanding during the period. Common share equivalents are outstanding securities which arise from assumed exercise of stock options (granted to officers and key employees of the company) and convertible debt (bonds which can be converted into common stock).

SOME KEY TERMS INTRODUCED IN THIS CHAPTER

1. **Change in accounting principle.** Adopting a generally accepted accounting principle different from the one used in a previous period.
2. **Comprehensive income.** Change in equity of a firm arising from transactions and other events from non-owner sources.
3. **Discontinued operations.** Disposal of a major segment of a business.
4. **Earnings per share (EPS).** A disclosure on the face of an income statement, reflecting management's success in achieving profits for the owners. Earnings are related to the weighted average of common shares and common share equivalent outstanding.
5. **Extraordinary items.** Unusual and non-recurring gains and losses.
6. **Fixed charges.** Noncontrollable indirect costs such as interest expense, depreciation expense, insurance expense and property taxes, which are deducted from income after undistributed operating expenses according to the uniform system for the lodging industry (USAL).
7. **Foreign currency translations.** Gains and losses arising from the conversion of foreign currency into dollars. It is included under comprehensive income.
8. **Gross margin or gross profit.** Revenues minus cost of sales.
9. **Income after undistributed operating expenses.** Operated departmental income less undistributed operating expenses.
10. **Multistep income statement.** Form of income statement that arrives at net income in steps.
11. **Noncontrollable costs or expenses.** Costs that are not under the control of management or department heads in a company
12. **Operated departments.** First section of a statement of income based on the USAL. It includes revenues arising from the operation of revenue producing departments and activities of the lodging establishment less expenses directly associated with those revenues.

13. **Prior-period adjustments.** The correction of an error in a financial statement from a prior period, shown as an adjustment to the opening balance of retained earnings.

14. **Single-step income statement.** Form of an income statement, which arrives at net income in one step.

15. **Undistributed operating expenses.** Costs incurred for the benefit of the overall organization; not allocated to specific departments since they are not under the control of operated departments.

16. **Uniform System of Accounts for the Lodging Industry (USAL).** A standardized system that provides a uniform classification, organization and presentation of financial information for the lodging industry. The ninth revised edition was published in 1997 and was approved by the American Hotel and Motel Association.

17. **Unrealized gain (loss).** A gain or loss recognized in the financial statements but not associated with an asset sale. It is included under comprehensive income.

QUESTIONS

1. What is the main objective of the statement of income?
2. Define (a) revenues, (b) expenses, (c) gains and losses.
3. Describe the single-step format and the multistep format used in the preparation of an income statement.
4. What are the major sources of revenue for (a) a table-service restaurant, (b) a fast-food operation, (c) a hotel, (d) a travel agency, (e) an airline company?
5. What is meant by revenue recognition?
6. How are gains and losses shown on the income statement? Give three examples.
7. What are the major differences between a hospitality firm income statement and that of other commercial enterprises?
8. Describe four major goals of the Uniform System of Accounts for the Lodging Industry (USAL).
9. In an income statement based on the USAL (seventh edition), what information is reported in the operated departments section?
10. What are undistributed operating expenses? Give one example of each category of such expenses under the ninth edition of the USAL.
11. What is the significance of Income after Undistributed Operating Expenses?
12. What are fixed charges? List three examples.
13. What is gain (or loss) on sale of property?
14. What is the basic objective of the short-form income statement?
15. What are extraordinary items? Give three examples.
16. What is earnings per share (EPS)?
17. Describe the main items that explain the change in retained earnings between two periods.
18. Describe the proper treatment of gains and losses from the disposal of a major segment of a hospitality business.
19. What are prior-period adjustments? How do they affect (a) retained earnings and (b) current income? Give two examples.
20. What is comprehensive income?
21. How are changes in accounting principles reported on the financial statements?

EXERCISES

1. Using the following information, prepare the food departmental schedule of Precious Inn for the period ended December 31, 2009:

Coffee shop	$ 70,000
Restaurant	20,000
Banquets	25,000
Other income	5,000
Employee meals	4,000
Cost of food consumed	80,000
Salaries, wages, and related expenses	50,000
China, glassware, silver, and linen	5,000
Licenses	1,000
Laundry and cleaning	700
Printing, stationery, and postage	800
Supplies	1,000
Other expenses	1,200

2. Consider the following operating data of the E&R Restaurant for the month of June 2010:

Food sales	$100,000
Beverage sales	60,000
Cost of food sold	38,000
Cost of beverages sold	15,000
Loss from tornado	5,000
Other income	3,000
Salaries and wages	40,000
Operating supplies	7,000
Payroll taxes	2,000
Laundry and cleaning	5,000
China, glassware, silver, and uniforms	8,000
Depreciation and amortization	25,000
Interest	12,000
Gain on sale of building	8,000

What were the restaurant's (1) total revenue, (2) total expenses, (3) gains or losses, (4) extraordinary items, and (5) net income or net loss in June?

3. Consider the partial information (not all the income statement items are included) of IRA Inn from its 2009 summary statement of income based on the USAL (ninth edition):

Room sales	$300,000
Rentals and other income	30,000
Net income	25,000
Income after undistributed operating expenses	80,000
Depreciation and amortization	10,000
Rent, property taxes, and insurance	20,000
Total undistributed operating expenses	75,000
Rooms—payroll and related expenses	120,000
Rooms—other expenses	90,000
Food income	50,000

Based on the foregoing information, answer the following questions:
(a) What is the rooms department income (or loss)?
(b) What is the total operated departments' income (or loss)?
(c) Assuming that the only operated department not listed above was the telecommunication department, what was its department income (or loss)?
(d) What is the income before income taxes? (Income tax rate is 40 percent).

4. Selected accounts appearing in the income statement and balance sheet columns of the financial statement worksheet of Air Travel Services for the year ending December 31, 2009 are listed in alphabetical order below:

Accumulated depreciation: building	$ 28,000
Cash	10,000
Commissions earned	230,000
Depreciation and amortization	10,000
Dividends payable (only dividend declared in 2009)	2,000
Interest expense	5,000
Inventories	6,000
Notes payable	30,000
Operating expenses	70,000
Prepaid expenses	6,000
Rental income	10,000
Retained earnings, beginning balance	22,000
Salaries and wages	70,000
Selling expenses	50,000

   (a) Prepare a single-step income statement for the year 2009.
   (b) Determine the amount of retained earnings to be reported in the balance sheet at the end of the year 2009.

SHORT PROBLEMS

1. Consider the following operating data (in thousands of dollars) given in random order for Income Motels, Inc., at November 30, 2010, the end of its fiscal year:

Room rentals	$ 59,000
Utilities	7,000
Rentals of real estate property	2,200
Maintenance and repairs	5,800
Loss on settlement of lawsuit	2,000
Food sales	20,000
Beverage sales	11,500
Direct operating expenses: motels	16,200
Direct operating expenses: restaurants	24,700
Telecommunication net revenue	24,100
Administrative and general expenses	20,000
Cost of sales: telecommunication	17,700
Interest expense	8,400
Depreciation and amortization	6,400
Other income	7,000
Income taxes	4,700
Licenses and taxes	2,000
Cash dividends	1,000
Gain from property disposition	3,000

   (a) Prepare a single-step income statement for the year ended December 31, 2010 (for external users).
   (b) Prepare a statement of retained earnings for the year ended December 31, 2010 (retained earnings balance at December 31, 2009 is $25,000).
2. Consider the following partial information (not all income statement items are included) taken from the summary statement of income of Big Mac

Place for the year ending December 31, 2009 (based on the ninth edition of the Uniform System of Accounts for the Lodging Industry (USAL).

Income before income taxes	$ 73,000
Rooms net revenue	980,000
Depreciation and amortization	100,000
Interest expense	80,000
Rooms payroll and related expenses	220,000
Income tax rate	30%
Income after undistributed operating expenses	330,000
Total undistributed operating expenses	350,000
Rentals and other income	5,000
Rooms departmental income	500,000

Required:

Answer the following questions:

(a) What is the amount of rooms other expenses?

(b) What is the amount of total operated departmental income or (loss)?

(c) What is the net income?

3. The adjusted trial balance of Cherished Restaurant is shown below, with the accounts listed in alphabetical order.

CHERISHED RESTAURANT
Adjusted Trial Balance
December 31, 2009

Accounts payable		$ 23,000
Accounts receivable	$ 30,000	
Accrued interest payable		1,000
Accumulated depreciation		55,000
Administrative and general expenses	85,000	
Building	325,000	
Cash	10,000	
Common stock		150,000
Cost of sales	180,000	
Depreciation expense	15,000	
Food inventory	20,000	
Furniture and equipment	60,000	
Income taxes expense	20,000	
Income taxes payable		20,000
Insurance expense	15.000	
Land	35,000	
Long-term investments	20,000	
Miscellaneous expenses	15,000	
Mortgages payable (current portion $15,000)		160,000
Notes payable (due 2010)		20,000
Prepaid insurance	6,000	
Retained earnings		57,000
Salaries and wages	150,000	
Sales		500,000
	$986,000	$986,000

(a) Prepare a simple-form income statement for the year ended December 31, 2009.

(b) Prepare a statement of retained earnings for the year ended December 31, 2009.

(c) Prepare a classified balance sheet as of December 31, 2009.

LONG PROBLEMS

1. The following represent the account balances of RF Inn, Inc., for the year ended December 31, 2009:

Accounts receivable—net of allowance for doubtful accounts of $5,000	$ 85,000	Interest income	$ 2,000
		Rooms other expenses	150,000
Accounts payable	65,000	Rooms—payroll	120,000
Accrued expenses	25,000	Store rentals	3,000
General and administrative—payroll and related expenses	30,000	Information Systems—payroll	5,000
		Preopening costs	12,000
General and administrative—other expenses	60,000	Food—payroll	130,000
		Food—other	112,000
Building	800,000	Utility costs—payroll	20,000
Accumulated depreciation	100,000	Repairs and maintenance—payroll	20,000
Amortization expense	1,000	Mortgages payable due in installments to 2013, installment due in 2010 $20,000	720,000
Common stock—par value $1.00	100,000		
Paid in additional capital	40,000	Land	150,000
Repairs and maintenance	10,000	Income taxes payable	35,000
Utility costs—other	30,000	Dividends payable—declared on Dec. 26, 2009	20,000
Depreciation expense	34,000		
Furniture and equipment	50,000	Loss on sale of property	(10,000)
Cost of sales—food	200,000	Interest expense	15,000
Cost of sales—telecommunications	14,000	Property taxes and insurance	28,000
Inventories	70,000	Marketing—other	20,000
Prepaid expenses	5,000	Marketing—payroll	25,000
Food sales	490,000	Telecommunications—payroll	12,000
Cash	25,000	Telecommunications—other	9,000
Room sales	600,000		
Telecommunications—sales	30,000		

Using the foregoing data, answer the following questions related to the balance sheet and the USAL income statement of RF Inn, Inc., as of, and for, the year ended December 31, 2009:
   (a) Rooms department income (loss)—year 2009
   (b) Rentals and other income—year 2009
   (c) Total operated departments income (loss)—year 2009
   (d) Total undistributed operating expenses—year 2009
   (e) Income after Undistributed Operating Expenses—year 2009
   (f) Income before income taxes and gain (or loss) on sale of property—year 2009
   (g) Income before income taxes—year 2009
   (h) Net income for the year 2009 (income tax rate 40 percent)
   (i) Total current assets at December 31, 2009; list items as they would appear on the balance sheet
   (j) Total current liabilities at December 31, 2009; show individual items as they would appear on the balance sheet
   (k) Net book value of property and equipment at December 31, 2009
   (l) Total assets at December 31, 2009
   (m) Total retained earnings at December 31, 2009 (Retained earnings at December 31, 2008, $70,000)
   (n) Total shareholders' equity at December 31, 2009
2. Using the following data for Topper Resorts, as of January 31, 2010 (the end of its fiscal year), prepare (1) a statement of income (under USAL) for the year ended January 31, 2010 and (2) a balance sheet as of January 31, 2010.

Accounts receivable—net of allowance for doubtful accounts of $3,000	$ 120,000	Depreciation	$ 80,000
Accounts payable	155,000	Prepaid insurance	6,000
General and Adm.—payroll and related expenses	50,000	Land	300,000
General—other expenses	97,000	Building	1,500,000
Telecommunications—cost of sales	20,500	Furniture and equipment	100,000
Room sales	780,000	Cash	65,000
Food sales	550,000	Loss on sale of land	30,000
Telecommunications sales	43,000	Income tax expense	70,000
Marketing—other expenses	50,000	Insurance	10,000
Property operations and maintenance—payroll	40,000	Real estate taxes	45,000
Property operations and maintenance—other expenses	20,000	Income taxes payable	14,000
Utility costs	40,000	Bonds payable	1,000,000
Accumulated depreciation	350,000	Bad debt expense	3,000
Investments	30,000	Accrued expenses	55,000
Store rentals	20,000	Inventories	105,000
Interest expense	110,000	Common stock—400,000 shares outstanding—$1 par value	400,000
Other income	40,000	Dividends payable (representing the only dividends declared during the year ended January 31, 2010)	50,000
Rooms—payroll	150,000		
Rooms—guest supplies	15,000	Retained earnings—balance Feb. 1, 2009	182,000
Rooms—linen and laundry	50,000	Food—cost of sales	200,000
Telecommunications—payroll	28,000	Food—payroll	180,000
Telecommunications—other expenses	2,500	Food—other expenses	70,000
Transportation—other	2,000		

3. Prepare a statement of income and expense for APB Hotels in accordance with USAL, based on the following ledger balances for the year ended September 30, 2010:

Utility costs—payroll and related expenses	$ 22,000	Marketing—payroll and related expenses	$ 1,000
Garage and parking—other expenses	400	Property operation and maintenance—other expenses	42,100
Telecommunications sales	31,500	Store rentals	18,000
Property operations and maintenance—payroll and related exp.	11,300	Rooms payroll and related expenses	214,000
Property taxes	96,500	Depreciation expense	138,000
Room sales	927,000	Food—other expenses	44,000
Telecommunications—cost of sales	43,000	Telecommunications—payroll and related expenses	14,000
Garage and parking—payroll and related expenses	600	Interest expense	67,000
General and administrative—other expenses	105,000	Beverage—payroll and related expenses	40,900
Garage and parking—cost of sales	28,000	Telecommunications—other expenses	1,000
Other income	24,150	Marketing—other expenses	45,000
Food—payroll and related expenses	322,000	Food sales	734,150
Beverage—sales	209,200	Provision for income taxes	30%
Utility costs—other expenses	74,300	General and Administrative payroll and related expenses	117,000
Beverage—cost of sales	64,000	Garage and parking net sales	32,100
Rooms—other expenses	79,000	Food—cost of sales	313,000
Fire insurance	2,400	Beverage—other expenses	9,600

SELECTED TOPICS

Property and Equipment, and Inventories | 11

The learning objectives in this chapter are:

- To become familiar with the various types of property and equipment, and how to record and dispose of these assets.
- To calculate depreciation and amortization as well as learn the various depreciation methods.
- To become familiar with some tax implications of owning property and equipment.
- To learn how to record inventory, determine cost of sales, and record employee meals.
- To learn the various inventory valuation methods, and their tax impact.
- To learn the procedure for taking a physical inventory, as well as the impact of errors in the physical inventory count.

Rendering the types of services typical to hospitality firms—lodging, board, and travel—requires a large investment in costly property and equipment such as hotel buildings, restaurants, cruise ships and airplanes. In the case of hotels, for instance, revenues are determined by multiplying:

- Number of available rooms (size of the hotel) by
- Average room rate (class of the hotel), and by
- Percentage occupancy

Similar calculations may be made for cruise ships, airplanes, and restaurants. The first two of these factors are directly related to the amount of investment in property and equipment which comprise more than 80 percent of the total assets of the typical hospitality industry firm.

The principal source of revenue for the hospitality industry in general is the sale of services such as lodging and travel. Nevertheless, transporting and lodging customers also often requires feeding them. Therefore, although the sale of food and beverages is the primary source of revenue only for restaurants, it is of some importance to most hospitality enterprises. Because food is highly perishable, only small amounts are kept on hand. Furthermore, supplies and spare parts inventories require a big investment only in the transportation segment of the industry. Consequently, hospitality industry firms tend to have small inventories relative to their total assets.

Nevertheless, for those firms that do have food and beverage inventories, the use of proper accounting procedures to record their purchase and consumption is essential in order to determine cost of sales accurately. When earnings in relation to inventories are small, the method used to account for these inventories may make the difference between reporting a profit or a loss. Furthermore, because in a restaurant up to 40 percent of every sales dollar can be consumed by cost of sales, even a slight lack of control in the area of inventories can cause a significant decrease in net income

In this chapter certain more advanced accounting procedures related to property and equipment, and inventories are presented. First, property and equipment is defined and the different types of property and equipment used in the hospitality industry are described. Then the procedure for recording the acquisition of property and equipment is explained, followed by a description of the most commonly used depreciation methods and an explanation of the amortization procedure. The procedure for disposing of property and equipment is then presented, followed by a brief discussion of some tax implications involved in the depreciation and sale of property and equipment.

With regard to inventories, this chapter first presents the accounting procedure for recording the purchase of inventories, followed by a brief discussion of periodic and perpetual inventories, purchase discounts and employee meals. The various inventory valuation methods used in accounting for inventories are then explained, followed by a comparison of the impact of these different valuation methods on the results of operations and financial position of a business, as well as some related tax considerations. Finally, the procedure for taking a physical inventory is described, accompanied by a short explanation of the impact of inventory valuation errors.

PROPERTY AND EQUIPMENT

Property and equipment includes all (1) tangible assets, (2) acquired for use in the ordinary operation of the business, and (3) having a useful life of more than one year. Leaseholds and leasehold improvements are included in this classification, even though they are intangible assets, because they give a hospitality firm the right to use tangible, physical assets. With the exception of land, which does not wear out, and construction in progress, which includes property and equipment not yet in service, all property and equipment are subject to a decline in value resulting from the process of aging. This loss of value may be produced by the asset wearing down or merely by some effect of the passage of time (obsolescence or changing markets, for instance). As described in Chapter 5, this decline in value (cost expiration) is recorded through a procedure called depreciation. In the case of leasehold and leasehold improvements, amortization is used to account for this cost expiration because they are intangible assets. Amortization will also be explained in this chapter.

Property and Equipment Categories

The Uniform System of Accounts for Lodging (USAL) includes the following categories in the property and equipment classification:

- Land
- Building
- Leaseholds and leasehold improvements
- Construction-in-progress

- Furniture and equipment
- China, glassware, silver, linen, and uniforms

The property and equipment categories are normally listed in order of permanence, as shown above. Restaurants and clubs have their own uniform system of accounts, which provide for similar property and equipment categories.

The land account includes all land used by a firm directly or indirectly to generate revenues during its ordinary course of operations. Land used for golf courses and parking lots is included along with land on which buildings are constructed. When a building is constructed upon it, the cost of the land must be segregated from the value of the building constructed to allow depreciation of the buildings exclusive of the land. As stated before, *land is never depreciated.*

Leasehold and leasehold improvements include expenditures made to acquire the rights to a lease or to improve property on which the hospitality firm already has leasehold rights.

Construction-in-progress includes all expenditures related to the construction of property or equipment. This account is charged with the cost of materials, labor, and advances on contracts involved in the construction of buildings, ships, airplanes and any other property and equipment. It should also be charged with the interest incurred due to the fact that the hospitality firm has its money invested during the construction period. Because the construction-in-progress does not generate income, the matching concept requires that the cost of this money, interest, be added to the cost of the construction, just as are labor and materials. This is an important category in the hospitality industry because hotel and restaurant chains tend to expand continually, and airlines and cruise lines are constantly contracting for the construction of new equipment to expand or replace outdated equipment. Property and equipment under construction is not depreciated. When construction is completed, the asset under construction is transferred to the appropriate property and equipment account, where the depreciation process begins.

The furniture and equipment category includes all the furniture, furnishings, and removable equipment owned by a firm. Room furniture, office furniture and equipment, kitchen equipment, and vehicles are included in this asset category. If an item can be removed from a building without harming it or the building, then it is furniture or a fixture.

The category of china, glassware, silver, linen, and uniforms includes all dishes, glasses, stemware, and silverware used by a restaurant or hotel. Also included are bed linen and restaurant linen as well as employee uniforms. Kitchen utensils are usually expensed when purchased, but are included in this category when it is not management policy to expense them.

The major property and equipment categories may be divided into subcategories such as furniture, furnishings, equipment, and vehicles. The degree to which account categories are subdivided depends upon the materiality or significance of the assets to be recorded therein. Also, subsidiary ledgers may be created to record cost and accumulated depreciation for individual single items of property or equipment when they are of very high value.

RECORDING CAPITAL LEASES

Sometimes a hospitality firm (lessee) will lease property and equipment from another firm (lessor) for a period of time that is 75 percent or more of the useful life of the asset and/or under such conditions that most of the risks and benefits incident to ownership are transferred to the lessee. These leases are commonly referred to as capital leases and must be recorded on the balance sheet as if the related asset had been purchased.

The conditions requiring capital lease treatment of what would normally be recorded as an operating lease are specified in FASB statement No. 13. When these conditions exist it is assumed that the lease contract is an installment purchase and the lease payments cannot be recorded as rent expense. According to FASB Statement No. 13, the future contractual lease payments over the life of the lease are totaled and discounted using a procedure called present value calculation. The present value of these future lease payments is debited to the appropriate property and equipment account as if the asset had been purchased, and a corresponding liability, called "capital lease obligation" is reported in the long term debt section of the balance sheet. The current portion of any long term lease obligation is included among the current liabilities. This capitalized lease is then amortized.

RECORDING PROPERTY AND EQUIPMENT

Property and equipment are recorded at cost. The matching concept requires that transportation and preparation expenses be added to the cost of an asset rather than be considered current period expenses. Some representative expenditures of this type are:

- Transportation costs
- Sales taxes, legal fees, and sales commissions
- Site preparation expenses
- Installation costs

Exhibit 11–1 shows the journal entry to record the cash purchase of an electric generator.

Since, by definition, property and equipment assets benefit a business over more than one annual accounting period (refer to the definition of an asset in Chapter 1), expenditures to make such assets operational will also benefit future accounting periods. Therefore such expenditures should be included as part of the cost of their related asset. When an expenditure is not expensed in the current accounting period but rather added to the cost of an asset on the balance sheet, we say that the expenditure has been *capitalized*, or that it is a capital expenditure.

Assumptions	
Purchase price	$5,000
Sales tax	250
Transportation cost	1,000
Cost to tear down existing wall	500
Installation cost	750

Journal Entry	Dr	Cr
Equipment	7,500	
Cash		7,500
To record the acquisition of an electric generator		

Exhibit 11–1   Journal entry to record purchase of an electric generator.

Thus, as stated earlier, interest on funds invested in construction-in-progress should be capitalized, or added to the cost of construction.

But interest paid in relation to the purchase of equipment that is ready for use should not be capitalized. Such interest should be expensed because, contrary to the situation of construction-in-progress, the related asset in this case is generating revenue, and consequently the matching concept requires that the interest expense be reported in the same period as the revenue it helps to generate.

Recording Improvements Versus Maintenance and Repairs Expense

The need to differentiate between expenditures that should be capitalized and expenditures that should be expensed in the current accounting period goes beyond the initial purchase phase of property and equipment. Expenditures related to property and equipment incurred after the purchase of a property and equipment asset should be recorded as maintenance and repairs expense (expensed) when they merely restore the property or equipment to its original condition. But expenditures should be added to the cost of the particular property or equipment (capitalized) when the expenditure (1) increases the capacity of the property or equipment, (2) improves its quality, or (3) extends its life beyond that expected when originally purchased. Such expenditures should be depreciated over the remaining useful life of the property or equipment they affect because they are now part of that property or equipment. If the useful life of the improvement is shorter than the remaining life of the related asset, then it should be depreciated over the improvement's useful life.

Suppose that the electric generator we purchased were now seven years old and needed to be repaired because it broke down. The repair shop tells us that to restore it to its original condition will cost $1,000, but for $2,500 they will do a complete overhaul that will extend its life by five years beyond its originally estimated 12 year useful life. The journal entry to record this transaction is shown below:

	Dr	Cr
Repairs expense	1,000	
Equipment	1,500	
Cash		2,500

Also, the remaining undepreciated original cost of the electric generator could be depreciated over the new remaining life of ten years. This would not be a violation of the consistency concept because an event had occurred which provides reasonable cause for changing the remaining depreciation life.

RECORDING DEPRECIATION OF PROPERTY AND EQUIPMENT

For reasons explained previously the cost of property and equipment must be allocated to the future periods that it will benefit. This is done by gradually writing-off, or expensing, the asset through a process called depreciation. Depreciation is a system of accounting which aims to distribute the cost or other basic value of tangible capital assets, less salvage (if any), over the estimated useful life of the unit (which may be a group of assets) in a systematic and rational manner.

According to this definition the three factors involved in depreciating property and equipment are:

1. The estimated useful life of the property or equipment
2. Its salvage value
3. The depreciation method used

Estimated Useful Life

The useful life of an asset is the period during which an asset will be of value to a firm in the firm's revenue-generating process. Since this period cannot be determined with certainty, it must be estimated by management. In making this estimate management must take into consideration the three factors that may, singly or in combination, cause an asset to lose value for their particular firm:

1. Physical deterioration caused by wear and tear
2. Obsolescence produced by technological developments
3. Inadequacy arising out of growth of the firm or changes in the industry (e.g., small airplanes may be inadequate after an airline opens new and longer routes)

Salvage Value

Property and equipment that is no longer useful to one firm may still have value for another firm. The salvage value (or residual value) of property and equipment is the amount that can be obtained for it when no longer of use to the original owner. In some instances the only value that can be obtained is the asset's scrap value. Because salvage value is based on estimates and the end of an asset's useful life may be so far in the future, it is often assumed to be zero. The value of an asset that is depreciated is called the *depreciable base* and is equal to cost less salvage value. This is the depreciable base for all four methods of depreciation described in this text. An asset should never be depreciated in excess of its depreciable base because that would leave a lower salvage value than that which was estimated.

DEPRECIATION METHODS

The definition of depreciation given above states that the cost of property and equipment must be distributed in a systematic and rational manner. In order to be rational, depreciation must record the expiration of an asset's value reasonably over its useful life. Some property or equipment loses value at a constant rate over its useful life—for example, buildings. In other cases, property loses value in relation to the amount of use given to it—for example, tour buses. In yet other cases, it loses value more rapidly in the early years of its life than in the later years—for example, an oven or other kitchen equipment. In order to allow for systematic and rational depreciation under these differing circumstances, four depreciation methods are available:

1. Straight-line method
2. Units-of-output method
3. Declining-balance method
4. Sum-of-years'-digits method

Reporting Accumulated Depreciation

Although it was covered in a previous chapter, it is important here to again explain the entry for recording depreciation expense. Whatever the method of calculating the amount of depreciation expense it is always entered the same way. Assuming that depreciation expense is $3,000, the entry to record it is:

	Dr	Cr
Depreciation expense	3,000	
Accumulated depreciation		3,000
To record $3,000 depreciation expense		

Straight-Line Depreciation

The straight-line depreciation method is based on the assumption that the cost of a particular property or equipment will expire at a constant rate over its useful life. This method expenses an asset's cost less salvage value, its depreciable base, evenly over its useful life. The formula for calculating annual straight-line depreciation is:

$$\frac{\text{cost} - \text{salvage value}}{\text{estimated useful life of asset}} = \text{annual depreciation expense}$$

Thus, a tour bus costing $12,000, with a $2,000 salvage value and a useful life of five years, would be subject to a $2,000 annual depreciation expense calculated as follows:

$$\frac{\$12,000 - \$2,000}{5 \text{ years}} = \$2,000$$

Another way of calculating this depreciation is to calculate what is called the *straight-line depreciation rate.* This is done by dividing the number "1" by the years in the asset's life, in this case 5. The depreciable base is then multiplied by the resulting decimal amount to obtain the annual depreciation. The tour bus straight-line depreciation is calculated using this method below:

$$\text{straight line rate} = .20$$
$$\text{then } .20 \times (\$12,000 - \$2,000) = \$2,000 \text{ annual depreciation}$$

Thus, the straight-line depreciation rate can also be expressed in terms of a percentage. The straight-line depreciation rate of our tour bus, for example, is 20 percent since it has a useful life of five years and 1/5, or 20 percent, of its depreciable base is depreciated annually.

Exhibit 11–2 shows the depreciable base, depreciation expense, accumulated depreciation, and net book value (cost less accumulated depreciation) of the tour bus over its useful life.

Units-of-Output Method

The units-of-output method is based on the assumption that the cost of a particular property or equipment will expire at a constant rate in proportion to the amount of use given to the asset. In the case of the tour bus, the amount of miles

Year	Depreciable base	Straight-line rate			Depreciation expense	Accumulated depreciation	Net book value
	$10,000	×	0.20	=	$2,000	$2,000	$10,000
2	10,000	×	0.20	=	2,000	4,000	8,000
3	10,000	×	0.20	=	2,000	6,000	6,000
4	10,000	×	0.20	=	2,000	8,000	4,000
5	10,000	×	0.20	=	2,000	10,000	2,000

Exhibit 11–2   Straight-line depreciation of tour bus.

Year	Depreciable base	Depreciation per mile		Miles traveled		Depreciation expense	Accumulated depreciation	Net book value
1	$10,000	$0.05	×	40,000	=	$2,000	$ 2,000	$10,000
2	10,000	0.05	×	20,000	=	1,000	3,000	9,000
3	10,000	0.05	×	60,000	=	3,000	6,000	6,000
4	10,000	0.05	×	50,000	=	2,500	8,500	3,500
5	10,000	0.05	×	30,000	=	1,500	10,000	2,000

Exhibit 11–3   Units-of-output method for depreciating tour bus.

that it is expected to travel before being sold for its salvage value, or scrapped, would have to be estimated. Its annual depreciation expense would then depend on the number of miles the tour bus traveled during the year. The formula for calculating annual depreciation under the units-of-output method is

$$\text{annual depreciation expense} = \frac{\text{cost} - \text{salvage value}}{\text{estimated units of output over entire life}} \times \text{annual units of output}$$

This formula multiplies the depreciation per unit of output times the annual units of output. Assuming that the same tour bus with a $12,000 cost and a $2,000 salvage value will travel 200,000 miles before it is worthless, the depreciation rate is

$$\frac{\text{cost} - \text{salvage}}{\text{estimated units of output during life}} = \frac{12,000 - 2,000}{200,000 \text{ miles}} = \$0.05 \text{ per mile depreciation}$$

If the bus travels 14,000 miles in a specific year, then for that year the depreciation expense will be:

$$\$0.05 \times 14,000 \text{ miles} = \$7,000 \text{ depreciation}$$

Exhibit 11–3 shows the depreciable base, depreciation expense, accumulated depreciation, and net book value of the tour bus under the assumption that the tour bus will travel the 200,000 miles in five years by traveling the number of miles each year that are indicated in the chart.

Accelerated-Depreciation Methods

In addition to these two depreciation methods, two other depreciation methods are available. These methods are called accelerated-depreciation methods because they result in higher depreciation expense during the first years of the asset's useful life than over the later years. The two most commonly used methods are the declining-balance method and the sum-of-the-years'-digits method.

Sum-of-the-Years'-Digits Method

The sum-of-the-years'-digits (SYD) method is a method of accelerating depreciation in the early years of an asset's useful life. As in the other two depreciation methods we have discussed, the depreciable base of an asset is its cost minus salvage value. This depreciable base is multiplied by a fraction the denominator of which is the sum of the years of estimated useful life of the asset. The numerator corresponds to each year of the asset's useful life, applied in reverse order. The last year of an asset's useful life is the numerator for the first year's fraction and the first year's digit (always the number 1) is the numerator for the fraction used in the final year of the asset's life. The yearly fractions for the tour bus with a five-year useful life are calculated as follows:

Year	Fraction		
1	$\dfrac{5}{1+2+3+4+5}$	$=\dfrac{5}{15}$	$=\dfrac{1}{3}$
2	$\dfrac{4}{1+2+3+4+5}$	$=\dfrac{4}{15}$	$=\dfrac{4}{15}$
3	$\dfrac{3}{1+2+3+4+5}$	$=\dfrac{3}{15}$	$=\dfrac{1}{5}$
4	$\dfrac{2}{1+2+3+4+5}$	$=\dfrac{2}{15}$	$=\dfrac{2}{15}$
5	$\dfrac{1}{1+2+3+4+5}$	$=\dfrac{1}{15}$	$=\dfrac{1}{15}$

Adding the number of years in an asset's life is a practical method of calculating the denominator of the fraction only when the asset's useful life is short. For assets with useful lives longer than five years (buildings can have useful lives as long as 50 years for instance) the following formula should be used, where N is the useful life of the asset in years:

$$\text{sum of years in asset's life} = \frac{N(N+1)}{2} = \frac{5(5+1)}{2} = 15$$

Once the yearly fraction is determined, it is applied according to the following formula to calculate the annual sum-of-year's-digit depreciation:

annual depreciation expense = annual fraction × cost less salvage value

For our sample tour bus the first year's depreciation would be calculated as follows:

$$\text{first year depreciation expense} = \frac{5}{15} \times (\$12,000 - \$2,000) = \$3,333$$

Exhibit 11–4 indicates the annual depreciation expense, accumulated depreciation, and net book value of our tour bus, which, as in the first two examples, has a $12,000 cost, a $2,000 salvage value, and a five-year useful life.

Declining-Balance Method

One of the ways that the declining-balance method differs from the other depreciation methods is that it uses net book value (cost minus the ever-increasing accumulated depreciation) in its calculations, rather than using the depreciable base (cost minus salvage value). Although salvage value is not taken into account in

Year	Depreciable base		Fraction		Depreciation expense	Accumulated depreciation	Net book value
1	$10,000	×	5/15	=	$3,333	$ 3,333	$8,667
2	10,000	×	4/15	=	2,667	6,000	6,000
3	10,000	×	3/15	=	2,000	8,000	4,000
4	10,000	×	2/15	=	1,333	9,333	2,667
5	10,000	×	1/15	=	667	10,000	2,000

Exhibit 11–4 Sum-of-the-years'-digits method for depreciating tour bus.

the formula for calculating declining-balance depreciation, an asset should never be depreciated below its salvage value.

To calculate declining-balance depreciation the decreasing net book value for each successive year is multiplied by the selected depreciation rate. This rate is usually double the straight-line rate, although 1.5 times the straight-line rate is also often used. When double the straight-line depreciation rate is used, this method is called the double-declining-balance (DDB) method. The formula for calculating double-declining-balance depreciation is:

$$\text{Asset's annual depreciation expense} = 2 \times \text{straight-line depreciation rate} \times \text{Asset's cost less accumulated depreciation}$$

As previously explained, the annual straight-line depreciation percentage rate is obtained by dividing the asset's useful life into the digit 1. Our tour bus with a five-year useful life has a straight-line depreciation rate of 1/5 or 20 percent and a double-declining-balance rate of 40 percent (2 × 20%). The net book value (cost less accumulated depreciation) for successive years is multiplied by this 40% rate to determine the annual depreciation expense.

The depreciable base, annual depreciation expense, accumulated depreciation, and net book value of the tour bus over its useful life are shown in Exhibit 11–5.

Fractional-Years Depreciation

When property or equipment is acquired on a date other than the beginning of an entity's accounting year, fractional-years depreciation must be used in order to include the proper amount of depreciation in each accounting period. For example, if a restaurant on a calendar accounting year purchases an oven on September 1, 2007, then one-third of the oven's first-year depreciation must be recorded in the accounting year ended December 31, 2007, and two-thirds in the 2008 accounting year. The example in Exhibits 11–6 and 11–7 serves to clarify this procedure. It shows the annual depreciation expense for a restaurant that is on an accounting year beginning September 1 (the date on which the oven was purchased) as opposed to that of a company on a calendar accounting year. The sum-of-years'-digits depreciation method is used.

Recording the Cost Expiration of China, Glassware, Silver, Linen, and Uniforms

China, glassware, silver, linen, and uniforms are assets with very short lives when compared to other property and equipment. Because of their special nature, cost expiration of assets in this category usually occurs because of physical

Year	Depreciable base	Depreciation expense	Accumulated depreciation	Net book value
1	$10,000	$12,000 × 0.40 = $4,800	$ 4,800	$7,200
2	10,000	7,200 × 0.40 = 2,880	7,680	4,320
3	10,000	4,320 × 0.40 = 1,728	9,408	2,592
4	10,000	592	10,000	2,000
5	10,000	0*	10,000	2,000

*With this method, the tour bus would have been depreciated below its $2,000 salvage value in year 4. Since an asset should never be depreciated below its salvage value, only $592 of depreciation expense should be recorded in year 4. Accordingly, no depreciation expense is recorded in year 5.

Exhibit 11–5 Double-declining-balance method for depreciating tour bus.

September 1–August 31

Year	Depreciation year dates	SYD annual depreciation expense
1	Sept. 1, 2007–Aug. 31, 2008	$ 3,333
2	Sept. 1, 2008–Aug. 31, 2009	2,667
3	Sept. 1, 2009–Aug. 31, 2010	2,000
4	Sept. 1, 2010–Aug. 31, 2011	1,333
5	Sept. 1, 2011–Aug. 31, 2012	667
Total		$10,000

Assume the oven cost $10,000 and had no salvage value.

Exhibit 11–6 Accelerated depreciation for restaurant on fiscal year September 1 to August 31.

deterioration caused by wear and tear and/or physical disappearance because of theft or breakage.

Depreciation of these assets, therefore, merely requires recording the cost of those items that are no longer serviceable or have disappeared. A count of the assets is made at the end of an accounting period and the original cost of all missing items is debited to their related cost expiration expense account.

The following example should serve to illustrate this process. Assume an establishment purchases $1,000 worth of china plates. Further assume that $500 worth of these are put into service and that only $400 worth are still in existence at the end of the year according to a physical count. The $100 worth of missing or broken china would be debited (charged) to an expense account called "china expense." The journal entry to record this is shown below.

	Dr	Cr
China expense	100	
China inventory		100

Notice that the cost expiration of china, glassware, silver, linen, and uniforms is deducted directly from their related asset inventory account. No contra-asset account is used.

Amortization

Amortization differs from depreciation in three ways: (1) theoretically it should be used only to record the cost expiration of intangible assets; (2) it is always calculated on a straight-line basis; and (3) it is credited directly to the asset account

Year	Depreciation year dates	Fractional depreciation	Annual depreciation expense
1	Sept. 1, 2007–Dec. 31, 2007	1/3 ($3,333)	$ 1,111
2	Jan. 1, 2008–Dec. 31, 2008	2/3 ($3,333) + 1/3 ($2,667)	3,111
3	Jan. 1, 2009–Dec. 31, 2009	2/3 ($2,667) + 1/3 ($2,000)	2,444
4	Jan. 1, 2010–Dec. 31, 2010	2/3 ($2,000) + 1/3 ($1,333)	1,778
5	Jan. 1, 2011–Dec. 31, 2011	2/3 ($1,333) + 1/3 ($667)	1,111
6	Jan. 1, 2012–Dec. 31, 2012	2/3 ($667)	445
Total			$10,000

Exhibit 11–7 Restaurant on calendar year January 1 to December 31.

instead of being credited to an accumulated amortization account. Below is shown the journal entry to record the amortization of ten year franchise rights that cost $100,000. Notice that no accumulated amortization account is credited, but rather the asset itself—franchise rights—is credited. If this were depreciation the accumulated depreciation account would be credited.

Example of ordinary treatment of amortization

	Dr	Cr
Amortization expense	10,000	
Franchise rights		10,000

To record one year's amortization of franchise rights that cost $100,000

We discuss amortization in this chapter because leasehold and leasehold improvements are intangible assets and must be amortized. They are actually out of place in the property and equipment section. Property and equipment theoretically includes only tangible assets. But they are closely associated with buildings and are a significant asset in the hospitality industry and so, by exception, they are included among the property and equipment. Their useful life is usually limited by the length of the lease contract, although in the case of longer leases physical deterioration may be the life-limiting factor.

Not only is the category of leaseholds and leasehold improvements exceptional because it is included among the property and equipment, but also because the amortization associated with this category is credited to an accumulated amortization account instead of being credited directly to the leasehold and leasehold improvements account, as is normal for amortization. This exception is allowed in order to establish consistency with the way accumulated depreciation is presented in this section.

Amortization is always calculated on a straight-line basis. Assume we are making modifications costing $5,000 on a property with five years remaining on its lease. We would divide the $5,000 cost by the five years remaining on the lease and amortize $1,000 each year as follows. Because leaseholds and leasehold improvements are, as an exception, included in the property and equipment section of the balance sheet, we will credit the amortization to an accumulated amortization account instead of crediting it directly to the leasehold and leasehold improvements account.

Example of the exceptional treatment of the amortization
of leaseholds and leasehold improvements

	Dr	Cr
Amortization expense	1,000	
Accumulated amortization		1,000

To record $1,000 amortization of leasehold improvements

As stated earlier, in the case of all intangible assets other than leaseholds and leasehold improvements the credit side of this entry would be made to the asset account itself, not to an accumulated amortization account.

Comparison of Depreciation Methods and Their Income Tax Impact

Exhibit 11–8 indicates the annual depreciation expense for the hypothetical tour bus under the four depreciation methods. As can be verified by the reader, the two accelerated-depreciation methods result in the depreciation of more than half of the tour bus' depreciable base during the first half of its useful life. These methods should, therefore, be used to depreciate assets whose cost expires more rapidly in their early years than in their later years of life. The straight-line

Year	Straight-line	Units-of-output	Double-declining-balance	Sum-of-the-years'-digits
1	$ 2,000	$ 2,000	$ 4,800	$ 3,333
2	2,000	1,000	2,880	2,667
3	2,000	3,000	1,728	2,000
4	2,000	2,500	592*	1,333
5	2,000	1,500		667
Total	$10,000	$10,000	$10,000	$10,000

*Depreciation required to arrive at salvage value.

Exhibit 11–8   Comparative depreciation expense chart.

method results in equal annual depreciation expense over an asset's useful life and should be used to depreciate assets that lose their value at a constant rate over time. The units-of-output method produces an erratic depreciation expense pattern. However, this pattern is due to the fluctuations in tour bus usage and is based on a constant rate of depreciation per mile of operation. This method should be used when an asset's loss of value is directly proportional to the amount of use it is given, thereby relating depreciation to the asset's productive output. It should be used to depreciate assets whose cost expires in direct proportion to the wear and tear caused by usage.

Exhibits 11–9 and 11–10 show graphically the results of plotting the depreciation amounts shown in Exhibit 11–8. Notice how depreciation expense is high in the early years of the tour bus' life and then decreases sharply under the double-declining-balance and sum-of-years'-digits depreciation methods. In contrast, the straight-line rate (it is actually a straight line on the graph) remains constant throughout the life of the asset. Exhibit 11–10 indicates that depreciation expense under the units-of-output method fluctuates according to the tour bus' annual mileage. This is consistent with the way depreciation is calculated under this method.

The use of accelerated depreciation methods has a direct impact on the calculation of a hospitality firm's net income. Because depreciation is higher than under the straight-line method over the early years of an asset's life, net income will be lower than under the straight-line method. Conversely, over the latter part of an asset's life there will be less depreciation expense than under the straight-line method, and consequently higher net income. Because managers should not try to manipulate or "manage" net income these consequences of using accelerated depreciation should not be taken into account when deciding on a depreciation method. However, as will be pointed out in the next paragraph, the manager can choose to use accelerated depreciation methods for tax reporting purposes and straight-line depreciation for financial reporting.

Other Income Tax Considerations in Accounting for Property and Equipment

This chapter has dealt with the procedures of accounting for property and equipment according to GAAP. However, the Internal Revenue Code (IRC), the compendium of laws governing the calculation of taxable income, in an effort to provide tax relief to businesses, permits the use of certain accounting procedures related to property and equipment that provide a lower current tax liability than that recognized under GAAP. This allows a company to postpone the payment of a portion of its taxes due. Another tax provision which will be discussed later, the

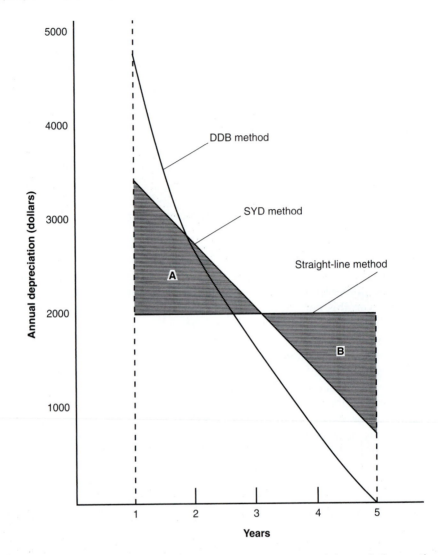

Exhibit 11–9   Comparison of straight-line and accelerated depreciation methods.

historical building investment tax credit, reduces a company's tax rate without the company ever having to pay back this credit.

Income Tax Impact of Accelerated Depreciation.   The most commonly used method of postponing tax payments involves accelerating the depreciation of property and equipment, regardless of whether or not this depreciation matches the useful life of an asset, when calculating taxable income. Taxable income is the income reported on a company's tax return and is calculated according to the rules stipulated by the Internal Revenue Code. The Modified Accelerated Cost Recovery System (MACRS) is the method allowed by the IRC for accelerating depreciation when calculating taxable income. It permits the recovery of the cost of property and equipment over a period shorter than its useful life and based on the double declining balance method of depreciation.

When using MACRS, taxable income will be lower than book income (the net income calculated according to GAAP) during the early part of an asset's life because book income must be calculated using a depreciation method that matches the useful life of an asset. These depreciation methods allowed by GAAP usually depreciate assets more slowly than MACRS. Consequently, the income

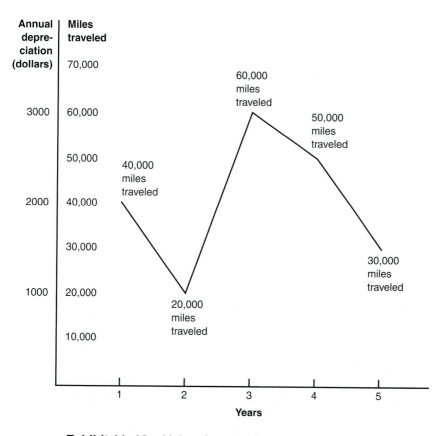

Exhibit 11–10   Units-of-output depreciation method.

tax payable, that is calculated using the faster (MACRS) depreciation method, and that is the tax amount actually paid to the government in any current accounting period, will also be lower over the early years of an asset's life.

As is the case with all accelerated depreciation methods, over the later years of an asset's life, this situation is reversed. During the later years of an asset's life, using MACRS produces a higher taxable income than book income because most of the depreciation for tax purposes was used up over the early years. Thus during these later years, the hospitality firm must pay the income taxes that accelerating depreciation enabled it to save during the early years. As you can see, using accelerated depreciation methods does not reduce a hospitality firm's income taxes, it just postpones them. But when millions of dollars of assets, with very long lives are involved, this postponement can amount to what is equivalent to a huge interest-free loan by the government to a business.

This "loan effect" through tax postponement is called deferred income tax, and can be observed in the example presented through Exhibits 11–11 and 11–12. In this example, an asset with a cost of $10,000 and no salvage value is depreciated over five years (using percentages provided in MACRS depreciation tables based on the half-year convention) for purposes of calculating taxable income and income tax payable. For calculating income tax expense and net income it is depreciated using the straight-line depreciation method over its useful life of five years. An income tax rate of 40 percent is assumed. The MACRS method uses the half-year convention or the mid-quarter convention. We will use the half-year convention, which means that we take only one half year's depreciation the first year and the remaining half year depreciation the sixth year of the asset's life. Therefore we will compare the straight-line method to MACRS over a six year period.

Year	Earnings before depreciation and taxes	Straight-line depreciation	Book income	Income tax expense
1	$10,000	$2,000	$ 8,000	$3,200
2	10,000	2,000	8,000	3,200
3	10,000	2,000	8,000	3,200
4	10,000	2,000	8,000	3,200
5	10,000	2,000	8,000	3,200
6	10,000	– 0 –	10,000	4,000
		$10,000	$20,000	

Exhibit 11–11   Calculation of book income and income tax expense.

By comparing the last columns in these two exhibits you can see the amount of loan that a firm is receiving as a result of using MACRS. The income tax expense column in Exhibit 11–11 indicates what a business would have to pay if it used straight line depreciation. The income tax payable column in Exhibit 11–12 indicates the amount of tax it actually has to write a check for each year. The difference is the amount on loan from the government as a result of using MACRS. This difference is shown on a cumulative basis in Exhibit 11–13. Notice when comparing Exhibit 11–11 and Exhibit 11–12 that the total income tax amount is the same in both cases—$20,000. It is just paid more slowly as a result of using MACRS than it would be using straight-line depreciation. Exhibit 11–13 indicates that the firm would have had available to it up to $480 of additional funds in year two of the asset's life because of postponement of income tax payments through the use of MACRS, and smaller amounts in other years. In years three to six the firm must pay back this $480 amount and the balance in the deferred income tax account goes to zero.

Historical Building Investment Tax Credit.   As of this writing, the Internal Revenue Code also provides tax relief to businesses through a special investment tax credit (ITC) for historical buildings. A tax credit is deductible from the amount of income tax payable rather than being treated as a deductible expense used in determining taxable income. An investment tax credit of up to 25 percent is allowed on all expenditures incurred in rehabilitating such buildings. This provides opportunities for hospitality firms to convert historic sites to hospitality use. An additional credit is also allowed for energy-saving investments.

Companies that take advantage of these latter two investment tax credits must reduce the depreciable base (for tax calculation purposes only) of the

Earnings before depreciation and taxes	MACRS depreciation (half-year convention)	Taxable income	Income tax payable
$10,000	$ 2,000	$8,000	$ 3,200
10,000	3,200	6,800	2,720
10,000	1,920	8,080	3,232
10,000	1,152	8,848	3,539
10,000	1,152	8,848	3,539
10,000	576	9,424	3,770
	$10,000		$20,000

Exhibit 11–12   Calculation of taxable income and income tax payable.

Year	Income tax expense	Income tax payable	Deferred income taxes	Balance in deferred income tax account
1	$3,200	$3,200	$0	$0
2	3,200	2,720	$480	$480
3	3,200	3,232	($32)	$448
4	3,200	3,539	($339)	$109
5	3,200	3,539	($339)	($230)
6	4,000	3,770	$230	$0

Exhibit 11–13   Interest-free funds available to a firm in the deferred income tax account.

affected assets by 50 percent of the investment tax credit. The use of an ITC results in a real reduction of a firm's tax rate. It is not like the use of an accelerated depreciation method, where the tax that is saved in earlier years must be repaid in later years of an asset's life.

DISPOSAL OF PROPERTY AND EQUIPMENT

Property and equipment may be disposed of by (1) sale, (2) retirement, (3) exchange, or (4) accidental destruction. In this text, we shall only cover the accounting treatment for the most common of these, namely the (1) sale and (2) retirement of property or equipment. Dealing with exchanges or accidental destruction involves more complex procedures that are beyond the scope of this text.

Sale of Property and Equipment

When property or equipment is sold, its cost must be deducted from the appropriate asset account and its related accumulated depreciation from the appropriate contra-asset account. Additionally, any gain or loss must be reported on the income statement. This gain or loss is the difference between the asset's net book value (NBV) and its sale price.

The entry to record the sale of a freezer with a cost of $12,000 and accumulated depreciation of $10,000 is shown below. The freezer is sold for $3,000 in cash.

	Dr	Cr
Cash	3,000	
Accumulated depreciation	10,000	
Equipment		12,000
Gain on sale of property		1,000

To record sale of freezer for $1,000 above its net book value

The above gain was calculated as follows:

Cost of freezer	$12,000
Less:	
Accumulated depreciation	10,000
Net book value	$ 2,000
Sale price	$ 3,000
Less:	
Net book value	2,000
Gain on sale	$ 1,000

A loss would be calculated similarly.

To comply with GAAP, a special account called "gain or (loss) on sale of property" is provided by the USAL to report such transactions. Since sales of property or equipment are considered to occur infrequently, accounting pronouncements require that gains or losses from such sales must be reported separately on the income statement, after all normal operating revenues and expenses and before extraordinary items. A material event or transaction that is unusual in nature or occurs infrequently, but not both, and therefore does not meet both criteria for classification as an extraordinary item, should be reported as a separate component of income from continuing operations. It is not reported net of its income tax effect.

In the case of certain hotel or restaurant chains that are constantly buying and selling properties, gains and losses from such sales do occur frequently and are considered usual because they involve the operating assets of the corporation. Therefore, they may be reported along with other ordinary operating revenues or expenses as part of the normal operations of the company.

Retirement of Property and Equipment

Property or equipment is retired when it cannot be sold or exchanged. Ideally, management should have foreseen that the asset would not be sellable and no salvage value would have been estimated, leaving the asset fully depreciated to a net book value of zero at the time of sale. Assuming this to be the case, the entry to retire a fully depreciated oven that cost $8,000 is shown below:

	Dr	Cr
Accumulated depreciation	8,000	
Equipment		8,000
To record retirement of a fully depreciated oven		

When an asset is netted against an amount in its related contra-asset account, thereby removing both amounts from a company's books, the asset is said to be written off against its accumulated depreciation account.

If an asset is not fully depreciated upon retirement then its write-off produces a loss. The entry to record the write-off of an oven that cost $8,000 and has accumulated depreciation of $6,000 is presented below:

	Dr	Cr
Loss on retirement of equipment	2,000	
Accumulated depreciation	6,000	
Equipment		8,000
To record retirement of an oven with a net book value of $2,000		

If it is not independently significant, the gain or loss on retirement of property may be reported on the income statement along with gains or losses from sales of property in a combined classification called "gain or loss on disposal of property."

Capital Gains Tax

When business property and equipment owned by a company for more than one year is sold at a gain, the normal income tax rate for the firm may not be applicable to this gain. Owners of businesses organized as sole proprietorships, partnerships or S-corporations benefit from a tax rate lower than the standard rate. This tax rate is called the long term capital gains tax rate. This tax provision results in a reduction in the amount of tax that must be paid in the current period, and not just a postponement. No income tax payment is deferred to future accounting periods. If you manage one of these types of organizations then you may want to consider postponing the sale of property and equipment to convert a regular gain into a long-term gain

INVENTORIES

Recording Inventories and Determining Cost of Sales

Inventory is used herein to designate the aggregate of those items of tangible personal property which (1) are held for sale in the ordinary course of business, or (2) are to be currently consumed in the production of goods or services to be available for sale. In a hospitality firm, inventories for sale may include (1) food, (2) beverages, (3) sundry merchandise for sale (candy, souvenirs, etc.), and (4) equipment for sale (to franchisees). Inventories not for sale (to be consumed by the hospitality entity itself) may consist of (1) spare parts and (2) supplies.

Spare parts inventories are usually associated with airlines and other transportation-oriented firms with a large investment in equipment. Supplies inventories in the hospitality industry include guest gratuities, office, advertising, maintenance, and—the most important category—housekeeping (cleaning) supplies. Housekeeping supplies consist of brooms, detergents, dishwashing compounds, disinfectants, insecticides, mops, pails, polishes, soaps, and any other materials used in cleaning.

The procedure of accounting for supplies inventory and spare parts inventories and their related expense accounts is the same as that explained in Chapter 5. In this chapter, we will describe the procedures for valuing and recording inventories for sale.

Two steps are involved in measuring inventories: (1) determining the number of physical units in inventory, and (2) determining the value of these units.

In order to determine the number of units in inventory, their physical flow must be recorded and controlled. In order to value the units in inventory, some assumptions must be made regarding the flow of inventory costs, which (as explained in a later section) are not always the same as the physical flow of the individual inventory items.

The two systems for recording and controlling the physical flow of inventory units are the periodic-inventory system and the perpetual-inventory system. Under the periodic-inventory system, purchases are recorded as they occur but inventory issues are not recorded until the end of the accounting period, whereas under the perpetual-inventory system, both purchases and issues are recorded as they occur.

Recording and Flow of Inventories

Lower of Cost or Market.   Before proceeding with a discussion of the details of inventory recording methods, it must be mentioned that whatever method is used, if market value is lower than historical cost inventories should be reported at their market value, recognizing the loss on the income statement. Extreme drops in prices, and sometimes physical deterioration or obsolescence causes the market value of inventories to decline below their original cost. When this occurs, they must be marked down to the lower of cost or market (LCM) in compliance with the principles of conservatism and matching.

The market value of inventories is their replacement cost. Since this is an estimate an upper and a lower limit on market value is placed to prevent exaggeration. These limits are that the market value of inventories:

- Cannot be higher than their net realizable value (NRV), and it
- Cannot be lower than net realizable value less a normal profit margin.

Net realizable value is the value received upon the sale of inventories net of any expenses incurred in their sale. Thus if a $500 advertisement were required to sell 10 bottles of wine at $300 each, their net realizable value would be $3,000 (10 × $300) less the $500 cost of the advertisement, or $2,500. It should be noted that the concept of conservatism does not allow inventories to be marked up again should their market value increase at a later date.

After the lower of cost or market has been determined, the loss is recorded in an income statement account called "loss on markdown of inventory to LCM." The credit entry is recorded either as a direct reduction of the inventory account or in an inventory contra-asset account called "allowance for markdown of inventory to LCM."

The direct-inventory-reduction method is preferable under the periodic-inventory system because the cost of sales calculation is less cumbersome without the "allowance for markdown" contra-asset account. It is preferable to use the allowance contra-asset account under the perpetual-inventory system to keep better track of the impact of changing prices on the firm.

Perpetual Inventory.   There are two ways to record the flow of inventories: (1) the perpetual-inventory system, and (2) the periodic-inventory system. In the perpetual inventory system, an account called "inventory" is created in the general ledger and purchases are debited to the account while issues, as the inventory is consumed, are credited to the same account. This flow of inventory is illustrated by means of a "T" account below:

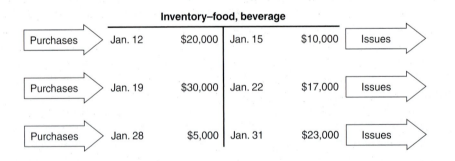

The key to understanding the diagram is to realize that inventory *issues* are being *recorded the same day that they occur*. Therefore the inventory account always indicates the current actual balance in inventory. This is the way a perpetual inventory works. It is perpetually updated and contains useful, timely information.

The journal entries to record the first purchase and issue are presented below to refresh your memory:

Purchase	Dr	Cr
Inventory	20,000	
Cash or accounts payable		20,000

Issue	Dr	Cr
Cost of sales	10,000	
Inventory		10,000

A perpetual inventory system is easy to understand because it is so straightforward. However, it is more expensive to maintain than a periodic-inventory system because someone must maintain physical control over the inventory at all times. Someone must be in the storeroom at all times to receive inventory purchases and to issue inventory as it is required by the using departments. This same person, or persons, must send daily receiving reports and issues reports to the accounting department for updating the balance in the inventory account. Either the storeroom keeper or the accounting department, or both, use these reports to maintain perpetual-inventory cards for each item in inventory. A sample perpetual-inventory card is presented in Exhibit 11–14. This card is self-explanatory. It indicates a beginning balance for each item, amounts purchased, amounts used and the units and value of current amounts on hand. Because of its greater control over the inventory, a perpetual-inventory system is more expensive to install and maintain. For this reason, it is only used for large inventories and inventories of high value goods.

Periodic Inventory. The periodic-inventory system is used for small inexpensive inventories, where the cost of maintaining a perpetual inventory is not justified, and for inventories to which employees need immediate access, such as kitchen pantries. Chefs do not have the time to prepare issues requisitions and wait while a storeroom clerk brings them what they need. Instead a certain amount of inventory is taken out of the storeroom, recorded as "purchases" in the pantry purchases account, and made available to the kitchen.

A physical count is made at the end of the day. This physical count is key to the periodic-inventory system because, unlike in the perpetual-inventory system, issues of inventory items have not been recorded as they occur. The only way to know the amount of inventory consumed is to calculate the difference between the value of inventory at the end of the previous day and the value of inventory at the end of today, after adding any items received during the day. The value of any additions to inventory plus any decreases in beginning inventory is logically the amount of inventory consumed and constitutes cost of sales expense. Thus a periodic-inventory system differs from a perpetual-inventory system in four ways:

- There is no one controlling the inventory on a perpetual basis.
- Because of this, *issues are not recorded as they occur,* and the inventory "T" account for the pantry does not contain the correct balance, except at the moment a physical inventory is taken and the "T" account is adjusted to reflect the value of the inventory count.

Perpetual–Inventory Card—FIFO Valuation Method							
Item name: Frozen turkeys					Inventory minimum: 2		
					Balance		
Date	Receipts	Issues	Unit cost	Total cost	Units	Unit cost	Total cost
3-1-05	2	—	10.00	20.00	2	10.00	20.00
3-2-05	5	—	10.50	52.50	5	10.50	72.50
3-2-05	—	2	10.00	20.00			
		1	10.50	10.50	4	10.50	42.00
3-8-05		1	10.50	10.50	3	10.50	31.50

Exhibit 11–14   Perpetual-inventory card.

- It is possible, however, to keep track of the items that are brought into the pantry daily. We can call these items "purchases" and in a periodic-inventory system a special "purchases" account is created to record these "purchases," regardless of whether they are real purchases or come from a storeroom.
- Because of the above, recording cost of sales in a periodic-inventory system involves making several journal entries. It is not a simple matter of crediting inventory and debiting cost of sales expense, as is the case in a perpetual-inventory system.

To illustrate the functioning of a periodic-inventory system we will post the following transactions. Let us assume that there is a beginning balance of $7,000 in the pantry. This balance, of course, is based on the physical count made at the end of the previous accounting period, March 31. The pantry inventory account would appear as follows:

Pantry inventory	Remember that this inventory is only accurate on March 31. After that date new amounts of inventory have been brought into the pantry, which we shall call purchases. Let us assume that during the month of April $28,000 worth of inventory is brought into the pantry. This would be recorded through the following journal entry
March 31-7,000	

	Dr	Cr
Purchases	28,000	
Accounts payable, or cash		28,000

Purchases	Note that this entry is posted to an account called "purchases." It would not make sense to post the $28,000 to the inventory account because we would be mixing an outdated, meaningless inventory value with a meaningful amount for purchases. If we mixed the two amounts the inventory value would still be meaningless but we would also contaminate the accurate meaningful value for purchases, and it, too, would now be meaningless.
April-28,000	

Now we know how much inventory we had at the beginning of the period, and we know how much we added during the period (purchases). But we don't know how much we used because, unlike in the perpetual-inventory system, no record of issues is kept in the periodic system. To calculate cost of sales (inventory consumed), we must go into the pantry and take a physical inventory count of what is left.

Let us assume we did this and found $9,000 worth of inventory remaining in the pantry. We can now calculate our cost of sales (inventory consumed) through the following calculation:

Beginning inventory	$ 7,000
plus: Purchases	28,000
equals: Goods available for sale	35,000
minus: ending inventory (per our count)	9,000
equals: cost of sales (inventory consumed)	$26,000

What this calculation states is that the cost of sales is equal to the purchases, plus any decrease in the beginning inventory, and minus any increase in inventory over the beginning inventory amount. In this case, the inventory increased from $7,000 to $9,000, so this means we did not consume all of what we purchased. Of the items we purchased, $2,000 went to increase inventory. So the cost of sales expense is $26,000, that is the sum of the $28,000 purchases minus this $2,000 increase in inventory.

The cost of sales calculation is transferred to the accounting records through the following journal entries. These journal entries can be made every time a physical inventory is taken, or at the end of every accounting period. In any case, they must be made before financial statements can be prepared.

	Dr	Cr
Cost of sales	28,000	
Purchases		28,000

To close (transfer) the purchases to the cost of sales account

	Dr	Cr
Inventory	2,000	
Cost of sales		2,000

To reduce cost of sales for unconsumed purchases

The inventory, purchases and cost of sales accounts are shown below after making these entries:

Inventory			Purchases			Cost of Sales		
Mar 31	7,000		April	28,000	Apr 30 28,000	Apr 30 28,000	Apr 30	2,000
Apr 30	2,000					Bal. 26,000		
Bal.	9,000							

The inventory now reflects the increase in inventory because of the fact that $2,000 of the purchases were not consumed, and the cost of sales account also shows that because $2,000 of the purchases were not consumed, the cost of sales is $2,000 less than the value of the purchases.

Decreases in Inventory. What would be done if the inventory decreased by $2,000? That would mean that not only were the purchases for the period consumed, but also some of the beginning inventory was consumed. In that case, the cost of sales would be greater than the purchases by the amount of inventory that was consumed. The second journal entry above would be made as follows:

	Dr	Cr
Cost of sales	2,000	
Inventory		2,000

To increase cost of sales in the amount of beginning inventory consumed

Purchase Discounts. Suppliers will very often offer discounts for prompt payment of their invoices. These discounts should always be taken by paying within the discount period. The availability of such a discount is usually indicated by stamping or typing the following annotation on an invoice:

2,10/Net 30

This means that if the invoice is paid within 10 days you can deduct 2 percent of the invoice amount when making out your check, otherwise you must pay the full value of the invoice within 30 days. Now 2 percent may not seem like a large amount. However, it is actually the same as receiving 2 percent interest for paying 20 days early, and on an annualized basis it amounts to approximately a

36 percent return on your money because there are about 18 periods of 20 days length within a 360-day year. The 36 percent annual rate of return is obtained by multiplying the 2 percent earned per 20 period by the 18 periods within the year, as follows:

$$2\% \times 18 \text{ periods} = 36\%/\text{year}$$

When paying an invoice and purchase discounts are taken the full invoice amount is not paid. In these cases the debit to accounts payable is offset by a credit to cash and a credit to an account called purchase discounts. For example, the entry to pay a $10,000 invoice while taking the 2 percent discount is as follows:

	Dr	Cr
Accounts payable	10,000	
Cash		9,800
Purchase discounts		200
To record payment of a $10,000 invoice less a 2% purchase discount		

The purchase discounts account can be closed out to the cost of sales account, or it can be left on the income statement as a source of "other income." Because the benefits of taking discounts are so great, it is best to leave the purchase discounts account on the income statement as a separate account so that you, as managers, will be able to easily keep track of the activity in this account. If you notice that purchase discounts are decreasing you should look into the matter and find out why. If, for some legitimate reason, you are running short on cash, then it is better to borrow the money at a reasonable interest rate, for example, 10 percent to 12 percent per year (APR), in order to be able to have the money needed to pay within the discount period and earn 36 percent per year.

Employee Meals. In the hospitality industry, employee meals are often provided to employees while at work. The USAL includes these meals in the employee benefits account. Usually the food and beverage consumed in employee meals are automatically included in cost of sales because they will be missing when the physical inventory is taken. A separate record of food and beverage consumed for employee meals must be maintained, through an entry such as the following, so that these amounts may be deducted from cost of sales and included in employee benefits.

	Dr	Cr
Employee meals	350	
Cost of sales		350
To record $350 worth of food consumed for employee meals		

INVENTORY VALUATION METHODS

We have discussed the two systems of controlling the physical flow of inventories. This physical flow, however, does not always match the flow of costs associated with individual inventory items. For instance, in a room full of wine bottles, all of the same vintage, vineyard, and bottler, it may be impossible or impractical to maintain a record of which bottles were purchased first and which last. If the purchases were made at different prices, some practical assumption must be made regarding the assignment of costs to each individual bottle as it is consumed, rather than going through the unnecessary trouble of attaching a specific price to every bottle individually.

Four different methods acceptable under GAAP for allowing costs to flow through to cost of sales are discussed here:

1. Specific-units method
2. Weighted-average method
3. FIFO (first-in-first-out) method
4. LIFO (last-in-first-out) method

We will discuss these methods as they would be implemented under a periodic inventory system. Because a perpetual inventory system does not rely on an end-of-period physical inventory to calculate cost of sales, but rather computes this cost on a continuous basis, these flow-through assumptions will, of course, be implemented differently in a perpetual inventory system. In the following examples, therefore, we will be valuing the inventory units at the end of the period based on a physical inventory, rather than assigning each item a value as it is consumed, as would be done in a perpetual inventory system.

All of the explanations of the above cost flow-through assumptions will be based on the inventory transactions listed in Exhibit 11–15.

Specific-Units Valuation Method

Under the specific-units method the specific cost of each individual bottle sold is allowed to flow through to cost of sales. Thus, referring to Exhibit 11–15, if two bottles came from those on hand at the beginning of May, two came from the purchase on May 5, and four came from the purchase on May 17, then the ending inventory and the cost of sales would be calculated as shown in Exhibit 11–16. This is verified by the familiar cost of sales calculation as follows:

Beginning inventory	0
Purchases	$ 2,185
Product available for sale	2,185
Ending inventory	−1,295
Cost of sales	$ 890

The specific-units method of inventory valuation is only practical for use with readily differentiable high-value items that can easily be associated with their actual cost, elaborate cakes, for example, or unique bottles of expensive wine. It would be ridiculous, for instance, to assign each individual potato in a bushel a specific unit cost.

Transaction date	Units purchased	Unit cost	Total cost of units purchased	Sales	Units in inventory
May 1	2	$100	$200		2
5	5	105	525		7
10				3	4
15	2	115	230		6
17	4	120	480		10
20				5	5
31	6	125	750		11
Totals	19		$2,185	8	

Exhibit 11–15 Chateau d'Yquem wine inventory transactions to be used in sample inventory cost flow-through examples.

Ending Inventory—Specific-Units Method

Date purchased	Quantity		Unit cost		Total cost
May 5	3	×	$105	=	$ 315
15	2	×	115	=	230
31	6	×	125	=	750
Total	11				$1,295

Cost of Sales

Date sold	Units sold	Date purchased	Unit cost		Total cost
May 10	3	May 1	2 × $100		
		5	1 × 105	=	$305
20	5	5	1 × 105		
		17	4 × 120	=	585
Total	8				$890

Exhibit 11–16   Ending inventory and cost of sales calculation using the specific units valuation method.

Weighted-Average Valuation Method

Under the weighted-average method of determining the flow of inventory costs, the total cost of all units in inventory is divided by the total number of units on hand when the physical inventory is taken. This generates a weighted-average cost per unit for calculating cost of sales. Under the periodic inventory system this calculation for the entire period is made at the end of the period. Exhibit 11–17 shows the weighted-average unit cost of the Chateau d'Yquem wine inventory calculated under the periodic inventory method on the basis of the data presented in Exhibit 11–15.

Notice that under the periodic-inventory system the cost of sales is not deducted until the end of the period, when the physical inventory is taken. Under the perpetual-inventory system the weighted-average unit cost at the time of each sale is deducted from the cumulative inventory value as sales occur, resulting in a slightly lower cost of sales in times of inflation.

The procedure for determining the average inventory cost between the two purchases made up to May 5 is shown below as an example of how to make a weighted-average inventory calculation.

Date purchased	Units purchased		Unit cost		Total cost
May 1	2	×	$100	=	$200
5	5	×	105	=	525
Total	7				$725

The weighted-average between these two purchases (rounded to the nearest dollar) is then calculated as follows:

$$\frac{\text{cumulative inventory value on May 5}}{\text{total units in inventory}} = \frac{\$725}{7} = \$104 \text{ is the weighted average cost per bottle}$$

In Exhibit 11–17, this same procedure is applied to the entire ending inventory per Exhibit 11–15 to arrive at a final weighted-average unit cost as of May 31, amounting to $115. Once the unit cost is determined, the entire ending inventory

Ending Inventory Valuation Using Weighted Average Method

$$\frac{\text{total cost of units available for sale}}{\text{total units available for sale}} = \frac{\$2,185^*}{19^*} = \$115 \text{ weighted average cost per bottle}$$

*These amounts are from Exhibit 11.15.

weighted-average unit cost	$\times$	**bottles per physical count**	=	**ending inventory value**
$115	$\times$	11	=	$1,265

Exhibit 11–17   Ending inventory valued using the weighted-average inventory valuation method.

value can be calculated by multiplying this unit value by the number of units remaining in inventory. The cost of sales for the month can then be calculated as usual for a periodic inventory:

Beginning inventory	0
Purchases	$ 2,185
Product available for sale	2,185
Ending inventory	−1,265
Cost of sales	$ 920

The weighted-average inventory valuation method dampens the effect of price fluctuations throughout an accounting period. This method generates a cost of sales amount and inventory values that are intermediate between those produced by the FIFO and LIFO inventory valuation methods.

First-in-First-out (FIFO) Valuation Method

The first-in-first-out (FIFO) method of inventory valuation allows the oldest costs to flow through to cost of sales, applying the most recent costs to products remaining in inventory. Exhibit 11–18 shows the Chateau d'Yquem ending inventory and cost of sales under the FIFO valuation method. This is the simplest method to apply in practice, and it is easy to understand as well. You should remember, however, when following the calculations in Exhibit 11–18, that you are calculating the costs remaining in inventory, not the costs that flowed through to cost of sales. Therefore, you will select the most recent costs, $115, $120, and $125, those that remain in inventory, to value your ending inventory, while the first costs in are the costs that already flowed out to cost of sales.

Once you calculate the ending inventory value and its related cost of sales using the FIFO method you can verify it by using the familiar cost of sales calculation as follows:

Beginning inventory	0
Purchases	$ 2,185
Product available for sale	2,185
Ending inventory	−1,345
Cost of sales	$ 840

Because it allows the oldest costs (lower than current costs in times of inflation) to flow through to cost of sales, the FIFO method of inventory valuation generates the lowest cost of sales in an inflationary economic environment, and the highest inventory value. Also, because of their simplicity and because inventories in the hospitality industry tend to be consumed quickly (food is perishable), the weighted average and FIFO inventory valuation methods are the ones most often used in the hospitality industry.

Ending Inventory—FIFO Method

Date purchased	Units in FIFO inventory		Unit cost		FIFO inventory value
May 15	1	×	$115	=	$ 115
17	4	×	120	=	480
31	6	×	125	=	750
Total	11				$1,345

Cost of Sales

Date sold	Units sold	Date purchased	Unit cost		Total cost
May 10	3	May 1	2 × $100		
		5	1 × 105	=	$ 305
20	5	5	4 × 105		
		15	1 × 115	=	535
Total	8				$ 840

Exhibit 11–18 Ending inventory and cost of sales calculation using the FIFO valuation method in a periodic inventory system.

Last-in-First-out (LIFO) Valuation Method

The last-in-first-out (LIFO) inventory valuation method allows the most recent costs to flow through to cost of sales and applies the oldest costs to products remaining in inventory. Exhibit 11–19 shows the Chateau d'Yquem ending inventory and cost of sales under the LIFO method. Just bear in mind that when you are calculating the ending inventory you are dealing with the oldest costs because the most recent costs, the last in, have already flowed out to cost of sales. Once you have calculated the value of the ending inventory and obtained the cost of sales using the LIFO procedure, the ending inventory valuation can again be verified by the familiar cost of sales calculation as follows:

Beginning inventory	0
Purchases	$ 2,185
Product available for sale	2,185
Ending inventory	−1,195
Cost of sales	$ 990

Notice that since cost of sales is calculated at the end of the accounting period under the periodic-inventory system, the cost of May 31 purchases is applied to sales on May 10 and May 20 as if the sales had been made at the end of the month. If a perpetual inventory were being used, the cost of sales for each sale would be recorded when it occurred, on the basis of the latest purchase costs prior to the sale, thereby generating a slightly lower cost of sales in times of inflation.

In an inflationary economic environment, the LIFO inventory valuation method initially generates the highest cost of sales (until the older, lower costs flow through) and the lowest inventory value because it allows the most recent costs (the most inflated) to flow through to cost of sales and assigns the oldest (the lowest during inflation) to inventories. The higher cost of sales in turn reduces net income until the older, lower costs pass through to cost of sales, and therefore a firm pays less income taxes initially until these lower costs pass through. Because of its complexity, however, and because hospitality industry inventories tend to be consumed quickly (food is perishable) the tax advantages of using LIFO are not significant enough to justify its use.

Ending Inventory—LIFO Method

Date purchased	Units in LIFO inventory		Unit cost		LIFO inventory value
May 1	2	×	$100	=	$ 200
5	5	×	105	=	525
15	2	×	115	=	230
17	2	×	120	=	240
Total	11				$1,195

Cost of Sales Calculation

Date sold	Units sold	Date purchased	Unit cost		Total cost
May 10	3	May 31	3 × $125	=	$375
20	5	31	3 × 125		
		17	2 × 120	=	615
Total	8				$990

Exhibit 11–19 Ending inventory and cost of sales calculation using LIFO valuation method in a periodic inventory system.

Comparison of Inventory Valuation Methods

In order to visualize better the effects on net income of the four inventory valuation methods discussed in this text, they are presented in the context of a partial income statement in Exhibit 11–20.

In Exhibit 11–20 it is easy to verify that the weighted-average inventory valuation method produces cost of sales and ending inventory amounts that are intermediate between the corresponding FIFO and LIFO amounts. This is due to the moderating effect produced by averaging costs when they are either increasing due to inflation or declining in times of recession.

It is also evident that because the data presented in Exhibit 11–20 assumes a period of rising prices (inflation), the FIFO inventory valuation method produces the lowest cost of sales and highest ending inventory value. It allows the oldest and lowest costs to flow through to cost of sales. In contrast the LIFO inventory valuation method allows the most recent, highest costs to flow through to cost of sales. Hence it generates the highest cost of sales and lowest inventory valuation. If prices were declining the opposite would be true concerning FIFO and LIFO

	FIFO	Weighted average	LIFO	Specific units
Sales	$ 2,000	$ 2,000	$ 2,000	$ 2,000
Cost of sales				
Beginning inventory	0	0	0	0
Purchases	2,185	2,185	2,185	2,185
Product available for sale	2,185	2,185	2,185	2,185
Ending inventory	−1,345	−1,265	−1,195	−1,295
Cost of sales	840	920	990	890
Gross profit	$ 1,160	$ 1,080	$ 1,010	$ 1,110

Exhibit 11–20 Comparative gross profit calculations based on four inventory valuation methods.

inventory valuation, although the weighted-average method would still produce intermediate cost of sales and inventory values. The specific-unit valuation method is not subject to any type of predictability. In our example it produced a cost of sales higher than FIFO and lower than the weighted-average method because mostly older, low-cost bottles were sold. Depending upon which specific units are sold (high cost or low cost), this method can generate a cost of sales anywhere between the FIFO and LIFO methods.

A review of Exhibit 11–20 indicates that the value assigned to ending inventory is a critical factor in determining cost of sales. As the ending inventory value increases, cost of sales decreases. The major objective in selecting an inventory valuation method is to choose the one which, under the circumstances, most clearly reflects periodic income. Thus, priority should be given to realistic income determination as opposed to realistic inventory valuation when selecting an inventory cost flow method. Since the LIFO inventory valuation method allows the most recent costs to flow through to cost of sales, it would seem to meet this requirement best in periods of changing prices.

However, although FIFO tends to overstate income in times of rising prices and understate income when prices are declining it is the simplest inventory valuation method to use. When the difference in net income produced by the FIFO and LIFO inventory methods is not material, most companies will tend to use the FIFO method. This is particularly true in the hospitality industry where inventories are usually perishable and are consumed quickly. Hospitality entities tend to consume all of their inventories even back to the oldest cost layers, thus diminishing the potential difference between the FIFO and LIFO valuation methods.

Because of their impact on net income the choice of inventory valuation method has tax consequences of which the manager of a hospitality firm should be aware. These are discussed in the next section.

FOB Point of Origin and FOB Destination

When an asset, such as inventory, is shipped from a distant location it can either be purchased FOB point of origin or FOB destination. FOB means "free on board" the delivery vehicle. If the purchase is FOB point of origin, then goods are considered to be delivered once the supplier has placed them on the train, truck, ship, etc. at the supplier's location. The purchase can be recorded at the time the supplies are on board the delivery vehicle because that is when ownership is transferred to the buyer.

If the purchase is FOB destination, then the goods are not delivered, and consequently the purchase has not been consummated, until the delivery vehicle reaches the purchaser's destination. Consequently, a supplier's invoice marked FOB destination should not be recorded until the product has been received at the destination point agreed upon by seller and buyer.

TAX CONSIDERATIONS IN ACCOUNTING FOR INVENTORIES

Before discussing the potential tax implications of using different inventory valuation methods, it is important to understand that if all the remaining inventory of a firm were to be consumed without buying new inventory, there would be absolutely no difference in cost of sales, regardless of the inventory valuation method used. In this case, all of the inventory costs would flow through to cost of sales in one single accounting period. The various methods of inventory valuation can result in different cost of sales amounts only if there is partial consumption of inventory amounts. In this case part of the inventory costs flow through to cost of sales in one accounting period and another part flows through in another period. If only a part of the inventory values is allowed to flow through to cost of sales, then it does make a difference whether the lower costs or higher costs flow through first. This is what is known as "timing differences" for the purpose of calculating income taxes.

From a tax-planning point of view, it is evident that in times of inflation the LIFO method of inventory valuation tends to minimize net income initially because it allows the most recent cost (the highest in times of inflation) to flow through to cost of sales first.

The FIFO method initially maximizes net income in times of inflation because it allows the oldest costs (lowest in times of inflation) to flow through to cost of sales, and the weighted-average inventory method produces an intermediate net income. The specific-units valuation method is unpredictable because the cost of sales under this method depends on which specific units are actually sold.

If a firm wishes to postpone its tax payments as long as possible, it will use the LIFO method of inventory valuation when there is inflation in order to minimize taxable income. Use of the LIFO inventory valuation method in calculating taxable income for tax reporting purposes has some drawbacks. First of all, when this method is used to calculate taxable income, the IRS requires that it also be used to calculate book income for financial reporting purposes. A manager is thus required to minimize the net income reported to stockholders as well as the taxable income reported to the IRS. Also, the LIFO inventory valuation method is very complex to use because of present IRS regulations.

As stated earlier, when inventories are small, or are quickly consumed, there is no significant tax advantage in using LIFO. This method would produce meaningful tax savings for a hospitality firm that owns an expensive vintage wine inventory purchased for different prices at various stages of its maturity. In this situation, the firm would retain a significant amount of older, lower, values in inventory over a large number of years, and the higher most recent purchase costs would flow through to increase cost of sales and decrease taxable income in current years. As long as the firm had bottles of this type of wine in inventory it would not have to pay the higher income tax that consuming the lower, older costs would generate because the older, lower costs would be attached to these bottles even though they were the newest bottles. Unless it consumed all of the inventory that it owns of this type of wine these lower, older costs would never pass through to cost of sales because the most recent, higher costs would constantly be flowing through to cost of sales.

As far as the mark-down of inventory value is concerned, the IRS allows the markdown of inventories to the lower of cost or market (LCM) with the recognition of the related loss on the tax return as long as the inventories so marked down are actually scrapped. This is usually the case when dealing with perishables such as food. Otherwise, the markdown cannot be made and the loss cannot be recognized for tax reporting purposes, even though GAAP may require the markdown for financial reporting purposes without requiring the scrapping of any inventory items. In this case a deferred income tax charges account, the opposite of a deferred income tax payable account, must be created and listed under "current assets" or "other assets" on the balance sheet, depending on when the timing difference will be resolved. This account is amortized as the marked-down inventory is gradually consumed.

THE PHYSICAL INVENTORY COUNT

As you have learned, the correct valuation of inventories depends on recording accurately the physical flow of inventory items. When using the periodic inventory system, the only way of recording inventory consumption is to take a physical inventory at the end of the period. This procedure must therefore be executed with care because it is a major factor in the determination of a firm's net income. Taking a physical inventory involves the following steps:

- Prepare appropriate inventory sheets.
- Control access to the area being inventoried (during the entire inventory period) and keep a control sheet of the amount, date, and time of all inventory items entering or leaving the area.
- Count all items in the area and keep a record of the date and time each item was counted.
- Adjust the physical count for all inventory items that entered or left the area between the date and time of the count and the inventory cutoff date.
- Assign costs to the items in the inventory using an acceptable inventory valuation method such as specific units, FIFO, weighted average, or LIFO, and calculate the total cost of the inventory.

A sample inventory count sheet is presented in Exhibit 11–21. The adjustment columns in the inventory count sheet are necessary because of the impossibility of taking an inventory of a large number of products exactly at the inventory cutoff time. In the physical inventory sheet shown in Exhibit 11–21, the cutoff time is midnight, December 31. Since the items to be counted were so numerous, the inventory was taken on December 31 and January 1, between 8:00 A.M. and 5:00 P.M. The time span between the date the physical count is finished and the inventory cutoff date may require that one of four types of potential adjustments be made to the actual physical count. When the physical count is made before the inventory cutoff date:

1. Add to the physical count any items received after the count is made.
2. Subtract from the physical count any items issued after the count is made.

When the physical count is made after the inventory cutoff date:

3. Add to the physical count any items issued after the inventory cutoff time.
4. Subtract from the physical count any items received after the inventory cutoff time.

For example, on the inventory count sheet shown above, 4 cans of vegetable soup were counted at 4:55 P.M. on December 31. Between 4:55 P.M. and midnight, 1 can was consumed and 10 cans were received, and so the physical count at

Stock no.	Description of item	Date and time of count	Quantity counted	Adjustments				Qty. at cutoff date	Unit cost	Total cost
				Out	In	Out	In			
446J	Canned vegetable soup	Dec. 31 4:55 P.M.	4	(1)	10			13	0.30	3.90
447J	Canned chili	Dec. 31 5:00 P.M.	5					5	0.55	2.75
448J	Canned carrots	Jan. 1 8:00 A.M.	16	1	(10)			7	0.40	2.80

Exhibit 11–21   Sample inventory count sheet.

4:55 P.M., December 31, must be adjusted to show the correct inventory at midnight, December 31, as follows:

December 31	Number of cans
Physical inventory count at 4:55 P.M.	4
Less: Consumed between 4:55 P.M. and midnight	−1
Plus: Received between 4:55 P.M. and midnight	+10
Inventory in stock at midnight, December 31	13

Opposite adjustments would be made if the physical inventory count had been taken after the midnight cutoff time on December 31.

Any items purchased FOB point of origin that have been shipped by the supplier but not received by the purchaser constitute purchases-in-transit and should be included in the physical inventory count. As noted earlier, title to these items passed to the purchaser upon delivery by the supplier to the transportation company.

After the physical quantities in inventory have been determined, unit costs are assigned and the total inventory cost is determined by adding the total cost of all inventory items. This may be done on the same sheet used for making the inventory count or on separate value computation worksheets.

POTENTIAL SOURCES OF ERRORS IN INVENTORY VALUATION

Errors in valuing inventories have as many sources as there are steps in the computation process. Some of these sources are listed below:

- No company policy requiring occasional physical inventory counts to verify perpetual-inventory cards
- Errors in making the physical inventory count
- Errors in recording the physical count on value computation sheets (the sheets on which quantities are multiplied by cost) when such sheets are used
- Errors in applying purchase costs according to the inventory valuation method selected
- Errors in recording freight-in and purchases returns when computing costs
- Mathematical errors on value computation sheets or physical count sheets
- Improper physical control of inventory while making the inventory count
- When a perpetual inventory is used, unauthorized personnel may have access to a storeroom and fail to record issues
- When using a computerized system, errors may be made in entering amounts

	Year 1	Year 2	Year 3
Sales	$1,500,000	$1,500,000	$1,500,000
Correct value of			
Beginning inventory	100,000	100,000	100,000
Food purchases	500,000	500,000	500.000
Ending inventory	100,000	100,000	100,000

Exhibit 11–22 Gourmet restaurant—three years' sales, purchases, and inventory data.

	Year 1	Year 2	Year 3
Sales	$1,500,000	$1,500,000	$1,500,000
Value of			
Beginning inventory	100,000	100.000	50,000
Food purchases	500,000	500,000	500,000
Food available for sale	600,000	600,000	550,000
Ending inventory	−100,000	−50,000	−100,000
Cost of sales	500,000	550,000	450,000
Gross profit	$1,000,000	$ 950,000	$1,050,000

Exhibit 11–23   Food inventory understated in year 2.

- When a perpetual-inventory system is used, errors may be made in entering receipts and issues on the perpetual-inventory cards
- When a periodic-inventory system is used, errors may be made in entering purchases

It is no coincidence that some of the sources of errors mentioned above, if avoided, will not only result in the correct evaluation of inventories at year end, but will also promote good physical control over inventories throughout the year. Avoiding errors in these areas is known as exercising good "internal control." The objectives of internal control are to safeguard the assets of an entity and to avoid misinformation. The effects of inventory valuation errors on net income are highlighted in the following section.

Impact of Inventory Valuation Errors

The inverse relationship between inventories and cost of sales should have been clearly established in the reader's mind by now. In other words, given a specific amount of product available for sale, the higher the ending inventory value, the lower will be the cost of sales and the higher the current period net income, and the lower the ending inventory value, the higher will be the cost of sales and the lower will be the current period net income.

Thus, if the current period's inventory is understated the current period's cost of sales will be overstated. Also, since the current period's ending inventory is the following period's beginning inventory, an understatement in the current period's inventory will produce an understatement in the subsequent period's cost of sales.

The effects of inventory valuation errors on the current and subsequent period's gross profit and corresponding net income, are demonstrated by the

	Year 1	Year 2	Year 3
Sales	$1,500,000	$1,500,000	$1,500,000
Value of			
Beginning inventory	100,000	100,000	100,000
Food purchases	500,000	500,000	500,000
Food available for sale	600,000	600,000	600,000
Ending inventory	−100,000	−100,000	−100,000
Cost of sales	500,000	500,000	500,000
Gross profit	$1,000,000	$1,000,000	$1,000,000

Exhibit 11–24   Food inventory correctly stated in year 2.

	Year 1	Year 2	Year 3
Sales	$1,500,000	$1,500,000	$1,500,000
Correct value of			
Beginning inventory	100,000	100,000	150,000
Food purchases	500,000	500,000	500,000
Food available for sale	600,000	600,000	650,000
Ending inventory	−100,000	−150,000	−100,000
Cost of sales	500,000	450,000	550,000
Gross profit	$1,000,000	$1,050,000	$ 950,000

Exhibit 11–25   Food inventory overstated in year 2.

examples given in Exhibits 11–23 to 11–25, based on the data presented in Exhibit 11–22. They indicate the effects on gross profit of (1) under-valuation, (2) correct valuation, and (3) over-valuation of inventories based on the data from the Gourmet Restaurant given in Exhibit 11–22.

In Exhibit 11–23, an understatement of ending inventory in year 2 results in an overstatement of cost of sales in year 2 and an understatement of cost of sales in year 3. The opposite occurs in Exhibit 11–25, where an overstatement of the current period's inventory occurs. Only the example in Exhibit 11–24, in which inventories are correctly valued, shows the correct gross profit for all three years.

Errors in current inventory valuation should therefore be diligently avoided. Their effect will be felt over a two-year period with possible negative consequences respecting the company's credit rating and income taxes payable, in addition to the unfavorable emotional impact of earnings fluctuations on the owners of the business.

SOME KEY TERMS INTRODUCED IN THIS CHAPTER

1. **Amortization.** The method of recording cost expiration for intangible assets.
2. **Book income.** Income as calculated according to GAAP.
3. **Capital gains tax.** A tax paid on certain assets when they are sold at a profit. If the asset is owned more than one year, this tax is lower than the tax on ordinary income.
4. **Capital lease.** Long-term lease that transfers to the lessee the risks and benefits incident to ownership.
5. **Capitalize.** To add an expenditure to an asset account.
6. **Construction-in-progress.** Payments made to the builder of an asset as the construction of the asset progresses. When the construction is concluded, the asset is transferred to its corresponding property and equipment account.
7. **Double-declining balance method.** An accelerated depreciation method in which twice the straight-line rate is applied to the net book value of an asset to determine its annual depreciation expense.
8. **Deferred income taxes.** The amount of tax payment that is postponed and recorded as a future liability when income tax payable is less than income tax expense, usually due to the use of MACRS depreciation for calculating taxable income.
9. **Depreciable base.** The cost of a depreciable asset minus its salvage value. This is the value of the asset that is depreciated.
10. **Employee meals.** Meals provided by the employer for employees during their work shifts.

11. **FIFO valuation method.** Stands for "First-in-first-out." A method of inventory valuation that allows the oldest inventory costs to flow through to cost of sales first and the most recent costs to be used to value the inventory, regardless of which physical unit is actually consumed.

12. **Fractional-years depreciation.** A method of allocating an asset's annual depreciation expense between consecutive periods when the purchase date of a depreciable asset does not coincide with the beginning of a company's annual accounting period.

13. **Income tax expense.** The amount of income tax calculated on the basis of book income. When this amount is different from income tax payable a deferred income tax account must be created. *See also* deferred income taxes.

14. **Income tax payable.** The amount of income tax calculated on the basis of taxable income. This is the actual amount that is paid in any given year.

15. **Investment tax credit.** A permanent, one-time, reduction in income taxes allowed by the Internal Revenue Code, usually to achieve some social goal.

16. **Leasehold.** A payment made to buy a lease from another lessee (a lessee is the user of a property—not the owner).

17. **Leasehold improvement.** Improvements to a rental property made by a lessee. Such improvements usually belong to the owner (lessor) of the property, but the lessee who makes the improvements acquires the right to use them over the life of the lease. *See also* Leasehold.

18. **LIFO valuation method.** Stands for "Last-in-first-out." A method of inventory valuation that allows the most recent inventory costs to flow through to cost of sales first, and the oldest costs to be used to value the inventory, regardless of which physical unit is actually consumed.

19. **Lower of cost or market.** Accounting convention that requires valuing inventories and certain other assets at their current market value when it is lower than their historical cost.

20. **MACRS.** Modified accelerated cost recovery system is the method allowed by the IRS (Internal Revenue Service) for calculating the accelerated depreciation of eligible assets.

21. **Periodic inventory.** A process of inventory control wherein only receipts (not issues) of inventory are recorded in the accounting system as they occur. To record inventory issues (inventory consumed) a physical inventory count must be made, usually either monthly or annually.

22. **Perpetual inventory.** A process of inventory control wherein issues as well as receipts of inventory are recorded in the accounting system as they occur.

23. **Purchase discounts.** A discount sometimes offered by suppliers to customers who pay their invoices within a specified period of time.

24. **Specific-units valuation method.** A method of inventory valuation that assigns specific values to specific units in inventory. It is applicable to high value inventories consisting of unique individual units, as opposed to fungible items.

25. **Sum-of-years'-digits method.** An accelerated depreciation method that allocates depreciation expense to each period in a fractional proportion, the denominator of which is the sum of the years' digits in the estimated useful life of the asset, and the numerator is the years' digits applied yearly in inverse order.

26. **Taxable income.** Income before income taxes as calculated according to the Internal Revenue Code (IRC) for the purpose of calculating the amount of federal income tax due.

27. **Units-of-output method.** A method of depreciation based on the units of output produced by an asset during an accounting period.

28. **Weighted-average valuation method.** A method of inventory valuation that averages the cost of goods available for sale over all units, both those remaining in inventory and those consumed as cost of sales.

QUESTIONS

1. What is depreciation?
2. What three factors must be taken into account in determining the useful life of an asset?
3. What types of expenditures should be included in the cost of newly purchased property and equipment?
4. In what circumstances should expenditures related to property and equipment be capitalized?
5. Why are certain depreciation methods called accelerated-depreciation methods?
6. What is a deferred income tax payable account? When is it necessary to create such an account on the balance sheet?
7. ARB No. 43 describes two broad inventory classifications. What are they?
8. Why is there sometimes a difference between the physical flow of inventories and the flow of inventory costs?
9. What are the two methods of recording the physical flow of inventories? What are the advantages and disadvantages of each?
10. How do you determine cost of sales under the periodic-inventory method? Under the perpetual-inventory method? At what point of the accounting process is cost of sales recorded in a periodic inventory system?
11. What costs are charged to the inventory account when recording inventories?
12. Which inventory valuation method tends to minimize net income in an inflationary economy? Which method generates the largest net income in an inflationary economy? Explain.
13. If inventories are understated at the end of year 1, what effect will that have on the income statements for years 1 and 2, and on the balance sheet at the end of year 2?
14. What four types of adjustments may have to be made on the inventory sheet when taking a physical inventory?

EXERCISES

1. Determine which of the following expenditures should be capitalized and prepare the journal entry to record each expenditure. Assume all cash payments.
   (a) Fumigated a hotel for $3,000.
   (b) Paid $8,000 for annual painting of a motel.
   (c) Rewired a restaurant at a cost of $6,000. This extends the life of the electrical system by 10 years.
   (d) Constructed a wall to divide the banquet hall into two rooms at a cost of $10,000.
   (e) Paid $13,000 to remove rubble from an empty lot on which a restaurant will be constructed.
   (f) Spent $11,000 to insulate a hotel in order to reduce energy costs.
2. Prepare journal entries to record the following transactions.
   (a) Sold an airplane that cost $30,000,000 and had accumulated depreciation of $20,000,000 for $8,000,000 cash.
   (b) Scrapped an oven that cost $10,000 and was fully depreciated, with no salvage value.
   (c) Scrapped a refrigerator that cost $15,000 and was depreciated down to its salvage value of $2,000.

(d) Sold a building, used as a fast food restaurant, that cost $250,000 and had accumulated depreciation of $50,000 for $210,000.

(e) Sold for $2,000 an emergency generator that cost $20,000 and was depreciated down to its salvage value of $3,000.

3. A hamburger broiler with a conveyer cost $40,000. It has a useful life of three years and a salvage value of $4,000. On the chart below use the double-declining balance method of depreciation to fill in column (a) headed "Tax reporting" and use straight-line depreciation to fill in column (b) headed "Book income" for each year of the broiler's useful life. Then enter the difference between column (a) and column (b) amounts for each of the three years in the appropriate columns to the right-headed "Lower taxable income" and "Higher taxable income." Remember that when depreciation for tax reporting purposes is higher than for book income purposes, you will have a lower taxable income than book income. This usually occurs in the early years of an asset's life. Over the later years the book income is lower than taxable income.

Year	Tax Reporting	Book income	Lower taxable income	Higher taxable income
1				
2				
3				
Totals				

4. The Camps Restaurant purchased a lunch van for $36,000 on June 30, 2007. The salvage value of the van is $9,000 and its useful life is ten years. Calculate its annual depreciation and annual net book value using the sum-of-years'-digits method of depreciation.

5. Assume you bought an air-conditioning unit for your hotel. Based on the following information prepare the journal entry to record the purchase of this air-conditioning unit.

Cost	$25,000
Sales tax	1,000
Transportation cost	1,500
Cost to remove a wall in room where air conditioner will be installed	2,000
Installation cost	1,700

6. Prepare the journal entries to record the following events which took place with regard to the china and china expense accounts of the Grass Roots Restaurant.

(a) Bought on credit $20,000 worth of china on April 1, 2007, the first day of restaurant's accounting fiscal year.

(b) On May 1, 2007, the china was counted and it was found that the restaurant had only $16,000 worth of china left.

Remember that even though china, glassware, silver and linen are tangible assets their cost expiration is treated slightly differently than that of other tangible assets.

7. Suppose you purchased seventy-five bottles of exactly the same Burgundy from three different purveyors as follows:

		Total cost
Jan 1	25 bottles at $ 50	1,250
15	25 bottles at $ 75	1,875
30	25 bottles at $100	2,500

(a) If you used the specific unit method of inventory valuation and you sold fifty bottles in January, which bottles would you sell first if you wish to:
   1. Maximize your net income?
   2. Minimize your net income?
(b) Calculate the cost of sales for the fifty bottles sold using the FIFO and LIFO inventory valuation methods.
(c) Which inventory cost flow-through assumption maximizes net income in January? Why?
(d) Which inventory cost flow-through assumption minimizes net income in January? Why?

8. Suppose you purchased five bottles of an exceptionally good vintage of cabernet sauvignon wine. Because you purchased it at different stages of its maturing process, and its quality became more and more apparent, you paid significantly higher prices for each bottle. These prices are listed below.

Year bought	Price paid
1985	$125
1990	$185
1995	$220
1998	$300
2001	$400

(a) Would using the specific units method of inventory valuation give you some freedom to increase or decrease your net income? Explain.
(b) If you wanted to maximize net income which bottle would you sell first?
(c) If you wanted to minimize net income which bottle would you sell first?
(d) Which inventory valuation method, other than the specific units method, would allow you to initially maximize net income?
(e) If you wanted to smooth out your annual net income and eliminate big fluctuations, which method of inventory valuation would you use?

9. The following three-years' income statements for the No-A-Count Restaurant reflect a $10,000 overstatement in the 2007 ending inventory:

	2007	2008	2009
Sales	$600,000	$650,000	$630,000
Cost of food and beverages sold	170,000	205,000	189,000
Gross profit	430,000	445,000	441,000
Expenses	330,000	350,000	335,000
Net income	$100,000	$ 95,000	$106,000

(a) Prepare corrected income statements for 2007, 2008, and 2009 after eliminating the $10,000 ending inventory overstatement error in 2007. (Hint: What would your cost of food and beverages sold be in 2007 if your ending inventory were $10,000 lower than the ending inventory used to calculate the $170,000 cost of food and beverages sold that year? Is ending inventory added to cost of sales, or subtracted from cost of sales?)
(b) Calculate and explain the effect of this inventory valuation error on No-A-Count Restaurant's owner's equity for 2007, 2008, and 2009.

10. The Fish-R-Fresh Restaurant chain uses the periodic inventory system. Its fish inventory was determined to be $100,000 by physical count on November 30, 2007. This amount was used to prepare the company's income statement and balance sheet for the November 30, 2007 fiscal year-end. It was discovered later that the following information had not been considered in calculating this inventory:

1. $15,000 worth of fish had been purchased FOB point of origin but had not yet been loaded on the trucks as of November 30, 2007.
2. $6,000 worth of fish had been purchased FOB destination and was en route to the restaurant chain's warehouse on November 30, 2007.
3. $20,000 worth of fish had been purchased FOB point of origin and was en route to the restaurant chain on November 30, 2007.

(a) What is the correct fish inventory value for the Fish-R-Fresh Restaurant chain as of November 30, 2007 after taking the above information into account?

(b) What effect will changing the November 30, 2007 ending inventory to the above correct inventory value have on the current year's net income?

(c) What effect will this error have on the following year's net income if this correction is not made on November 30, 2007?

SHORT PROBLEMS

1. Ceci's Restaurant purchased a mixer for $4,000 on September 30, 2006. The mixer has a useful life of four years, a salvage value of $1,000, and will be depreciated using the sum-of-years digits method. Ceci's restaurant uses the calendar year as its accounting year. Calculate the amount of depreciation expense of the mixer for the years 2006, 2007, 2008, 2009 and 2010. (Remember that in 2006 you will only be able to deduct the depreciation for the months of October, November and December, one fourth of the mixer's first year depreciation. In 2007 you will deduct the remaining three fourths of its first year depreciation plus one fourth of the depreciation for the second year of the mixer's life. This process will continue until in 2010 you deduct three fourths of the depreciation corresponding to the fourth year of the asset's life.)

2. Your inventory cut-off time was midnight on March 31 but you required between 8:00 A.M. and 5:00 P.M. on March 31 and between 8:00 A.M. and 5:00 P.M. on April 1 to take the entire physical inventory. The activity that occurred between the time of your physical count indicated on the inventory count sheet shown here and the inventory cutoff time is listed below for four inventory items. Based on this activity make the required adjustments to your physical count and determine the correct amount in inventory at the inventory cutoff time.

Inventory Count Sheet

Stock no.	Item description	Date and time of count	Quantity counted	Adjustment		Quantity at cutoff time
				Out	In	
688P	Onions	Mar. 31 4:55 P.M.	30 lb			
689P	Carrots	Mar. 31 5:00 P.M.	20 lb			
690P	Potatoes	Apr. 1 8:00 A.M.	100 lb			
691P	Cauliflower	Apr.1 8:05 A.M.	20 lb			

Events between time of count and cutoff time:
1. At 6:00 P.M. on March 31, 10 lb of onions were received.
2. At 10:00 P.M. on March 31, 5 lb of carrots were consumed.
3. At 5:00 A.M. on April 1, 8 lb of potatoes were consumed.
4. At 7:30 A.M. on April 1, 10 lb of cauliflower were received.

3. On January 1, 2007 the Trundmore Restaurant purchased a pick-up truck in a city 300 miles away for $15,000. The truck needed $1,000 of repairs because it did not run at the time it was purchased, and was purchased "as is." The sales tax was $750 and the owner had to pay a driver $200 to drive it the 300 miles to the restaurant.
   (a) Prepare the journal entry to record the purchase of the pick-up truck.
   (b) Assume the truck had a seven year life, a salvage value of $3,000, and was depreciated using the straight-line rate. If it was sold for $9,000 on June 30, 2010, prepare the journal entry to record the sale.

4. On January 1, 2008 a restaurant purchased a franchise from Bumble Burger Co. that gave it the right to use the Bumble Burger name for 10 years. The cost of the franchise rights was $20,000. Prepare the journal entry
   (a) to record the purchase of these franchise rights, and
   (b) to record the cost expiration expense for the year ended December 31, 2008.
   (c) Indicate in what section of the balance sheet franchise rights appear.
   (d) Show how these franchise rights would appear on the balance sheet at December 31, 2008.

   Remember that franchise rights are an intangible asset and their cost expiration is recorded somewhat differently than for tangible assets, and that they are treated differently on the balance sheet.

5. Based on the following ending inventory values, answer the questions below. Assume inventory purchases each year are $100,000, and remember that the previous year's ending inventory is the current year's beginning inventory.

	2006	2007	2008
FIFO	$100,000	$97,000	$115,000
LIFO	95,000	90,000	110,000

   Which inventory valuation method (FIFO or LIFO) would you prefer if you want to:
   1. Maximize net income in 2007?
   2. Minimize net income in 2007?

LONG PROBLEMS

1. The Garden Restaurant, whose fiscal year ends on June 30, purchased a new oven for $8,000 on June 30, 2008. The oven was purchased and transported at a cost of $500. A sales tax of $750 was paid and transportation insurance cost $100. It also cost $650 to prepare the site where the oven was to be installed and certain expenses involved in testing the oven prior to commercial use amounted to $100. The room where the oven was installed was due for its regular annual coat of paint, which was done at a cost of $300. The $8,000 cost of the oven was paid for as follows: $1,000 paid by check, and a note payable was signed for the $7,000 balance. All other expenditures were on a credit basis.
   (a) Prepare the journal entry or entries to record all of the above expenditures.

(b) Calculate depreciation expense for the oven using the sum-of-years'-digits method. Assume a five-year useful life and a $1,000 salvage value. Remember that the company's fiscal accounting year ends on June 30, the same day that each year of the oven's useful life ends.

(c) Calculate depreciation expense using the straight-line method.

(d) Draw a single graph showing the two depreciation methods similar to the one in the text.

(e) Which method of depreciation allows a firm to deduct most of the oven's depreciation expense over the early years of the oven's useful life?

(f) Explain how the graph indicates this.

(g) Is the total depreciation expense under both methods the same over the life of the oven?

2. The Garden Restaurant, whose fiscal year ends on August 31, purchased a new refrigerator for $12,000 on August 31, 2009. The oven was purchased and transported at a cost of $600. A sales tax of $900 was paid and transportation insurance cost $150. It also cost $500 to prepare the site where the refrigerator was to be installed. The electric cables leading to the room where the refrigerator was to be installed had been accidentally cut and needed to be repaired. This cost $500. The $12,000 cost of the refrigerator was paid for as follows: $3,000 paid by check, and a note payable was signed for the $9,000 balance. All other expenditures were on a credit basis.

(a) Prepare the journal entry or entries to record all of the above expenditures.

(b) Calculate depreciation expense for the oven using the one-and-one-half-times declining balance method. Assume a five-year useful life and a $1,000 salvage value. Remember that the company's fiscal accounting year ends on August 31, the same day that each year of the oven's useful life ends.

(c) Calculate depreciation expense using the straight-line method.

(d) Draw a single graph showing the two depreciation methods similar to the one in the text.

(e) Which method of depreciation allows a firm to deduct most of the oven's depreciation expense over the early years of the oven's useful life?

(f) Explain how the graph indicates this.

(g) Is the total depreciation under both methods the same over the life of the refrigerator?

3. The Villamar Tour Bus Company purchased a small tour bus for $15,000 on April 30, 2009, the company's fiscal year end. Management estimates that it will be in usable condition for only 100,000 miles after a major overhaul, which cost $5,000. Its salvage value is estimated to be $5,000. Management expects to operate the bus as follows:

Fiscal year ended	Miles covered
April 30, 2010	30,000
April 30, 2011	25,000
April 30, 2012	30,000
April 30, 2013	15,000

(a) Calculate the annual depreciation for each year of the life of the bus using the four depreciation methods explained in this chapter. Assume a four-year life where needed.

(b) What is the effect of these different depreciation methods on net income?

(c) Which depreciation method is best to use in this situation? Explain.

(d) Under what operating circumstances would the units-of-output depreciation method achieve the same results as the straight-line depreciation method?

(e) Is the total depreciation under these different methods the same over the entire life of the bus?

4. The Covadonga Hotel purchased an adjacent tract of land and is building an extension to the hotel on the land. All the following expenditures were charged to the building account. You are reviewing the account on December 31, 2007—the hotel's fiscal year end—and discover that some items were charged (debited) to the construction-in-progress account that should not have been debited to the account.

Land appraisal fee	1,000
Title search related to new land	200
Attorney's fee related to purchase of land	800
Cost of new land	700,000
Cost of demolishing previous structure on land	20,000
Cost of leveling the new land	13,000
Cost of laying building foundations for the extension	80,000
Cost of reinstalling ducts in the air-conditioning system of the original Covadonga Hotel building	80,000
Cost of central air conditioning for the extension	60,000
Freight cost of air-conditioning unit for the extension	1,500
Cost to install air conditioner for extension	1,000
Cost of testing air conditioner for the extension	200
Cost of purchasing new freezer for original hotel	2,500
Architectural drawings for the extension	25,000
Construction materials for the extension	807,632
Construction labor for the extension	547,321
Total debited to construction-in-progress building account	$2,290,153

Additional Information:

- In addition to the above expenses the company employed a supervisor whose salary was $30,000 per year. He spent six months exclusively supervising this construction. His salary has been charged to the salaries and wages account on the income statement as of December 31, 2007.

- Also, the company borrowed funds specifically to finance this construction and had paid interest on these funds of $122,000. This interest has been charged to the interest expense account on the income statement as of December 31, 2007.

(a) In the above list there are two expenditures that should not have been charged to the construction-in-progress account. Can you identify them?

(b) To what accounts should these two expenditures have been charged?

(c) Based on the additional information given, were any expenditures charged to other accounts that should have been charged to the building account? What are they?

(d) Prepare a worksheet with six columns as indicated below. At the top of the columns enter the names of the correct accounts to be charged or credited. Then enter each expenditure amount in the column corresponding to the account where it belongs. Enter credits to remove amounts from the account columns by using brackets.

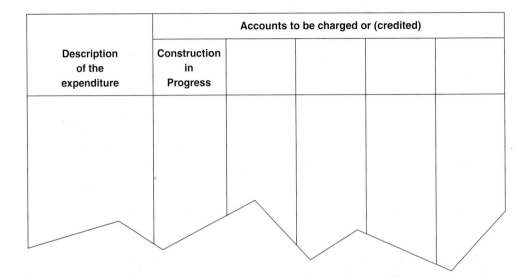

Description of the expenditure	Accounts to be charged or (credited)				
	Construction in Progress				

(e) Total the columns in the above worksheet and prepare one journal entry to correct all the accounts. Amounts recorded in wrong accounts should be removed from the expenditure column where they have been charged and transferred to the correct account column where they belong. For example, imagine that there were a $10,000 amount in the above construction-in-progress list that should actually be charged (debited) to the salaries and wages expense account. To correct this hypothetical error you would have written the $10,000 amount in parentheses in the construction-in-progress column, and would also have written the same amount, without parentheses, in a column to the right that you had labeled "salaries and wages." This would have removed the $10,000 amount from the construction-in-progress column and transferred it to the salaries and wages column where it belongs.

5. Prepare journal entries to record the following transactions of the Riverfork Restaurant under the periodic inventory system for the month ended June 30, 2008. Assume the inventory on May 31, 2008 is $1,000. Record the end-of-period cost of sales entries and then prepare a journal entry to close the cost-of-sales account to the income summary account. Assume the purchase discounts account is not closed to cost of sales but is shown on the income statement instead. Round amounts to the nearest dollar.

  1. June 10, 2008: Purchased 20 frozen ducks on 2/10, net 30 credit terms for $10 each. Shipping terms were FOB the Riverfork Restaurant.
  2. June 15, 2000: Sold 25 ducks for $750.
  3. June 19, 2000: Purchased 30 frozen ducks for $9 each on credit from another supplier that did not give a prompt payment discount. Shipping terms were FOB the Riverfork Restaurant.
  4. June 20, 2008: Paid for the 20 ducks purchased on June 10, 2008.
  5. June 24, 2000: Sold 15 ducks for $450.
  6. June 30, 2000: Purchased 10 ducks for $8 each from a supplier that did not give a prompt payment discount. Shipping terms were FOB the Riverfork Restaurant and it takes two days for the ducks to arrive at the restaurant.

6. Following are listed the sales and purchases of Chianti wine made by Mr. Xavier Camp's Restaurant in January, 2007. Assume there was no beginning inventory and that the periodic-inventory system is in use.

Transaction date 2007	Units purchased	Unit cost	Total cost	Unit sales
Jan. 10	20	$2.00	$40.00	
Jan. 13				8
Jan. 15	5	2.10	10.50	
Jan. 18				9
Jan. 26	6	2.10	12.60	

(a) Prepare abbreviated income statements showing sales, cost of sales (based on the periodic-inventory system), and gross profit for the month of January using the following inventory valuation methods:
1. FIFO
2. LIFO
3. Weighted-average

Assume the sales price in $6 per unit for all sales. When calculating weighted-average, round amounts to nearest hundredth of a cent.

7. Following are listed the sales and purchases of Bordeaux wine made by the ABC Restaurant in February, 2008. Assume the beginning inventory consisted of 10 units purchased at $2.10 each and that the periodic-inventory system is in use.

Transaction date 2008	Units purchased	Unit cost	Total cost	Unit sales
Feb. 10	7	2.15	15.05	
Feb. 20				7
Feb. 28	7	2.20	15.40	
Feb. 28				4

(a) Prepare abbreviated income statements showing sales, cost of sales (based on the periodic-inventory system), and gross profit for the month of February using the following inventory valuation methods:
1. FIFO
2. LIFO
3. Weighted-average

Assume the sales price is $6 per unit for all sales. When calculating weighted-average, round amounts to nearest hundredth of a cent.

8. Following are listed the sales and purchases of Bordeaux wine made by the Blue Bottle Restaurant in March, 2009. Assume the beginning inventory consisted of 8 units purchased at $2.20 each and that the periodic-inventory system is in use.

Transaction date 2009	Units purchased	Unit cost	Total cost	Unit sales
Mar. 10	7	2.15	15.05	
Mar. 13				3
Mar. 17	7	2.20	15.40	
Mar. 19				5
Mar. 23	5	2.30	11.50	
Mar. 27				6
Mar. 30				2

(a) Prepare abbreviated income statements showing sales, cost of sales (based on the periodic-inventory system), and gross profit for the month of March using the following inventory valuation methods:

    1. FIFO

    2. LIFO

    3. Weighted-average

Assume the sales price is $6 per unit for all sales. When calculating weighted-average round amouns to nearest hundredth of a cent.

9. The following mistakes were made by the Weineck Restaurant in accounting for its food and beverage inventory as of December 31, 2008, the restaurant's year-end. (The accounting records have already been adjusted to the physical inventory count.)

    1. Food amounting to $1,200 was purchased and recorded on the books on December 28, 2008, FOB point of origin, but had not been received when the physical inventory was taken and was therefore excluded from the inventory count.

    2. When the physical inventory sheets were totaled, one sheet was added incorrectly. An incorrect amount of $1,000 was used as a column total instead of the correct amount of $500.

    3. The Mouton-Cadet wine inventory was taken on January 1, 2009 and amounted to $5,600. Because of poor inventory-taking procedures, $1,000 worth of this wine was taken to the ballroom from inventory between midnight December 31, 2008 (the inventory cutoff date) and the time of the physical count, without being detected by those in charge of taking the inventory.

    4. The wrong invoice was used to determine the value of the Spanish ham inventory. Consequently, the 100 hams in inventory were erroneously valued at $25 each instead of $35 each, the correct amount.

    5. In order to avoid bothering the chefs during their preparations for midnight dinner on December 31, 2008, the food in the kitchen pantry was counted on December 30, 2008. No control was kept of the amount of food consumed subsequently in preparing the midnight dinner. The value of the food consumed during the dinner was $15,000.

(a) On the worksheet presented below indicate the effect of each error on inventory, cost of sales, and gross profit for the years 2008 and 2009. Indicate amounts to be subtracted in each column by using parentheses.

2008			
Mistake	Inventory	Cost of sales	Gross Profit
(1)			
(2)			
(3)			
(4)			
(5)			

2009			
Mistake	Inventory	Cost of sales	Gross Profit
(1)			
(2)			
(3)			
(4)			
(5)			

(b) Based on the above analysis prepare appropriate entries to correct the errors in 2008 and 2009. Assume 2008 closing entries have already been made.

Receivables, Payables and Corporation Accounting **12**

The learning objectives of this chapter are:

- To become familiar with the various receivables and their balance sheet presentation.
- To learn how to write off and restore an account receivable.
- To become familiar with the various current and long-term liabilities, including contingent liabilities, as well as their balance sheet presentation.
- To learn the accounting procedures involved in recording the formation of a corporation.
- To learn the characteristics of different types of stock.
- To become familiar with the accounting procedures involved in the declaration and payment of dividends.
- To become familiar with additional transactions that affect the retained earnings account.
- To briefly discuss treasury stock transactions.

This chapter will cover receivables, payables, and a brief overview of corporation accounting. Additional attention is given to receivables and payables because, together with the cash accounts, they are the most frequently used accounts in a hospitality accounting system. Then, to complete the more detailed review of the liabilities and equity side of the balance sheet, the impact of corporation accounting on the equity section of the balance sheet will be discussed. The corporate form of business entity is the major form of business enterprise in terms of economic power in the United States, and it is the most complex from the point of view of accounting transactions. It should be noted that the advantages and disadvantages of using the corporate form of business entity were mentioned in Chapter 1.

In this chapter, the more common receivables are first listed, followed by a discussion of the different methods of accounting for uncollectible accounts receivable, a discussion of credit card sales, and an explanation of notes receivable, including the accrual and the recording of interest on notes receivable.

The payables section of the chapter begins with a listing of the most common types of liabilities incurred by a hospitality firm. This includes a discussion of non-interest-bearing and interest-bearing current liabilities, followed by a discussion of long-term debt instruments, such as long-term notes payable, mortgages payable, bonds and long-term lease obligations. The chapter concludes with a discussion of other accounts that appear in, or affect, the liability section of the balance sheet, such as deferred income taxes, reserves, minority interest and future commitments and contingencies, all of which play an important role in the financing of hospitality industry firms.

The section on corporation accounting begins with a discussion of the formation of a corporation, its organizational structure, different types of stock and the significance of par value. This is followed by an explanation of the accounting for the issue of common stock, preferred stock, and no-par stock; as well as the issue of stock in exchange for non-cash assets. Treasury stock transactions, buying and reissuing, are dealt with next. In conclusion the chapter ends with a review of the retained earnings account and a description of transactions that affect retained earnings, such as the recording of cash dividends, stock dividends, stock splits, and mistakes made in recording prior years' earnings.

RECEIVABLES

Although trade accounts receivable and accounts payable are the most significant components of the receivables and payables accounts in terms of their impact on the operations of a hospitality firm, they are not the only components of these account groups. This chapter therefore will touch upon some non-trade accounts receivable and notes receivable as well as other payables, such as: accrued liabilities, taxes payable, short-term notes payable, dividends payable, unearned revenue, long-term debt, deferred taxes payable and contingent liabilities.

Types of Receivables

The receivables account group can be subdivided into the following three major categories:

1. Trade accounts receivable
2. Other accounts receivable
   - Loans to employees
   - Refunds receivable
   - Interest receivable
3. Notes receivable

Trade accounts receivable represent amounts due the hospitality firm for goods sold or services rendered, and originate as the result of credit sales. Other accounts receivable include notes receivable, and all non-trade accounts receivable such as loans to employees, refunds receivable, and interest receivable. The non-trade receivables are described clearly by their individual names and need no explanation. Notes receivable are formal promises to pay the hospitality firm and are backed by a note signed by whoever has received services or property from the hospitality firm in exchange for the note.

Although credit sales imply an additional risk for a business entity, without credit sales growth in the hospitality industry would be greatly impaired. When sales are made on credit, the hospitality firm receives a commitment of future payment instead of immediate cash payment. In order to engage safely in making such sales, therefore, a firm should apply certain policies to reduce the risk of subsequent nonpayment.

Establish internal procedures for authorizing credit, such as:

1. Investigating the client's credit history, and
2. Requiring an officer's authorization before granting credit.

Establish specific collection procedures to remind customers of amounts that are due.

In larger firms, a credit department is established to assume responsibility for implementing the policies enumerated above. Proper control of credit enables a firm to minimize losses due to nonpayment and to maximize profits earned on credit sales.

Nevertheless, it is nearly impossible to avoid such losses altogether and it is difficult to ascertain the amount of current accounts receivable that will become uncollectible in the future. Management usually does not become aware of the uncollectibility of an account until a subsequent accounting period, since the creditworthiness of each client is well established at the time of the sale if proper credit policies are applied.

This is problematical because management does not know for sure which customers will fail to pay their accounts receivable. Yet, the matching concept requires that expenses be matched with the revenue they help to generate in the current period. To comply with this concept, management must, consequently, estimate what dollar amount of a firm's accounts receivable will eventually, probably in a later accounting period, prove to be uncollectible. The process of accounting for these uncollectible accounts is discussed next.

PROCESS OF RECORDING BAD DEBTS EXPENSE

There are two methods of accounting for accounts receivable that are not paid. These are:

- The direct write-off method, and
- The allowance method.

Direct Write-Off Method of Recording Bad Debts

The direct write-off method of recording bad debts expense requires waiting for an account to be proven uncollectible before it is charged to bad debts expense. After every effort to collect from a customer has failed, including sometimes taking legal action, the amount is charged to an account called bad debts expense on the income statement. Since this may occur in a period subsequent to the one in which the account was created and its related revenue was recorded, this method does not comply with the matching concept, and, if amounts to be written-off are material, it is not acceptable under GAAP. The write-off is recorded as follows:

	Dr	Cr
Bad debts expense	400	
Accounts receivable		400
To write off an uncollectible account under the direct write-off method.		

Although it is not acceptable for financial reporting purposes, this method is allowed by the IRS (Internal Revenue Service) for tax reporting purposes.

Allowance Method of Recording Bad Debts

The allowance method of recording uncollectible accounts enables management to estimate, for purposes of recording them in the current accounting period, potential future losses on accounts receivable. Because this entry is based on estimates and not actual facts, the charge to the bad debts expense account cannot be offset by a credit to accounts receivable. Such a credit would imply that accounts receivable had in fact been diminished, whereas it is only the possibility of future reduction that is being recorded. Consequently, under this method, the estimate of future uncollectible accounts is credited to a contra-asset account called "allowance for doubtful accounts." This account is called a contra-asset account because it contains a credit balance—the opposite, or "contra" to, the normal debit balance of assets—yet it appears on the asset side of the balance sheet. This account appears in parentheses to indicate that it has a balance opposite to the debit balance that assets should have, and immediately below accounts receivable on the balance sheet as follows:

Accounts receivable	$100,000
Less: Allowance for doubtful accounts	2,000
Net accounts receivable	$ 98,000

The debit side of the entry is made, as usual, to the bad debts expense account on the income statement. Under this method bad debts expense is recorded by the adjusting entry shown below:

	Dr	Cr
Bad debts expense	2,000	
Allowance for doubtful accounts		2,000
To provide for estimated uncollectible accounts.		

Estimating the Allowance for Doubtful Accounts

Having to estimate the amount of allowance for doubtful accounts raises the question of how this should be done. Management can estimate the amount of the allowance for doubtful accounts in two ways:

- The percentage-of-sales method, and
- The accounts receivable aging method.

Percentage-of-Sales Method

The percentage-of-sales method is the easier of the two methods to use. It focuses on the income statement and, as its name implies, is calculated by multiplying sales by a certain percentage to arrive at the amount of expected bad debts. This percentage rate is determined by looking at the amount of uncollectible accounts receivable in previous years. It should be based on an average of two or three previous years. The current year's sales would then be multiplied by this percent to determine the amount by which the allowance for uncollectible accounts should be increased in the current accounting period. This process is demonstrated below:

Year	Sales	Actual uncollectible accounts	Average uncollectible percentage
2008	$ 650,000	$19,500	
2009	890,000	15,300	
2010	1,120,000	18,400	
	$2,660,000	$53,200	2%

The average uncollectible percentage rate of 2 percent was calculated above based on the uncollectible accounts receivable of the previous three years. The final step of the percentage rate calculation is demonstrated below:

$$\frac{53,200}{2,660,000} \times 100 = 2\%$$

Let us assume that this year is 2011, and that this year's sales are $1,400,000. The entry to record management's estimate of uncollectible accounts based on the above previous experience percentage rate is indicated below. The $28,000 amount is obtained as follows: $1,400,000 × .02 = $28,000.

	Dr	Cr
Bad debts expense	28,000	
Allowance for doubtful accounts		28,000
To record 2 percent bad debts expense on year 2011 sales of $1,400,000.		

Accounts Receivable Aging Method

The accounts receivable aging method focuses on the balance sheet and instead of attempting to estimate the percentage of current period sales that is likely to be uncollectible it attempts to estimate the percentage of accounts receivable that is likely to be uncollectible. In order to arrive at this estimate, an accounts receivable aging schedule is prepared. This is a worksheet such as the one illustrated in Exhibit 12–1, in which each outstanding account is listed in columns according to how many days it has been outstanding. The column headings indicate that an account is current, 1 to 30 days past due, 31 to 60 days past due, 61 to 90 days past due, or over 90 days past due. The columns are then totaled and a percentage of each column total is calculated. These percentages, a different one for each column, are estimates based on previous experience. In Exhibit 12–1, for instance, it is indicated that management has estimated 1 percent of the current accounts, 3 percent of accounts 1 to 30 days past due, 4 percent of accounts 31 to 60 days past due, 15 percent of accounts 61 to 90 days past due, and 30 percent of accounts over 90 days past due will be uncollectible. When these percentages are multiplied by the total dollar amount of accounts receivable in each category the estimated uncollectible dollar amount for each category is obtained. These dollar amounts are then totaled to obtain the estimated balance ($742) that should be considered as the allowance for doubtful accounts.

The accounts receivable aging schedule in Exhibit 12–1 indicates that the allowance for doubtful accounts should have a credit balance of $742.

Preparing the Journal Entry to Record Bad Debts Expense Under the Aging Schedule Method

At this point, we must emphasize that there is another major difference between the percentage-of-sales method and the accounts receivable aging method. When using the percentage-of-sales method the estimated uncollectible amount is automatically credited to the allowance for doubtful accounts regardless of whatever balance this account already has in it. On the other hand, when using the accounts receivable aging method the estimated amount of uncollectible accounts is not automatically added to the allowance for doubtful accounts. The reason for this is that the accounts receivable aging method focuses on the balance sheet and the result of the calculation gives us the correct estimated balance that should appear on the balance sheet as allowance for doubtful accounts. Therefore, when preparing the journal entry to record bad debts expense the amount that is already in the allowance for doubtful accounts must be taken into account.

Client	Amount due	Current	30-Jan	31–60	61–90	Over 90
					Days past due	
John Wirth	520					520
William Blye	650				650	
Patricia Velez	1,200			1,200		
Karmon, Inc.	20,000	10,000	6,000	4,000		
	$22,370	$10,000	$6,000	$5,200	$650	$520
Precentage uncollectible		x .01	x .03	x .04	x .15	x .30
Amount uncollectible		$100	$180	$208	$98	$156

By totalling the estimated uncollectible amount in each aging category above, the appropriate estimated balance of "allowance for doubtful accounts" is determined below:

Total uncollectible = $100 + $180 + $208 + $98 + $156 = $742

Exhibit 12–1   Accounts receivable aging schedule.

For example, let us assume that the aging schedule indicates the allowance for doubtful accounts should be $742, and there is already a $300 credit balance in the account. This balance would have resulted from overestimating the amount of uncollectible accounts in previous years. In this case, the journal entry to record bad debts expense should be only for the difference between the $300 already in the account and the $742 balance that should be in the account according to the aging schedule. This calculation and the correct journal entry to record bad debts expense would be made as follows:

Balance that the aging schedule indicates should be in the allowance for doubtful accounts.	$ 742
Balance in the allowance for doubtful accounts from previous years.	−300
Required current year credit to the account	$ 442

The journal entry to record bad debts expense in the current period would then be:

	Dr	Cr
Bad debts expense	442	
Allowance for doubtful accounts		442

To record bad debts expense per the accounts receivable aging schedule.

If we had underestimated the amount of uncollectible accounts receivable in previous years, then the account allowances for uncollectible accounts would have had a debit balance. In that case, we would have had to add the debit balance to the $742 so that the ending balance in the account would be $742. Let us assume that there had been a $200 debit balance in the account allowance for uncollectible accounts. The general ledger "T" account for this account would have appeared as follows after making the appropriate entry debiting bad debts expense for $942 and crediting the allowance account for $942:

Allowance for doubtful accounts

Bal.	200	GJ	942
		Bal.	742

The journal entry to bring the balance to the correct amount of $742 in this case would have been as follows:

	Dr	Cr
Bad debts expense	942	
Allowance for doubtful accounts		942
To adjust the balance in the allowance for doubtful accounts to the amount indicated by the accounts receivable aging schedule.		

Generally, both the percentage-of-sales method and the accounts receivable aging schedule method are used by a firm at different stages of the accounting cycle. Throughout the year, the percentage-of-sales method is applied because of its simplicity. At year end, an aging schedule is prepared to adjust the allowance for doubtful accounts with greater accuracy.

Writing Off Uncollectible Accounts Receivable Under the Allowance Method

The allowance for doubtful accounts is recorded on the basis of estimates. When a customer goes into bankruptcy or gives evidence in some other way that it will be impossible to collect all or part of the amount owed the firm, then the loss on that account becomes a certainty. It is misleading to include such customers in accounts receivable after this point, and so their account must be written off the books. Because, under the allowance method, bad debts expense has already been charged, such accounts must be written off against the allowance for doubtful accounts. Assuming Ralf Auslin owed the firm $1,000, was declared bankrupt, and was thus unable to pay any of his debt, the entry to write off his account would be made as follows:

	Dr	Cr
Allowance for doubtful accounts	1,000	
Accounts receivable		1,000
To write off Ralf Auslin's uncollectible account receivable.		

This is the type of entry that will cause the allowance for doubtful accounts to end the year with a debit balance, instead of the usual credit balance. This will happen if management has underestimated the amount of uncollectible accounts, and has not created a sufficiently large allowance. Such a situation would be corrected, of course, at the end of the year when the aging schedule method is used to estimate the balance in the allowance account.

Recovering an Accounts Receivable That Was Previously Written Off

When a customer whose account was previously written off as uncollectible later pays all or part of the account, the above entry is reversed and a second entry to record collection of the restored accounts receivable is made. These two entries are shown below based on the assumption that Ralf Auslin later paid $500 of his account receivable that had been written off:

	Dr	Cr
Accounts receivable	500	
Allowance for uncollectible accounts		500
To reverse the write-off of $500 of Ralf Auslin's account receivable.		
Cash	500	
Accounts receivable		500
To record the collection of $500 of Ralf Auslin's partially recovered account receivable.		

OTHER RECEIVABLES

Accounts Receivable Credit Balances

The account of a customer who overpays will have a credit balance. In such cases, the account should be included in accounts payable when preparing financial statements. It would be misleading to offset this credit amount against the debit balances of other accounts receivable because the overpayment represents an amount actually owed by the firm.

Likewise, a firm cannot offset accounts payable generated by purchases from a supplier against accounts receivable generated by sales to the same supplier. Even though both the sales and purchase transactions occurred with the same firm, the receivable must be shown as a current asset and the payable must be shown as a current liability on the financial statements.

Credit Card Sales

Generating sales by accepting credit card payments is another way for the hospitality firm to grant credit. In this case, the hospitality firm is granting credit to the credit card firm, not to the customer. Formerly credit card companies took several days to pay these slips. Today, however, credit card slips can be deposited in a bank account like money because credit card companies maintain large balances in the major banks. When a credit card slip is deposited in the bank, the bank merely transfers money from the credit card account to the hospitality firm's account on an overnight basis.

Credit card companies assume the risk of granting credit to their cardholders, thereby relieving the hospitality firm of this risk. In return for this service, they charge member firms a percentage of sales effected through their cards. This percentage becomes an expense of the member firm.

For example, a $200 sale through a credit card is recorded by debiting the accounts receivable account of the credit card company as follows:

	Dr	Cr
Accounts receivable (from the credit card company)	200	
Sales		200
To record a $200 sale through a credit card.		

At the time the sale is made, the customer signs a sales slip, which is sent to the credit card company for payment. Payment is made for the amount of the sale less a commission. Assuming a 3 percent commission on the above sale, the entry to record payment by the credit card company is made as follows:

	Dr	Cr
Cash	194	
Credit card commission expense	6	
Accounts receivable (from credit card company)		200
To record payment by a credit card company of a $200 sales slip less 3% commission.		

If a credit card company has an account with a local bank, then the commission is recorded at the time the credit card slip is deposited by the hospitality firm in its bank account. It knows that the bank will only transfer to its account the amount of the deposit slip less the credit card company's commission. In this case, only one entry, which combines the deposit and commission charge, is made as follows:

	Dr	**Cr**
Cash	194	
Credit card commission expense	6	
Sales		200

To record credit card sales slip deposits when a direct payment agreement exists with a local bank.

Notes Receivable

Often, when a customer cannot pay the amount owed within the normal credit period, either because of the large size of the transaction, or because of a temporary cash shortage, the customer may negotiate extended credit terms with the hospitality firm. Usually, if the hospitality firm agrees to extend the credit period it will ask the client to sign a promissory note. Notes have two advantages over accounts receivable: (1) they are interest-bearing, and (2) they are negotiable instruments, legally transferable to a lender by endorsement. These two attributes facilitate a firm's converting its notes into cash and recompense it for the time value of the money being used by the customer.

To be negotiable a note must meet four conditions:

1. It must be signed by the maker (customer-borrower).
2. It must contain an unconditional promise to pay or order someone other than the maker to pay a specific amount.
3. It must be payable on demand or at a specific future time.
4. It must be payable to bearer or to the order of someone named specifically on the note (payee).

Although notes usually are interest-bearing and specify an interest rate on their face, they do not have to be interest-bearing to qualify as a promissory note. Even though they be interest-bearing, however, notes receivable are recorded at their face value, i.e., at the amount of the principal owed, exclusive of interest. Thus, if $1,000 of accounts receivable are converted into a note receivable due in six months and bearing interest of 12 percent APR (annual percentage rate), the note is recorded as follows:

	Dr	**Cr**
Notes receivable	1,000	
Accounts receivable		1,000

To record conversion of $1,000 in accounts receivable into a note receivable with a face value of $1,000.

If this were not a conversion from accounts receivable, but rather a prenegotiated sale on extended credit terms, then the credit would be directly to the sales account.

Interest Accrual on Notes Receivable. If a note receivable is interest-bearing, the hospitality firm must record the earning of this interest over time. It cannot record this interest when the note is received because the hospitality firm has not earned it yet. But, for example, after a period of three months, the firm has earned interest income that it can record. Invoices are usually not issued for interest receivable, so interest income is recorded through an adjusting accrual entry. The accrual entry can be made automatically each month, or it can be made only when financial statements are prepared. Let us assume that three months have passed since the above note was received and the hospitality firm needs to accrue the interest income because it is going to prepare financial statements. The entry to record three months of accrued interest income on the $1,000 note is presented below. The 12 percent annual rate is the same as a 1 percent monthly rate, so the firm has earned 3 percent of $1,000 over the three-month period.

	Dr	Cr
Accrued interest receivable	30	
Interest income		30

To accrue three months' interest at 12% on a $1,000 note receivable (3/12 × 0.12 = 0.03; 0.03 × $1,000 = $30).

When payment of the note is received, at the end of its six-month term, the following entry is recorded:

	Dr	Cr
Cash	1,060	
Interest income		30
Accrued interest receivable		30
Notes receivable		1,000

To record collection of a $1,000 note receivable plus six months' interest at 12%.

LIABILITIES

Types of Payables

Payables, as discussed in this text, include:

1. Liabilities, which are divided into three groups called:
   - Current liabilities
   - Long-term debt
   - Deferred income taxes, and other accounts
2. Future commitments and contingent liabilities.

Together, these comprise all amounts actually owed to others by a hospitality firm, as well as amounts that may be owed in the future (commitments and contingencies). The liabilities can be divided into the three categories listed above: (1) current liabilities, (2) long-term debt, and (3) deferred income taxes and other accounts.

CURRENT LIABILITIES

Current liabilities are debts that are payable within one year from the balance sheet date, and include the following accounts. These accounts can be divided into interest-bearing (on which the hospitality firm must pay interest), and non-interest-bearing:

- Accounts payable
- Accrued liabilities
- Unearned revenue
- Taxes payable
- Dividends payable
- Deferred income taxes

- Short-term notes payable
- Current portion of long-term debt

Of the above categories, the hospitality firm must pay interest on only the last two current liabilities: short-term notes payable and the current portion of long-term debt. All the other current liabilities constitute interest-free loans from suppliers, service providers, and others. This is why at the beginning of the section on Receivables we recommended that a hospitality firm should take advantage of the full discount period offered by suppliers, or the full credit period offered by a supplier if no discounts are offered. Paying liabilities at the very end of the discount period, or the end of the credit period, allows the hospitality firm to take advantage of discounts offered while making maximum use of the interest-free money of its suppliers, service providers, and others. This helps the hospitality firm to finance, interest-free, its investment in accounts receivable and other current assets.

Non-Interest-Bearing Current Liabilities

Accounts payable, also called trade accounts payable, are amounts owed to suppliers for purchases of goods or services. They are recorded when a supplier's invoice is received. Sometimes suppliers offer a discount of 2 percent if their invoice is paid within 10 days, instead of the normal 30-day credit period. When this discount is offered, the following is usually stamped on the invoice: 2,10/net 30. This offer should always be accepted and the invoice paid on the tenth day, no sooner of course, because the 2 percent represents an annual interest rate of approximately 36 percent. The difference between paying in 10 and 30 days is 20 days. In return for paying 20 days early, the hospitality firm receives a 2 percent discount, which is like receiving 2 percent interest on the invoice amount for lending it to the supplier over a period of 20 days. There are approximately 18 periods of 20 days in a year, so on an annualized basis, this 2 percent is equivalent to 36 percent interest per year.

Accrued liabilities, also called accrued expenses payable, are liabilities that must be entered on the accounting records of a hospitality firm by making an accrual adjusting entry because they have not been invoiced. Sometimes a firm is not invoiced for monthly rent, or interest expenses as a matter of policy. The firm is expected to know that it owes these amounts. However, if no invoice is received, the firms accounting clerks do not have enough knowledge about the business to record these expenses. Often, because an invoice has not been received, they are based on management estimates. Because of this fact, they must be kept in a separate account. The implication is that the balance in the accrued expenses account is not as precise as the balance in the accounts payable account.

Accounting personnel who do not have the general overview of a business that the manager and controller have are only aware of the debts of a business when they receive an invoice for processing. Debts that are not backed by an invoice must be entered on the books by accounting personnel who know of their existence because they have participated in some way in the management of the business, such as a controller, or by personnel who have been specifically instructed to record them. As stated before, they are entered on the accounting records by making adjusting entries, called accrual adjusting entries.

Accrued liabilities can also be divided into two subcategories. Some, such as accrued interest on notes payable or accrued vacations payable, must be accrued because they are never invoiced. Other liabilities, such as electricity expense, must be accrued because receipt of the invoice does not usually coincide with the end of an accounting period. A manager should know that this second type of accrued expenses involves an additional step in the accounting process, a step not required by the accrued expenses that will never be invoiced. This step, a reversing entry, is explained in Chapter 6.

Unearned revenue, such as customers' deposits or customer advances, represents the value of goods or services that must be rendered in return for advance payments made by customers. For example, if the firm is to cater a wedding next month and the customer pays for it in advance, the payment is recorded as a customer's deposit, or unearned revenue. This is a liability of the hospitality firm because it owes the service for which payment has been received, or it must pay back the money to the customer. The realization concept does not allow such receipts to be considered as earned revenue until the corresponding service has been rendered. Remember, receipt of cash does not constitute revenue. In those cases when a deposit is non-refundable then the hospitality firm may record the receipt of cash as revenue. But in these cases a service has been rendered—namely the guarantee to the customer that a room will be available, or that some other service will be rendered by the hospitality firm.

Taxes payable include both taxes owed by the firm directly and taxes collected from others for subsequent remittal to the federal and local governments. Income and property taxes payable are an example of the former. Sales taxes and taxes deducted from employees' pay, such as withheld income taxes and withheld social security taxes and medicare, fall into the latter category.

Corporations are not obliged to pay dividends unless the board of directors declares them. However, the moment that dividends are declared the amount of the dividend ceases to be a part of retained earnings, i.e., ownership rights, and becomes an actual liability of the hospitality corporation. Because dividends are not paid immediately on the declaration date, which is impossible for most corporations to do because of the complex processes involved, as well as the need to publicly establish a future date of record, they must be recorded on the books of the hospitality firm as current liabilities. Once a dividend has been declared, stockholders have the right to sue the corporation for non-payment of the dividend, if it is not paid on the payment date, because it is now a legal debt of the corporation.

Short-Term Notes Payable

Short-term notes payable are promissory notes signed by the firm. They are usually given to suppliers for goods or services that will be paid for over a longer term than the supplier's normal credit period, or they are given to banks for short-term loans.

The interest on notes payable may be stated separately on the face of the note as a percentage rate, or the actual dollar amount of interest may be included in the face amount of the note. In Exhibits 12–2 and 12–3, a sample of both types of notes

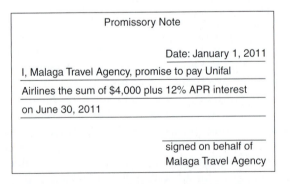

Exhibit 12–2 Promissory note with 12 percent interest rate stated on the face of the note.

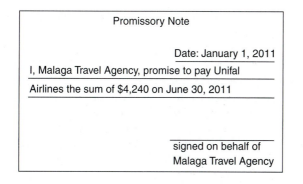

Exhibit 12–3 Promissory note with $120 of interest included in principal amount.

is presented. Both notes are identical in their principal amount of $4,000, their interest rate of 12 percent APR, and their 360-day term. But the first note has the interest stated as a percentage on the face of the note, and the second note has the interest included as a dollar amount added to the principal on the face of the note.

When the interest is stated as a percentage rate, then the hospitality firm (borrower) receives the full face value of the note. A $4,000, 180-day note bearing 12 percent APR interest would be recorded as follows:

2011		Dr	Cr
Jan. 1	Cash	4,000	
	Notes payable		4,000

To record a $4,000, 180-day note when the interest amount is not added to the principal amount on the face of the note.

When the interest is included in the note's face value, the note is recorded through the following journal entry because the borrower does not receive the full face value of the note:

2011		Dr	Cr
Jan. 1	Cash	4,000	
	Discount on notes payable	240	
	Notes payable		4,240

To record a $4,000, 180-day note when the interest amount is added to the principal amount on the face of the note.

In this case, the note would appear on the balance sheet as shown below:

Current Liabilities		
Notes payable	$4,240	
Less: Discount on notes payable	240	$4,000

If the firm's accounting period ends on March 31, 2011, then interest payable would have to be accrued for each type of note as follows. For interest not included in the face value of the note:

2011		Dr	Cr
March 31	Interest expense	120	
	Accrued interest payable		120

To accrue 90 days interest on a $4,000, 180-day note payable bearing 12% APR interest when the interest amount is not added to the principal amount on the face of the note
(12% × 90/360 × $4,000 = $120).

When the interest amount is included with the principal amount on the face of the note the entry to record 90 days interest accrual would be:

2011		Dr	Cr
March 31	Interest expense	120	
	Discount on notes payable		120

To accrue 90 days interest on a $4,000, 180-day note payable bearing 12 percent APR interest when the interest amount is added to the principal amount on the face of the note (12% × 90/360 × $4,000 = $120).

Payment of the note and interest at the end of its 180-day term is recorded as follows for each type of note:

For interest not included in the face value of the note:

2011		Dr	Cr
March 31	Accrued interest payable	120	
	Interest expense	120	
	Notes payable	4,000	
	Cash		4,240

To record payment of a $4,000 note payable whose interest is not added to the principal amount on the face of the note, and for which interest was accrued on March 31, 2011.

For interest included in the face value of the note:

2011		Dr	Cr
March 31	Interest expense	120	
	Notes payable	4,240	
	Discount on notes payable		120
	Cash		4,240

To record payment of a $4,000 note payable whose interest is added to the principal amount on the face of the note, and for which interest was accrued on March 31, 2011.

Current Portion of Long-Term Debt

The current portion of long-term debt is that portion of a firm's long-term debt that is due in the current year. If a firm borrows $1,000,000 on December 31, 2005 to be paid $100,000 annually, then the $100,000 installment due within twelve months of the balance sheet date is reclassified as a current liability account called current portion of long-term debt as follows:

2005		Dr	Cr
Dec. 31	Long-term debt	100,000	
	Current portion of long-term debt		100,000

To reclassify the portion of long-term debt payable within the current year based on single annual payments of $100,000 per year.

If a firm borrows $1.2 million dollars to be repaid at the rate of $10,000 per month, beginning on January 31, 2006, then the current portion would amount to $120,000 (12 × $10,000). To carry this exercise further, let us suppose that the hospitality firm begins to repay the $1 million on July 31, 2006. In this case, only six $10,000 payments would be made within one year from the balance sheet date, December 31, 2005, and the reclassification journal entry on December 31, 2005 would be:

2005		**Dr**	**Cr**
Dec. 31	Long-term debt	60,000	
	Current portion of long-term debt		60,000

To reclassify a portion of long-term debt payable within the first year of the loan's life based on monthly payments of $10,000 beginning in the seventh month after loan was received.

During the second to the tenth years of the above loan's life, the current portion will be $100,000. But then during the eleventh year of the loan's life only six monthly payments will remain, and the current portion will again be reduced to $60,000.

LONG-TERM DEBT

Long-term debt is that portion of a firm's debt that is payable more then one year in the future, in other words it is non-current. This is an important account classification in the hospitality industry because of the capital-intensive nature of the industry. Large amounts of long-term financing are needed to purchase the hotels, restaurants, airplanes, and cruise ships, etc. required by this expanding industry. Short-term notes, which might be renewable every six to twelve months, would be entirely inadequate for financing a hotel with a forty-year useful life. The major categories of long-term debt are:

- Long-term notes payable
- Mortgages payable
- Bonds payable
- Long-term lease obligations (for capital leases)
- Deferred income taxes payable

Long-Term Notes Payable

Long-term notes payable are similar to short-term notes payable except that they are payable after one year from the balance sheet date.

Mortgages Payable

Mortgages payable are similar to long-term notes payable except that they offer the lender, as guarantee or collateral, a specific property, usually real estate. If the borrower defaults on the mortgage notes, the lender may take possession of the property or equipment pledged.

Mortgages payable are usually paid in equal monthly installments that include both principal and interest, necessitating the recording of the interest portion of the mortgage in a discount on notes payable account similar to the one used for short-term notes payable. As is the case with all long-term debt, the payments due within one year from the balance sheet date are recorded as a current liability. For example, if a $100,000, 12 percent mortgage note were payable in $2,000 monthly installments, each installment would contain an interest portion and a principal portion. The amount of interest included in each payment decreases progressively with each payment and the principal portion of the note increases proportionately so that the monthly payments remain at $2,000 per month. To illustrate this, the first four payments on the $100,000 note described above are shown in Exhibit 12–4.

Month	Monthly payment	Monthly interest[1] (12% annually)	Principal reduction	Principal balance
Date	—	—	—	$100,000
Jan. 31	$2,000	$1,000	$1,000	99,000
Feb. 28	2,000	990	1,010	97,990
Mar. 31	2,000	980	1,020	96,970
June 30	2,000	970	1,030	95,940

[1](12%/12 months × remaining principal balance. All amounts rounded to the nearest dollar.)

Exhibit 12–4   Analysis of installments on a $100,000, 12 percent mortgage loan.

Bonds

Bonds are long-term debt instruments that enable a hospitality firm to borrow large amounts of money from many small lenders. Bonds usually have a face value of $1,000, thus making them accessible to many small- and medium-sized lenders.

Bonds may be classified according to whether they are collateral bonds (secured by some specific property or equipment) or unsecured debentures (secured by the general credit-worthiness of the hospitality firm only).

They may be registered bonds (the owner's name is registered with the company, which mails the interest checks when due) or coupon bonds. In the latter case, the issuing entity does not know who owns the bonds, and so the owner must clip interest coupons off the bonds when interest payments are due. These coupons are deposited in the bank, which then collects the interest anonymously from the borrower. Coupons may also be given to a third party, such as a lawyer, to collect on behalf of the true owner.

There are sinking fund bonds, which require a firm to deposit certain amounts annually to be invested in income-producing investments for the purpose of repaying the bond principal when they mature.

Serial bonds, though all issued on the same date, do not all fall due on the same date. They are repaid gradually (in series) over a specified period of years, providing the lender with a constant cash flow over the repayment period.

Then there are convertible debentures. This type of bond may be converted into a specific number of common shares at the bondholder's option, enabling the bondholder to participate in the growth of the company. Interest on bonds is fixed, but when a company is growing, its net income per common share (usually called earnings per share), and dividends, grow also, thus enabling common stock holders to participate in the company's growth, which is something that holders of non-convertible bonds cannot do.

Some bonds may be callable at the option of the issuing firm, thereby enabling it to take advantage of lower current interest rates to refinance its debt, or to sell stock to pay off its debt.

Bonds may be further subdivided into regular and subordinated debentures. When a bond is subordinated it means that in the event of liquidation, it becomes payable only after all liabilities to which they are subordinated have been discharged.

The entries to issue bonds, pay interest on the bonds, and retire (pay back) $1,000,000 worth of five-year bonds whose total principal is payable at maturity and which bear a 12% nominal interest rate printed on their face are presented below:

	Dr	Cr
Cash	1,000,000	
Bonds payable		1,000,000
To issue $1,000,000, 12%, five-year bonds.		
Interest expense	120,000	
Cash		120,000
To record annual interest payment on the 12% bonds.		
Bonds payable	1,000,000	
Cash		1,000,000
To retire the bonds.		

The above entries are valid only when bonds are issued, or sold, at their face or par value. The face or par value of a bond is the amount that the lender will have to repay at its maturity date. This seldom occurs, however. Usually bonds are issued at a discount from their par value, or at a premium. The interest rate a firm will have to pay when it issues bonds to the public depends on two factors that cannot be accurately measured beforehand: (1) the prevailing interest rate on the day of the sale, and (2) the public's reaction to the firm's recent earnings history. Because of these uncertainties, issuing firms print bonds with a predetermined par value of $1,000 and with an interest rate percent that approximates what the firm believes will be the market interest rate on the day the bonds are sold. For instance, annual interest of $120 is paid to the owner of a $1,000 (par value) bond with a 12 percent nominal interest rate printed on its face, regardless of what the bond was sold for, and regardless of what the prevailing interest rate is on the date of sale.

At the time the bonds are sold, however, the public may demand more than 12 percent interest on the bonds. It is impractical to reprint new bonds, and so, instead of changing the stated interest rate on the bonds, they are sold for less than their par value (at a discount).

Similarly, if potential buyers are willing to earn less than 12 percent interest on their investment because competing market interest rates have declined, then they will bid the issue price of the bonds up above their par value. In this case the bonds would be sold at a premium.

If a 12 percent bond is sold at a 20 percent premium this means that it will be sold for $1,200. Because it is a 12 percent bond the owner of the bond will receive $120 per year interest. But if the owner paid $1,200 for the bond, this $120 interest payment does not give the owner a 12 percent return on the $1,200 paid for the bond. It only gives the owner a 10 percent return ($120/$1,200 = 10 percent). Thus, a bond's rate of return can be adjusted down to the market interest rate by increasing the bond's price from $1,000 to $1,200. The opposite would, of course, be true if interest rates were higher than the face interest rate of a bond at the time the bond were sold. A further slight adjustment in the price of the bond (down from $1,200) is also made to compensate for the fact that the new owner will only receive the face value of the bond, $1,000, at its maturity, although he or she paid $1,200 to buy the bond.

Long-Term Lease Obligations

In the property and equipment section of Chapter 11 it was stated that the present value of the annual lease payments of certain long-term leases must be capitalized and included among the property and equipment category of the lessee (the party using the property, not the owner). When the present value of these payments is recorded as property or equipment the corresponding credit entry is made to the long-term lease obligations account. The entry to record the capital lease of a building with lease payments having a present value of $270,000 is made as follows:

	Dr	Cr
Property under capital leases	270,000	
Long-term lease obligations		270,000
To record the capital lease.		

When financial statements are prepared the current portion of the long-term lease obligations is reclassified to a current liability account on the balance sheet, as explained earlier in this chapter, under the heading: "Current Portion of Long-Term Debt."

OTHER ACCOUNTS

Deferred Income Taxes.   In the property and equipment section of the preceding chapter we also learned that because the IRC (Internal Revenue Code) allows a business to accelerate the deduction of certain expenses when calculating taxable income for income tax reporting purposes, part of a firm's income tax expense can be deferred for payment in later years. This deferred amount is recorded in an account called deferred income taxes. If a business is going to have to pay these credits during the current accounting period they appear in the current liabilities section of the balance sheet, otherwise the account appears on the balance sheet towards the bottom of the liabilities section. Financial Accounting Statement (FAS) No. 109, issued by the FASB (Financial Accounting Standards Board) in 1992, dramatically changed the procedure for calculating and presenting deferred income taxes on the balance sheet, however this topic is beyond the scope of this text.

Reserves.   Sometimes a hospitality firm will create reserves for future amounts that it may have to pay. One example of this type of liability is the reserve created for paying pensions or medical expense coverage of retired employees. Because this future liability is incurred while an employee is still working for the firm, as part of the remuneration due the employee, it is expensed during the employee's working lifetime, based on actuarial calculations, and a reserve is created indicating the approximate amount of the liability that the firm has incurred to pay the worker once he or she retires. Reserves can also be established when a firm wishes to insure itself against suits or other possible unfavorable contingencies.

Minority Interest.   When one corporation owns more than fifty percent of another corporation GAAP requires that the parent company (the owner of the other company's stock) consolidate (combine) its financial statements with those of its subsidiary (the company whose stock is owned) when public financial statements are prepared. This indicates to the reader of these financial statements that the two companies are more like one single company than like two separate companies. In this case the parent must show, as the last item at the bottom of the liability section of its balance sheet, the value of the combined companies' equity that belongs to those investors who own a minority share in the subsidiary corporation.

FUTURE COMMITMENTS AND CONTINGENCIES

This heading usually appears between the liabilities and equity sections of a balance sheet. It never has a dollar amount following it because it is intended only to refer the reader of the financial statements to a note to the financial statements. This note lists: (1) future commitments, and (2) contingent liabilities. Since neither of these categories represents actual debts of the business no dollar amount can be shown on the balance sheet for them.

Future commitments arise when a hospitality firm obligates itself for the payment of amounts based on the contracted-for performance of another party. Contracts for the construction of large, expensive assets, such as hotels, restaurants, cruise ships or airplanes constitute this type of commitment. Although the firm may not owe the contractors any money currently, it is important that the reader of the financial statements know that these future payment obligations will exist and that they will become actual liabilities of the company progressively as the contractor completes the construction of the asset. Long-term operating lease agreements are another type of commitment that firms must disclose in this note.

A contingent liability is a potential future liability that may become an actual liability subject to the occurrence of an uncertain event. Its existence and amount cannot be definitely established; therefore, it can, and if material, must be disclosed only in a note to the financial statements. Before a contingent liability can be considered an actual liability with an amount that can be included on the balance sheet of the hospitality entity, some event whose occurrence is uncertain must take place. For instance, the fact that a lawsuit directed against a hospitality firm exists does not mean the entity will necessarily lose the lawsuit and/or be required to pay the entire amount for which it is being sued. On the one hand the firm may win the lawsuit, and, on the other hand, even if it loses, extenuating circumstances may persuade the judge, or jury, to reduce the monetary award. Therefore, before the amount that the plaintiff is seeking in the lawsuit, or any other amount, becomes an actual liability of the hospitality firm, there must be a probability that the lawsuit will be won by the adversary and it must be possible to make a reasonable estimate of the amount that a judge, or jury, will award the plaintiff.

A contingent liability also arises when a hospitality firm guarantees a debt of another entity, such as when it discounts its receivables with recourse with a bank or other financial entity. When accounts receivable are discounted with recourse, a bank, or other financial entity, pays to the hospitality firm the value of all the discounted receivables minus an amount to cover the interest for discounting the accounts. Under these circumstances, the hospitality firm is still responsible for any amounts that its customers do not pay on their accounts. Thus it may have to pay back to the bank, or other financial entity, part of the money that it received for the discounted accounts receivable. This is not an actual debt when the firm discounts the notes, but it may become an actual debt contingent upon non-payment by some of its customers.

In conclusion, contingent liabilities should be presented with a specific amount on the balance sheet only if both of the following are true:

1. It is probable that the event upon which the liability is contingent will occur.
2. The absolute amount of the liability can be estimated with reasonable accuracy.

Otherwise, if they are material, they must be disclosed in the notes to the financial statements, usually in a note titled: Commitments and contingencies.

CORPORATION ACCOUNTING

Forming a Corporation

A corporation is a legal person, whose separate rights are recognized by law. Although each state has its own laws governing the creation of a corporation, usually one or more people (incorporators) must submit to the state an application accompanied by the articles of incorporation of the new entity. The articles of incorporation state the conditions under which the corporation will be formed, such as types of business it will engage in, number of shares, par value and types of stock, voting and dividend rights of each type of stockholder, and the names and addresses of the original subscribers to its stock. Because a corporation is governed by a board of directors, and this board cannot be elected until at least one common share of the corporation is sold (only common shareholders have the right to vote), a provisional board of directors is also named in the articles of incorporation.

Because of the complexities and subtleties involved in preparing the articles of incorporation, a lawyer is usually called upon to draw them up, to fulfill any other legal registration requirement, and to pay registration fees. An accountant may be called upon to design an accounting system for the corporation, and there may also be certain promotional fees involved in its conception.

All of these expenses of forming the corporation are called organization costs. Since they will benefit the corporation over its entire life and are intangible in nature, the matching concept would require that they be capitalized as intangible assets and amortized gradually over the life of the corporation. Although a corporation's life is indefinite, in practice GAAP require that organization costs be amortized over no more than forty years. A frequently used practical approach when organization costs are not material is to amortize them over five years, the shortest amortization period allowed by the IRS. Organization costs are an intangible asset and are included in the other assets classification of the balance sheet along with any other intangible assets.

Accounting for the Formation of a Corporation

The costs of forming a corporation mentioned above would be recorded as follows. If the lawyers' fees for creating a corporation were $2,700, registration fees $500, accountant's fees $2,000, and promoter's fees $4,000, the entry to record organization costs would be as follows:

	Dr	Cr
Organization costs	9,200	
Cash		9,200

To record various organization costs totaling $9,200.

To amortize these costs over a five-year life, the following entry would be made annually for five years:

	Dr	Cr
Amortization expense	1,840	
Organization costs		1,840

To amortize 1/5 of the $9,200 of organization costs.

Organizational Structure

As stated previously, individual stockholders do not manage a corporation. Instead, a separate management team is created to run its affairs. The composition of this team varies from corporation to corporation but must, from its inception, include a board of directors. This board hires a team of operating executives such as a president, one or more vice-presidents, a treasurer, a secretary, a controller, and various other managers at different levels of the corporation's structure. The president, also known as the chief operating officer is responsible for all the day-to-day operations of the firm. The president may delegate responsibility for certain geographical areas (United States, Europe, etc.) or for certain types of activity (hotels, airlines, etc.) to the vice-presidents. The treasurer reports to the president and has overall responsibility for the corporation's funds. He or she is assisted in managing them by the controller, or chief accountant, who is in turn responsible for establishing accounting systems, establishing and implementing internal control procedures, preparing accounting records, tax returns, and other financial records. The secretary is responsible for fulfilling the corporation's legal requirements such as sending meeting notifications and maintaining the minutes of stockholders' meetings and of the meetings of the board of directors.

The stockholders exert control over the executives in charge of the day-to-day operations through the board of directors. The board of directors is elected by the stockholders, usually at an annual stockholders' meeting. The board may have as many members as provided for in the articles of incorporation and is presided over by the chairman of the board, also known as the chief executive officer (CEO). It is responsible for selecting the corporation's president and for overseeing the activities of the corporation throughout the year.

In addition to voting for the board of directors, other matters having great impact on the corporation, such as merger decisions, may be voted upon by stockholders directly at stockholders' meetings. If stockholders cannot attend a stockholders' meeting, they may assign their right to vote to someone else. When a stockholder assigns his or her right to vote on corporate matters to someone else he or she is said to vote by proxy, or by a proxy vote.

TYPES OF STOCK

Although all the stockholders of a corporation are the owners of the corporation to some degree, each type of stock issued may have different stockholder rights assigned to it by the issuing corporation. Generally, there are two broad categories of stock: common stock and preferred stock, distinguishable by the differences in stockholder rights associated with them, which are listed below.

Common Stock

The rights of common stockholders may include some or all of the following:

- The right to sell their shares to whomever they wish
- The right to vote at stockholders' meetings
- The right to receive dividends when declared by the board of directors
- The right to share in the distribution of a corporation's assets upon liquidation in proportion to the number of shares owned
- The right of first refusal on a number of shares proportionate to their current ownership percentage if additional shares are issued and sold. This is known as a stockholder's preemptive right. Its purpose is to enable stockholders to maintain their original percentage ownership of a corporation's shares

Common stockholders do not necessarily enjoy all of these rights, nor do they necessarily enjoy them to the same degree. Before stock may be sold by a corporation the stock issue for each particular type of common stock must be authorized by the board of directors of the corporation and by the state. When the authorization is requested, the stockholder rights attached to those shares must be specified.

All corporations must issue some common stock with the right to vote because such voting shares are necessary to elect a board of directors, which then creates a management structure for the corporation. When different groups of common stock give different rights to stockholders they are differentiated by calling them type A common, type B common, etc.

Preferred Stock

The rights of preferred stockholders usually differ from the rights of common stockholders in three ways:

1. Preferred stockholders do not have voting rights.
2. Preferred stockholders do not share in the corporation's growth. They are only entitled to the fixed dividend amount specified on the face of their stock certificates. Also, in case the corporation is dissolved or, as this process is usually called, liquidated, the preferred stockholders are only entitled to a distribution of the corporation's assets up to the liquidation value specified on the preferred stock certificate—usually the par value.
3. Preferred stock derives its name from the fact that preferred stockholders have the right to receive their fixed dividend before common stockholders receive any dividend at all, and from the fact that upon liquidation, preferred stockholders also have the right to receive the liquidation value of their stock before common stockholders receive any assets from the corporation.

There are many types of preferred stock, such as regular, cumulative, participating, and convertible. No dividends may be paid by a corporation unless declared by its board of directors. Thus, if in any year the board of directors does not deem it to be in the best interest of the corporation to declare a dividend on preferred stock, the preferred stockholders will not receive a dividend in that year. If the preferred stock is noncumulative, the stockholders lose their right to receive this dividend in future years. In the case of cumulative preferred, this right is never lost and the dividend accumulates from year to year so that the following year preferred stockholders are entitled to two years' dividends before any dividends can be declared on common stock. Unpaid dividends on cumulative preferred stock are said to be in arrears. Dividends in arrears must be disclosed in the notes to the financial statements because they present a barrier to the distribution of any common stock dividends.

Regular preferred stock is nonparticipating, that is, the preferred stockholders are entitled only to the fixed dividend amount specified on their stock certificate and do not have the right to share in the future earnings growth of the corporation. Owners of participating preferred stock do have this right, however. After they have received their preferred stock dividend they are entitled to participate with common stockholders in any dividends declared on common stock.

Certain preferred stock issues give their stockholders the right to convert their shares into a specified number of shares of common stock. Such stock is called convertible preferred stock. This type of preferred stock also benefits from the growth of the corporation because its market value increases along with the market value of the underlying common stock into which it is convertible.

Par Value

When a corporation is formed or a new stock issue is authorized, the board of directors arbitrarily designates the minimum legal capital in the corporation per share of stock. This amount is called the par value of each share of stock and it is printed on the face of each stock certificate. The total par value of all the outstanding shares is called the legal capital of the corporation. It is the minimum amount of capital that creditors of the corporation have the right to expect to be invested in the corporation. Thus, if stock with a par value of $10 is issued for $8, the creditors of the corporation can demand legally that all the stockholders invest the additional $2 per share to pay the corporation's debts.

In order to avoid this dilemma and sometimes to avoid giving the impression that the par value is the true value of a stock, some corporations issue no-par stock. However, a few states require that a minimum issue price be given to no-par stock to protect the creditors. This minimum issue price is called the stated value of the stock.

It should be understood by the reader that the par or stated value of a stock is not the value at which it is sold. However, it does constitute the minimum price at which a share of stock can be originally issued by a corporation. The initial sales price of a stock may be higher than the par or stated value depending upon the strength of demand for the stock on the day it is issued—but by law it cannot be lower. The higher the earnings expectations for the corporation selling the stock, the greater will be the demand for the stock and consequently the higher its selling price will be. Stocks that are listed on the major stock exchanges, such as the New York Stock Exchange and the American Stock Exchange, have a ready and liquid market allowing for constant daily price fluctuations to occur in the stock in response to recent news concerning the company or the economy. Therefore, it is impossible to know beforehand what the selling price at the issue date will be. The par value is usually set far enough below the market value of a stock to assure that a sudden drop in market value will not prevent a corporation from selling a stock issue—it being illegal for a corporation to initially sell stock at below its par or stated value.

Par value is especially significant with regard to preferred stock because in the absence of a specifically stated liquidation value, it represents the liquidation value of a share. Also, preferred dividends are sometimes expressed in terms of a percentage of par value.

Issuing Common Stock

Before stock can be issued (sold) the shares must be authorized by the board of directors of the corporation and by the state. The original stock issue is included in the articles of incorporation and is authorized when the corporation is registered with the state. After a stock issue is authorized it may be sold to investors, thereby becoming stock that is issued and outstanding. When all of the shares authorized originally have been issued, subsequent issues must be authorized both by the board of directors and by the state.

If 1,000,000 shares of common stock with a par value of $1 are authorized and 500,000 shares are sold, the sale would be recorded as follows:

	Dr	Cr
Cash	500,000	
Common stock		500,000

To record the sale of 500,000 shares of $1 par common stock at $1 per share.

They would appear in the stockholders' equity section of the balance sheet as shown below:

Stockholders' equity
Common stock—$1 par, 1,000,000 shares authorized,
    500,000 shares issued and outstanding $500,000

In the above example the common stock was sold at its par value of $1. When it is sold for more than its par value, the amount paid in excess of par is recorded in a separate account called additional paid-in capital. Thus, if the above company had initially sold its shares at $1.50 per share they would be recorded through the following journal entry:

	Dr	**Cr**
Cash	750,000	
Common stock		500,000
Additional paid-in capital		250,000

To record the sale of 500,000 shares of $1 par common stock at $1.50 per share.

They would appear in the stockholders' equity section of the balance sheet as shown below:

Stockholders' equity

Common stock—$1 par value, 1,000,000 shares authorized, 500,000 shares issued and outstanding	$500,000
Additional paid-in capital	250,000

The $250,000 amount paid in excess of par corresponds to the $0.50 ($1.50 selling price less $1.00 par value) per share collected in excess of the par value of each share times the number of shares sold (500,000 shares × $0.50 = $250,000).

Because stockholders can be legally obliged by creditors and other stakeholders in a corporation to pay at least the par value for shares of stock that they buy, it is now illegal for a corporation to initially sell stock below its par value.

Issuing Preferred Stock, No-Par Stock, and Stock in Exchange for Non-Cash Assets

The only difference between the recording of a sale of preferred stock and common stock is the fact that preferred stock is always listed first in the stockholders' equity section of the balance sheet. If the above company sold 200,000 shares of $2.00 par value preferred for $3.00 per share, they would be recorded in the same way as the sale of common stock. After the above sales of preferred and common stock the stockholders' equity section would appear as follows:

Stockholders' equity

Preferred stock—$2 par value, 5% non-cumulative, 200,000 shares authorized, issued and outstanding	$400,000
Additional paid-in capital—preferred stock	200,000
Common stock—$1 par value, 1,000,000 shares authorized, 500,000 shares issued and outstanding	500,000
Additional paid-in capital—common stock	250,000

When no-par common stock is sold, the full selling price of the stock is recorded in the stock account. In this case there is no additional paid-in capital.

Sometimes stock is exchanged for assets other than cash, or for services. In this case the entry to record the sale of stock includes a debit to the accounts of the assets or services being received. For example, the exchange of 50,000 shares of $1 par value common stock for land with a market value of $75,000 is recorded as follows:

	Dr	Cr
Land	75,000	
Common stock		50,000
Additional paid-in capital—common stock		25,000

To record the exchange of 50,000 shares of $1 par common stock for land worth $75,000.

When stock is exchanged for non-cash assets or services, it may be difficult to determine the exchange value for the transaction. The proper procedure is to record the exchange at either the market value of the asset or service received, or at the market value of the stock sold, whichever is more easily determinable accurately.

TREASURY STOCK

Sometimes it is advisable for a corporation to repurchase its own stock. It may use this stock for employee stock purchase plans, to increase or decrease the control of certain stockholders, or simply as a good investment, if it feels the market price of its stock is unreasonably low. When a corporation repurchases its own stock this stock is called treasury stock.

Treasury stock reduces the number of shares outstanding but not the number of shares issued. Issued shares can only be reduced by retiring, or cancelling, them. Also, treasury stock is not entitled to vote or to receive dividends.

The acquisition of treasury stock is usually recorded at cost and is presented on the balance sheet as a reduction of stockholders' equity. The cost of repurchased stock is recorded in an account called treasury stock, and is deducted at the bottom of the stockholders' equity section.

Suppose our hypothetical corporation repurchased at $2 per share 10,000 shares of the $1 par common stock it had originally sold for $1.50. This transaction would be recorded as follows:

	Dr	Cr
Treasury stock	20,000	
Cash		20,000

To record purchase of 10,000 shares of treasury stock at $2 per share.

This purchase of treasury stock would appear as follows in the stockholders' equity section of the balance sheet:

Stockholders' equity

Common stock—$1 par value, 1,000,000 shares authorized, 500,000 shares issued and outstanding	$500,000
Additional paid-in capital	250,000
	750,000
Less: Treasury stock at cost	20,000
Total stockholders' equity	$730,000

If 5,000 shares of the above treasury stock were reissued at $3, $1 more than their purchase price, the treasury stock account is credited for the amount of the original purchase price of $2 and the additional paid-in capital–treasury stock account is credited for the difference from the original purchase price as follows:

	Dr	Cr
Cash	15,000	
Treasury stock		10,000
Additional paid-in capital—treasury stock		5,000

To record the reissue of 5,000 shares of treasury stock at $3 per share when the original purchase price was $2 per share.

When treasury stock is reissued at a price lower than its original purchase price, the difference between the original purchase price and the reissue price is debited to the additional paid-in capital-treasury stock account. If this account does not have a balance sufficient to absorb this difference, the retained earnings account is debited for the remaining amount.

Retiring Treasury Stock

A corporation may wish to retire or cancel some of its treasury stock. This is done by reducing all balances in the capital stock account, additional paid-in capital account, and treasury stock account related to the stock being cancelled. Any net debit difference is debited to retained earnings, and any net credit difference is credited to an account called capital from stock retirement, which appears in the stockholders' equity section following the additional paid-in capital-common stock account.

RETAINED EARNINGS

The retained earnings account normally consists of the cumulative total of all prior periods' net earnings and losses, less any dividends declared. As stated earlier, this account may also be affected by adjustments of prior periods' transactions, some treasury stock transactions, and, in some cases, the retirement of stock. Furthermore, as we shall see, a portion of retained earnings may be appropriated, or designated, by the board of directors for a special use.

Net income is recorded in the retained earnings account by debiting the income summary account and crediting the retained earnings account as explained in Chapter 6. A $40,000 net income would be recorded as follows:

	Dr	Cr
Income summary	40,000	
Retained earnings		40,000

To close $40,000 of net income to retained earnings.

A net loss would be recorded by crediting the income summary account and debiting the retained earnings account. If a corporation's losses exceed its retained earnings, this account is reported as a deficit.

Although the amount of retained earnings is not indicative of a corporation's total previous earnings (dividends and other non-operating transactions may have reduced this amount), it is important because no dividends may be declared in excess of the current retained earnings of an ongoing corporation.

In the following, final, sections of this chapter some transactions that affect, or may affect, the retained earnings account are discussed and, in conclusion, a more complex statement of retained earnings is presented.

Cash Dividends

Dividends are the partial or total distribution of a corporation's earnings to its stockholders in proportion to the number of shares each stockholder owns. No dividends may be declared in excess of a corporation's retained earnings unless the corporation is being liquidated, in which case they are called liquidating dividends. Dividends may be paid annually, quarterly, or at any other time determined by the board of directors. Although normally dividends are paid in cash, they may also be distributed in the form of assets, such as stock in other corporations owned by the corporation distributing the dividend.

Corporations are not obliged to pay dividends. If the board of directors does not deem it in the best interest of the corporation to do so, the corporation need not pay any dividend, even on preferred stock. No dividends may be paid to common stockholders, however, until the full dividend due has been paid to the preferred stockholders. The amount of this dividend is designated on the preferred stock certificate either as an absolute dollar amount or as a percentage of the par value of the stock. Thus the term preferred stock—$10 par value, 5 percent non-cumulative indicates a preferred stock with a $10 par value and paying a non-cumulative dividend of $0.50 per share (5 percent of $10). Alternatively, the absolute dollar amount ($0.50) of the dividend might be specified on the stock certificate.

When a dividend is to be paid, three dates are of significance: (1) the declaration date, (2) the date of record, and (3) the payment date. The declaration date is the date the dividend is declared by the board of directors. When a dividend is declared it becomes a liability of the corporation and must be recorded as such. The date of record is usually determined by the board of directors at the time the dividend is declared. This is the date used to determine ownership of a stock for the purpose of receiving the dividend. For instance, if the date of record is October 3, 2013 and a stockholder sells stock on October 2, 2013, then the new stockholder is entitled to the entire dividend. The payment date is the date the dividend is actually paid.

Suppose a corporation had the following capital structure and the board of directors decided to declare a $200,000 dividend:

Stockholders' equity

Preferred stock—$20 par value, 3% cumulative, 100,000 shares authorized, issued, and outstanding	$ 2,000,000
Additional paid-in capital—preferred stock	1,000,000
Common stock—$10 par value, 1,000,000 shares authorized, issued and outstanding	10,000,000
Retained earnings	1,000,000
Total stockholders' equity	$14,000,000

The preferred stockholders would receive $60,000 in dividends (3 percent of the $2,000,000 total par value of preferred stock outstanding) and the common stockholders would receive the remaining $140,000 (i.e., $200,000 − $60,000) in dividends. If the declaration date is June 15, 2010, the date of record is October 15, 2010, and the payment date is February 15, 2011, the following entries would be required to record this dividend:

	Dr	Cr

Declaration date

June 15, 2010

Retained earnings	200,000	
Dividends payable on preferred stock		60,000
Dividends payable on common stock		140,000

To record declaration of cash dividends, 3% of $2,000,000 par to preferred stockholders and $0.14 per share to common stockholders.

Date of record

October 15, 2010

No entry required. The stockholders registered on the corporation's stock records as of the date will receive the dividend.

Payment date

February 15, 2011

Dividends payable on preferred stock	140,000	
Dividends payable on common stock	60,000	
Cash		200,000

To record payment of $200 000 in cash dividends.

Stock Dividends

If the board of directors wishes to (1) make a nontaxable distribution to stockholders, (2) make a distribution that will transform the increase in retained earnings resulting from profits into sellable stock without using the corporation's cash, or (3) reduce the market price of the stock by increasing the number of shares outstanding, it can declare a stock dividend instead of a cash dividend. A stock dividend does not reduce stockholders' equity since no assets are distributed. The only effect of a stock dividend is that retained earnings equivalent to the amount of the fair market value of the stock on the declaration date is transferred to the capital stock accounts in the stockholders' equity section, the par value to the stock account, and any excess to the additional paid-in capital account.

Stock Splits

If the market price of a corporation's stock increases excessively, this makes it difficult for small investors to purchase the stock. Many investors only have small amounts of money to invest. If the market value of one particular stock is too high, then they may not be able to diversify their portfolio sufficiently if they buy this stock.

Therefore, corporations often try to reduce the market price of their shares. They do this by executing a stock split. In a stock split every stockholder receives two or more new shares in exchange for every share owned. If the split is two-for-one two new shares are exchanged for every old one; if the split is three-for-one, three new shares are received for every old share, etc. In a two-for-one or a three-for-one split, the new shares have a par value, or stated value, that is one-half or one-third the par value of the original shares, respectively. The reduction in the par value depends on the extent of the split. If the split is four-for-one and the market price of an old share was $100, then each new share (after the split) will be worth $25 on the market. The par value of the shares will also be one-fourth the par value of the original shares. Since a corporation's account balances do not change as a result of a stock split, no journal entry is required to record the stock split, except a memo entry to record the new par value of the shares and a change in the number of shares issued as stated in the stockholders' equity section of the balance sheet. The difference between a stock dividend and a stock split is that in the case of a stock dividend, a portion of retained earnings equivalent to the market value of the shares (or the par value in case of stock dividends of 20 percent or more) is transferred to the capital stock accounts.

Correction of Prior Years' Earnings

Sometimes, due to a mistake in recording a revenue or expense amount, an incorrect net income or loss amount is closed out to the retained earnings account. Usually this occurs as the result of not posting an adjusting entry or not recording an invoice received, or received late, from a supplier. When this occurs, and the incorrect retained earnings amount has been distributed with the financial statements to all stakeholders in a business, it is necessary to correct this error in the next statement of retained earnings. In the more complex statement of retained earnings shown at the end of this chapter, depreciation expense for the year ended December 31, 2006 was understated by $12,000. After deducting the reduction in income tax payable that this additional expense produced, and assuming an income tax rate of 40 percent, the net effect on the prior year's net income and on the retained earnings account would be $7,200 (i.e., $12,000 − [40 percent × $12,000]). Stated another way, if the business has an additional $12,000 expense, it will have to pay $4,800 less income tax because its taxable income will be $12,000 lower.

More Complex Statement of Retained Earnings

In Chapter 2, a statement of retained earnings was presented in its simplest form. In this chapter it has been explained that some additional events, other than net income or loss, and the declaration of cash dividends, can impact the retained earnings account. Three of these events that have impact on the statement of retained earnings presented in Chapter 2 are:

1. Adjustments of a prior period's earnings (usually to correct an error),
2. Declaration of a stock dividend, and
3. The sale of treasury stock at less than cost when there is no additional paid-in capital is shown in the statement of retained earnings illustrated in Exhibit 12–5.

Because the purpose of the statement of retained earnings is to show all the activity in the account, the effect of these events on the retained earnings account is clearly evident.

FRB RESTAURANTS, INC.
Statement of Retained Earnings
for the Year Ended December 31, 2007

Beginning balance, December 31, 2006		$65,000
Less: Prior period correction of depreciation		
(net of $4,800 tax effect)		7,200
Restated balance, December 31, 2006		57,800
Add: Net income for year 2007		28,000
		85,800
Less: Cash dividends	8,000	
Stock dividends	15,000	
Treasury stock sold below cost	10,000	
		33,000
Ending balance, December 31, 2007		$52,800

Exhibit 12–5 Statement of retained earnings showing additional transactions.

SOME KEY TERMS INTRODUCED IN THIS CHAPTER

1. **Accounts receivable aging method.** A method for calculating the balance in the account allowance for doubtful accounts. It is based on preparing a schedule of all accounts receivable listed in different columns according to how much time has transpired since the sale was made. Each column is then multiplied by an appropriate percentage, based on historical experience, to determine an amount to which the account allowance for doubtful accounts should be adjusted. *See also* Allowance method, Direct write-off method, and Percentage of sales method.

2. **Accrued liability.** A liability for which no invoice has been received at the time the financial statements are prepared. To record the incurred expense in this situation an accrual adjusting entry must be made. Because these entries are often based on estimates, the account accrued expenses payable is credited to differentiate such estimated amounts from accounts payable, which are based on specific invoices.

3. **Allowance method.** An estimate is made of the accounts that may become uncollectible in the future, and this estimated amount is debited to bad debts expense and credited to a contra-asset account called Allowance for doubtful accounts, instead of being credited directly to accounts receivable. *See also* Accounts receivable aging method, Direct write-off method, and Percentage of sales method.

4. **Arrears.** Because dividends on cumulative preferred stock accumulate from one year to the next, if a dividend is not declared by the board of directors in any year it is said to be in arrears. No common stock dividend can be declared until all cumulative preferred dividends in arrears are paid.

5. **Authorized.** This statement usually appears below a stock account in the stockholders' equity section of the balance sheet. It indicates the number of shares that were authorized to be issued (sold) by the board of directors of a corporation and by the state authorities.

6. **Bond payable.** A bond is a debt instrument that allows businesses to borrow large sums of money from many small lenders. Businesses sell bonds to borrow needed funds. They usually have a face value of $1,000 and are interest-bearing.

7. **Chief executive officer (CEO).** The chief executive officer is the chairman of the board of directors.

8. **Convertible preferred stock.** Preferred stock that can be converted into a specific number of common shares.

9. **Cumulative preferred stock.** Because the board of directors is never obligated to declare a dividend, in any year in which a dividend is not declared the preferred stockholders lose it forever. In the case of cumulative preferred stock, however, a cumulative preferred dividend that is not declared in any year accumulates to future years. It is said to be in arrears. *See also* Arrears, and Non-cumulative preferred stock.

10. **Current portion of long-term debt.** This is the portion of long-term debt that is due to be paid within one year from the balance sheet date.

11. **Date of record.** Whoever owns a share of a corporation's stock on this date receives the entire dividend, the amount of which is specified on the declaration date.

12. **Declaration date.** The date on which the board of directors of a corporation declares (1) that a dividend will be paid, (2) the amount of the dividend, (3) the date of record, and (4) the payment date. *See* Date of record, and Payment date.

13. **Deficit.** A debit balance in the retained earnings account produced when the accumulated losses of a business are greater than the accumulated undistributed profits.

14. **Direct write-off method.** No debit to bad debts expense is made until an accounts receivable is proved uncollectible. When it does become uncollectible the account is credited directly to the accounts receivable account and debited to bad debts expense. *See also* Accounts receivable aging method, Allowance method, and Percentage of sales method.

15. **Discount period.** In order to accelerate the collection of their accounts receivable, suppliers often offer their customers a discount from the full invoice price if the customer pays the invoice before the end of the entire period granted the customer under the credit agreement between the supplier and customer. For example, a customer may be granted 30 days credit, but the supplier will offer a 2 percent discount if the customer pays within 10 days, instead of taking the full 30 day credit period to pay the invoice. This is usually indicated by writing or stamping the following on an invoice: 2,10/net 30.

16. **Distribution date.** The date that a stock dividend is distributed to the stockholders. It is equivalent to the payment date when cash dividends are declared.

17. **Issued.** This statement usually appears below a stock account in the stockholders' equity section of the balance sheet. It indicates the number of shares that were initially sold to investors in the corporation.

18. **Legal capital of the corporation.** This is the minimum amount of money that the owners of a corporation have committed themselves to invest in the corporation. It is usually represented by the par value of the stock that the corporation has sold, exclusive of any additional paid-in capital.

19. **Liquidating dividends.** Dividends paid to the owners of a corporation from any money that remains after it has sold, or liquidated, all its assets and paid all its creditors.

20. **Liquidation value.** Usually refers to the par value of preferred stock. This is the value that preferred stockholders will receive if a corporation has sufficient funds left upon liquidating, or selling, all its assets and paying all its creditors.

21. **Long-term lease obligation.** A contract to rent an asset over a period longer than one year from the balance sheet date.

22. **Long-term note payable.** A note that is payable later than one year from the balance sheet date.

23. **Minutes of meetings.** A record of what events took place, what decisions were made, and/or what was said, during a meeting.

24. **Non-cumulative preferred stock.** Non-cumulative preferred stock is stock whose dividends are lost forever if the board of directors does not declare them in any year. *See also* Cumulative preferred stock.

25. **Non-interest-bearing liability.** A liability on which no interest is payable. Accounts payable are usually non-interest-bearing liabilities.

26. **No-par stock.** Stock that does not have a par value, but may have a stated value. *See also* Stated value, and Par value.

27. **Non-trade accounts receivable.** Accounts receivable from persons or entities that are not customers of the business. For example, advances to employees is a non-trade receivable.

28. **Note (receivable or payable).** A note is a signed formal promise to pay a specific monetary amount, on a specific date, to a specific person or to bearer. In addition, it usually includes a promise to pay interest on the amount due.

29. **Outstanding.** This statement usually appears below a stock account in the stockholders' equity section of the balance sheet. It indicates the number of shares that were initially sold to investors in the corporation and are still owned by investors, i.e., that are not treasury stock. *See* Authorized, Issued, Outstanding, and Treasury stock.

30. **Participating preferred stock.** Preferred stock that entitles the owner to receive the preferred dividend corresponding to it before any common stock dividends are paid, and then entitles the owner to participate with the common stockholders in any common stock dividends that are paid.

31. **Payment date.** The date on which a dividend will be paid. This date is declared by the board of directors of a corporation on the date the dividend is declared (declaration date). *See* Date of record, and Declaration date.

32. **Percentage-of-sales method.** A method for calculating bad debts expense based on multiplying sales by a percent determined by previous years' uncollectibility experience. *See also* Accounts receivable aging method, Allowance method, and Direct write-off method.

33. **Proxy vote.** When a stockholder gives someone else the authority to vote his or her shares the stockholder is said to give them their proxy vote, or the stockholder can be said to vote by proxy.

34. **Stated value.** When a corporation issues no-par stock some states require it to assign a stated value to the shares.

35. **Stock certificate.** A document that transfers ownership of a part of a corporation to its owner.

36. **Stock dividend.** A dividend that is paid for by distributing stock of a corporation to its stockholders, rather than by distributing cash.

37. **Stock split.** A process whereby the number of outstanding shares of a corporation is increased, but without issuing new shares. Instead of issuing new shares, the outstanding shares' par value is split, or reduced. If a company that has 1,000 shares of $10 par stock outstanding splits its stock 2 for 1, then the 1,000 shares will be transformed into 2,000 shares and their par value will be cut in half to $5 per share. Because after the split the par value per share is reduced to half of what it was before the split, the total par value of all the corporation's stock will remain the same.

QUESTIONS

1. Why do hospitality entities make credit sales? Is there any added expense when making credit sales?
2. What are two ways of recording losses from bad debts? Which method is acceptable under GAAP? Why?
3. What is the difference between an accounts receivable and a note receivable? When should a note receivable be used to extend credit?
4. When is a 180-day note dated January 1, 2007 due? Who is the maker of a note? Who is the payee?
5. What are current liabilities? Give four examples of current liabilities.
6. Under what circumstances would a hospitality entity report money received from a customer as a current liability.
7. What is a contingent liability? Give one example of a contingent liability. Is a contingent liability recorded in the body of the financial statements? Under what circumstances?
8. What is the difference between mortgage bonds, unsecured debentures, and subordinated debentures?
9. How do bond premiums and bond discounts arise?
10. What is the difference between the face interest rate on bonds and the effective interest rate?
11. What are organization costs? How should they be recorded on the accounting books of a corporation?
12. Name and describe three rights of common stockholders.

13. Name and describe three fundamental differences between common stock and preferred stock.
14. What are dividends in arrears? How should they be treated on the financial statements?
15. What is the significance of par value and why is it unwise for a corporation to issue stock with a high par value?
16. Who designates the board of directors of a corporation? What is the relationship between the board of directors and the management of a corporation?
17. What does it mean to state that a corporation's stock is authorized? Issued? Outstanding?
18. What is the preemptive right of stockholders?
19. What is the difference between a stock dividend and a stock split?
20. What is treasury stock? Where in the stockholders' equity section of the balance sheet should it appear?
21. What is the significance of the following dates: (a) declaration date, (b) date of record, (c) payment date?
22. What are retained earnings?

EXERCISES

1. John Worthee owed the Spicey Palate Restaurant $560 on account. Because the account was 120 days past due and John Worthee could not be found, the restaurant decided to write off his account. After it had been written off, however, John Worthee mailed in a payment of $560.
    (a) Prepare the journal entry to write off John Worthee's account.
    (b) Prepare the journal entry to record the subsequent payment by John Worthee.
    (c) Explain the effect on net accounts receivable (not gross accounts receivable) of writing off John Worthee's account.
2. Paul Rover owed $4,000 and Marly Stuart owed $2,000 to the Beaumont Hotel. The Beaumont Hotel had a credit balance in its allowance for doubtful accounts account amounting to $1,800. Paul and Marly declared bankruptcy and the court awarded the Beaumont Hotel the amount of $4,000 of the $6,000 that they owed. The restaurant wrote off the $2,000 difference.
    (a) Prepare the journal entry to write off this $2,000 amount.
    (b) Prepare a "T" account of the account allowance for doubtful accounts, showing the balance in the account after the write-off.
    (c) Is this the type of balance you would normally expect this account to have? Explain your answer.
    (d) What method of calculating the allowance for doubtful accounts would you want to use if you were preparing a balance sheet to present to a bank? Why?
3. Assume that you have $300,000 of sales for the current year, ended December 31, 2007. The balance in your account allowance for uncollectible accounts is a credit balance of $3,000 because you had an unusually low amount of uncollectible accounts from sales in the year 2006. Your aging schedule, based on sales in the year 2007, tells you that you should have a balance of $7,100 in the account. Your previous history tells you that on average over the past three years you have been unable to collect more than 3 percent of your sales. You are trying to obtain a reasonably accurate approximation of how profitable your company is on a consistent annual basis. What amount would you include in the adjusting entry to record the allowance for doubtful accounts to make this determination? Explain why.

4. A cruise line sold the following tour packages in January, 2009:

Quantity	Name of tour	Price
200	Caribbean Cruise	$1,200
1,000	West Coast Cruise	1,500
500	Gulf Cruise	800

These cruises were to take place sometime within the period March to December of 2009.

(a) Prepare the journal entry to record the sale of the cruises in January 2009.

(b) Prepare the journal entry to record that the cruises had all taken place, based on the assumption that all cruises were taken in 2009.

5. Wiley Willy owed the Bastille Hotel $1,050. His account was 90 days past due and so the manager of the hotel asked him to sign a 90-day note dated June 30, 2009, bearing 12 percent interest. (Hint: When the due-date of the note is stated in days, instead of in months, you should calculate interest by dividing the number of days transpired by the total number of days of the note.)

(a) Prepare the journal entry to record the replacement of the account receivable by the note receivable when the note is signed.

(b) If the hotel wishes to prepare financial statements on July 31, how much interest would it have to accrue on this note? (Hint: How many days have gone by?)

(c) Prepare the journal entry to record the accrual of this interest.

(d) Assume Wiley Willy paid the note when due, on September 28, 2009. Prepare the journal entry to record receipt of payment on this note.

6. Harry's Bar was authorized to issue 100,000 shares of $5 par common stock. It sold 50,000 shares at $7 per share.

(a) Prepare the journal entry to record the sale.

(b) Show the stockholders' equity section of the balance sheet immediately after the sale of the stock. (Be sure to include all the proper text that applies to the stock issue in the stockholders' equity section of the balance sheet.)

7. Tom's Pub was authorized to issue 100,000 shares of $6 par common stock. The market value at the time of issue was $5 per share. Could Tom's Pub sell the 100,000 shares? Why or why not?

8. The Palmera Hotel was authorized to issue 200,000 shares of $50 par, 2% preferred stock, and 500,000 shares of $10 par common stock. It issued 100,000 shares of the preferred stock for $60 per share, and 200,000 shares of the common stock for $15 per share.

(a) Prepare the journal entries to record the two sales.

(b) Show the stockholders' equity section of the balance sheet after both sales of stock. (Be sure to include all the proper text that applies to each issue of stock.)

9. The stockholders' equity section of the Rodant Hotel is presented below:

Stockholders' equity

Common stock, $10 par, 1,000,000 shares authorized, issued and outstanding	$10,000,000
Additional paid-in capital	2,000,000
Retained earnings	3,000,000
Total stockholders' equity	$15,000,000

(a) Prepare the journal entry to record the purchase of 100,000 shares of treasury stock at $20 per share.

(b) Show the stockholders' equity section of the balance sheet immediately after the purchase of the treasury stock.

10. The Ponteverde Hotel Corporation was authorized to issue 42,000,000 common shares of $20 par value. It recently sold 500,000 shares for $12,500,000 and exchanged 200,000 shares for land with an estimated market value of $6,000,000. The Ponteverde Hotel Corporation is a well-established corporation, and had sold 40,000,000 of the authorized common shares many years ago at $22 per share. Its stock is traded on the New York Stock Exchange, where a ready and liquid market exists for its shares. At the time the 200,000 shares were exchanged for the land, the Ponteverde Hotel's stock was selling for $25 per share.

   (a) Prepare the journal entries to record the issue of the 700,000 additional shares of common stock.

   (b) Show the stockholders' equity section of the balance sheet immediately after the issue of these shares.

   Assume the hotel has retained earnings of $30,000,000.

11. Juan Romero wanted to build a restaurant on an acre of land. He had recently sold the acre of land adjacent to it for $100,000. He contributed the acre in his possession to the Tropicale Corporation, a new corporation that he recently formed, in exchange for 10,000 shares of $5 par common stock of the corporation.

   (a) Prepare the journal entry to record the exchange of the acre of land for the common stock.

   (b) Show the stockholders' equity section of the Tropicale Corporation's balance sheet after this exchange (include all pertinent text in the stockholders' equity section).

SHORT PROBLEMS

1. Annual sales and the dollar amount of uncollectible accounts for 2007 to 2009 are listed below:

Year	Sales	Uncollectible accounts
2007	$245,000	$ 4,900
2008	$380,000	$11,400
2009	$470,000	$ 4,700

   Based on this historical data, and on the assumptions specified below, prepare the journal entry to record bad debt expense for the year 2010 using the percentage-of-sales method.

   (a) Base your percentage of uncollectible accounts on the average uncollectibility percent over the past three years and assume that the allowance for uncollectible accounts already has a credit balance of $1,000.

   (b) Base your percentage of uncollectible accounts on the average uncollectibity percent over the past two years and assume that the allowance for uncollectible accounts already has a credit balance of $500.

   (c) Base your percentage of uncollectible accounts on the average uncollectibility percent over the past three years and assume that the allowance for uncollectible accounts already has a debit balance of $100.

2. Prepare the requested journal entries for the following situations:

   (a) Assume that the allowance for uncollectible accounts already has a $3,000 credit balance in it. How would you record the following? These events are not cumulative, they are totally independent of each other.

(b) You are using the aging schedule method and it indicates that the balance in the allowance for uncollectible accounts should be $15,000.

(c) You are using the percentage-of-sales method and the percentage of sales calculations indicate that the accounts estimated to be uncollectible amount to $15,000.

(d) Assume that the allowance for uncollectible accounts already has a $3,000 debit balance in it.

(e) How would you record the following? These events are not cumulative, they are totally independent of each other.

(f) You are using the aging schedule method and it indicates that the balance in the allowance for uncollectible accounts should be $15,000.

(g) You are using the percentage-of-sales method and the percentage-of-sales calculations indicate that the accounts estimated to be uncollectible amount to $15,000.

3. Prepare the requested journal entries for the following situations:

(a) Assume that the allowance for uncollectible accounts already has a $1,000 credit balance in it. How would you record the following? These events are not cumulative, they are totally independent of each other.

(b) You are using the percentage-of-sales method and the percentage of sales calculations indicate that the accounts estimated to be uncollectible amount to $9,000.

(c) You are using the aging schedule method and it indicates that the balance in the allowance for uncollectible accounts should be $8,000.

(d) Assume that the allowance for uncollectible accounts already has a $2,000 debit balance in it.

(e) How would you record the following? These events are not cumulative, they are totally independent of each other.

(f) You are using the aging schedule method and it indicates that the balance in the allowance for uncollectible accounts should be $7,000.

(g) You are using the percentage-of-sales method and the percentage-of-sales calculations indicate that the accounts estimated to be uncollectible amount to $6,000.

4. The stockholders' equity section of the Ubiquitous Travel Agency Corporation is presented below:

Stockholders' equity

Preferred stock—$10 par, 10% participating, 200,000 shares authorized, 100,000 shares issued and outstanding	$ 1,000,000
Additional paid-in capital—preferred stock	500,000
Common stock—$5 par, 1,000,000 shares authorized and issued.	5,000,000
Additional paid-in capital—common stock	2,000,000
Retained earnings	10,000.000
	18,500,000
Less: Treasury stock at cost (100,000 shares)	1,000,000
Total stockholders' equity	$17,500,000

If the board of directors wishes to pay $3,000,000 in dividends to the preferred and common stockholders combined, how much will the shareholders receive:

(a) for each preferred share they own?

(b) for each common share they own?

LONG PROBLEMS

1. The Paydmor Hotel prepared a list of the following open accounts on May 31, 2009:

Date	Client	Invoice Amount
Jan. 1	Joe Weingard	$ 156
Jan. 15	Marylinn Ops	342
Feb. 5	Larry Warmon	98
Feb. 18	Stan Welton	998
Mar. 3	Karl Josephs	320
Mar. 8	Bill Gordner	144
Mar. 14	Frank Ross	788
Mar. 20	Mary Smith	842
Mar. 25	Orlin Thomas	1,120
Apr. 4	Grif Dugood	88
Apr. 16	Marvin Fenton	2,112
Apr. 28	Grace Filigree	1,642
May 10	Ron Stacroft	450
May 14	Philip Herrera	676
May 15	Cecilia Debayle	771
May 21	Steve Murhous	1,342
May 24	Griselda Ferguson	2,231

(a) Prepare an aging schedule for the above accounts. Group the accounts in columns such as those shown below:

Hypothetical Aging Schedule as of December 31, XXXX

Invoice Date	Customer	All Invoices	Current	31–60 Days Old	61–90 Days Old	Over 90 Days Old
Oct. x, xxxx	John Doe	12,000			12,000	
Nov. x, xxxx	Paula Doe	7,000		7,000		
Dec. x, xxxx	Mark Good	6,000	6,000			
Totals:		25,000	6,000	7,000	12,000	

(b) Based on the aging schedule as of May 31, 2009, prepare the journal entry to record the allowance for doubtful accounts. You are told that the amount of bad debts was underestimated in prior years and the allowance for doubtful accounts has a debit balance of $450. You are also told that based on prior experience 1 percent of current accounts, 1.5 percent of accounts 31 to 60 days old, 2 percent of accounts 61 to 90 days old, and 20 percent of accounts more than 90 days old are estimated to be uncollectible.

(c) Show how the above accounts receivable would appear on the balance sheet after recording the journal entry you made in part (b).

2. (a) Record the following transactions in the general journal of Flywait Airlines for 2007:

May 12   Sold $2,400 worth of tickets to the Trustworth Co. on credit.
May 20   Wrote off a $1,200 balance due from John Peilaiter.
May 31 $1,000 worth of tickets are used.
Jun. 5   Sold $5,200 worth of tickets to the L. Argess Co.
Jun. 10   Sold $2,400 worth of tickets to Mr. I. M. Slopei on credit.
Jun. 30 $3,100 worth of tickets are used.

Aug. 5 Received signed notes from Trustworth Co. and L. Argess Co. to cover their accounts receivable. The notes are 60-day notes and bear 10% interest.

Aug. 31 $1,400 worth of tickets are used.

Sept. 2 Received $200 checks from John Peilaiter in the mail.

Sept. 5 Accrued interest on the notes receivable from Trustworth Co.

Sept. 30 Sold $3,100 worth of tickets on an international credit card to M. N. Ernest. The credit card company charges a 5% commission and has an arrangement with a local bank to reimburse Flywait Airlines when it deposits the credit slip. This commission is recorded when the credit slip is deposited.

Sept. 30 $3,500 worth of tickets are used.

Oct. 1 The credit slip for the sale to M. N. Ernest is deposited in the bank.

Oct. 5 The Trustworth Co. honors its note and pays all amounts due.

Oct. 5 The L. Argess Co. dishonors its note but promises to pay all amounts due, plus a $10 protest fee, in 10 days. Flywait Airlines accepts this oral promise and agrees not to charge any more interest.

Oct. 30 $1,100 worth of tickets are used.

Oct. 31 There is a $2,400 credit balance in the allowance for doubtful accounts.

(b) Prepare the journal entry to record bad debts expense assuming Flywait Airline's accounts receivable aging schedule indicates it should have a credit balance of $3,100 in its allowance for doubtful accounts.

(c) Assuming it had a $60,000 balance in trade accounts receivable before the above transactions, show the accounts receivable amount net of the allowance for doubtful accounts as it would appear on the balance sheet after the above transaction. Round amounts to nearest dollar.

3. The Swellmont Hotel Corporation sold two bond issues during 2010. Following are listed the transactions relating to these bond issues.

Jan. 1 Issued $3,000,000, 12%, 10-year bonds, dated January 1, 2010, interest payable on June 30 and December 31. The bonds were sold at full face value (no discount or premium was involved).

Feb. 1 Issued $5,000,000, 10%, five-year bonds, dated February 1, 2010, interest payable on July 31 and January 31. The bonds were sold at face value (no discount or premium was involved).

June 30 Paid interest due on the $3,000,000 bond issue and accrued interest on the $5,000,000 bond issue.

July 31 Paid interest due on the $5,000,000 bond issue.

Dec. 31 Paid interest due on the $3,000,000 bond issue and accrued interest on the $5,000,000 bond issue.

Dec. 31 Retired the $5,000,000 bond issue before it was due.

(a) Record the above transactions in general journal entry format.

(b) Show how the bonds and interest payable would appear on the balance sheet at December 31, 2010.

4. The Cucharita Restaurant Corporation was recently formed and has not begun operations yet.

(a) Prepare journal entries to record the following transactions in the year 2010:

June 1 Received an invoice from the lawyer who handled the incorporation for $2,000.

June 2 Received an invoice from the accountant who developed the accounting system for $3,000.

June 4   Received an invoice for a finder's fee of $5,000 from the person who brought together the original investors in the corporation.

June 15   Sold 50,000 shares of $20 par common stock for $1,500,000.

June 30   Repurchased 5,000 shares of common stock at $25 per share.

July 1   Sold 2,000 shares of treasury stock at $15 per share.

(b) Show the stockholders' equity section of the Cucharita Restaurant Corporation's balance sheet immediately after recording all of the above transactions. Assume 50,000 preferred shares and 600,000 common shares authorized. Also, assume the company has a $30,000 accumulated deficit as of July 1, 2010.

5. The stockholders' equity section of the Sleepmore Hotel, Inc. as of August 31, 2007 is presented below. It is on a calendar year basis.

Stockholders' equity

Preferred stock—$5 par, 10% non-cumulative shares, 200,000 authorized, issued, and outstanding	$ 1,000,000
Common stock—$10 par, 2,000,000 shares authorized, 1,000,000 shares issued and outstanding	10,000,000
Additional paid-in capital—common stock	2,000,000
Retained earnings	15,000,000
Total stockholders' equity	$28,000,000

(a) Prepare journal entries to record the following transactions on the corporation's accounting books:

Sept. 1   Purchased 100,000 shares of its own common stock for $1,500,000.

Sept. 3   Declared a cash dividend of $100,000 to preferred stockholders.

Sept. 30   Paid the cash dividend to preferred stockholders.

Oct. 15   Sold 40,000 shares of treasury stock for $10 per share.

Dec. 30   Sold 50,000 shares of treasury stock for $20 per share.

Dec. 26   10,000 shares of common stock are retired.

(b) Show the stockholders' equity section of the Sleepmore Hotel Corporation's balance sheet immediately after recording all of the above transactions.

(c) Show the stockholders' equity section of the Sleepmore Hotel Corporation's balance sheet immediately after recording all of the above transactions.

6. The stockholders' equity section of the Nicoya Hotel Corporation's balance sheet as of the corporation's fiscal year end, January 31, 2008, is presented below. For the first time since the company was formed no dividends were declared in the fiscal year ended January 31, 2008. The market value of a common share was $15 during the month of February 2008.

Stockholders' equity

Preferred stock—$50 par, 5% cumulative, 100,000 shares authorized, issued, and outstanding	$ 5,000,000
Preferred stock—$20 par, 10% non-cumulative, 50,000 shares authorized, issued, and outstanding	1,000,000
Additional paid-in capital—preferred stock	500,000
Common stock—$10 par, 900,000 shares authorized, and issued	9,000,000
Retained earnings	1,500,000
	17,000,000
Less: Treasury stock at cost (100,000 shares)	300,000
Total stockholders' equity	$16,700,000

(a) If the board of directors wishes to declare a dividend of $1,000,000 on February 5, 2008, how much must be distributed to each type of stock-holder on a per share basis? Assume the date of record is February 15, 2008, and that no new shares of any kind were issued between January 31 and February 15, 2008.

(b) Prepare the journal entry to record the declaration of this dividend, and then prepare the journal entry to record the payment of this dividend.

(c) If the common stock were split five-for-one, what entry would have to be made on the accounting books of the corporation?

7. Based on the information given below, prepare a statement of retained earnings for the XYZ Restaurant Corporation at its November 30, 2010 fiscal year end. The retained earnings account of the XYZ Restaurant Corporation had a balance of $450,000 at the November 30, 2009 fiscal year end of the corporation. Ignore any information given below that does not affect retained earnings. The market value of a common share should be assumed to be $30 for all transactions listed.

Dec. 15, 2009	It was discovered after the books were closed that an expense of $10,000 had not been recorded on the books of the corporation as of November 30, 2009, and had therefore not been included in the calculation of its net income for the year ended November 30, 2009.
Jan. 15, 2010	The restaurant sold for $7,000 an oven that cost $12,000 and that had accumulated depreciation of $5,000.
March 12, 2010	A cash dividend of 10,000 shares was declared. There are 80,000 shares of common stock outstanding.
Aug. 1, 2010	10,000 shares of treasury stock that had been purchased for $15 per share were sold for $30 per share. The corporation has no additional paid-in capital accounts.
Sept. 2, 2010	The corporation repaid a $50,000 loan.
Nov. 30, 2010	The corporation earned a net income of $65,000 during the fiscal year ended November 30, 2010.

Understanding Financial Statements | 13

The learning objectives of this chapter are:

- To introduce various analytical tools and techniques that are used to interpret and evaluate financial statements.
- To present an overview of how these techniques of financial analysis are evaluated both by parties outside the hospitality firm and by the firm's management.
- To present a brief review of four major tools of financial statement analysis: trend analysis, common-size analysis, ratio analysis, and cash flow analysis.
- To examine information contained in annual reports.
- To understand the auditor's opinion letter and notes to the financial statements or footnotes.
- To identify the nature and limitations of financial statements, which are to be fully recognized in order to perform an effective analysis and evaluation of financial and operating data.

Throughout this book we have seen how the primary aim of accounting is to provide information for management and other interested parties, which will serve as a basis to make business decisions and to direct business activities.

As previously noted, financial statement users must be armed with a very good understanding of the nature and limitations of the accounting system in order to use the accounting information effectively to make economic business decisions. Once this knowledge is acquired, management and other users will be better able to evaluate whether the data shown on the statements indicate good, bad, or indifferent performance.

It is of the utmost importance to recognize that financial statements are of no value unless they are properly understood. The analysis and interpretation of financial statements entails the compilation, comparison, study, and evaluation of financial and operating data. Financial analysis will help determine the overall position of the hospitality firm and establish future trends, thus clarifying and enhancing the usefulness of the financial statements.

Financial statements are read and interpreted in many different ways, depending on who is doing the reading—management, creditors, investors, or employees. All these users might emphasize a specific aspect of the firm's position. For example, a prospective investor will be primarily concerned with the company's earning prospects, whereas a creditor will be mainly interested in the determination of the hospitality firm's debt-paying ability.

Financial statement analysis employs various tools and techniques developed by business analysts as a means to assist financial statement users in the interpretation and understanding of key trends that serve as a guide for evaluating future business success. By using these tools, the users should gain insight into the company's operations and form an opinion about future performance. This is done by subjecting the financial data to scrutiny, looking for trends, and ascertaining strengths and weaknesses.

The purpose of this chapter is to introduce several analytical tools by which financial statements will be better understood, interpreted, and evaluated for decision-making purposes. We describe, to a limited extent, how these techniques are used both by parties outside the hospitality firm and by the firm's own management.

First, four major tools of financial statement analysis are discussed: trend analysis, common-size analysis, ratio analysis, and cash flow analysis.

The next section of the chapter examines information contained in annual reports that is in addition to the financial statements. Accordingly, the auditor's opinion letter and the notes to the financial statements (footnotes) are reviewed. These footnotes are dictated by the full disclosure principle of accounting with the basic objective of disclosing all items that might influence the decision-making process. Finally, this chapter discusses the nature and limitations of financial statements, which are to be fully recognized in order to perform an effective analysis and evaluation of financial and operating data.

OBJECTIVES OF FINANCIAL STATEMENT PRESENTATION

The objectives of financial statement presentation are to provide useful information (1) for credit and investment decisions, (2) in assessing cash flow prospects, and (3) about business economic resources, including claims to those resources and changes in them. The two primary qualities that make accounting information useful for decision-making purposes are: relevance, which is the capability of the accounting information to make a difference in user decisions, and reliability, which means that the information must be verifiable and give a clear and accurate picture of a business' condition and performance.

In FASB Statement No. 130, which was enacted in June 1997, additional criteria for the recognition of revenues and gains, and a new distinction between earnings and comprehensive income were established. Comprehensive income includes earnings, the cumulative effect of accounting changes, and certain other nonowner changes in equity (e.g., decline in market value of marketable securities). The new rules require companies to display items of other comprehensive income either below the total for net income on the income statement, in a separate statement of comprehensive income, or in a statement of changes in equity. The latter is the alternative that has been followed by many companies.

FINANCIAL ANALYSIS

No matter how relevant and reliable financial statements are, they only tell what happened to the hospitality firm during a particular period of time. Yet most financial statement users are concerned with what will happen to the firm in the future. The future item that financial statement users are most interested in determining is earnings. Earnings provide a basis for creditors to lend funds to a restaurant or tourism firm, and earnings, in most instances, make hotel and restaurant expansion possible. However, the prediction of earnings is rather uncertain, necessitating the use of certain analytical tools and techniques to facilitate the interpretation of key trends. These tools will aid in the evaluation of the financial condition and operating results of the hospitality firm as well as in the determination of earnings prospects.

Although the analysis and interpretation of financial statements is the subject of more specialized and advanced textbooks, it is helpful at this point to give an overview of the principal tools of financial analysis: common-size analysis (trend, vertical, and horizontal), ratio analysis, and cash flow analysis.

TREND ANALYSIS

Trend analysis involves reviewing past performance in order to determine the direction in which the business appears to be headed. It is primarily used to predict earnings by forecasting future revenues and expenses. That is, past experience is projected into the future, taking into consideration known or planned changes.

It is important to note that analysis of trend results requires the use of comparative financial and operating data for several years. Looking at results over a period of time is usually far more meaningful than reviewing data for two consecutive periods, particularly if an unusual event distorted the figures for either of the two periods (e.g., an airline strike). Trend analysis will provide the reader with an added perspective in evaluating the firm's progress and in determining signs of future improvement or deterioration. In fact, trend analysis permits corrective action to be made prior to the actual occurrence of forecasted unacceptable operating results, thereby avoiding these anticipated unfavorable conditions.

In evaluating and analyzing trends we must keep in mind, however, that trends do not necessarily continue into the future, and thus other crucial factors are to be considered. For example, future poor economic conditions affecting travel might result in a decrease in room sales growth for a hotel in spite of a positive trend of sales growth denoted by trend analysis.

VERTICAL ANALYSIS

Vertical common-size analysis compares all figures on the statement with a base figure selected from the same statement. On the balance sheet, all items (in both the asset and equity sections) are stated as a percentage of total assets. This will show the significant changes that have taken place in the composition of the various asset categories, showing the relative importance of individual assets as compared to total assets.

At the same time, by placing all items on the common-size income statement as a percentage of net sales, it is possible to see the relative significance of the various costs, expenses, and income items. Vertical analysis is also very helpful in bringing to the analyst's attention certain facts that otherwise might go unnoticed. If a restaurant's marketing costs go up by $25,000 over the previous period, for instance, this might appear as a major increase. However, when the common-size income statement of the restaurant is analyzed, it might indicate that marketing costs as a percentage of net sales were no higher than the previous year, evidence that there is no cause for concern.

Vertical analysis is, indeed, a very valuable tool when comparing several companies within the same segment of the hospitality industry. It is also helpful for comparing individual restaurants or hotel properties owned by a large chain, since vertical analysis would place various units of different size and volume on comparable terms.

	Year ended Dec. 31		Year ended Dec. 31	
	2007	**2006**	**2007 (%)**	**2006 (%)**
Net sales	$980,000	$760,000	100.0%	100.0%
Cost of sales	371,000	305,000	37.9	40.1
	609,000	455,000	62.1	59.9
Other expenses	519,000	388,000	52.9	51.1
Net income	$ 90,000	$ 67,000	9.2%	8.8%

Exhibit 13–1   Vertical common-size analysis of Regal Restaurant.

Vertical common-size analysis is illustrated in Exhibit 13–1, using the condensed income statements of Regal Restaurant for the years ended December 31, 2007 and 2006.

We can see how the net income as a percentage of sales increased from 8.8 percent in 2006 to 9.2 percent in 2007. This was mainly attributable to the decreasing trend in cost of sales as a percentage of sales (from 40.1 to 37.9 percent), a possible result of improved control procedures, or an increase in menu prices in relation to food costs.

HORIZONTAL ANALYSIS

Horizontal common-size analysis compares all figures on one financial statement with the same account selected from a base year. It is useful in detecting trends in revenue, costs, and income items over time.

By showing changes between years in percentages, the evaluation of the relative significance of the changes that have taken place is greatly enhanced. To illustrate, an increase of $1,000,000 in the current year's sales will most likely be considered a reflection of normal growth if the preceding year's sales were $10,000,000 for a typical hotel company (a 10 percent increase). Conversely, the same $1,000,000 increase in sales would be viewed as extremely significant for the hotel if the previous year's sales were $2,000,000 inasmuch as it would represent a 50 percent increase.

In short, horizontal common-size analysis should enable financial statement users to gain insight into the trends, deficiencies, and strong points of a business.

RATIO ANALYSIS

Ratio analysis indicates the strengths and weaknesses of a hospitality firm by calculating basic relationships. A ratio is the mathematical expression of the relationship between two financial and/or operating figures. Nonetheless, a single ratio in itself is meaningless since it does not furnish a complete picture. The ratio becomes meaningful when compared with company or industry standards, or both.

Ratio analysis has become an integral part of most computerized financial analysis programs, demonstrating its widespread use. Ratios can serve as a guide for comparisons with historical data or industry performance, and to analyze trends. Management will select for further review any items showing material variance with hospitality industry standards (better known as hospitality industry averages) and/or company standards to determine the reason(s) for each major change. In this manner, problem areas in need of managerial attention are highlighted.

Ratio analysis can measure most aspects of a hospitality company's performance. In discussing ratios we identify four major types of evaluation based on ratio analysis: liquidity, solvency and leverage, profitability, and operating performance.

Evaluation of Liquidity

Liquidity ratios measure the hospitality firm's ability to meet its short-term obligations as they become due, normally referred to as the firm's short-term debt-paying ability. In the evaluation of liquidity we assume that current assets are used for fulfilling short-term obligations.

Although the primary parties interested in the evaluation of the firm's current debt-paying ability are the short-term creditors, it is important to recognize that lack of liquidity in its more extreme form could lead to the dissolution of the hospitality company (i.e., bankruptcy) and thus will affect all financial statement users.

Three major measures of liquidity in the hospitality industry are the current ratio, the quick ratio, and the accounts receivable turnover. Although working capital is also referred to as a measure of liquidity, it is not as effective as the aforementioned ratios. Working capital is calculated by deducting current liabilities from current assets, and thus it is considered an absolute number as opposed to the current, quick and accounts receivable turnover, which are relative measures of liquidity.

Current Ratio. The current ratio is computed by dividing total current assets by total current liabilities. The computation of the current ratio for Outback Steakhouse for the years 2000 and 1999 (expressed in thousands of dollars) is shown below (refer to the consolidated statements of Outback Steakhouse, Inc. and affiliates in Appendix B):

	2000	1999
Current assets	$182,047	$143,211
Current liabilities	$168,045	$130,935
Current ratio	1.08 to 1	1.09 to 1

In 2000 Outback (see Appendix B) had approximately $1.08 of current assets for each dollar of current liabilities. As shown on its balance sheet in Appendix B, a major portion of Outback's current assets are in the form of cash and cash equivalents intended as a source of cash for the construction of specific properties ($131.6 million in 2000 and $92.6 million in 1999).

While a low current ratio may spell potential financial trouble by suggesting that a hospitality firm is unable to pay its bills, a high current ratio may point to poor management if it reflects an excessive amount of cash on hand or too large an investment in receivables and inventories. In the latter case, it will suggest an unproductive use of assets.

As a result of the typical large investment in inventories and receivables, the industry average for the current ratio of commercial and industrial companies is normally 2 to 1. In the hospitality industry, on the other hand, because of the relatively small amounts of inventories, the industry average for the current ratio is 1 to 1 or lower for some segments of the industry such as restaurants. That is, an average firm in the hospitality industry would have $1 of current assets for each dollar of current liabilities. Therefore, the current ratios of Outback's as of December 31, 2000 and 1999 serve as evidence of fairly high liquidity, resulting primarily from the large amounts of cash and cash equivalents.

Quick Ratio. The quick ratio (or acid-test ratio) supplements the current ratio by taking into consideration the composition of the current assets in the evaluation of liquidity. It measures the extent to which cash and near cash items (short-term investments and receivables) cover current liabilities as follows:

$$\text{Quick ratio} = \frac{\text{Cash} + \text{short-term investments} + \text{receivables}}{\text{Current liabilities}}$$

Thus the quick ratio will serve as a reflection of the hospitality firm's ability to pay its current liabilities by converting its most liquid assets into cash. Inventories and prepaid expenses are excluded from the calculation because they are not readily converted into cash.

In most segments of the hospitality industry, based on the small amounts and fast turnover of inventories (they are sold and converted into accounts receivable very quickly), the industry average has been somewhat less than 1 to 1 for the quick ratio.

Accounts Receivable Turnover. The accounts receivable turnover shows the number of times that accounts receivable is converted into cash during the period. It is obtained by dividing net sales by the average accounts receivable (the sum of the beginning and ending balances divided by 2), as follows:

$$\text{Accounts receivable turnover} = \frac{\text{Net sales}}{\text{Average accounts receivable}}$$

The accounts receivable turnover ratio serves to assess the quality of the current and quick ratios in the evaluation of the hospitality firm's short-term debt-paying ability. This is done by determining the liquidity of receivables, that is, the likelihood of collection of the accounts without incurring a loss, since experience has indicated that the longer receivables remain uncollected the higher the chances that they will not be collected in full.

In the hospitality industry, an average accounts receivable turnover is typically between fifteen and thirty times. In other words, a typical hospitality firm will collect its average receivables between fifteen and thirty times during the year (or between twelve and twenty-four days).

Other measures of the quality and liquidity of the receivables include average collection period and the accounts receivable percentage.

Evaluation of Solvency and Leverage

A major aspect of financial analysis deals with the determination of the proportion of equity (common stock) and debt financing in a hospitality firm's capital structure. This is viewed as an indicator of the company's ability to meet its long-term obligations as they mature (both principal and interest).

Financial leverage refers to the use of borrowed funds with the major objective of increasing the owner's well-being through increased returns. When leverage works to the advantage of the borrowing firm, it is said to be favorable or positive (i.e., when the return to the owners—common shareholders—is higher than the cost of borrowing—interest).

Solvency and leverage ratios measure the contribution of owners used to finance the hospitality firm's assets in relation to the financing provided by creditors. Obviously, if owners provide a small proportion of the firm's financing, the major risk of insolvency of the company will be borne by creditors.

Two principal ratios used to appraise the hospitality firm's long-term debt paying ability are the debt-to-equity ratio and the interest coverage ratio.

Debt-to-Equity Ratio. The debt-to-equity ratio is an expression of the creditors' financing in relation to the owners' financing:

$$\text{Debt to equity ratio} = \frac{\text{Total liabilities}}{\text{Total equity}}$$

In making credit decisions, creditors prefer moderate debt-to-equity ratios inasmuch as the lower use of leverage would constitute a greater cushion against creditors' losses in the event of liquidation. Conversely, owners may seek high leverage in order to magnify earnings per share or because of the dilutive effect of reduction of legal control when raising new equity capital.

Most businesses have a 1 to 1 debt-to-equity ratio (approximately), showing that 50 percent of their financing has been provided by creditors and the remaining 50 percent by owners. Hospitality firms, however, are highly leveraged companies evidenced by an average debt-to-equity ratio of 2 to 1. That is, an average firm in the hospitality industry has $2 of debt financing for each dollar of equity financing. Some segments of the hospitality industry (e.g., airlines) have had average debt-to-equity ratios even higher than 2 to 1.

Interest Coverage Ratio. The interest coverage ratio measures the ability of the company to meet its annual interest costs. Failure to meet this obligation can bring legal action by creditors, which may lead to the dissolution of the hospitality firm.

The interest coverage ratio is determined by dividing earnings before interest and taxes (since interest was deducted in the computation of income before income taxes, it must be added back) by the annual interest charges, or:

$$\text{Interest coverage} = \frac{\text{Earnings before interest and taxes}}{\text{Interest expense}}$$

Industry averages for interest coverage for typical hospitality firms have fluctuated between 2 and 5 times. The higher the interest coverage, the better the chances to obtain additional debt financing since it will represent a margin of safety for creditors.

Evaluation of Profitability

The evaluation of profitability centers on the measurement of a hospitality firm's ability to generate earnings from the available resources. This is done by relating earnings to sales, assets, and equity investment. It is based on the fact that both owners and long-term creditors measure the success of the firm by its ability to generate earnings.

Important measures of profitability in the hospitality industry include return on equity, return on assets, profit margin, and operating efficiency ratio. Additionally, the earnings per share, the price-earnings ratio and the dividend yield are very significant profitability measures for publicly owned companies in the hospitality industry.

Return on Equity. The return on equity, or ROE, is a fundamental measure of profitability from the standpoint of current and prospective investors. From their viewpoint, capital is invested with the primary objective of earning an acceptable return. ROE is calculated by dividing net income by the average shareholders' equity. The calculation of the return on equity for Outback's for the year 2000 (based on the 2000 financial statements included in Appendix B which are stated in thousands of dollars) is:

$$\text{Return on equity} = \frac{\text{Net income}}{\text{Average shareholders' equity}} = \frac{\$141,130}{\$750,278} = 18.8\%$$

where the average shareholders' equity is calculated as follows:

$$\$807,590,000 + \$692,965,000 \text{ divided by } 2 = \$750,277,500.$$

The above return on equity of 18.8 percent for 2000 would be in line with the restaurant industry average of 18 percent. This showing of return on equity served as evidence of Outback's overall success in achieving acceptable returns for its owners.

Return on Assets. Return on assets, or ROA, has been regarded as a measure of the return obtained on all the company's assets without consideration of the method used to finance them. It is computed as follows:

$$\text{Return on assets} = \frac{\text{Earnings before interest and taxes}}{\text{Average assets}}$$

In order to determine the total benefit (if any) of financial leverage, return on assets is compared with the annual interest rate on borrowed funds. If the return on assets is higher, leverage is said to be favorable.

Profit Margin. Profit margin expresses the net income per dollar of sale. It serves as an indication of the magnitude of protection against future losses resulting from decreases in sales revenue or increases in costs. The calculation of profit margin is made as follows:

$$\frac{\text{Profit margin}}{\text{Net sales}} = \text{Net income}$$

Companies that tend to need a substantial investment in assets normally require a higher profit margin to offset the less effective utilization of resources in the generation of sales. For instance, a hotel company will generally require a higher profit margin than a restaurant due to the very significant investment in assets needed by the hotel firm.

The industry average of the profit margin of hotel companies for the year 2000 was reported by *www.marketguide.com* to be 10.86 percent whereas the industry average for restaurants for the same period was reported as 9.20 percent.

Operating Efficiency Ratio. The operating efficiency ratio expresses the ability of a hotel firm to operate profitably by relating income before fixed charges to revenues:

$$\text{Operating efficiency ratio} = \frac{\text{Income before fixed charges}}{\text{Total revenues}}$$

The operating efficiency ratio is, indeed, one of the most important profitability measures from the standpoint of operating management since it serves to appraise overall managerial performance.

For restaurants and other companies within the hospitality industry the operating income margin is regarded as the equivalent measure of operating profitability. This is done by relating operating income to revenues.

Earnings per Share. Earnings per share (EPS) reflect management's success in achieving earnings for the owners. A rise in earnings per share will normally trigger an increase in market prices for publicly held companies. As a result, earnings per share have become the most widely published financial ratio of interest to all investors, both current and prospective.

The calculation of earnings per share for companies with a simple capital structure is presented below:

$$\text{Earnings per share} = \frac{\text{Net income less preferred dividends}}{\text{Weighted average number of common shares outstanding}}$$

Price-Earnings Ratio. The price-earnings ratio (P/E) serves as a reflection of how much the investing public is willing to pay for the company's prospective earnings. A high price-earnings ratio means that investors are confident in the company's future earnings prospects and are willing to pay a greater price in relation to the firm's current earnings.

The calculation of the price-earnings ratio is made by dividing market price per share by earnings per share. For example, if a hotel firm's common stock is traded at the price of $50 and its earnings per share for the most recent year is $2, the price-earnings ratio is computed as follows:

$$\text{Price-earnings ratio} = \frac{\text{Market price per share}}{\text{Earnings per share}} = \frac{\$50}{\$2} = 25 \text{ times}$$

In this case, the investors are willing to pay $25 for each dollar of current earnings. Similarly, prospective investors will determine if the stock is priced too high or reasonably by comparing the price-earnings ratio against industry averages. According to *www.marketguide.com* (May 11, 2001), the price-earnings ratio five-year industry average has ranged from a low of 13 to a high of 47 in the lodging industry.

Generally, companies with ample opportunities for growth have very high price-earnings ratios. Conversely, companies with limited growth prospects have a low price-earnings ratio.

Dividend Yield.   Dividend yield relates the current price of the company's common stock to the annual dividend:

$$\text{Dividend yield} = \frac{\text{Dividend per share}}{\text{Market price per share}}$$

The dividend yield is of specific interest to investors whose primary objective is to receive a current return on their investment (in the form of dividends). Nevertheless, many successful hospitality firms invest their earnings for expansion purposes rather than distributing them as dividends. In those cases, the dividend yield will be relatively low.

Evaluation of Operating Performance

Activity and operating ratios measure the effective utilization of the hospitality firm's assets while relating business success to the company's ability to generate revenues and control expenses. Among the activity and operating measures used by hospitality firms in the evaluation of operating performance are inventory turnovers, cost percentages, annual occupancy percentages, average room rate, and average food check. A brief description of each of these measures is presented below.

Inventory Turnovers.   Inventory turnovers show how rapidly goods (e.g., food and beverages) are being sold and replaced during the period. They are computed by relating the cost of sales to the average inventory (to eliminate seasonal fluctuations):

$$\text{Inventory turnover} = \frac{\text{Cost of sales}}{\text{Average inventory}}$$

The main factors that affect the food and beverage inventory turnovers are:

- Sales forecasting
- Purchasing policies
- Control procedures
- Property location
- Type of operation
- Perishable nature of food inventory

Whereas a low food inventory turnover can serve as an indication of over-buying, poor sales forecasting, waste, spoilage, or pilferage, or a combination of them, a higher turnover might not be desirable at all times. A high turnover can lead to dissatisfied customers if the firm runs out of inventory items constantly.

In addition to the foregoing, the beverage inventory turnover will depend on the class of operation. Luxury hotels and restaurants that carry a large assortment of wines and spirits will turn over their inventory at a very slow pace (possibly only three or four times a year). Conversely, an average commercial hotel or restaurant with a limited selection of wines and spirits will be turning over its inventory seven to nine times a year. Furthermore, the traditional large discounts taken by the hospitality industry for volume purchases of beverage inventories result in a slower beverage inventory turnover (lower) because of the over-investment in inventories.

Cost Percentages.   Both the food and the beverage percentages measure the relative efficiency of the food and the beverage operations by relating the cost of food or beverages sold to the revenues generated from the sale of food or alcoholic beverages:

$$\text{Cost percentage} = \frac{\text{Cost of sales}}{\text{Sales}}$$

Food and beverage cost percentages are mainly affected by the adjustment of menu prices (or list prices), the product mix, control procedures (particularly in the kitchen and the bar), and purchasing policies.

Continuous review and evaluation of the beverage cost percentage is essential due to the high cost of the alcoholic beverages. In doing so, a major factor to be considered is the class of operation since this will affect the type of beverages sold. For instance, operations selling a high proportion of beer will normally have a higher beverage cost percentage in view of the fact that beer has a lower markup than most other liquors.

Annual Occupancy Percentage.   The annual occupancy percentage measures the use of facilities through the generation of revenues from the sale of space. This is done by relating the total rooms sold to the number of rooms available for sale, as follows:

$$\text{Annual occupancy percentage} = \frac{\text{Rooms sold}}{\text{Number of available rooms}}$$

Factors affecting occupancy include location, rate structure, management, seasonal nature of the operation, and the general state of the world, national, and local economies. The calculation of the double occupancy percentage serves as an added measure of the profitable utilization of resources by the hotel operation. This results from the surcharge for the additional person in the room.

Average Daily Rate.   The average daily rate (or average room rate) serves as an indication of the rate structure and/or salesmanship ability. It reflects the receipts per unit sold:

$$\text{Average daily rate} = \frac{\text{Total room sales}}{\text{Number of rooms sold}}$$

Average Food Check.   The average food check is a widely used statistic in the food service industry. It measures the ability of the food operation to generate revenues by relating the food sales to the number of food covers (customers) served:

$$\text{Average food check} = \frac{\text{Food sales}}{\text{Number of food covers}}$$

In addition to the activity and operating ratios enumerated and briefly discussed above, there are a multitude of operating measures designed to evaluate a hospitality company's operating performance. Some of those ratios include the average daily room rate per guest, food and beverage sales to room sales, payroll and related expenses to total revenue, and food and beverage departmental income to room sales.

CASH FLOW ANALYSIS

As stated in Chapter 1, the statement of cash flow reflects the sources and uses of cash during an accounting period. Such a statement shows specifically where the cash of the hospitality firm has been obtained and how it has been used by management.

The statement of cash flow adds significantly to the understanding of what happened to the business during the year, providing insights into its financial and investing activities. In examining the details of the statement of cash flow, owners, creditors, and others can obtain data concerning changes in cash, the dividend payment policies of the company, its investment in property and equipment, and the firm's financing policies.

The statement of cash flow provides clues to important future concerns such as future dividend policies, ability to meet future debt requirements, and sources of financing.

In general, the statement of cash flow serves as a summary of the overall investment and financing aspects of the hospitality firm, providing more reliable and credible evidence of the company's actions and intentions than any statements or speeches by its management. It breaks down cash sources and uses into three sections: operating activities, financing activities and investing activities.

Cash flow analysis encompasses a review of the major sources and uses of cash appearing on the statement of cash flow. The sources of cash can be divided into two main groups: internal—operations, and external—common stock, preferred stock, long-term debt, sales of property and equipment, or long-term investments. Funds generated by operations are, by far, the most significant since they reflect the firm's ability to finance expansion (additions to property and equipment) and meet future debt requirements internally.

Cash is used for many different purposes: additions to property and equipment, dividends, repayment of long-term debt, purchase of long-term investments, and the like. It is evident that hospitality firms undergoing rapid growth (opening new areas, new hotels, or new restaurants) will show an extremely large proportion of cash used for additions to property and equipment. It becomes very important to evaluate how the company's expansion is being financed, that is, through operations, long-term debt or common equity financing. In reviewing Outback's statement of cash flow included in Appendix B, it was determined, for instance, that Outback was expanding very rapidly, using most of its funds for additions to property and equipment. This aggressive expansion was primarily financed by cash provided by operations.

EXAMINATION OF SUPPLEMENTAL INFORMATION

As a means to acquire an adequate understanding of a hospitality firm's financial and operational data, it becomes important to examine certain supplemental information to the financial statements. The two main sources of supplemental information are the auditor's opinion and the notes to the financial statements, also referred to as footnotes.

AUDITOR'S OPINION

Publicly owned corporations, companies whose securities are usually traded on a stock exchange (e.g., New York Stock Exchange) or over the counter, are required by federal securities laws to have their annual report audited by an independent CPA firm. Furthermore, there may be a legal need for an independent audit when raising new debt or equity capital or when borrowing money from a bank.

Indeed, the review of the CPA's report is a most essential step to be followed in understanding financial statements since it places the statements in proper perspective by providing the readers with crucial information concerning the fairness of the financial statement presentation.

The main purpose of the CPA audit is to provide external parties with a reasonable degree of assurance as to the validity of the information contained in the financial statements. CPAs examine sufficient evidential matter as a basis to express their professional opinion regarding the fairness of the financial statements. The audit steps entail the inspection and observation of invoices, bank statements, and other internal evidence, as well as external inquiries.

Again, it is important to recognize that the responsibility for financial statements (including footnotes) rests with management. Yet, the auditor's opinion adds credibility to the financial statements, serving as an indication of whether the financial statements have been prepared in accordance with GAAP and are fairly and consistently presented. Any departures are properly noted in order to enable readers better to interpret the statements.

The CPA's opinion letter includes a scope paragraph and an opinion paragraph. If upon completion of the audit, the CPA is satisfied that the financial statements are fairly presented in accordance to GAAP, an unqualified (clean) opinion is issued. Appendix B includes an example of an unqualified opinion covering the financial statements of Outback Steakhouse, Inc. for the years 1999 and 2000 (issued by PriceWaterhouseCoopers LLP).

If the opinion is other than unqualified (e.g., qualified, disclaimer of opinion, or adverse opinion) the financial statement users should proceed with caution. Readers should fully understand the reason(s) given by the auditors for their reluctance to issue a clean opinion on the fairness of the financial statement presentation.

NOTES TO THE FINANCIAL STATEMENTS

Notes to the financial statement are considered an integral part of the statements. They are governed by the accounting principle requiring the full disclosure of all facts needed by statement users to reach informed conclusions, and thus make the financial statements not misleading.

These footnotes amplify and clarify the information contained in the three basic financial statements. As a result, it becomes evident that a review of the notes to the financial statements is essential for a complete and accurate interpretation of the hospitality firm's financial and operating data.

We shall examine some of the more significant footnotes, referring to the notes of Outback's 2000 financial statements included in Appendix B.

Summary of Significant Accounting Policies

A particularly important footnote is the summary of the hospitality firm's accounting policies, usually the first note to the financial statements. The information in the statement of accounting policies is fundamental for understanding and evaluating the data contained in the statements. Further, it will be helpful in assessing the credibility and quality of earnings, and in comparative analysis.

The following are some of the most frequent disclosures found in the summary of significant accounting policies:

- Basis of presentation
- Use of estimates
- Method of determining inventory cost and basis of stating inventories
- A general description of the method(s) used in the computation of depreciation with respect to major classes of depreciable assets
- Basis for accounting for revenue recognition and related costs (e.g., unearned revenue, franchise fee revenue)
- Accounting methods and principles peculiar to the industry in which the reporting entity operates
- Basis of presentation of earnings per share
- Basis of allocating asset costs to current and future periods (e.g., deferred charges, goodwill)

Note 1 to Outback's 2000 financial statements provides an actual illustration of the preceding discussion.

Commitments and Contingencies

An examination of commitments and contingencies is vital in assessing the earnings prospects and the probable future success of a hospitality firm. Contingencies refer to existing conditions whose ultimate effect is uncertain, and their resolution depends on specific future events. They include the cosigning of a note by another party, pending lawsuits, and tax assessments. Disclosures normally include the nature of the contingency and give an estimate of the possible loss (if any) or states that a reasonable estimate cannot be made.

The major commitments disclosed by a hospitality firm are construction, leasing, and restrictions pursuant to the terms of long-term debt agreements. Disclosures of leasing commitments contain the general description of the leasing arrangement(s), including restrictions imposed by the lease agreement. For leases that transfer the risks and benefits incident in ownership to the lessee, referred to as capital leases the future minimum lease payments and the imputed interest rate are also disclosed. Note 9 to Outback's 2000 financial statements (see Appendix B) illustrate the disclosure of commitments and contingencies.

Segment Reporting

Based upon FASB Statement No. 131 (i.e., disclosures about segments of an enterprise and related information), issued in 1997, the operations and assets of publicly held companies are to be apportioned into reportable business segments. This disclosure includes revenue, operating earnings or losses, identifiable assets, depreciation expense, and capital asset expenditures relating to each material reporting segment or industry in which the company operates.

Pension Plans

When applicable, it is necessary to disclose the nature of the hospitality company's pension plan, describing the employee groups covered, funding policies, and provision for the current period pension cost. Other disclosure requirements for pension plans are governed by APB Opinion No. 8 and FASB Statement No. 36.

Long-Term Debt Obligations

Important features and provisions of long-term obligations for each major type of debt are the general character of each issue, interest rates, assets mortgaged, maturity dates and amounts; and restrictive debt agreements relating to working capital, dividends, or other restrictions.

Note 5 to Outback's 2000 financial statements in Appendix B serves as an illustration of the type of disclosures pertaining to long-term debt.

Subsequent Events

Disclosures of events that occurred subsequent to the balance sheet date are required by GAAP to prevent the financial statements from being misleading. Examples of subsequent events are the purchase of new companies, mergers or business combinations, losses resulting from fire or other casualties, settlement of litigations, and the sale of bonds or capital stock.

Other Disclosures

Additional disclosures often found in notes to the financial statements of hospitality firms are as follows:

1. Accounting changes. This includes a clear explanation of the nature of and justification for changes in accounting principles, and their effect on earnings and on the related earnings per share amounts.
2. Marketable securities. Disclosure of the aggregate cost and aggregate market value with an indication as to which amount is reported on the balance sheet.
3. Stock options. Disclosure of the status of the plan at the balance sheet date, including the number of shares under option, option price, and how many shares are exercisable is required. (See note 11 to Outback's 2000 financial statements in Appendix B.)
4. Income taxes. Disclosure of significant amounts of unused credits, the nature of significant differences between pretax accounting income (income before income taxes) and taxable income, and tax effects of timing differences are also disclosed. (See note 8 to Outback's 2000 financial statements in Appendix B.)

LIMITATIONS OF FINANCIAL STATEMENTS

As demonstrated, financial statements provide useful information for making rational decisions concerning the hospitality enterprise. However, financial statements have a number of shortcomings and weaknesses that all financial statement users must recognize during their evaluation and appraisal of the hospitality firm's financial and operating data. Some of these are enumerated and discussed below.

1. Conventional financial statements are prepared under a constant dollar assumption, which is, in fact, not valid since declines in purchasing power resulting from the changing value of the dollar (or inflation) are not taken into account.

2. Facts and conditions not specifically reflected on the financial statements could have a major impact on the future of a hospitality firm. Some examples are changes in consumer tastes, seasonal nature of operations, management changes, and economic conditions. To illustrate, a change in an upper management position might serve as a basis for favorable earning projections, in spite of poor performance denoted by the historical financial statements.

3. Judgmental factors pertaining to diverse accounting treatments of inventory, depreciation, capitalizing vs. expensing expenditures, and the like make meaningful comparisons of hospitality firms doubtful.

4. Only those facts that can be expressed in monetary terms are included in the financial statements. As a result, a number of very significant items might not appear on the statements. For instance, the ability and expertise of hospitality firms' personnel, a prime hotel location, and the impact of political or economic factors are not included in the financial statements due to the nonmonetary nature of these data. Nonetheless, this information needs to be considered for a complete understanding of the hospitality firm.

SOME KEY TERMS INTRODUCED IN THIS CHAPTER

1. **Acid-test ratio.** *See* Quick ratio.
2. **Annual occupancy percentage.** *See* Occupancy percentage.
3. **Average daily rate.** A measure of the rate structure and/or salesmanship ability of a hotel. It reflects the average receipt per unit sold, and it is calculated by dividing total rooms sales by the number of rooms sold during a certain period of time.
4. **Average food check.** A widely used statistic in the foodservice industry that measures the ability of the food operation to generate revenues by dividing food sold by the number of customers served.
5. **Average room rate.** *See* Average daily rate.
6. **Common-size analysis.** The expression of financial statement items in percentage form.
7. **Cost percentages.** Measures of the relative efficiency of the food and beverage operations by relating the cost of food or beverages sold to the revenues generated from the sale of food or alcoholic beverages.
8. **Current ratio.** A measure of short-term debt paying ability computed by dividing total current assets by total current liabilities.
9. **Debt-to-equity ratio.** The expression of creditors' financing in relation to owners' financing.
10. **Dividend yield.** The relationship of the current price of the company's stock to the annual dividend.
11. **Financial leverage.** *See* Leverage.

12. **Horizontal analysis.** The comparison of each account on one financial statement with the same account selected from a base year.
13. **Leverage.** The use of borrowed funds with the intention of enhancing the rate of return on invested capital of the owners of the corporation.
14. **Liquidity.** Measure of a firm's short-term debt paying ability.
15. **Occupancy percentage.** Measure of the use of facilities through the generation of revenues from the sale of space. It is calculated by dividing the total rooms sold by the number of available rooms.
16. **Price-earnings ratio.** An indication of how much the investing public is willing to pay for a company's prospective earnings.
17. **Profit margin.** Net income per dollar of sale.
18. **Quick ratio.** A measure of liquidity that divides cash, cash equivalents and receivables by current liabilities.
19. **Ratio.** A mathematical expression of the relationship between two financial and/or operating numbers.
20. **Ratio analysis.** The indication of the strengths and weaknesses of a firm by calculating strategic relationships (i.e., ratios).
21. **Return on assets.** A measure of the return obtained on all the company's assets without considering the method used in financing those assets.
22. **Return on equity.** A measure of return on investment that divides net income by average shareholders' equity.
23. **Solvency.** The ability of the company to pay its long-term obligations.
24. **Summary of significant accounting policies.** A note to the financial statements that discloses which generally accepted accounting principles the company has followed in the preparation of said statements, usually the first footnote.
25. **Trend analysis.** Review of past performance in order to analyze the direction and strength of the trend.
26. **Vertical analysis.** The comparison of financial statement figures with a base figure selected from the same statement.

QUESTIONS

1. What is the primary objective of financial statements? How do financial statement users accomplish this objective?
2. What is meant by financial analysis? Cite four major analytical tools.
3. What is the primary purpose of comparative analysis?
4. What is trend analysis?
5. What is common-size analysis? What are three forms of common-size analysis?
6. What is ratio analysis? What are the most common evaluations performed using ratio analysis?
7. How is the liquidity of a hospitality company measured?
8. Is a high debt-to-equity ratio a sign of financial trouble for a hotel? Explain.
9. What are the most common measures of profitability and how do they differ?
10. Describe three common measures of operating performance in the hospitality industry.
11. What is cash flow analysis? What are the major sources and uses of cash of a growing company?
12. What is meant by an auditor's clean opinion? In which manner can a financial statement user evaluate the auditor's opinion letter concerning the fairness of the financial statements?

13. What is meant by full disclosure? How does full disclosure relate to the information contained in the notes to the financial statements?
14. What type of information is normally included in the summary of significant accounting policies footnote? List four examples.
15. What are commitments and contingencies? List two examples of each.
16. Describe three typical notes to hospitality firms' financial statements.
17. What are some limitations of financial statements? What are some of the influences that are not specifically reflected in the financial statements?
18. What is meant by the diversity of accounting alternatives?

EXERCISES

1. What ratios or other analytical tools will assist in answering the following questions? Discuss each answer.
   (a) Is there adequate protection for short-term creditors?
   (b) How liquid are the accounts receivable?
   (c) Is there an over-investment in inventories?
   (d) Is the level of earnings adequate?
   (e) How are the company's assets being financed?
   (f) Are the shareholders receiving an adequate return on the money invested in the business?
   (g) What is the overall efficiency of the food operation?
   (h) Is management doing a good job in achieving profits for the owners?
2. Go to your university library web page and locate a recent annual report of a publicly held restaurant chain. Answer each of the following questions by using the information included in the annual report:
   (a) What was the net income earned per dollar of sales in the most recent year?
   (b) Are international operations significant for the company?
   (c) Who are the independent auditors of the company?
   (d) Does the company use leverage to finance expansion?
   (e) How does the company account for inventories?
   (f) What is the firm's return on equity at the beginning and end of the most recent year?
   (g) What depreciation method(s) are used for property and equipment?
   (h) List the company's commitments and contingencies.
   (i) How significant are the company's commitments related to lease obligations?
3. Go to your university library web page and locate a recent annual report of a publicly held hotel chain. Answer each of the following questions by using the information included in the annual report:
   (a) What was the net income earned per dollar of sales on the most recent year?
   (b) Are international operations significant for the company?
   (c) Who are the independent auditors of the company?
   (d) Does the company use leverage to finance expansion?
   (e) How does the company account for inventories?
   (f) What is the firm's return on equity at the beginning and end of the most recent year?
   (g) What depreciation method(s) are used for property and equipment?
   (h) List the company's commitments and contingencies.
   (i) How significant are the company's commitments related to lease obligations?

SHORT PROBLEMS

1. Z Company owns two restaurants, AZ and BZ, in the same city. Operating results for the current year for each restaurant follow:

	Restaurant AZ		Restaurant BZ	
Sales		$300,000		$400,000
Cost of sales	$110,000		$170,000	
Salaries and wages	120,000		155,000	
Other expenses	40,000	270,000	50,000	375,000
Net income		$ 30,000		$ 25,000
Customers served		110,000		120,000

The owners of the company are concerned that Restaurant BZ has higher sales and lower earnings than Restaurant AZ. Use common-size analysis, and activity and operating ratio analysis, to analyze both operations and comment about the results.

2. Consider the data for TRX Inn and answer the following questions:

	2007	2006	Industry average
Current ratio	2.9 to 1	1.9 to 1	1 to 1
Quick ratio	2.5 to 1	1.7 to 1	Somewhat less than 1 to 1
Accounts receivable turnover	5 times	5 times	25 times
Debt-to-equity ratio	3.12 to 1	3.59 to 1	2 to 1
Return on equity	9.6%	10.1%	15%
Number of times interest earned	2 times	3 times	5 times
Sales	$100,000	$80,000	Not applicable
Operating efficiency ratio	20%	21%	26%
Price/earnings ratio	11	9	20 times
Earnings per share	0.10	0.12	Not applicable

(a) Is it becoming easier for the company to pay its bills as they become due? Discuss.
(b) Is the total amount of accounts receivable increasing?
(c) Is the company employing leverage to the advantage of the common shareholders? Discuss.
(d) Are the investors confident about the future of the company? Discuss.
(e) Evaluate managerial performance. Speculate on the reasons causing improvements (or deterioration) in specific ratios.

3. Using Outback's financial statements (see Appendix B), complete the following:
(a) An in-depth analysis of the major accounting policies of Outback. Relate your discussion to Outback's quality of earnings.
(b) A review of other significant information revealed by the footnotes, indicating their possible impact on prospective earnings and financial position.

LONG PROBLEMS

1. The condensed balance sheet and income statements of Simple Restaurant are presented below:

SIMPLE RESTAURANT
Balance Sheet
December 31, 2007

Assets		Liabilities & shareholders' equity	
Current assets	$ 80,000	Current liabilities	$ 75,000
Investments	10,000	Long-term debt	270,000
Property and equipment	300,000	Common stock	50,000
Goodwill	18,000	Retained earnings	13,000
Total Assets	$408,000	Total Equities	$408,000

SIMPLE RESTAURANT
Income Statement
for the Year Ended December 31, 2007

Sales		$500,000
Cost of sales		150,000
Gross margin		350,000
Other operating expenses	$250,000	
Depreciation	30,000	
Interest	35,000	315,000
Income before income taxes		35,000
Income taxes		16,000
Net income		$ 19,000

Using ratio analysis, complete the following:

(a) Evaluate the short-term debt-paying ability of Simple Restaurant.

(b) Calculate the (1) debt-to-equity ratio and (2) interest coverage as a basis to evaluate Simple Restaurant's use of leverage.

(c) Evaluate the ability of the company to generate earnings.

(d) Discuss the firm's operating performance assuming that food is the only revenue-producing department and 100,000 customers were served in 2007.

2. Using the financial statements and auditors' report of Outback (see Appendix B), answer the following questions:

(a) Did the amount of working capital increase or decrease from 1999 to 2000? By how much?

(b) What was the largest source of cash in 1999 and 2000? Is this trend favorable?

(c) Did the company's independent auditor think that the financial statements presented fairly the financial status of Outback for the pertinent periods?

(d) Did the quick ratio improve from 1999 to 2000? Is this an indication of the firm's better debt-paying ability? Explain.

(e) Discuss Outback's dividend policies.

(f) Was Outback undergoing material expansion during 1999 and 2000? How was expansion financed during this period?

(g) Is the company employing leverage to the advantage of its owners? Explain.

(h) Did the capital structure of Outback change from 1999 to 2000? Explain.

(i) Is the earnings trend favorable? Explain.

3. Using the summary data taken from the financial statements of Glorious Inn for the past three years that appears next, do the following:

Current assets	$ 150,000	$140,000	$130,000
Total assets	1,100,000	800,000	700,000
Current liabilities	145,000	150,000	135,000
Long-term debt	800,000	500,000	450,000
Shareholders' equity	155,000	150,000	115,000
Sales	500,000	450,000	430,000
Net income	30,000	25,000	22,000
Interest expense	8,000	7,000	6,500

Required:

(a) Using the common measures to evaluate liquidity, determine the firm's short-term debt-paying ability.

(b) Is the company in a good position to borrow additional funds? (Assume an income tax rate of 40%.)

(c) What is the ability of the company to generate earnings from the available resources?

(d) Using common-size analysis, comment on the significant trends indicated by the financial and operating data of Glorious Inn.

Sample Chart of Accounts | A

INSTRUCTIONS

Account numbers are assigned based on the chart of accounts presented below by combining a two-digit department prefix with a three-digit asset, liability, equity, revenue, or expense account number. Thus every account has a five-digit number. In the case of accounts applicable to the hotel as a whole, the first two digits are zeros. For example, the account number for rent expense would be 00-581, and the account for food sales would be 15-400.

Department Prefixes (00-90)

00	Hotel as a whole (no specific department)
10	Rooms department
15	Food department
20	Beverage department
25	Food and beverage department (combined)
30	Casino department
35	Telephone department
40	Garage-parking lot department
45	Golf department
50	Laundry department
55	Swimming pool-cabanas department
60	Tennis department
65	Other revenue-producing department
70	Administrative and general department
75	Marketing department
80	Guest entertainment department
85	Property operation, maintenance, and energy department

Assets (100-199)

Current Assets (100-149)

100	Cash
101	House funds
103	Checking account
109	Petty cash
110	Short-term investments
121	Accounts receivable–guest ledger
122	Accounts receivable–credit card accounts
123	Accounts receivable–direct bill

124	Notes receivable (current)
125	Due from employees
127	Other accounts receivable
129	Allowance for doubtful accounts
131	Food inventory
132	Liquor inventory
133	Operating supplies inventory
137	Cleaning supplies inventory
138	China, glassware, silver, linen and uniforms (unopened stock)
139	Other inventory
141	Prepaid insurance
142	Prepaid taxes
144	Prepaid supplies
146	Deferred tax assets (current)
149	Other prepaids

Investments (150-159)

| 150 | Non-current receivables |
| 155 | Investments (long-term) |

Property and Equipment (160-189)

161	Land
162	Buildings
163	Accumulated depreciation–buildings
164	Leasehold and leasehold improvements
165	Accumulated depreciation–leasehold and leasehold improvements
166	Furniture and fixtures
167	Accumulated depreciation–furniture and fixtures
168	Machinery and equipment
169	Accumulated depreciation–machinery and equipment
170	Information systems equipment
171	Accumulated depreciation–information systems equipment
172	Automobiles and trucks
173	Accumulated depreciation–automobiles and trucks
174	Construction-in-progress
175	China
176	Glassware
177	Silver
178	Linen
179	Uniforms
180	Accumulated depreciation–China, glassware, silver, linen and uniforms

Other Assets (190-199)

191	Security deposits
192	Deferred charges
193	Long-term deferred tax asset
197	Goodwill
199	Miscellaneous

Liabilities (200-299)

Current Liabilities (200-249)

201	Accounts payable
207	Notes payable
210	Employee withholdings

215   Employer payroll taxes
220   Federal and state income taxes
225   Advance deposits (Unearned revenue)
230   Accrued expenses
235   Current portion–long term debt
240   Other current liabilities
245   Current deferred tax liability

Long-Term Debt (250-299)

255   Long term debt
270   Capital leases
275   Long term deferred tax liability
280   Other non-current liabilities

Equity (300-399)

For proprietorships and partnerships:

300–349   Owner's or partners' capital accounts
350–398   Owner's or partners' withdrawal accounts
399   Income summary

For corporations:

300   Preferred stock
301   Additional paid-in capital–preferred
310   Common stock
311   Additional paid-in capital–common
350   Retained earnings
351   Dividends
355   Treasury stock
360   Unrealized gain (loss) on marketable equity securities
370   Cumulative foreign currency translation adjustments
399   Income summary

Revenue (400-499)

400   Sales
450   Space rentals
460   Other income
470   Allowances
480   Cash discounts

Expenses (500-599)

Cost of Sales (500-529)

500   Cost of sales
505   Purchases
510   Trade discounts
515   Transportation charges
520   Other cost of sales
523   Cost of employee meals
527   Bottle deposit refunds
529   Grease and bone sales revenue

Payroll (530-539)

530   Salaries and wages
533   Payroll taxes
537   Employee benefits

Other Expenses (540-579)

540	Operating supplies
542	China, glassware, silver, linen and uniforms
544	Contract cleaning expenses
546	Laundry and dry cleaning
548	Laundry supplies
550	Licenses
552	Kitchen fuel
555	Music and entertainment expenses
557	Reservations expenses
560	Information systems expenses
565	Human resources expenses
567	Administrative expenses
569	Credit card commissions
570	Marketing expenses
572	Franchise fees
570	Property operation expenses
575	Utility costs
577	Guest transportation
579	Other expenses

Fixed Charges (580-589)

580	Management fees
581	Rent or lease expenses
582	Tax expense
583	Building and content insurance
584	Interest expense
585	Depreciation and amortization

Other Revenue and Expense Accounts (590-599)

591	Gain or loss on sale of property
595	Income taxes

Financial Statements | **B**

OUTBACK STEAKHOUSE, INC.

2000 Annual Report

REPORT OF INDEPENDENT CERTIFIED PUBLIC ACCOUNTANTS

To the Board of Directors and
Stockholders of Outback Steakhouse, Inc.

In our opinion, the accompanying consolidated balance sheets and the related consolidated statements of income, stockholders' equity and cash flows present fairly, in all material respects, the financial position of Outback Steakhouse, Inc. (the "Company") at December 31, 2000 and 1999, and the results of their operations and their cash flows for each of the three years in the period ended December 31, 2000, in conformity with accounting principles generally accepted in the United States of America. These financial statements are the responsibility of the Company's management; our responsibility is to express an opinion on these financial statements based on our audits. We conducted our audits of these statements in accordance with auditing standards generally accepted in the United States of America, which require that we plan and perform the audit to obtain reasonable assurance about whether the financial statements are free of material misstatement. An audit includes examining, on a test basis, evidence supporting the amounts and disclosures in the financial statements, assessing the accounting principles used and significant estimates made by management, and evaluating the overall financial statement presentation. We believe that our audits provide a reasonable basis for our opinion.

As discussed in Note 12 of Notes to the Consolidated Financial Statements, the Company changed its method of accounting for the costs of start-up activities in 1998.

Price waterhouse Coopers LLP

Tampa, Florida
February 14, 2001

Outback Steakhouse, Inc. and Affiliates
Consolidated Statements of Income

(IN THOUSANDS, EXCEPT PER SHARE AMOUNTS)

	Years Ended December 31,		
	2000	**1999**	**1998**
REVENUES			
Restaurant sales	$1,888,322	$1,632,720	$1,392,587
Other revenues	17,684	13,293	10,024
TOTAL REVENUES	1,906,006	1,646,013	1,402,611
COSTS AND EXPENSES			
Cost of sales	715,224	620,249	543,770
Labor and other related	450,879	387,006	327,261
Other operating	358,514	299,829	259,757
Depreciation and amortization	58,109	50,709	40,771
General and administrative	75,410	61,173	51,859
Provision for impaired assets and restaurant closings		5,493	
Income from operations of unconsolidated affiliates	(2,457)	(1,089)	(514)
	1,655,679	1,423,370	1,222,904
INCOME FROM OPERATIONS	250,327	222,643	179,707
OTHER INCOME (EXPENSE), NET	(2,058)	(3,042)	(1,870)
INTEREST INCOME (EXPENSE)	4,617	1,416	(1,357)
INCOME BEFORE ELIMINATION OF MINORITY PARTNERS' INTEREST AND PROVISION FOR INCOME TAXES	252,886	221,017	176,480
ELIMINATION OF MINORITY PARTNERS' INTEREST	33,884	29,770	21,914
INCOME BEFORE PROVISION FOR INCOME TAXES	219,002	191,247	154,566
PROVISION FOR INCOME TAXES	77,872	66,924	53,638
INCOME BEFORE CUMULATIVE EFFECT OF A CHANGE IN ACCOUNTING PRINCIPLE	141,130	124,323	100,928
CUMULATIVE EFFECT OF CHANGE IN ACCOUNTING PRINCIPLE (NET OF INCOME TAXES)			(4,880)
NET INCOME	$ 141,130	$ 124,323	$ 96,048
BASIC EARNINGS PER SHARE			
Income before cumulative effect of a change in accounting principle	$ 1.82	$ 1.61	$ 1.33
Cumulative effect of change in accounting principle (net of income taxes)			(0.06)
Net income	$ 1.82	$ 1.61	$ 1.27
Basic weighted average number of common shares outstanding	77,470	77,089	75,702
DILUTED EARNINGS PER COMMON SHARE			
Income before cumulative effect of a change in accounting principle	$ 1.78	$ 1.57	$ 1.30
Cumulative effect of change in accounting principle (net of income taxes)			(0.06)
Net income	$ 1.78	$ 1.57	$ 1.24
Diluted weighted average number of common shares outstanding	79,232	79,197	77,484
PRO FORMA (unaudited) (See Notes 8 and 17):			
PRO FORMA PROVISION FOR INCOME TAXES		$ 68,849	$ 55,003
PRO FORMA INCOME BEFORE CUMULATIVE EFFECT OF A CHANGE IN ACCOUNTING PRINCIPLE		122,398	99,563
CUMULATIVE EFFECT OF CHANGE IN ACCOUNTING PRINCIPLE (NET OF INCOME TAXES)			(4,880)
PRO FORMA NET INCOME		$ 122,398	$ 94,683

(continued)

(IN THOUSANDS, EXCEPT PER SHARE AMOUNTS)

	Years Ended December 31,		
	2000	**1999**	**1998**
PRO FORMA BASIC EARNINGS PER SHARE			
Pro forma income before cumulative effect of a change in accounting principle		$ 1.59	$ 1.31
Cumulative effect of change in accounting principle (net of income taxes)			(0.06)
Pro forma net income		$ 1.59	$ 1.25
PRO FORMA DILUTED EARNINGS PER COMMON SHARE			
Pro forma income before cumulative effect of a change in accounting principle		$ 1.55	$ 1.28
Cumulative effect of change in accounting principle (net of income taxes)			(0.06)
Pro forma net income		$ 1.55	$ 1.22

The accompanying notes are an integral part of these Consolidated Financial Statements.

Outback Steakhouse, Inc. and Affiliates
Consolidated Balance Sheets

(IN THOUSANDS)

	December 31, 2000	December 31, 1999
Assets		
CURRENT ASSETS		
Cash and cash equivalents	$ 131,604	$ 92,623
Inventories	27,871	26,088
Other current assets	22,572	24,500
Total current assets	182,047	143,211
PROPERTY, FIXTURES AND EQUIPMENT, NET	693,975	607,028
INVESTMENTS IN AND ADVANCES TO UNCONSOLIDATED AFFILIATES, NET	29,655	21,272
OTHER ASSETS	116,858	80,771
	$1,022,535	$852,282
Liabilities and Stockholders' Equity		
CURRENT LIABILITIES		
Accounts payable	$ 37,162	$ 33,974
Sales taxes payable	11,580	10,354
Accrued expenses	46,266	29,628
Unearned revenue	54,458	45,188
Income taxes payable	13,621	10,166
Current portion of long-term debt	4,958	1,625
Total current liabilities	168,045	130,935
DEFERRED INCOME TAXES	14,382	4,659
LONG-TERM DEBT	11,678	1,519
OTHER LONG-TERM LIABILITIES	4,000	4,500
Total liabilities	198,105	141,613
COMMITMENTS AND CONTINGENCIES (Notes 5 and 9)		
INTEREST OF MINORITY PARTNERS IN CONSOLIDATED PARTNERSHIPS	16,840	17,704
STOCKHOLDERS' EQUITY		
Common stock, $0.01 par value, 200,000 shares authorized; 78,514 and 77,519 shares issued; and 76,632 and 77,404 outstanding as of December 31, 2000 and 1999, respectively	785	775
Additional paid-in capital	214,541	194,251
Retained earnings	638,383	501,384
	853,709	696,410
Less treasury stock, 1,882 shares and 115 shares at December 31, 2000 and 1999, respectively, at cost	(46,119)	(3,445)
Total stockholders' equity	807,590	692,965
	$1,022,535	$852,282

The accompanying notes are an integral part of these Consolidated Financial Statements.

Outback Steakhouse, Inc. and Affiliates
Consolidated Statements of Cash Flows

(IN THOUSANDS)

	Years Ended December 31,		
	2000	1999	1998
Cash flows from operating activities:			
Net income	$ 141,130	$ 124,323	$ 96,048
Adjustments to reconcile net income to net cash provided by operating activities:			
Depreciation	52,946	47,184	38,873
Amortization	5,163	3,525	1,898
Provision for impaired assets and restaurant closings		5,493	
Cumulative effect of change in accounting principle			4,880
Minority partners' interest in consolidated partnerships' income	33,884	29,770	21,914
Income from operations of unconsolidated affiliates	(2,457)	(1,089)	(514)
Change in assets and liabilities:			
(Increase) decrease in inventories	(1,783)	(6,171)	779
Decrease (increase) in other current assets	1,928	(5,252)	(3,623)
Increase in other assets	(34,265)	(25,754)	(7,820)
Increase (decrease) in accounts payable, sales taxes payable and accrued expenses	21,052	(7,310)	21,962
Increase in unearned revenue	9,270	8,672	8,697
Increase in income taxes payable	3,455	10,166	
(Decrease) increase in other long-term liabilities	(500)	500	(500)
Increase in deferred income taxes	9,723	7,924	4,878
Net cash provided by operating activities	239,546	191,981	187,472
Cash flows from investing activities:			
Capital expenditures	$(139,893)	$(116,065)	$(108,148)
Payments from unconsolidated affiliates	841	220	1,596
Distributions to unconsolidated affiliates	(2,707)	(1,470)	(690)
Investments in and advances to unconsolidated affiliates, net	(4,060)	(9,704)	(1,936)
Net cash used in investing activities	(145,819)	(127,019)	(109,178)
Cash flows from financing activities:			
Proceeds from issuance of common stock	$ 13,315	$ 13,292	$ 19,121
Proceeds from issuance of long-term debt	15,400		1,013
Proceeds from minority partners' contributions	4,450	1,250	5,525
Distributions to minority partners and stockholders	(39,198)	(38,755)	(24,952)
Repayments of long-term debt	(1,908)	(37,516)	(32,231)
Payments for purchase of treasury stock	(48,615)	(7,230)	(6,345)
Proceeds from reissuance of treasury stock	1,810	12,585	3,451
Net cash used in financing activities	(54,746)	(56,374)	(34,418)
Net increase in cash and cash equivalents	38,981	8,588	43,876
Cash and cash equivalents at the beginning of the year	92,623	84,035	40,159
Cash and cash equivalents at the end of the year	$ 131,604	$ 92,623	$ 84,035
Supplemental disclosures of cash flow information:			
Cash paid for interest	$ 215	$ 491	$ 2,476
Cash paid for income taxes	68,095	41,572	40,170
Supplemental disclosures of non-cash items:			
Purchase of minority partners' interest	$ 6,985	$ 17,082	$ 1,647

The accompanying notes are an integral part of these Consolidated Financial Statements.

Outback Steakhouse, Inc. and Affiliates
Consolidated Statements of Stockholders' Equity

(IN THOUSANDS)

	Common Stock Shares	Common Stock Amount	Additional Paid-In Capital	Retained Earnings	Treasury Stock	Total
Balance, December 31, 1997	75,028	$762	$157,903	$292,617	$(13,900)	$437,382
Issuance of common stock	946	9	19,112			19,121
Distributions				(2,639)		(2,639)
Purchase of treasury stock	(300)				(6,345)	(6,345)
Reissuance of treasury stock	544		719	(5,266)	9,420	4,873
Net income				96,048		96,048
Balance, December 31, 1998	76,218	771	177,734	380,760	(10,825)	548,440
Issuance of common stock	442	4	16,230			16,234
Distributions				(2,522)		(2,522)
Purchase of treasury stock	(239)				(7,230)	(7,230)
Reissuance of treasury stock	983		287	(1,177)	14,610	13,720
Net income				124,323		124,323
Balance, December 31, 1999	77,404	775	194,251	501,384	(3,445)	692,965
Issuance of common stock	995	10	20,290			20,300
Purchase of treasury stock	(1,980)				(48,615)	(48,615)
Reissuance of treasury stock	213			(4,131)	5,941	1,810
Net income				141,130		141,130
Balance, December 31, 2000	76,632	$785	$214,541	$638,383	$(46,119)	$807,590

The accompanying notes are an integral part of these Consolidated Financial Statements.

Outback Steakhouse, Inc. and Affiliates
Notes to Consolidated Financial Statements

1. Summary of Significant Accounting Policies

Basis of Presentation - Outback Steakhouse, Inc. and Affiliates (the "Company") develops and operates casual dining restaurants primarily in the United States. The Company's restaurants are generally organized as partnerships, with the Company as the general partner.

Profits and losses of each partnership are shared based on respective partnership interest percentages, as are cash distributions and capital contributions with exceptions defined in the management agreement.

Additional Outback Steakhouse restaurants in which the Company has no direct investment are operated under franchise agreements.

The Company completed its merger with its New England franchisee ("Tedesco") on November 30, 1999. This merger was accounted for under the pooling of interests method of accounting; and accordingly, all historical information has been restated to reflect the merger.

Principles of Consolidation - The consolidated financial statements include the accounts and operations of the Company and affiliated partnerships in which the Company is a general partner and owns more than a 50% interest. All material balances and transactions between the consolidated entities have been eliminated.

The unconsolidated affiliates are accounted for using the equity method.

Reclassification - Certain amounts shown in the 1998 and 1999 consolidated financial statements have been reclassified to conform with the 2000 presentation. These reclassifications did not have any effect on total assets, total liabilities, stockholders' equity or net income.

Use of Estimates - The preparation of financial statements in conformity with generally accepted accounting principles requires management to make estimates and assumptions that affect the reported amounts of assets and liabilities and disclosure of contingent assets and liabilities at the date of the financial statements and the reported amounts of revenues and expenses during the reporting period. Actual results could differ from those estimated.

Cash and Cash Equivalents - Cash equivalents consist of investments which are readily convertible to cash with an original maturity date of three months or less.

Inventories - Inventories consist of food and beverages, and are stated at the lower of cost (first-in, first-out) or market. The Company will periodically make advance purchases of various inventory items to ensure adequate supply or to obtain favorable pricing. At December 31, 2000 and 1999, inventories included advance purchases of approximately $10,699,000 and $7,692,000, respectively.

Preopening costs - Prior to the adoption of Statement of Position 98-5 ("SOP 98-5"), "Reporting on the Costs of Start-up Activities" during 1998 which requires that preopening and other start-up costs be expensed as incurred rather than capitalized, preopening costs, consisting of training costs and other direct costs related to new restaurant openings, were amortized primarily over twelve months. Accordingly, since the adoption of SOP 98-5, all further preopening costs have been expensed in the period incurred.

Goodwill - Goodwill is included in the line item entitled "Other Assets" in the Company's Consolidated Balance Sheets and is amortized using the straight line method from 5 to 20 years. On an annual basis, the Company reviews the recoverability of goodwill based primarily upon an analysis of undiscounted cash flows of the related investment asset as compared to the carrying value.

Unearned Revenue - Unearned revenues primarily represent the Company's liability for gift certificates, which have been sold but not yet redeemed, recorded at the anticipated redemption value. When gift certificates are redeemed, the Company recognizes restaurant sales and reduces the related deferred liability.

Property, Fixtures and Equipment - Property, fixtures and equipment are stated at cost, net of accumulated depreciation. Depreciation is computed on the straight-line method over the following estimated useful lives:

Buildings and building improvements....................................	20 to 31.5 years
Furniture and fixtures............................	7 years
Equipment...	2 to 15 years
Leasehold improvements......................	5 to 20 years

Periodically, the Company evaluates the recoverability of the net carrying value of its property, fixtures and equipment by estimating its fair value which is generally measured by discounting expected future cash flows. The Company estimates fair value based on the best information available making the appropriate estimates, judgements and projections that are considered necessary. The fair value is compared to the carrying amount in the consolidated financial statements. A deficiency in fair value relative to the carrying amount is an indication of the need to reduce the carrying value of the assets. If the total of future undiscounted cash flows were less than the carrying amount of the property, fixtures and equipment, the carrying amount is written down to the estimated fair value, and a loss resulting from value impairment is recognized by a charge to earnings.

Construction in Progress - The Company capitalizes all direct costs incurred to construct its restaurants. Upon opening, these costs are depreciated and charged to expense based upon their property classification. The amount of interest capitalized in connection with restaurant construction was approximately $215,000, $0 and $850,000 in 2000, 1999 and 1998, respectively.

Revenue Recognition - The Company records revenues from normal recurring sales upon the performance of services. Revenue from the sales of franchises are recognized as income when the Company has substantially performed all of its material obligations under the franchise agreement. Continuing royalties, which are a percentage of net sales of franchised restaurants, are accrued as income when earned.

Advertising Costs - The Company's policy is to report advertising costs as expenses in the periods in which the costs are incurred. The total amounts charged to advertising expense were approximately $68,993,000, $54,320,000 and $49,540,000 in 2000, 1999 and 1998, respectively.

Income Taxes - The Company uses the asset and liability method which recognizes the amount of current and deferred taxes payable or refundable at the date of the financial statements as a result of all events that have been recognized in the consolidated financial statements as measured by the provisions of enacted tax laws.

The minority partners' interest in affiliated partnerships includes no provision or liability for income taxes as any tax liability related thereto is the responsibility of the individual minority partners.

Stock Based Compensation - The Company accounts for stock based compensation under the intrinsic value method of accounting for stock based compensation and has disclosed pro forma net income and earnings per share amounts using the fair value based method prescribed by SFAS No. 123, "Accounting for Stock Based Compensation."

Earnings Per Common Share - Earnings per common share are computed in accordance with SFAS No. 128 "Earnings Per Share," which requires companies to present basic earnings per share and diluted earnings per share. Basic earnings per share are computed by dividing net income by the weighted average number of shares of common stock outstanding during the year. Diluted earnings per common share are computed by dividing net income by the weighted average number of shares of common stock outstanding and dilutive options outstanding during the year. All applicable share and per share data have been restated to reflect the retroactive effect of a three-for-two stock split effective on March 2, 1999.

Recently Issued Financial Accounting Standard - In June 2000, the FASB issued Statement No. 138, "Accounting for Certain Hedging Activities," which amended Statement No. 133, "Accounting for Derivative Instruments and Hedging Activities." Statement No. 138 must be adopted concurrently with the adoption of Statement 133. The Company expects to adopt these new Statements effective January 1, 2001.

These Statements will require the Company to recognize all derivatives on the balance sheet at fair value. The Company does not anticipate that the adoption of these Statements will have a significant effect on its results of operations or financial position. As of December 31, 2000 the Company does not have any derivative instruments as defined in SFAS No. 133.

Outback Steakhouse, Inc. and Affiliates
Notes to Consolidated Financial Statements

2. Other Current Assets

Other current assets consisted of the following (in thousands):

	December 31,	
	2000	1999
Deposits (including income tax deposits)	$ 1,543	$ 1,253
Accounts receivable	5,549	6,116
Accounts receivable - franchisees	5,100	6,291
Prepaid expenses	8,315	9,444
Other current assets	2,065	1,396
	$22,572	$24,500

Outback Steakhouse, Inc. and Affiliates
Notes to Consolidated Financial Statements

3. Property, Fixtures and Equipment, Net

Property, fixtures and equipment consisted of the following (in thousands):

| | December 31, | |
	2000	1999
Land	$135,710	$120,978
Buildings and building improvements	322,078	289,261
Furniture and fixtures	82,347	72,452
Equipment	212,713	168,705
Leasehold improvements	139,426	115,340
Construction in progress	32,360	19,495
Accumulated depreciation	(230,659)	(179,203)
	$693,975	$607,028

Outback Steakhouse, Inc. and Affiliates
Notes to Consolidated Financial Statements

4. Other Assets

Other assets consisted of the following (in thousands):

	December 31,	
	2000	**1999**
Intangible assets, net (consisting primarily of goodwill)	$ 77,329	$61,508
Other assets	39,529	19,263
	$116,858	$80,771

During 1999, the Company entered into life insurance agreements for five officers whereby the Company pays the premiums on the policies held in trust for these individuals. The primary purpose of these agreements is to provide the officers' estates with liquidity in the event of the officers' death to avoid the need for the estate to liquidate its holdings of the Company's stock. The Company will recover the premiums it pays through policy withdrawals or proceeds from the policy benefits in the event of death. The Company has included the amount of its collateral interest in the policies in Other Assets.

Outback Steakhouse, Inc. and Affiliates
Notes to Consolidated Financial Statements

5. Long-Term Debt

Long-term debt consisted of the following (in thousands):

	December 31, 2000	1999
Revolving line of credit, interest at rates ranging from 6.78% to 7.14% at December 31, 2000	$10,000	
Other notes payable, uncollateralized, interest at rates ranging from 4.49% to 9.50%	6,623	$ 2,378
Note payable to corporation, collateralized by real estate, interest at 9.0%	13	119
Notes payable to banks, collateralized by property, fixtures and equipment, interest at rates ranging from 8.02% to 9.9% at December 31, 1999		647
	16,636	3,144
Less current portion	4,958	1,625
Long-term debt	$11,678	$ 1,519

The Company has an uncollateralized revolving line of credit which permits borrowing up to a maximum of $125,000,000 at 57.5 basis points over the 30, 60, 90 or 180 day London Interbank Offered Rate (LIBOR) (6.20% to 6.56% at December 31, 2000 and 5.82% to 6.13% at December 31, 1999). At December 31, 2000 and 1999, the unused portion of the revolving line of credit was $115,000,000 and $125,000,000, respectively. The line includes a credit facility fee of 17.5 basis points. The agreement was amended in December 2000 to increase the maturity from December 2002 to December 2004.

The revolving line of credit contains certain restrictions and conditions as defined in the agreement which requires the Company to maintain: net worth of $501,363,000, a fixed charge coverage at a minimum of 3.5 to 1.0, and a maximum total debt to EBITDA ratio of 2.0 to 1.0. At December 31, 2000, the Company was in compliance with all of the above debt covenants.

The Company has a $15,000,000 uncollateralized line of credit bearing interest at rates ranging from 57.5 to 95 basis points over LIBOR. Approximately $3,110,000 of the line of credit is committed for the issuance of letters of credit.

The Company has a $7,500,000 uncollateralized line of credit bearing interest at rates ranging from 50 to 75 basis points over LIBOR. Approximately $770,000 of the line of credit is committed for the issuance of letters of credit, $670,000 of which is to collateralize loans made by the bank to certain franchisee's.

The Company has a $10,000,000 uncollateralized line of credit to support the Company's international operations bearing interest at rates 75 basis points above the three month CD rate. On December 31, 2000, the outstanding balance was approximately $4,323,000.

The Company is the guarantor of an uncollateralized line of credit which permits borrowing of up to $25,000,000, maturing in March 2002, for one of its franchisees. At December 31, 2000 and 1999, the outstanding balance was approximately $22,470,000 and $19,220,000, respectively. Subsequent to December 31, 2000, the guarantee was increased to $35,000,000.

The Company is the guarantor of an uncollateralized line of credit which permits borrowing of up to a maximum of $12,000,000, maturing in December 2003, for one of its joint venture partners. At December 31, 2000, the balance on the line of credit was approximately $6,552,000.

The Company is the guarantor of approximately $9,445,000 of a $68,000,000 note for an unconsolidated affiliate in which the Company has a 22.22% equity interest. At December 31, 2000, the outstanding balance was approximately $65,000,000.

The aggregate payments of long-term debt outstanding at December 31, 2000, for the next four years subsequent to 2001, are summarized as follows: 2002-$492,000; 2003-$573,000; 2004-$10,354,000; 2005-$259,000.

The carrying amount of long-term debt approximates fair value.

Outback Steakhouse, Inc. and Affiliates
Notes to Consolidated Financial Statements

6. Accrued Expenses

Accrued expenses consisted of the following (in thousands):

| | December 31, | |
	2000	1999
Accrued payroll and other compensation	$15,722	$11,132
Accrued insurance	11,012	7,837
Accrued property taxes	6,129	5,078
Other accrued expenses	13,403	5,581
	$46,266	$29,628

Outback Steakhouse, Inc. and Affiliates
Notes to Consolidated Financial Statements

7. Stockholders' Equity

During 2000, the Company repurchased 1,980,000 shares of its Common Stock, $.01 par value, for an aggregate purchase price of approximately $48,615,000. During 1999, the Company repurchased 239,000 shares of its Common Stock, $.01 par value, for an aggregate purchase price of approximately $7,230,000. Repurchased shares are carried as Treasury Stock on the Consolidated Balance Sheets and are recorded at cost. During 2000 and 1999 the Company reissued approximately 213,000 and 983,000 shares of treasury stock, respectively, that had a cost of approximately $5,941,000 and $14,610,000 respectively.

Distributions in the Consolidated Statements of Stockholders' Equity represent distributions to Subchapter S Corporation shareholders of Tedesco prior to the merger in 1999.

On March 2, 1999, a three-for-two split of the Company's Common Stock was effected through distribution of one additional share for every two shares already issued. All applicable share and per share data have been restated to give retroactive effect to the stock split.

Outback Steakhouse, Inc. and Affiliates
Notes to Consolidated Financial Statements

8. Income Taxes

Provision for income taxes consisted of the following (in thousands):

	Years Ended December 31,		
	2000	1999	1998
Federal:			
Current	$63,606	$46,656	$37,936
Deferred	9,075	11,146	5,197
	72,681	57,802	43,133
State:			
Current	4,543	7,363	9,261
Deferred	648	1,759	1,244
	5,191	9,122	10,505
	$77,872	$66,924	$53,638

The Company's effective tax rate differs from the federal statutory rate for the following reasons:

	Years Ended December 31,		
	2000	1999	1998
Income taxes at federal statutory rate	35.0%	35.0%	35.0%
State taxes, net of federal benefit	2.5	3.3	4.0
Earnings not subject to corporate income taxes		(1.2)	(0.8)
Other, net	(1.9)	(2.1)	(3.5)
Total	35.6%	35.0%	34.7%

The income tax effects of temporary differences that give rise to significant portions of deferred tax assets and liabilities are as follows:

	December 31	
	2000	1999
Deferred income tax assets (in thousands):		
Insurance reserves	$ 5,076	$ 6,737
Advertising expense reserves	1,544	1,164
Intangibles	12,705	13,285
Other, net	1,830	852
	21,155	22,038
Deferred income tax liabilities (in thousands):		
Depreciation	35,537	26,697
	35,537	26,697
Net deferred tax liability	$(14,382)	$(4,659)

As discussed in Notes 10 and 17, the Company's net income included earnings attributable to Tedesco in all periods presented. Tedesco had elected under Subchapter S of the Internal Revenue Code to have their shareholders pay any federal income tax due on their earnings. Although Tedesco's income prior to the merger is included in the Company's consolidated financial statements, the Company is not required to pay income taxes on the income since they are the responsibility of the Tedesco shareholders.

Outback Steakhouse, Inc. and Affiliates
Notes to Consolidated Financial Statements

9. Commitments and Contingencies

Operating Leases - The Company leases restaurant and office facilities and certain equipment under operating leases having initial terms expiring between 2001 and 2016. The restaurant facility leases primarily have renewal clauses of five to 20 years exercisable at the option of the Company. Certain of these leases require the payment of contingent rentals based on a percentage of gross revenues, as defined by the terms of the applicable lease agreement. Total rental expense for the years ended December 31, 2000, 1999 and 1998 was approximately $31,155,000, $27,015,000 and $23,430,000, respectively, and included contingent rent of approximately $3,220,000, $2,902,000 and $2,391,000, respectively.

Future minimum lease payments on operating leases (including leases for restaurants scheduled to open in 2001), are as follows (in thousands):

2001	$ 31,966
2002	30,577
2003	27,916
2004	25,374
2005	22,676
Thereafter	60,369
Total minimum lease payments	$198,878

During 1999, the Company formed joint ventures to develop Outback Steakhouses in Brazil and the Philippines. The Company also entered into agreements to develop and operate Roy's restaurants and Fleming's. Under the terms of the Fleming's agreement, the Company purchased three existing Fleming's for $12,000,000 and committed to the first $13,000,000 of future development costs of which approximately $6,048,000 has been expended as of December 31, 2000.

The Company is subject to legal proceedings claims and liabilities which arise in the ordinary course of business. In the opinion of management, the amount of the ultimate liability with respect to those actions will not materially affect the Company's financial position or results of operations and cash flows.

The Company retains direct liability for the first $250,000 of all individual workers compensation claims, except for 1999, and general liability claims and $230,000 of all individual health insurance claims. The Company believes it has adequate reserves for all self insurance claims.

Outback Steakhouse, Inc. and Affiliates
Notes to Consolidated Financial Statements

10. Business Combinations

During 2000, the Company issued approximately 273,000 shares of Common Stock to four area operating partners for all their interests in 33 Outback Steakhouses in Arizona, New Mexico, Northern New Jersey, New York Metropolitan area, North Texas and Virginia.

During 1999, the Company issued 2,256,000 shares of Common Stock for all of the outstanding shares of its New England franchisee (Tedesco) which owned 17 Outback Steakhouses in Connecticut, Massachusetts, New Hampshire, and Rhode Island. The merger was accounted for by the pooling-of-interests method using historical amounts and the financial statements presented herein have been restated to give retroactive effect to the merger for all periods presented.

During 1999, the Company issued approximately 160,000 shares of Common Stock to three area operating partners for all of the outstanding interests in 25 Outback Steakhouses in Colorado, Georgia and West Florida.

During 1998, the Company issued approximately 80,250 shares of Common Stock to one area operating partner for the outstanding interest in Outback Steakhouses in Indiana and Kentucky.

The acquisitions of the area operating partners' interests in 2000, 1999 and 1998 were accounted for by the purchase method and the related goodwill is included in the line item entitled "Other Assets" in the Company's Consolidated Balance Sheets.

Outback Steakhouse, Inc. and Affiliates
Notes to Consolidated Financial Statements

11. Stock Option and Other Benefit Plans

The Company's amended and Restated Stock Option Plan (the "Stock Option Plan") was approved by the shareholders of the Company in April 1992, and has subsequently been amended as deemed appropriate by the Company's Board of Directors or shareholders. There are currently 22,500,000 shares of the Company's Common Stock which may be issued and sold upon exercise of stock options ("Options"). The term of Options granted is determined by the Board of Directors and optionees generally vest in the Options over a five year period.

The purpose of the Stock Option Plan is to attract competent personnel, to provide long-term incentives to Directors and key employees, and to discourage employees from competing with the Company.

Options under the Stock Option Plan may be Options which qualify under Section 422 of the Internal Revenue Code ("Incentive Stock Options") or Options which do not qualify under Section 422 ("Nonqualified Options"). To date, the Company has only issued Nonqualified Options. The term of Options granted is generally five years and the price generally cannot be less than the fair market value of the shares covered by the Option.

To provide long term incentives to its restaurant managers, the Company periodically grants them options to purchase its common stock. The Stock Option Committee estimates the fair market value of the grants by using a three month weighted average stock price to eliminate the daily trading increases and decreases in the stock price. This averaging method may result in option grants that are above or below the closing price as of the exact grant date. The Company believes that the averaging of the price is a more fair method of determining fair market value for long term incentives. Compensation expense results if the exercise price of these options is less than the market price on the date of grant.

As of December 31, 2000, the Company had granted to employees of the Company a cumulative total of approximately 19,769,000 options to purchase the Company's Common Stock at prices ranging from $0.19 to $38.33 per share which was the estimated fair market value at the time of each grant. As of December 31, 2000, Options for approximately 1,845,000 shares were exercisable.

Options to purchase 3,076,855, 3,619,385 and 1,433,013 of the Company's Common Stock were issued to employees during 2000, 1999, and 1998 with exercise prices ranging from $23.69 to $32.06, $20.05 to $37.94 and $19.28 to $26.71 for each respective period.

The remaining contractual life for options granted was approximately four to ten years, three to nine years and two to eight years for the options granted during 2000, 1999 and 1998, respectively.

Activity in the Company's Stock option Plan was:

Outstanding at	Shares	Weighted Average Exercise Price
December 31, 1997	8,766,282	$15.11
Granted	1,433,013	23.03
Exercised	(1,407,063)	11.77
Forfeited	(75,969)	19.41
Outstanding at December 31, 1998	8,716,263	16.96
Granted	3,619,385	26.60
Exercised	(1,192,550)	12.85
Forfeited	(80,323)	19.00
Outstanding at December 31, 1999	11,062,775	20.59
Granted	3,076,855	26.73
Exercised	(807,888)	14.03
Forfeited	(141,790)	24.57
Outstanding at December 31, 2000	13,189,952	$22.93

Had the compensation cost for the Company's Stock Option Plan been determined based on the fair value at the grant dates for awards under the plan consistent with SFAS No. 123, the Company's net income and earnings per share on a pro forma basis would have been (in thousands, except per share data):

| | December 31, | | |
	2000	1999	1998
Net income	$135,838	$119,294	$87,184
Basic earnings per common share	$ 1.75	$ 1.55	$ 1.15
Diluted earnings per common share	$ 1.71	$ 1.51	$ 1.13

The preceding pro forma results were calculated with the use of the Black Scholes option-pricing model. The following assumptions were used for the years ended December 31, 2000, 1999, 1998, respectively: (1) risk-free interest rates of 5.03%, 6.36%, and 5.30%,; (2) dividend yield of 0.0% in all three periods presented; (3) expected lives of 3.5 years in all three periods presented; and (4) volatility of 35%, 36%, and 40%. Results may vary depending on the assumptions applied within the model. Compensation expense recognized in providing pro forma disclosures may not be representative of the effects on net income for future years.

Tax benefits resulting from the exercise of non-qualified stock options reduced taxes currently payable by $3,290,000 and $9,153,000 in 2000 and 1999, respectively. The tax benefits are credited to additional paid in capital.

The Company has a qualified defined contribution 401(K) plan covering substantially all full-time employees, except officers and certain highly compensated employees. Assets of this plan are held in trust for the sole benefit of the employees.

Outback Steakhouse, Inc. and Affiliates
Notes to Consolidated Financial Statements

12. Adoption of Statement of Position 98-5, "Reporting on the Costs of Start-up Activities."

The Company adopted the new accounting standard, Statement of Position 98-5, "Reporting on the Costs of Start-up Activities," which requires that pre-opening and other start-up costs be expensed as incurred rather than capitalized. The adoption was made effective as of the beginning of the Company's 1998 fiscal year. As a result of the adoption, the Company expenses start-up cost as incurred rather than through future amortization. The cumulative effect of the change in accounting principle, which was approximately $4,880,000 net of income taxes or $0.06 per share diluted, was recorded as a one-time charge in the Company's 1998 Financial Statements.

Outback Steakhouse, Inc. and Affiliates
Notes to Consolidated Financial Statements

13. Related Party Transactions

During 1998, the Company leased/chartered an airplane from a Corporation owned by two officers/directors of the Company. Airplane lease/charter payments for the year ended December 31, 1998 totalled approximately $90,000. During December 1998, the Company purchased, at fair market value, an aircraft from a corporation owned by two officers/directors of the Company for a purchase price of $1,350,000.

During 1999, the Company purchased, at original price, an 18% ownership interest in a motor speedway for $592,000 from a partnership in which three officers/directors are partners. The investment is included in the line item in the Company's Consolidated Balance Sheets entitled "Investments in and advances to unconsolidated affiliates."

During 2000, a member of the Board of Directors made a $120,000 investment in limited partnerships of a joint venture. Subsequent to year end, Mr. Lee Roy Selmon, a member of the Board of Directors invested approximately $101,000 for a 10% interest in the operations of a Company owned restaurant which bears his name and to which he is making a material image contribution.

Outback Steakhouse, Inc. and Affiliates
Notes to Consolidated Financial Statements

14. Subsequent Events

Subsequent to year end, the Company entered into a ten year licensing agreement with an entity owned by minority interest owners of certain non-restaurant operations. The licensing agreement transferred the right and license to use certain assets of these non-restaurant operations. License fees, payable over the term of the agreement, total approximately $22,000,0000. Under the terms of a line of credit agreement related to the licensing agreement, the Company loaned this entity approximately $900,000 to fund working capital needs.

Outback Steakhouse, Inc. and Affiliates
Notes to Consolidated Financial Statements

15. Segment Reporting

In June 1997, the FASB issued SFAS No. 131, "Disclosures about Segments of an Enterprise and Related Information." The Company operates restaurants under six brands that have similar investment criteria and economic and operating characteristics and are considered one reportable operating segment. Management does not believe that the Company has any material reporting segments.

Outback Steakhouse, Inc. and Affiliates
Notes to Consolidated Financial Statements

16. Provision for Impaired Assets and Restaurant Closings

In the fourth quarter of 1999, the Company recorded a pre-tax charge to earnings of $5,493,000 which includes approximately $3,617,000 for the write down of impaired assets, $1,876,000 related to restaurant closings, severance and other costs. The write down primarily related to Carrabba's restaurant properties and assets of ancillary businesses.

In accordance with SFAS No. 121, "Accounting for the Impairment of Long-Lived Assets," the Company identified certain long-lived assets which are held and used in the Carrabba's restaurants as impaired. An impairment was recognized when the future undiscounted cash flows of certain assets were estimated to be less than the assets' related carrying value. As such, the carrying values were written down to the Company's estimates of fair value. Fair value was estimated utilizing the best information available making whatever estimates, judgements, and projections were considered necessary.

Index